D1736793

PRAISE FOR *KNOWING WHAT PSYCHOANALYSTS DO AND DOING WHAT PSYCHOANALYSTS KNOW*

"In this groundbreaking book, David Tuckett et al. show how their sophisticated, nuanced research model, when applied to the clinical material from the long-standing Comparative Clinical Methods Working Party, allows them to present a sophisticated comparison of different psychoanalytic methods. It is beautifully written with numerous clinical examples that are discussed in an unbiased way. Every psychoanalyst can benefit from reading this book." —**Fred Busch, PhD, Boston Psychoanalytic Society and Institute**

"A groundbreaking exploration of psychoanalytic practice. Through their meticulous research, analysis of workshop discussions, and psychoanalytical writings, the authors offer a shared theoretical framework for self-enquiry. I participated in the work that led to this book and the one that preceded it, always gaining a better understanding of the models with which my colleagues worked and the model I used myself. This book challenges and guides psychoanalysts to reflect on their practice, fostering a deeper understanding of the analytic situation, recognition of the unconscious, and transformative interventions. A must-read for professionals seeking to enhance their therapeutic approach and contribute to the evolution of psychoanalysis."
—**Antonino Ferro, MD, past president, Italian Psychoanalytic Society**

"In terms of the history of science, the Comparative Clinical Methods project has the great merit of having led psychoanalysis from the time of ideological struggles between different psychoanalytic schools into the time of plurality in psychoanalysis. A treasure of clinical case material as well as sophisticated conceptual thinking."
—**Marianne Leuzinger-Bohleber, German Psychoanalytic Association and senior scientist**

"This pioneering work from the Comparative Clinical Methods (CCM) project accomplishes Freud's wished-for Junktim of practice and theory—elaborating the traditional case study into a research method with group validation of findings. Using case reports of well-known analysts, the CCM team develops and demonstrates a new theoretical frame that all clinicians will find illuminating." —**William Glover, PhD, past president, American Psychoanalytic Association**

"Extraordinarily astute, this book represents a milestone. The authors create a framework both for unity in diversity in the international cooperation of psychoanalysts and for self-reflection based on conceptual empiricism for the everyday work of each individual clinician. The knowledgeable re-translation of some of Freud's central terms correct some previously common misconceptions. A gift to all international psychoanalysts, including psychoanalysts-in-training." —**Heribert Blass, MD, German Psychoanalytic Association, EPF President, IPA President-elect**

ing What Psychoanalysts Do and Doing What Psychoanalysts Know

David Tuckett
Elizabeth Allison
Olivier Bonard
Georg J. Bruns
Anna L. Christopoulos
Michael Diercks
Eike Hinze
Marinella Linardos
Michael Šebek

with assistance from
Abbot Bronstein
Marie Rudden

ROWMAN & LITTLEFIELD
Lanham • Boulder • New York • London

Published by Rowman & Littlefield
An imprint of The Rowman & Littlefield Publishing Group, Inc.
4501 Forbes Boulevard, Suite 200, Lanham, Maryland 20706
www.rowman.com

86-90 Paul Street, London EC2A 4NE

Copyright © 2024 by David Tuckett

British Library Cataloguing in Publication Information Available

Library of Congress Cataloging-in-Publication Data

Names: Tuckett, David, author.
Title: Knowing what psychoanalysts do and doing what psychoanalysts know / David Tuckett, Elizabeth Allison, Olivier Bonard, Georg J. Bruns, Anna L. Christopoulos, Michael Diercks, Eike Hinze, Marinella Linardos, Michael Šebek ; with assistance from Abbot Bronstein, Marie Rudden.
Description: Lanham : Rowman & Littlefield, [2024] | Includes bibliographical references and index.
Identifiers: LCCN 2023038845 (print) | LCCN 2023038846 (ebook) | ISBN 9781538188095 (cloth) | ISBN 9781538188101 (paperback) | ISBN 9781538188118 (epub)
Subjects: LCSH: Psychoanalysis. | Psychoanalysts.
Classification: LCC BF173 .T839 2024 (print) | LCC BF173 (ebook) | DDC 150.19/5—dc23/eng/20231116
LC record available at https://lccn.loc.gov/2023038845
LC ebook record available at https://lccn.loc.gov/2023038846

Contents

Preface and Acknowledgments

The ideas described in this book are the outcome of a twenty-year international research project inspired by the realization that when psychoanalysts share what they do in their consulting rooms, which many are reluctant to do, they have difficulty knowing what they do sufficiently clearly to describe it even to another psychoanalyst. They also have great difficulty with being clear about and learning from the different ways other psychoanalysts work, particularly if they are separated by geography or culture. Hence the title of the book.

To answer the two questions in the title has not been easy. We will describe how our attempt to do so required two things: (1) a method that allowed different psychoanalysts safely to say what they did with examples that made sense to a diverse group of peers, and (2) a framework to bring out and compare different practices.

The first task, the development of a two-step comparative clinical discussion method that respected difference and diversity, took about five years. Its key strength was to enable a focus on what people did and why, rather than judging what they did. The main outlines of the method and how it was arrived at were published by the group in 2008 (Tuckett et al., 2008). Over one thousand workshops using the method have been conducted in numerous countries across four continents.

The second task proved much more difficult. In fact, only the need to complete the writing of this book enabled it to gain momentum. The challenge was to find a framework that enabled the different ways psychoanalysts approached their work to surface and to be described so that they could be meaningfully compared, bearing in mind that we wanted to hold to the view that all the clinical work presented to us was competent and could be effective. The solution we arrived at rests on the presumption that anyone who wishes to define themselves as working as a psychoanalyst must, whether they describe it like that or not, be putting into practice their version of four sets of suppositions that necessarily govern any psychoanalytic investigation: (1) about the investigation's setting, (2) about how the "otherwise inaccessible" ideas that patients have are to be inferred, (3) about how those "otherwise inaccessible" ideas and impulses repetitively create a patient's troubles, and (4) about how the process brings about change. We refer to the implicit ideas governing these four issues as suppositions about the analytic situation, unconscious inference, unconscious repetition, and furthering a transformational process, respectively. In each case we have used what we call an "ideal type" methodology to characterize several different types of supposition each analyst made. In the book we use this framework to analyze the work of sixteen psychoanalysts who presented to our workshops, the published work of seven leading international colleagues, and some of Freud's clinical work and thinking.

Our analysis points up the extent to which, from Freud onward, psychoanalysis is necessarily a highly subjective and fragile enterprise inherent in which are very considerable ethical dangers. Practice must rely on the analyst's intuition and must necessarily be the outcome of an analyst's unconscious (and therefore inherently uncertain) relation to his or her patient as a person influenced in turn by the patient's unconscious (and therefore inherently uncertain) relation to his or her analyst as a person. It was when Freud realized this—realized that, however inconvenient, unconscious cognition was a fact—that he and his immediate circle demanded that analytic training include personal psychoanalysis. However, as we discuss, that cannot, logically, solve the problem.

It all points to a further conclusion—namely, that the grounds on which analysts construct their understanding of their patients and their past are fundamentally insecure. Relational analysts in the United States have discussed this "constructivist dilemma" and in so doing have questioned the value of traditional interpretation and approaches. We will propose that our framework can contribute to this dilemma, and in our final chapter we offer eleven questions any analyst can ask themselves about sessions they have just completed and also address several of today's most pressing controversies.

We hope this book and the ideas in it will be useful to every psychoanalyst or psychoanalytic psychotherapist, as well as to trainees and educators. Meanwhile, we have many people to thank, starting with our sixteen presenters whose work is represented, as well as all those several hundreds of others who presented their work in workshops and all their peers who used the new method to discuss the work. All cases have been anonymized in numerous ways in the clinical descriptions, so of course we cannot mention names.

Special thanks go to the original members of the European Psychoanalytic Federation's Comparative Clinical Methods Working Party: Roberto Basile (Italy), Dana Birksted Breen (United Kingdom), Tomas Bohm (Sweden), Paul Denis (France), Antonino Ferro (Italy), Helmut Hinz (Germany), Arne Jemstedt (Sweden), Paola Mariotti (United Kingdom), and Johan Schubert (Sweden), as well as to Haydée Faimberg (France) and Jorge Canestri (Italy), who participated in some of our most crucial early discussions. With the help of the International Psychoanalytic Association (IPA) at this time we also established comparative clinical methods working parties in North and South America. In North America Abbot Bronstein and Marie

Rudden led the groups and have also crafted papers in journals and the IPA book on working parties. In Latin America Jose Calich (Brazil), Alfonso Pola (Chile), Elisabeth de Rocha Barros (Brazil), and Clara Nemas (Argentina) are still running groups and have also contributed ideas.

After 2008, the European group was led by Olivier Bonard (Switzerland) for the next ten years with all the authors of this book and also Paola Mariotti (United Kingdom), Dana Birksted Breen (United Kingdom), and Paul Denis (France) remaining for many more years. Angela Mauss Hanke (Germany), Jordi Sala (Spain), Manuel Fernandez Criado (Spain), Marc Hebbrecht (Belgium), Dimitris James Jackson (Greece), Regine Prat (France), and Brigitte Moïses-Durand (France) also joined for varying lengths of time. Over the last two or three years, Elizabeth Allison (United Kingdom), Olivier Bonard (Switzerland), Georg Bruns (Germany), Anna Christopoulos (Greece), Michael Diercks (Austria), Eike Hinze (Germany), Marinella Linardos (Italy), Michael Sebek (Czech Republic), and I have drafted, read, and commented on the various chapters, and we have also had assistance from Abbot Bronstein and Marie Rudden from the United States.

For many years, we held workshops at European Psychoanalytic Federation conferences and IPA congresses, and thanks to the generosity of the Paris Psychoanalytical Society (Société Psychanalytique de Paris, SPP), we met for moderator discussion in Paris at their beautiful building in the rue St. Jacques. In later years we continued to meet in Paris and have organized workshops in Vienna—thanks to the generosity and considerable effort of Michael Diercks and the Vienna Psychoanalytic Society. In 2022, we met in Rome, superbly hosted by Marinella Linardos.

In particular, I am deeply grateful to Ron Britton, Bernard Reith, Bruce Reis, Patrick Miller, and Fred Busch, who kindly read and commented on significant parts of the manuscript, as well as to Otto Kernberg, Antonino Ferro, Peter Fonagy, Marianne Leuzinger Bohleber, Bill Glover, Heribert Blass, Beth and Elias Mallet de Rocha Barros, Gerard Sobnosky, Dana Birksted Breen, Marina Altmann de Litvan, and Nasir Ilahi for very rapid reviews.

Charu Mangla Goel, Mary Heller, Alejandra Perez, Anssi Peräkylä, Anne Ward, and Maria Parissis conducted significant empirical work and transcription in the past.

I would like to thank my colleagues in the Psychoanalysis Unit at UCL for all kinds of support.

Finally, Mark Kerr, Lilith Dorko, Sarah Reinhardt, Alden Perkins, and Jennifer Kelland at Rowman & Littlefield have made this book possible in rapid time, and Carol Ladewig has generously given permission for her painting to be reproduced for the book cover.

David Tuckett
London, September 2023

1

Toward a Shared Common Framework for Self-Enquiry

This book tries to answer the question of what psychoanalysts do when they are practicing psychoanalysis.

To achieve our aim, we have collected a unique dataset of everyday clinical sessions using a two-step workshop discussion method designed to reveal and understand different ways of working. We have also had to evolve a new common theoretical framework to surface and then make sense of the differences in the data. Finally, to present our findings in this book, we have had to develop a lively means to convey to any psychoanalyst reading it a sense of the crucial differences. The overall aim is to create a structure that psychoanalysts can use to ask themselves what they do and where they think their practice fits, if they are minded to review and reflect on their clinical work.

Capturing diversity and making it intelligible have proved much more challenging tasks than they might immediately appear. First, they have required a commitment to acknowledging and respecting diversity in a field in which different ways of doing psychoanalysis have been hotly contested and the external boundary between what some psychoanalysts think is psychoanalysis and not psychoanalysis is hazy. Second, they have required us to elaborate a new common theoretical framework to compare different practices along a set of shared dimensions.

To achieve the first goal, we began by inviting a range of experienced practitioners from many different psychoanalytic societies and orientations to present what *they considered ordinary everyday sessions of psychoanalysis*, and we created specially designed workshops in which their work could be discussed by a similarly diverse selection of colleagues. Most crucially, we arranged the workshops so that we could demand of ourselves and our workshop members that we all take active steps to put aside the usual practice of understanding and critiquing another psychoanalyst's practice in terms of our own approach. Instead, we would actively try to focus on what the presenter seemed to be doing and why they seemed to be doing it, from their point of view.

This "self-denying ordinance" was challenging to implement (Tuckett et al., 2008, p. 278) and is always only imperfectly achieved. Experience shows that it is and will always be difficult to set aside one's own (often not fully realized) preconceptions, which are always emotionally saturated. Indeed, to some of our critics and even to an extent to some in our groups, the attitude of tolerance to diverse practice has sometimes seemed close to heresy (Blass, 2023). In the groups one reason for this is that it is both emotionally and intellectually challenging to listen to descriptions of often disturbing or tragic clinical events and circumstances, to be open to the situations, and yet to retain curiosity rather than rush to judgment—particularly when many of the dynamics are unconscious.

In any case, the two-step method discussion workshops we first created in 2002 and described six years later (Tuckett et al., 2008) to facilitate focusing on what psychoanalysts do have by now accumulated the largest database of ordinary psychoanalytic practice yet assembled in the field. Presentations by over three hundred psychoanalysts (well over three-quarters of whom were training analysts) working in many countries have been discussed in special workshops using the two-step method for eight or more hours at a time. Well over one thousand psychoanalysts have taken part in the workshops over the years, many of whom have participated multiple times. Reports have been compiled by the moderators of nearly every workshop.

The two-step method took about five years to evolve. To achieve the second goal, to evolve a new common theoretical framework for analyzing and presenting the data on how psychoanalysts work, has proved far more difficult, taking three times as long!

Data, however well collected with attention to diversity, do not "speak" for themselves. To "speak" clearly, to convey a meaningful picture of how different psychoanalysts work, data must be placed inside a theoretical framework of meaning that is as common and transparent as possible.

For the past fifteen years the main authors of this book (along with other collaborators[1]) have met in person two or three times a year for long weekend meetings, as well as more recently by remote means, to take part in what we call moderator meetings. They are nine individuals, each practicing psychoanalysis in different ways, trained at eight different psychoanalytic institutes, and practicing in at least six different languages! At times this diversity (and the diversity also evident in the workshop groups and sometimes inconsistent reporting) created chaos. But, we argue, and readers will judge if we are right, it has ultimately provided a decisive advantage. Over the past fifteen years, trying to understand the data iteration by iteration, we have developed a common theoretical framework that both makes sense of core differences we find in how the psychoanalysts we studied do psychoanalysis and provides a heuristic methodology for any practitioner to "know" what they are doing.

The concepts we use within our new theoretical framework are the product of a rigorous iterative process that turned out to be greatly enhanced by writing and

---

1. Paola Mariotti, Dana Birksted Breen, and Paul Denis remained for a further ten years approximately. Angela Mauss Hanke, Jordi Sala, Marc Hebbrcht, Dimitris James Jackson, Regine Prat, and Brigitte Moïse-Durand also took part for many years.

agreeing on each of the main chapters (and before that composing and discussing the working papers on which each one was based)!

For years the authors, as moderators of the most recent workshop they had conducted, had repeatedly presented the outcome of workshops to each other at moderator meetings. Each time, first the moderator and then, independently, each of the rest of us tried collectively to characterize and write up the presenting analyst's implicit suppositions across the four crucial but overlapping dimensions of their work already identified in the second step of the two-step method (Tuckett et al., 2008). How we understood and applied this second step evolved first in one way and then another as we tried to arrive at common definitions to apply. But in headline theoretical terms, discussion of how the analysts who presented were working always stayed close to four dimensions: (1) how they appeared to understand and use transference and countertransference, (2) how they appeared to infer unconscious meanings from their patients' talk, (3) what they appeared to think about the repetitive problems from which their patients were suffering, and (4) what sort of process they appeared to believe needed to be set in motion in sessions to alter it.

What we were doing in the fifteen years of our meetings, iteratively, was trying to find a more and more useful fit between our growing understanding of the practice of everyday sessions presented in the workshops, viewed from the presenting analyst's point of view, the understanding of it developed in the workshop, and an evolving common theoretical framework we could use to ask crucial questions (Figure 1.1). Very gradually the framework began to solidify so that we began to feel meaningfully able to surface differences that were useful—first about transference and then about the other dimensions. The process accelerated when we were faced with the demand for rigor required by having to produce written explanations in this book.

In fact, Chapters 3 to 6 of this book develop the four topic areas mentioned in the last paragraph but one. From their origins in the formulation of Step 2 and through successive elaboration, the four topics remain the core dimensions of the new common framework. But they have been elaborated, on the one hand, by the demand

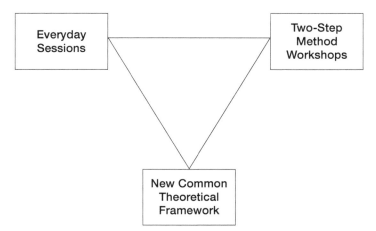

Figure 1.1. Creating a Common Framework

to make sense of the data from the workshops in the many moderator meetings held over fifteen years and, on the other and more recently, through a "conversation" between our concepts and Sigmund Freud's writings. Particularly thanks to the German-speaking members, as we began to read each other's drafts of the different chapters and gained a growing familiarity with the issues, we also began to study the subtle nuances on the same topics present in Freud's writings, which sometimes seem to have become obscured in translation, preconception, or controversial debate.

Each main chapter in the book begins by indicating what it is we are trying to compare—for example, in Chapter 3 the presenting analyst's suppositions as to how an unconscious script energizing the patient's life reveals itself in the situation with the analyst in the regular sessions (i.e., through a specific view of how transference operates). Examples of different suppositions on this topic are then presented and discussed with detailed material from presentations and the conversations in the workshops that discussed them. The outcome is to show both what the new common concepts that emerged are and to suggest how they provide useful ways to highlight differences.

A turning point, as just mentioned, arrived when we began to elaborate and test the framework alongside what we could derive as to the obvious differences in Freud's own suppositions in each of these areas, as set out in his core technical writings. We had not turned to Freud, as has so often been done, in search of legitimation. Rather we found, in fact unexpectedly, that conjoining our struggle to understand what the psychoanalysts in our workshops were doing with Freud's own struggle to develop his thoughts in each of these core areas—a specialist research area initiated by Michael Diercks—was highly productive. It assisted our analysis of differences in the way sessions were conducted, our development of a common theoretical framework through which we sought to apprehend them, and our understanding of Freud's own uneven and sometimes halting development.

We describe this set of insights in their context in four successive chapters beginning with Chapter 3. In this respect, Freud's writing seems to have functioned for us as a kind of third pillar (Figure 1.2) from which to reflect both on what the presenters were doing, as envisaged in the workshops, and how we could characterize it within a common theoretical framework, alternately helping us to understand ways to conceptualize Freud's changing clinical strategies and those of our presenters.

It is this overall process of iteration from a succession of third viewpoints, we think, that has led us to the new common theoretical framework we consider our principal achievement. It has emerged from the process and bears both on the initial question of what psychoanalysts do, but more importantly on how they might know they are doing it—in this way permitting the development of some key technical questions that may be of use to any analyst, trainee, or supervisor. We develop these in Chapters 8 and 9.

Because psychoanalysts tend to "live" in relatively close-networked groups apparently sharing an orientation, the level of diversity in the field is only encountered by those who read or travel widely across networks.

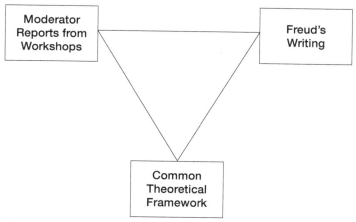

Figure 1.2.   A Third Pillar

To make plain the extent of difference that might not always be apparent, in the remainder of this chapter we look a little more closely at diversity in psychoanalytic technique since Freud's death in 1939. To do so, we have selected published examples from the work of seven international psychoanalysts from both sides of the Atlantic Ocean—Kurt Eissler, Fred Busch, Otto Kernberg, Wilfred Bion, André Green, Donnel Stern, and Philip Bromberg—who should be widely recognized as practicing within different schools. Our selection was not systematic or intended to be representative along demographic lines. We could have chosen many more. Rather, what influenced selection was the availability of suitably comprehensible and brief clinical vignettes.

As far as possible, while trying to keep the clinical stories these analysts tell alive, we focus each extract on the aspects of their approach that are relevant to identifying apparent differences in their ideas about transference, recognizing unconscious content, the repetitive forces causing a patient's troubles, and what they apparently do to further a psychoanalytic process and its purpose. Unlike in the case of the data from our workshops, which we will present in subsequent chapters, in the case of these published presentations we did not have the opportunity to discuss their presentations with them, which necessarily limits our inferences. The full-length accounts from which we took these extracts are very well worth examining in detail in their original form, and we strongly recommend readers do so.

KURT EISSLER

Fourteen years after Freud's death, at the time when he was widely considered the magisterial voice of psychoanalytic orthodoxy in the United States (Cooper, 2008), Kurt Eissler (1953), whose original analytic training was in Vienna, provided rather clear guidance as to the "proper" way to do psychoanalysis, starting from the "basic rule":

A patient is informed of the *basic rule* and of his obligation to follow it. He adheres to it to the best of his ability, which is quite sufficient for the task of achieving recovery. The tool with which the analyst can accomplish this task is *interpretation*, and the goal of interpretation is to provide the patient with insight. *Insight* will remove the obstacles which have so far delayed the ego in attaining its full development. The problem here is only when and what to interpret; for in the ideal case the analyst's activity is limited to interpretation; no other tool becomes necessary. (p. 108; our emphasis)

Eissler's use of the word "interpretation" demands attention. He is using the word simultaneously to denote a way of making sense of the unconscious meaning of the material (which must necessarily be highly subjective) and the form of intervention to make to the patient. He emphasizes that the term, as intervention, always presupposes "the proper use of this technique," stressing that "it would be foolish to suggest that just any kind of interpretation, or the mere act of interpreting, will do." He provides a brief but otherwise rather precise clinical example of this approach in the same paper:

A patient of superior intelligence . . . filled long stretches of his analysis with *repetitive complaints* about trivial matters regarding his wife. He did not show any understanding of the obvious fact that the discrepancy between the intensity of his complaints and the triviality of their content required a discussion and explanation. One day he reported, somewhat abruptly, that he enjoyed his wife's doing the very things he had always complained of and that he knew how secretly to manipulate situations in such a way as to make his wife act the way he had considered so obnoxious and which *gave him occasion to be cold and unfriendly to her*. (p. 138–39; our emphasis)

Eissler explains how what he selects from these associations, what he "listens to" or "attends to" to make sense of its unconscious meaning, is what he pictures as his patient's hidden but repetitive sadistic, aggressive impulse to be unfriendly and cold to his wife. Based on this subjective interpretative understanding of what he was hearing and his idea that the cause of this repetitive marital problem was that the patient gained unconscious sadistic pleasure from his sadistic impulses without feeling guilty, Eissler then intervened. He "explained"—that is shared insight with—his patient about what he was doing with his wife. Apparently, Eissler's patient acknowledged this "interpretation." In further associations, the patient then volunteered that really he had known this for a long time and, according to Eissler, now "showed some understanding of the uncanny sadistic technique with which he maneuvered his wife into the situation of a helpless victim without giving her an opportunity of defending herself" (p. 139).

But conveying this understanding that he had reached did not end the matter due to what Eissler terms his patient's "resistance." While the patient could agree that he was behaving in the way he did toward his wife in the sessions, he "tried to prove to himself and to the analyst that he was not cruel, but that he deserved pity owing to his wife's deficiencies." In Eissler's view this could be understood by *assuming* his patient could not cope with the guilt feelings that accompany being conscious of the meaning of his activity with his wife. Faced with this appeal to recognize his reasons for behaving as he was, Eissler then tried to show the patient that his "incessant complaining" about being a victim of the situation—a phrase possibly indicating Eissler was still feeling some irritation with his patient long after—served the purpose of assuaging his feelings of guilt.[2] "The more successful he was in gratifying his sadism in the camouflaged way he used so expertly, the more he had to present himself the next day as injured and unjustly treated by fate in being married to an allegedly unsatisfactory partner."

Sharing this further interpretation of what was happening with his wife was not accepted by the patient. "He could not understand it; he could not follow me; and he insisted upon the validity of his complaints, although he had just agreed that he himself secretly induced his wife to behave in the manner about which he habitually complained to me the following day." They seem to have struggled, and we do not learn more about the outcome.[3] But from what Eissler writes, it seems there was something of an impasse. He thought his patient "had come to a point when he would more readily forego the sadistic gratification and acquire mastery over this force than he would sacrifice the feeling of being unjustly treated by fate."

FRED BUSCH

The next clinical example is from the work of Fred Busch—who describes himself as a "modern American Freudian" writing sixty years later in 2013 (Busch, 2013). His patient, Jim, at this point seven years into an analysis, is said to be good at letting his mind roam freely. He came into the session reported, saying that he had lost his mind over the weekend. The excerpt shows how Busch helps him to realize that he is becoming conscious of unconscious beliefs that had made him very anxious.

BOX 1.1. BUSCH

FB 1: It sounds like there was something dangerous about putting into words that your wife's excitement over something you were excited about led to a concern you could lose something valuable.

Jim: I'm talking to someone. Now that I think about it, I was in a subterranean all white room. (At this point Jim waves his hand around my white, subterranean office.) This other person was saying something about this guy, Eric, a friend from High School. He was very popular, a good athlete and friends with everyone (like Jim in H.S.). This other person was telling me that Eric had a disease where they got black eyes as a <u>symptom</u>.

Continued on next page

---

2. Eissler uses this example to demonstrate what he called secondary resistance from the superego.
3. Eissler is intent on focusing his patient on what is happening with his wife. He does not examine the possible situation going between them—for example, that the patient is perhaps provoking and frustrating his analyst and gaining satisfaction from that or perhaps that Eissler is taking on the role of superego himself and "beating up the patient for it." Such different approaches to the "analytic situation" are discussed in Chapter 3, using a number of metaphors.

BOX 1.1, continued

Like they were beat up. I heard somewhere that Eric was having serious difficulty, with job problems. I'm wondering now if Eric represents me in the dream, as my job isn't going so great. Then there was this other part of the dream. You went out of the room to make a phone call. I'm <u>thinking</u> it was to Fox news. They were inviting you to appear on a show, and in this phone call, you were working out the details. When I think of Fox news, I think of Republicans. I went out into the corridor and was listening at the closed door. Then I realized that if you came out of the room you would catch me and I'd have no reason for being there. So I went back into the other room.

   I saw an Obama sticker on your car, so I don't know why I saw you as a Republican.

[There was then a long pause.]

   I don't feel like I have any more to say.

[Pause.]

FB 2: It's when you think we're not so different . . . i.e., maybe I'm not a Republican . . . that your thoughts stop.

Jim: I just thought of the old *Saturday Night Live* routine about "the 2 wild and crazy guys," and how they talked about going after foxes. Then I thought about those trips you took a few years ago and how I was convinced you were going to visit your "floozy" with her lap dog. The plot thickens.

FB 3: So it seems like in the dream you are curious about what I'm doing with this foxy, floozy, but it feels dangerous. [Referring back to his fear of getting caught by me in his interest of what I'm doing with this foxy, floozy behind closed doors.]

Jim: In the old movies I've seen guys are always getting black eyes for their interest in some other guy's woman. My mind now goes back to those times when my mother asked me about male teachers and how I felt about them. It was really confusing.

[His thoughts then went to a few situations that came up during the weekend where he had difficulty making a decision. He would be interested in working out the details, but when it came to making a decision, he backed away.]

FB 4: Maybe it's like in the dream, where you're curious about what I'm doing, maybe in detail, with this foxy woman, or interested yourself in the details of this foxy woman, but then worry you'll get caught, and get a black eye.

Jim: I just thought about this whole thing with our handshake at the end of sessions. (At the end of each session we shake hands.) I just thought of something else. Saturday night Kathy and I met some friends for drinks. Harvey was there with his brother, who is openly and flagrantly homosexual, and he was hitting on me. I didn't think it was in a serious way. I think I had to say that. At one point, I realized I was pleased that it was me he was flirting with, and not Gary (his oldest and best friend). I found myself enjoying it, and *thinking* that I wasn't feeling anxious. Later that night, I thought about it and became anxious, and then forgot about it. At least I thought I did.

FB 5: The end of curiosity, and its beginning.

Just before the excerpt in Box 1.1, Busch describes how Jim came into a session saying he felt dull and that there was nothing new in his thoughts. He then mentioned he had been angry with his wife all weekend but couldn't think about it. Jim felt she spent too much money, and he got angry when she brought up ideas about all the things they needed to buy. As an example, he mentioned that she had done a ton of research on the new BMW X5 and how excited she was. He was afraid that Kathy was becoming like his parents, who preached thrift but would always spend beyond their means. He added details of their latest financial fiasco. Busch eventually interpreted (FB 1) that it sounded like there was something dangerous being put into words.

In his paper, Busch was, he said, attempting to represent (put into words) a *defense against an anxiety* he sensed his patient was experiencing. In any case, his comment led Jim to remember a dream, after which he mentioned he thought he saw an Obama sticker on his analyst's car. He then became manifestly and increasingly inhibited. This emergence of inhibition allows Busch to point out (FB 2) that it's when he thinks his analyst is "not so different" that his thoughts stop, so that what happened at the weekend is now happening before them in the here and now. Busch is then able to mention the dream (FB 3) and, as patient and analyst develop their respective association and interpretation, to arrive at what Busch calls the Oedipal unconscious dynamics operating between them, eventually including Jim's homosexual anxieties.

The excerpt shows an analyst encouraging a patient's free associations and then using signs of inhibition to begin to infer and then gradually to elaborate the unconscious ideas he infers to be behind the patient's anxieties. Nothing is forced. Meanings emerge gradually from a process that helps the analyst to elucidate (and helps his patient to grasp) the unconscious causes of his patient's fear that he was losing his mind: a range of anxieties caused by his unconscious wishes and feelings toward his analyst but with wider application to his life.

OTTO KERNBERG

The next example is from the work of Otto Kernberg published in 1979—midway between the accounts of Eissler and Busch (Kernberg, 1979). Kernberg, who was born in Vienna but migrated to Chile with his parents before undertaking medical training, is a North American analyst trained in South America with an interest in merging a variety of theoretical and technical approaches, including those of Melanie Klein. His patient, whom we will call Karl, a professional in his late forties, had been describing a powerful father and a submissive mother. He came for treatment because of chronic marital conflicts, severe work inhibition, and sexual conflicts. He was sometimes sexually impotent with his wife but not with prostitutes, with whom, at the time reported, in the second year of his psychoanalysis, he would engage in sadistic sexual behavior.

Kernberg reports that for several months, it had become apparent to him that Karl was presenting him with his "shameful" and self-defeating submission to his wife, implicitly blaming his analyst for not helping him to become more assertive in his relationship with her. Among other things, she imposed strict regulations upon him about bedtimes, turning out the light, and staying silent, which all interfered with his research work. Kernberg also felt blamed for Karl's work failures and observed that his efforts to help were disparaged compared to the more active encouragement and sympathy he had obtained from a previous therapist—one whom Karl had in fact persuaded to give him advice on how to handle his wife.

Meanwhile, Kernberg's interpretations were examined and found wanting compared to what Karl read about how psychoanalysis should be done. He would often react to Kernberg's interpretations with an amused, ironical expression, implying that he could do better than that or that Kernberg was not on his best form, and so forth. Kernberg writes that his overall hypothesis at the time was that Karl was attempting to maintain him at a devalued, impotent level "in order to avoid" an unconscious and frightening image of Kernberg as "a brutal, overpowering father" whom he had to placate and hide from.

For several sessions Kernberg reports that he had experienced a sense of impotence, "an incapacity to know how I could convey to him an understanding that would be useful to him." Meanwhile, Karl had changed from his air of ironic superiority into a complaining, nagging protest over not getting any better and the lack of any "original contribution" from Kernberg.

The session that we have partially excerpted in Box 1.2 began when, feeling himself to be in a role with Karl like the role his patient described himself to be in with his nagging wife, Kernberg verbalized his sense that Karl was repeating in that session his relationship with his wife, but with inverted roles. Hearing this, Karl became tense. He said he remembered that his analyst had pointed out to him in the past that he had been attracted by masculine features in his wife. He then associated further to say that he felt Kernberg was accusing him of being homosexual, just like his wife. He then talked about his efforts to persuade his wife or prostitutes to have anal sex and a time when his mother and father had jointly held him to give him an enema.

Growing more anxious, Karl now associated to his analyst forcefully blowing his nose the day before. This had seemed to him to express "brutally uninhibited" power. From there he imagined his analyst both as all-powerful in sex and taking no nonsense.

Simultaneously, Kernberg himself noticed he was feeling incredibly clear and intellectually powerful (in contrast to his earlier helplessness) and understood this reaction of his to suggest that he was now being represented as the all-powerful bullying father forcing Karl into homosexual submission. It now became clear this picture of Kernberg was the role Karl was unsuccessfully trying to take on and enact in his relationships. Kernberg elaborates to suggest that maybe the recent increase in activity with prostitutes was an attempt to escape and reassure himself that this role was working. To this idea Karl (3) responds with deep regret and awareness that how he had been behaving had caused him to miss out.

BOX 1.2. KERNBERG

Karl 1: Now becoming tense remembered that OK had pointed out to him in the past that he had been attracted by masculine features in his wife. He said he felt OK was accusing him of identifying with his wife and implicitly telling him that he was a homosexual. His associations then shifted to his wife's rage with him because once, when he attempted to have anal intercourse with her, she had felt brutally attacked and now, years later, still accused him of having behaved sadistically toward her. He then thought of prostitutes he had engaged to participate masochistically in sexual games in which he "playfully" acted like a sadist and had fantasies about giving such prostitutes enemas. He next remembered his mother and father jointly holding him while giving him enemas in his childhood.

OK 1: [*Throughout these associations, I sensed an increasing fearfulness in him*], I pointed this out to him.

Karl 2: Now remembered that OK had blown his nose forcefully in the previous session, and that this seemed something "brutally uninhibited" to him. He then thought that OK wouldn't take all that abuse from his wife if he were married to her, and also imagined him standing up to his boss very effectively, in fact, intimidating him, in contrast to the patient's always trying to play the nice boy.

OK 2: [*At this moment, I also experienced a sudden sense of intellectual clarity and power, quite in contrast to the helpless insecurity that I had experienced earlier. I felt that I now represented his powerful and brutal father, forcing him into homosexual submission, and that he was engaged in a pathetic effort to identify with me in his sadistic role with prostitutes, while leaving—in his* **fantasy**—*his wife and his work to me.*] I proceeded to interpret the patient's image of me as a powerful man, strong, ruthless, and brutal with women—as he had perceived his father—and I raised the question whether his fear of my branding him as a homosexual might reflect his fear of his *masculinity's* being destroyed if he dared to compete with me, as father, in his behavior toward his wife and toward his boss. I later added that his intense search for sadomasochistic relations with prostitutes in recent weeks might serve the purpose of reassuring him against his fear of me and his temptation to submit to me (father).

Silence.

Karl 3: He now said that it was very painful to think that because of his neurotic behavior he had lost valuable opportunities for advancement in his research work. He added, almost with a shudder, that he had never before thought that the reason why he had no child with his wife was because he had never dared to stand up to her unrealistic excuses for not wanting to have a child, and now it was probably too late.

Like those of the other two analysts described so far, Kernberg's report describes a process of association and interpretation. It is also rather different from the previous two in that it is obvious that Kernberg uses the feelings and thoughts that Karl's associations provoke in him in the sessions as a data source on which to reflect. He combines what he is feeling with the content of the material to imagine the content of Karl's unconscious image of his analyst and his intentions toward him and their effects, both in the session and in Karl's life. By understanding Karl's defensive efforts to protect himself against his unconscious beliefs about his analyst's competitive intentions toward him in sessions, Kernberg comes to understand what happens to Karl in his relationships outside analysis and gains empathy for him and his predicament.

WILFRED BION

Kernberg's patient was on his second attempt to find help. Wilfred Bion (1950), one of Melanie Klein's leading followers, also describes a patient, to whom we give the name Brian, whose previous psychotherapy had ended in difficulty. In fact, it was such a deadly impasse that the psychotherapist had given up and advised that the solution for Brian was a leucotomy.

Bion notes that when Brian first arrived in his consulting room, Brian was visibly upset. For many sessions once they started, however, the upset was not easily apparent. Associations often contained a theme of contamination. Bion reports how he interpreted as best as he could and that as far as he could tell, Brian further associated as best as he could. Moreover, as they reached the end of the second year of treatment, occasional reports reached Bion from outside that Brian was doing better. The problem was, Bion writes, he did not feel the same way. However, with more time, gradually a change seemed to be noticeable.

"At first it seemed as if my interpretations were only meeting with more than usually stubborn indifference, and then as if I was a parent issuing ineffectual exhortations and warnings to a refractory child," Bion wrote (p. 56). He also noticed *a further* change, which he said was not easily formulated:

> There was still the dreary monotone of associations but there was now a quality which derived from what I can best describe as the rhythm of his associations. It was as if two quite separate co-existent scansions of his material were possible. One imparted an overpowering sense of boredom and depression; the other, dependent on the fact that he introduced regularly spaced pauses in the stream of his associations, an almost jocular effect as if he were saying "Go on; it's your turn." (pp. 56–57)

Gradually, Bion also noticed that he thought Brian's associations were "stale associations inviting a stale response" (p. 57). He faced a dilemma: "If I broke the rhythm, he showed signs of anxiety or irritability; if I continued to give the interpretations, which it now became clear he both invited and expected, there emerged a sense of having reached a dead-end" (p. 57).

Although he doesn't use the term in the paper, Bion was describing a growing impasse, which, given the gradual denudation of meaning, he was not surprised by.

BOX 1.3. BION

Brian: He felt the treatment was getting nowhere and was doing no good. Did Bion (in Bion's words, "very reasonably" [p. 57]) think it was worthwhile going on?

Bion 1: Replied that although estimations of progress in analysis were difficult to make there was no reason why they should not accept Brian's evaluation as correct. But, "Before we pass on to consider what should be done about it, we need to know what is meant by *treatment*" [our emphasis]. "It might mean psychoanalysis; in which case it would appear that some other method of approach to his problems would have to be sought. A perhaps more obvious meaning would be, psycho-analysis as practised by myself, in which case the remedy would lie in a change of analyst rather than a change of method. There was, however, yet another possibility. We had already had reason to suppose that alleviation of symptoms was sometimes achieved by factors incidental to analysis; for example, the sense of security obtained from feeling there was someone to go to. It was possible that he was unconsciously referring to some factor of that kind" (p. 57).

There was a silence.

Bion 2: What was Brian thinking about?

Brian: A woman with rheumatic pain was in his mind. "She's always complaining about something or other and I thought that she's very neurotic. I just advised her to buy some amytal and packed her off" (p. 59).

One day (Box 1.3) Brian came in to say he wondered if the treatment should be stopped. Bion's reply (summarized as Bion 1) is a striking example of a psychoanalyst maintaining a psychoanalytic position in the face of impasse and resistance—that is, a position defined by curiosity rather than judgment or action. It led to silence and a prompt from Bion before Brian revealed that what was in his mind was a complaining woman.

For Bion this association, to someone complaining who needed to be given a sedative to calm down, had a clear meaning, even if one not immediately accessible to Brian. It was, Bion thought, a compact unconscious description of the patient's treatment experience with his complaining analyst right now. Box 1.4 presents the interpretations, constructing the emotional situation between them and Brian's hitherto unconscious picture of his complaining analyst and how he dealt with him, which Bion then gave at length. Bion reported that Brian's response was *striking*.

The remainder of the case material traces the further associations and interpretations through which, gradually, what Bion calls a "reinvestigation" was now possible, based on this new shared understanding of what had been unconsciously going on between them and its development. Restored as more of an analyst for his patient,

BOX 1.4. BION CONTINUED

Bion: Perhaps you feel me to be someone who makes interpretations which are vague complaints to which, consequently, it seems you need pay scant attention. . . . [F]or this reason "his associations were, many of them, stale associations employed more for the soporific effect they shared with amytal than for their informative value." They were designed to keep his analyst employed "without bothering him." "We should also consider," he said to Brian, how Brian nonetheless manages to make the situation tolerable for himself.

[Bion elaborated by drawing Brian's attention to peculiarities in his behavior he had observed, notably the rhythm of "association–interpretation association (p. 59)," which indicated that Brian saw his analyst as a twin of himself who supported him in a jocular evasion of his complaints—and that this softened his resentment. In fact, Bion had elaborated, he could identify how he, Bion, might very well seem to be in any of the various roles.]

Brian: [His voice changing and in a depressed tone], he felt tired and unclean.

It was as if, writes Bion, "in a moment, I had in front of me, unchanged in every respect the patient as I had seen him at the first interview" (p. 59).

Bion was able to bring out Brian's deeper underlying unconscious (inaccessible) belief that he had a poisonous (contaminating) family inside him linked to a wide range of primitive infantile sexual anxieties enacted in other relationships. Brian feared, Bion conjectured, that if he were to have a relationship with his analyst, both of them being recognized by each other as "experienced" sexually, it would be bound to result in mutual jealousy and hatred.

Curiously, by a very different route, Bion's patient was in fact discovered to be suffering a similar set of unconsciously constructed and repetitive problems to those Busch and Kernberg described as the problem of their two patients.

There are several aspects of the way Bion was doing psychoanalysis that stand out in this excerpt. First, he very obviously takes up an equidistant observational position both inside and outside the relationship he and Brian are having. This means that when Brian wonders if the relationship has become unproductive, Bion can be both open to the idea as reasonable and able to think about it with Brian without in any way becoming defensive—in other words he can take a neutral or third position as well as be involved. Second, it seems Bion uses the patient's words as data but also treats as data his observation of the rhythm of their exchanges and their effect on him. In this way, this is no ordinary conversation but a special type of investigation of what is inaccessible to the patient using the method of free association as well as evenly hovering attention[4] (see Bion Talamo, 1997). Third, Bion is highly attentive

---

4. This is our translation of Freud's phrase *gleichschwebende Aufmerksamkeit*, which he used to describe the analyst's attentive stance. There is further discussion in Chapter 4 and the glossary of this important phrase.

and, so to speak, critically reflective of his own responses, constantly keeping what is happening in question. Although he does not make it explicit, he strongly implies that he has been a participant in a rhythm they established mutually to ward off both their anxieties. Fourth, his view of Brian's troubles, when it finally emerges clearly, identifies unconscious and so hitherto inaccessible ambivalent beliefs that are the outcome of infantile and subsequent difficulties negotiating the conflicts Freud labeled as characteristic of the Oedipal situation—sexual rivalry and ambivalent relationships (full of love and hate).

ANDRÉ GREEN

A fifth clinical example, nearly fifty years after Bion's, is taken from the work of French psychoanalyst André Green (2000). Green had a classical French training, was influenced by and critical of Jacques Lacan, and was strongly influenced by his own contacts with both Bion and Donald Winnicott.

As with Bion's and Kernberg's patients, other therapeutic attempts to help Gabriel had failed. According to him, his last therapist had complained that Gabriel prevented him from doing his work and had become exasperated. That analysis had in fact gone on for a long time in almost total silence before the therapist decided to put an end to it. Green wrote that he empathized with the difficulty that he imagined the therapist had had but also felt that perhaps his patient was right to suppose he had not been understood. Like Kernberg's and Bion's excerpts, Green's also concerns a moment of difficulty in an analysis.

The patient, Gabriel, now in the fifth year of analysis, had come to see Green because of chronic anxiety. In the session, some of which is excerpted in Box 1.5 (next page), Gabriel is late.[5] Manifestly very anxious, he begs to sit in front of his analyst rather than to lie on the couch. His analyst does not reply in words but gestures toward the couch. Gabriel lies down and explains his claustrophobic feelings before remembering the last session and a wish to "jump out of the bed." As his analyst remains silent and leaves him to associate, he becomes more and more anxious. He struggles on but eventually cannot continue. Green (1) makes an interpretation that designates what sort of person Green has become for Gabriel. Gabriel is now able to continue, and the subjective situation he is experiencing on the couch becomes more and more elaborated and confused with experiences with his mother. Green (2) makes a complex but parsimonious intervention. Gabriel elaborates and eventually produces the terrifying image of being with a whale.

In his paper, Green gradually traces Gabriel's anxieties to infantile unconscious fantasies and impulses that, he thought, lay behind the phobia of allowing himself to have thoughts—literally to have his next thought—for years. Green explains in his paper how, for years, "I was looking for my way in the fog. I thought at first that I

---

5. Green's published account is minimally supplemented here by additional material he made available to one of us twenty years ago (David Tuckett).

BOX 1.5. GREEN

Gabriel: Became claustrophobic on the underground railway on his way to the session and feels trapped and pricked all over his body. Staying on the couch makes him feel afraid of being overwhelmed. Then he thinks about the last session. He recalls saying to himself in the silence that he had to "jump out of the bed." At this point, it became increasingly apparent that the that fact his analyst was remaining silent was difficult for him. He found it very difficult to bear. Maybe what I said was not interesting, Gabriel then ventured. I feel very bad. He trailed off and became fully silent.

Green 1: "You seem to feel my silence not as if I was listening, not only as if I was not interested, but *as if I took pleasure* to let you down alone and not to give you any help."

Gabriel: Said that he felt very threatened. It now came to his mind powerfully that he was feeling like a whale beached on the seashore—although, he says, he knows that he is not at all like that physically. Then he adds that he cannot bear to picture himself on the couch now. "It is as if I find myself in a situation where I'd have to look at myself in the mirror, it is unbearable." "Then I say to myself, if I stood up and if I could see you and, particularly, if you could look at me—it's that look from you that is important—I would feel more reassured." Then he says that the couch is like a bed, like the bed he was in in his early childhood with his mother.

Green 2: "If you were not on that couch and you could look at me and I could look at you, then you would be surer that I am not *in* you but *outside* you. We wouldn't be mixed up. We could be separate."

Gabriel: "Yes, but it is this whale that I feel I am. I know what am I asking you about is this whale? I want you to throw it back to the sea."

The session continues with more ideas about the whale and the sexual connotations that came to the analyst's mind associated with the word for it in the patient's language.

Gabriel: "I see her, I see her throwing looks everywhere, right and left, with enormous anxiety and without legs or arms." Although he knows very well that a whale has no legs or arms, it's how he feels, he adds.

Note: Gabriel's and Green's actual words in this excerpt supplement the paper and were provided to David Tuckett by Green in 1999.

was faced with an attitude stemming from a massive and extensive repression. But then I understood that if he needed to stop himself associating freely in this way, it was not deliberately but as expressing a sort of compulsion. . . . It was not from a lack but rather from a potential excess of associations."

Green says about his clinical approach in his paper that in sessions he tries to hear the statements the patient makes and their meaning "*outside the framework of the logical connections* associated with secondary process" (our emphasis). Crucially and gradually, he believes meaning will emerge out of dispersion—that is, out of the ideas dispersed around the frightening ideas, which are not themselves what is frightening. His eventual construction of the missing ideas emerged from the feeling he had of periodically losing the thread of what Gabriel was saying and then a gradual realization that this was due to persistent ruptures in the associative process at particular points. Over time, rather than as interruptions or changes of theme, Green came to view ruptures (more conventionally, resistances) to freely associating as revealing a deeper discourse. It was one that expressed a conflictual relationship to making connections. For protection they needed "to be kept at a distance, developed at length on the basis of generalities expressed in broken speech" (p. 431).

Summarizing his way of working in a quite different paper, Green (1999) writes,

> I place myself in the analyst's position, when, having forced myself to maintain as much as possible freely floating attention . . . I hear the analysand's communication from two points of view at once. That is to say, on the one hand, I try to perceive the internal conflicts that inhabit it and, on the other, I consider it from the point of view of something addressed, implicitly or explicitly, to me. The conflicts to which I refer . . . [are] the way in which the discourse in turn approaches and moves away from a kernel of meaning. . . . One does not have to have a very precise idea of what activates or, on the contrary, impedes or diverts communication to perceive the movement. . . . [O]ne may, therefore, perceive these variations intuitively without knowing the exact nature of the focus around which they gravitate and that will often appear more or less suddenly, sometimes perfectly clearly, sometimes in a more accidental way, in the course of the dialogue. . . . [O]ne's floating attention turns into investigatory acuteness . . . an instant of reorganisation in the analyst's mind of what has slipped under the fluidity of the reception of verbalisation of the patient's more or less free associative discourse in a state of suspended attention. (p. 278)

Green and his patient had a high tolerance for anxiety when together. It is interesting that as Gabriel became able to associate more to his anxieties and as his analyst constructed their unconscious meaning, as exemplified in the material above, Gabriel's associations became accompanied by not less but more and more anxiety at being with his analyst. But Green was undeterred. As Gabriel responded eventually, Green became able to construct for him a picture of his situation with his analyst: Gabriel felt like he did when he was with a frightened mother as a very frightened and helpless little boy.

Four features stand out about Green's approach: (1) his tolerance of his patient's anxiety and his own frustration and confusion and his determination to stay curious in an investigative mode; (2) his belief that via maintaining an analytic procedure with free association and evenly hovering attention, unconscious meaning would emerge; (3) his focus on sensing the internal conflict producing anxiety for Gabriel linked directly to his unconscious image of his analyst and his intentions (e.g., even taking pleasure at his discomfort) and its infantile origin; (4) his attention to the patient's words and their potential multiple meanings (e.g., bed/couch, etc.).

DONNEL STERN

The sixth example comes from Donnel Stern (2019), a North American relational analyst, who has been very critical of standard North American technique. His patient, Alan, like Gabriel, was also very anxious but additionally suffered bouts of what sounds like alternating mania and depression.[6] The experience Alan and his analyst are having, like those in the previous examples, is difficult for both. A central issue is that Alan misses sessions, something he had also done prior to giving up entirely with his previous therapist.[7] With Stern the problem emerged gradually: "First, he missed one or two per week (out of three); then, within a month, he was missing most of them. Eventually he was missing almost every one. He was depressed, yes, but that wasn't even close to being the whole story" (p. 341).

Stern explains that because he realized getting out of his apartment to come was such a problem for Alan, he had to telephone him. As he put it,

> As I began to know his difficulty just getting himself out of his apartment, I started calling him when he was late, having a pretty good idea that he was still at home. Sometimes he picked up his phone, often he didn't. He always had long, complicated explanations for missing the session, and he kept insisting that he would get there if he could. But something always stymied him. I've often heard explanations like these; we all have. But Alan is a champion explainer. Over and over again something happened that seemed unavoidable. (p. 341)

Eventually, Stern asked Alan if he wanted to continue in treatment. He told Alan that it wasn't necessary to force himself to do something he really didn't want to do and added that he thought that, if really the issue was that he didn't want to be there, he'd have a terrible time telling Stern. "I also told him that I knew he felt he was wasting my time and his father's money, and that he hated that" (p. 341).

But Alan insisted that he did want to come, that he wanted and needed to be in therapy, and that his difficulty getting to it didn't reflect the wish not to be there. Stern responded that he thought the two of them got along pretty well, with which the patient agreed, and "this fact made his claim that he did indeed want to continue our work seem plausible." Stern concluded that it didn't seem that he was avoiding treatment to avoid his analyst.

---

6. These are not Stern's terms. He writes that his patient "has started working for several hedge funds, and in each, he is almost immediately recognized as a wunderkind, and is given a surprising amount of responsibility. And each time he fails, because, after starting by firing on all cylinders—enthusiastic, impressive, and full of energy—Alan simply cannot get himself out of bed and into the office. . . . Alan finds a way to pick himself up, to rebuild his hopes and try again" (pp. 338–39).

7. Eissler's, Bion's, Green's, and Stern's sessions were selected from many others with the conscious belief only that the analysts had provided enough detail and it appeared to be relatively easy to summarize the method of investigation briefly. It was only afterward, in the process of writing this chapter, that it emerged (1) that many of the analysts were struggling with potential impasse, and (2) that many of their patients had had previous treatments, all of which seemed to have got stuck! A conclusion might be that psychoanalysts often write about periods of impasse and its overcoming and that is how psychoanalysis proceeds—when it is working.

Stern reports how the sessions that followed often focused on offering Alan interpretations (i.e., explanations) of this problem of getting to his sessions, most frequently understood in terms of a conflict between two different parts of him: one that wanted to come and another that didn't. The idea was that, just as with his parents, he had a wish to be a good boy with his analyst but was then resentful about it. His resolution of this conflict, Stern suggested, was to attribute nonattendance to unattributable acts of God rather than to himself.

As things progressed without change, Stern felt his interpretations more and more stale and stereotyped, while Alan kept saying he couldn't understand them. At this point, Alan both stopped coming and stopped answering his analyst's phone calls. Instead, he would sometimes send texts.

Eventually, but not at all for the first time, Stern received a very long text saying that Alan felt terrible that he wasn't responding to Stern's texts, couldn't listen to the phone messages because he feared it would make him worse, and felt pushed and pulled in every direction and so very anxious. He had now escaped to his parent's vacation home. He had wanted to speak this morning but could not, giving a long explanation of the trap he felt he was in.

Stern stresses this was not the first such text but that for reasons he could not explain, this particular one "unlocked my capacity to think," shifting the field, although he didn't recognize that had happened at the time. On this occasion, in his answering text, he wrote, "I have a thought about how we might proceed that might just make it unnecessary to keep pulling on the Chinese finger trap[8]—at least between you and me, and then maybe elsewhere as well. Please see if you can come to the session tomorrow and we'll talk about it" (p. 344).

Alan did come for the next session. Alan had apparently "heard" something compelling in Stern's text, just as Stern thinks he had heard something compelling in Alan's. Stern now told Alan that, from then on, he thought they should ignore everything "except what was in his head in the session, whether that made sense or not, and whether it was connected to something obviously meaningful or not." They needed to stop going over and over his attendance issues.

Stern writes that "what was important about this" "was that I meant it." As he put it,

> I felt that I just couldn't stand to keep hitting him over the head and feeling intellectualized. Of course, my suggestion was hardly radical. It was nothing more than a restatement of free association, *although I didn't think of that at the time*. I thought that what I said came completely from me. And I think I was right, actually, even though of course I probably could not have thought of this particular alternative without being a psychoanalyst. (p. 344; our emphasis)

For Stern the crucial point about this type of technical approach to psychoanalysis is the sense of authenticity—"it came completely from me." As he elaborated, for Stern, "unconscious process is potential experience, what conscious experience

---

8. A toy of Alan's that had often come up.

might become"; and for that reason, he says, he does not "accept that the contents of the unconscious are aptly described as unconscious phantasy" (p. 337). Rather, for Stern, unconscious process is "unformulated experience"—states of potential meaningfulness that are "vaguely organized, primitive, global, non-ideational, and affectively saturated" (p. 337).

From Stern's frame of reference, the most crucial clinical events in a psycho-analytic treatment, as it evolves moment to moment, as we saw in his description, can happen both *inside* and *outside* the consulting room. His view is that, skillfully handled, events can resolve aspects of the ambiguously unformulated experience patients experience into some sort of explicit, more consciously meaningful shape. And, crucially, the most significant influence on such resolution is the current con-figuration of the interpersonal field. So that what matters, according to Stern, is the nature of the "analytic relatedness" between analyst and patient. He elaborates to clarify that what he means is that to the extent "to which the field is free to develop spontaneously between analyst and patient" (p. 337), the conscious thoughts and feelings of both analyst and patient are free to do the same. And to the extent that the field is frozen or constricted, the depth and spontaneity of the participants' conscious experience is compromised.

Stern does interpret, as we saw, but in his frame of reference, stating that "the rev-elation of unconscious content is not really the point, and interpretation is not neces-sarily the means of therapeutic action . . . [although he does also say that] what we say to our patients is an important influence on the next generation of clinical events" (p. 337). As in his example, it is when the analyst is capable of knowing or feeling some-thing new toward or about the patient—that is, when the analyst becomes capable of a new experience or of making a new interpretation—that the patient can move. Clinical attention is on the ways "relational freedom" is compromised.

PHILIP BROMBERG

A seventh example of psychoanalytic development since Freud died is taken from the work of Philip Bromberg, another North American relational analyst. Bromberg (2000) also describes a difficult clinical situation.

A patient he calls Alec had been in analytic treatment with him for about one year, on the couch. He had come regularly to sessions four times a week but, at the time of the report, had for several months been more and more openly dissatisfied that the treatment was not, as he put it, moving fast enough. Alec could not describe the details of what "fast enough" meant or what the sessions felt like to him, other than to say it felt pointless to just lie on the couch and discuss how pointless the sessions felt. He also asserted that, despite his wishing not to come to sessions, he had every intention of staying in treatment, even though he did not quite know why. All he did know was that he wished he could get something out of it.

Bromberg writes that he did not at first feel consciously uncomfortable with this development and was curious to see where this new "material" would go. He reports that ordinarily his approach is to use his "own feelings as a source of data as well as my patient's difficulty in articulating" theirs. He anticipated that this feeling relationship would become clearer so that the "work" would then move along (p. 20).[9]

But "No such luck!" he wrote. His patient arrived for a session and told him that he had joined a group run by a [behavior] therapist, who was an established rival. Alec informed Bromberg, with more enthusiasm than he had shown in months, that he wanted to see if he could help the analysis move along faster. He expressed some concern about what he had done but attributed it to his own insecurity that his analyst might disapprove. Bromberg writes,

> I'm taken completely off guard by this development and experience some anxiety and mild irritation; but I realize that if whatever is going on between us can be explored, this might start to provide the clarity I'd been hoping for. Determined to maintain empathic contact with my patient's own viewpoint while inquiring into the interaction between us, I shift my perspective on the situation to one that sees Alec's behavior as an act of self-expression that requires respect and acknowledgment, though not necessarily agreement. I'm now feeling able to encompass, at least consciously, what I experience as going on in myself at that moment (including my negative feelings toward Alec) as simply "more grist for the analytic mill," and I'm more curious about my irritation than threatened by it. (p. 20)

So Bromberg reports he said to himself something like "Okay, Alec will either stay in this rational-emotive therapy group or he won't, but whatever he does we will have a chance to explore the meaning of it to him, along with his experience that I didn't invalidate the importance of it to him. He thinks to himself that perhaps this will all prove 'good.'" In this way, he thinks to himself, "My anxiety and irritation are, at least for the moment, held in a professionally containable framework of meaning through this empathic identification" (p. 20).

Contained by these thoughts, Bromberg then asks Alec to tell him in more detail about the feeling of disapproval he is anticipating from him, expecting the answer will start to make more sense of both his and his patient's feelings.

Alec, however, raises the stakes. He responds by saying that the additional cost of the group makes him now unable to continue paying for four sessions per week, at least for the next year, and he is going to have to cut back to three!

In his brave and honest account Bromberg reports,

> I can now feel myself getting hot under the collar. My anger is now feeling somehow "personal." I am even able to recognize that my patient's infuriatingly "impersonal" manner must be a corresponding part of the same context as my own feelings, but the awareness isn't feeling like "material." The concept of "setting limits," usually an idea I employ only with great reluctance, suddenly feels like a weapon. I realize that it would be useful to have my own feelings under better control before saying anything further, and decide to wait and remain silent as I think about what is happening. (Pp. 20–21)

---

9. Bromberg (1986) has further described these ideas and this vignette in his essay "Love and Hate in Psychoanalysis."

It is Alec who breaks the silence by saying that he feels his analyst is "very mad at him right now and that using the couch feels 'wrong.'"[10]

Moreover, before Bromberg is able to think out a response, Alec sits up and tells him that he "feels much better sitting up and being able to look at each other. In fact, he wants to try sitting up for a while." "Perhaps," he says, "between the group and sitting up, the analysis may move faster" (p. 21).

Bromberg now describes himself as "on the ropes"—pushed back in a fight. He writes that he "[can] feel my own hatred in my body and in every sentence that I formulate in my mind, but reject saying. I also know that my feeling shows in my face and that Alec, now sitting up, can probably see it" (p. 21).

Bromberg decides that, if he were able to communicate what he was feeling to Alec, it might be useful because he might then be freer to deal more openly with what he already sees but cannot fully use. He says to Alec, "I don't know what to make of what is happening between us right now, but I'd like to see if we can make some sense of it from both of our perspectives. How are you experiencing what is going on?" (p. 21).

His patient replies that he does not know what there is to look at and that now he is totally confused and upset because he feels like nothing he said was understood. "But," he goes on, "I know that I have so many problems it makes me wonder if I'm seeing this all wrong. After all, I did come to you because you're the expert. Maybe I should have a consultation with another analyst to get clear on that. Would that be all right with you, and would you give me someone's name since I don't know any other analysts?" (p. 21). We leave the discussion hanging at that point.

Bromberg's purpose here is to show what he sees as the limitations of "trying to do the right thing." His preferred alternative is to work with patient's and analyst's respective experiences. He writes, "What started as a therapeutic enactment had become a potential abyss" (p. 22). He says he offered himself numerous rationalizations and options until he discovered each to be "wrong." It was only when he ran out of "techniques" and gave up trying to do the "right thing" that he and Alec ultimately made personal contact and openly worked with their respective experiences, including the extent of their undisclosed anger toward one another and the warded-off shame it masked.

His overall point is that shifts in state of mind, whether the patient's or the analyst's, provide the core context for a genuine analytic experience to take shape. The clinical implication he draws is that the locus of therapeutic action is not in the material that is told to the analyst, as if it were a buried fantasy uncovered by piecing together the links between a patient's associations. Rather, therapeutic action is organized affectively, through the process of enactment between patient and analyst,[11] where it then has a chance to be symbolized by the verbal meaning attached to the affective perception of what is taking place in the here and now.

---

10. "Mad" in American English means angry.

11. The usual psychoanalytic definition of "enactment," from Freud's use of the word *Agieren*, has the meaning of acting out or actualization of an unconscious wish or fantasy (see glossary). But that is not the meaning here: in an American relational context, it simply means interpersonal interaction, implying no underlying unconscious ideation.

SURFACING DIFFERENCE

These seven examples demonstrate a variety of ways psychoanalysts from within different networks of practice have been doing psychoanalysis that are available in the literature since Freud's death. Describing them, we have tried to bring out some of the more obvious differences, but it will be apparent that to do a more systematic analysis or to ask a question like "Do I work more like Kernberg, Busch, or Green?" requires precisely the kind of common framework that defines significant differences that we discussed earlier.

The approach to developing such a framework that we will elaborate in subsequent chapters rests on the idea, argued in the first book produced by the Working Party on Comparative Clinical Methods (Tuckett et al., 2008), that every practitioner attempting to do psychoanalysis must necessarily be being guided by a theoretical framework of some kind, even if it is only implicit. That framework is what distinguishes psychoanalytic practice, at least in principle, from the practice of a chest physician, life coach, physiotherapist, or priest. As Dana Birksted Breen observed in our first book, "Psychoanalysis cannot be psychoanalysis without the structure of a theoretical model, even if models vary" (Tuckett et al., 2008, p. 1).

She was stressing that although the psychoanalytic setup is two people talking regularly, how practice is conducted in it depends crucially on the ideas about psychoanalysis, whether implicit or explicit, that the analyst puts into practice. Practice may vary between practitioners (and be pushed and pulled by their daily experiences of success and failure with their patients), but every analyst's theory of day-to-day psychoanalytic practice must necessarily structure what their psychoanalysis will look like.

Methodologically, to orient our efforts to capture core elements of an analyst's practice, we borrowed the anthropologist's term "explanatory model." It is a term used to abstract, make sense of, and compare organized belief systems and practices, such as religious or medical practices, existing within different communities so that particular related features can be drawn out and compared. It has proved particularly useful when applied to the success or failure of communicative practices in psychiatry and medicine (Kleinman, 1980; Tuckett et al., 1985), or more generally to explore situations of potential misunderstanding between participants who give different meanings, embedded in different causal models, to events and processes (Tuckett et al., 2020). In a modern political context, it can be applied to Democrats and Republicans in the United States. They view much of the world, such as the origins of Covid-19, in very different ways, not only because they have various different beliefs but because these are "organized" into two differing explanatory models.

The clinical illustrations from the seven psychoanalysts just shared can be analyzed theoretically as considered "performances" (to use a term from sociological analysis) of the explanatory model each of those psychoanalysts was working inside. The advantage of this way of thinking for comparative analysis is that explanatory models, for our purposes, as for anthropological study, do *not* imply that the different analysts necessarily knew the models they were performing or could even describe their components. They "did" their psychoanalytic sessions just as great musicians play their instruments, great chefs cook, or great surgeons perform operations. Although we would expect that they could, to a degree, be nudged to elaborate components of what they were doing and some of their reasons why they did it, fundamentally they just did it. The issue here is not whether they were conscious or unconscious of their method, in a psychoanalytic sense; it is rather that most expert practice works, as when we drive a car. What a comparison using an explanatory model approach brings to understanding cannot replace the "something more" that true expertise always involves. But it can postulate and describe some core elements that a particular practice must achieve in *one way or another* to constitute that practice.

The four dimensions developed for Step 2 and mentioned above were our starting point for defining some essential elements of psychoanalytic practice. In our common framework they are modified into four different lines of enquiry into *the core suppositions* that psychoanalysts put into practice when they are doing psychoanalysis:

1. How did the psychoanalysts we studied suppose that what is inaccessible to a patient's consciousness (for shorthand, an unconscious script) but is nonetheless driving their experience and responses becomes evident in and/or influences a psychoanalytic session, so that they can recognize it? (Transference and counter-transference suppositions are reported in Chapter 3.)
2. What sources of data did the psychoanalysts we studied suppose they needed to draw on in their sessions, and how did they create the conditions for this to be possible, to infer what is otherwise inaccessible to their patients? (Suppositions about inferring unconscious content are reported in Chapter 4.)
3. What did the psychoanalysts we studied suppose was inaccessible but repeatedly reproducing their patients' problems and how did they know this was so? (Suppositions about what is unconsciously repeated to create patients' problems and why are reported in Chapter 5.)
4. How did the psychoanalysts we studied suppose they could make a difference, and what did they need to put in train in their sessions for that to work? (Suppositions about making a difference through a psychoanalytic process are reported in Chapter 6.)

These four questions are the basis of the common theoretical framework we will set out in subsequent chapters, beginning with Chapter 3. We will return to the seven analysts again in Chapter 8.

SUMMARY

This book tries to answer the question of what psychoanalysts do when they are practicing psychoanalysis. In this chapter we have described how, to achieve our aim, we collected a unique dataset of everyday clinical sessions using a two-step workshop discussion method designed to reveal and understand different ways of working. We have also described how we had to evolve a new common theoretical framework to surface and then make sense of the differences in the data, which we did during fifteen years of iterative meetings, trying to apprehend and understand the differences we could sense from the workshop materials and fit the clinical data to theory and vice versa. We have also described how we found that Freud's writing, particularly in German, offered a third pillar to support our efforts. Trying to conceptualize not only how the presenters in our workshops differed in the suppositions they put into practice but also how Freud's suppositions changed as his work evolved improved our understanding of our framework and the ways it could be used.

Finally, to present our findings in this book, we have had to develop a lively means to convey to any psychoanalyst reading it a sense of the crucial differences. The overall aim is to create a structure that psychoanalysts can use to ask themselves what they do and where they think their practice fits, if they are minded to review and reflect on their clinical work.

In the next chapter we will elaborate on our two-step method for discussion and on the new approach to researching and reflecting on psychoanalytic work that it has enabled. Thereafter, the chapters will explore what we concluded that the different analysts who presented in our workshops were doing, when viewed through the lens of the four suppositions just outlined.

2

Our Method and Our Data

As we have just set out, this book aims to answer questions about what we are doing when we do psychoanalysis. To do so, it will combine what we could find out about the suppositions held by the presenters in our workshops with those we infer were held by Sigmund Freud and the seven clinicians described in Chapter 1. This exercise will lead us to a list of questions all psychoanalysts should find useful to ask themselves and reflect on in their own work.

Surprisingly, what we are attempting—that is, a systematic look at significant numbers of psychanalytic cases conducted by many different psychoanalysts—is in fact rather novel. One reason is theoretical. As discussed in Chapter 1, a consistent framework against which to describe and discuss different practices hasn't been available. The second reason is practical and methodological. Psychoanalysts do not organize routinely to present their ordinary clinical work to each other in the systematic way that is required to make comparisons between different approaches. The two reasons together have so far proved decisive.

Consequently, students of psychoanalysis or even mature practitioners have very little solid ground on which to compare what they are trying to do with the practice of others.

Chapter 1 introduced the need for a new common theoretical framework to study differences between psychoanalysts and suggested it could be based on "four suppositions" that every psychoanalyst necessarily must make. We will elaborate the framework we developed in later chapters. Meanwhile, the purpose of this chapter is to describe how we gathered our observations of psychoanalytic practice from which to draw the conclusions we present in this book.

There were two principal challenges: first, where to get the examples of clinical practice to try to understand (data selection) and, second, how meaningfully to infer from the data what the different psychoanalysts providing examples were supposing (data interpretation and analysis).

The latter task, given the lack of any existing comparative framework (Tuckett et al., 2008) and the fact that understanding what an analyst is doing inevitably requires interpretation, was the most challenging. As Widlöcher (1994) pointed out, "A case is not a fact" (p. 1233); in other words, in slightly different language, the data simply does not speak for itself. This problem, of course, exists even in biological or physical sciences as well as in psychological and social sciences. But in all those fields, some confidence that conclusions are more than mere opinion rests on method. Careful definition, repetition, and the use of numbers as summary devices for measuring well-defined concepts, aided by the formality of the experimental method, go a long way toward surfacing subjective issues of interpretation and so establishing the meaning of data. In psychoanalysis, the concepts, not to mention ways of indicating them, are fuzzy. Moreover, as we will discuss in Chapter 4, the twin facts that the clinical aim is unconscious inference and that the psychoanalyst must be an actor in the process being described clearly raise momentous issues.

An interpretation of the absence of existing work indicates a lack of belief that we can do better. However, if we are not to face the consequences, which are some combination of "anything goes" and authoritarian "diktat," efforts toward solution of both the data-selection and data-interpretation problems are required.

COLLECTING OBSERVATIONS: TWO-STEP WORKSHOPS TO CREATE THE DATA

When we began in 2003, our solution to the data-selection problem was to create a series of specialized workshops in Europe, using the Comparative Clinical Method (CCM) or two-step method, broadly described previously (Tuckett, 2012; Tuckett et al., 2008). They have continued until the present day, numbering around three hundred in all.[1]

Each workshop had a presenter, whose work was discussed by a small group of colleagues from different psychoanalytic centers using different approaches and languages. The members of the moderators' group and the authors of this book also come from diverse traditions.

Who made up the "sample" of presenters at these workshops?

For several years, they were limited to very experienced "training analysts" from Europe as well as North and South America. For this reason, we can conclude that many of the psychoanalysts presenting their work over this time included many of the most distinguished of the era. Latterly, we have continued to ask such very experienced colleagues but also extended the net more widely. By now, those accepting the invitation have come from all the main centers and, at least in a formal sense, represent all the main traditions of clinical work currently practiced—albeit with a bias toward English speakers.[2]

---

1. Other workshops have been organized by "sister" groups in North and South America. They are organized a little differently, so the data is not used here.

2. We have conducted workshops in Spanish, Portuguese, French, and Russian, but the method is most successful when the participants come from diverse analytic cultural and theoretical backgrounds.

Although we have held groups on three continents, the groups were mostly run in English—this is unfortunate, but it facilitates the interchange of views. It may introduce some bias as although some presenters spoke French, Spanish, and Italian, discussants of their work mostly came from Germany, the Netherlands, Scandinavia, eastern Europe, the United Kingdom, and the United States.

In the workshop, a psychoanalyst presents a brief history and between one and three verbatim sessions of what they consider a working psychoanalysis, usually making the case anonymous in terms of names, place-names, and other identifying details. Further editing work has been done for this book—so that here we focus on presentations, which were originally discussed with all relevant facts but have now been made general and limited to just the crucial information needed to support the points being made. This is a necessary limitation to protect both patients and analysts.

In each workshop, a group, usually of around twelve to fifteen other well-qualified psychoanalysts, listens to the presentation with a moderator. They then discuss—first so that they feel confident they know the relevant details and the reasons the analyst has for what he or she said, insofar as these can be articulated. The groups then complete the two steps described below. The workshop usually lasts not less than ten hours over two to three days.

Each workshop group is set up with some organizational principles and has a moderator. Moderators have previously had the experience of being a presenter and of taking part in discussion with the other moderators. They have a working knowledge of the concepts and principal assumptions, but each has their own style. Because the concepts (like psychoanalytic method) are hard to internalize, the way groups discussed them did differ. We will try to bring out where we think this might matter for conclusions.

Before the workshop starts, moderators will usually have spoken with the presenter to explain what will happen and at the beginning will outline the principal assumptions and roles. In the workshop itself moderators chair the discussion, ensure that the roles of the presenter and discussants are respected, and try to help group members to use the conceptual tools (Step 1 and 2 definitions below) that the CCM moderators' group has developed over twenty years. Moderators then write a report, sometimes assisted by others in the workshop group, and present it to the other moderators. This report is usually shared with the group and presenter, but the level of response meant practice could vary.

A core assumption during each workshop is that the presenter and everyone else present is a psychoanalyst and therefore that the sessions presented are to be considered typical of an ordinary working psychoanalysis. For this reason, presenters are asked to select a case that they believe demonstrates their psychoanalytic method.[3]

What can we conclude from this sample? Although the selection was clearly not random (which would be a challenge to implement anyway), we chose presenters with

---

3. Early on people manifestly brought cases to get "help." Probably there is always some element of this, but as we went on we asked presenters to find a case in which they thought a psychoanalysis was "in progress."

a reputation that could support the assumption that their significant peers thought they were doing psychoanalysis, albeit their way. For several years we used the heuristic that presenters should only be training analysts or equivalent others, because their status has usually been subject to some kind of collegial review.

All cases were discussed for many hours over the last twenty years. We will discuss below how, for the practical task of describing what the psychoanalysts did for this book, we eventually selected sixteen (mostly recent) cases to discuss in detail. We cannot say whether this sample is representative of all types of work, but we believe we have obtained a wide range, covering most of the techniques encountered in the past twenty years.

TWO STEPS

CCM workshops are organized with two core steps. Step 1 focuses on the analyst's "interventions," and Step 2, using what has been learned in Step 1, focuses on the suppositions behind them.

Step 1 was an innovation. It was designed to focus the group's attention on the details of what the psychoanalyst did, trying to alter for most participants what has been their usual focus: how to understand the patient. In practice, clinical discussion among psychoanalysts often becomes an opportunity to offer competitive evaluations of the way the presenting analyst or outspoken group members understand or would work differently with the patient. This might be called not discussion but supervision. Instead, the innovation behind Step 1 was to instill collective curiosity about the function of what the presenting psychoanalysts were doing and, behind that, their supporting suppositions.

As discussed in the first book produced by the Working Party on Comparative Clinical Methods (Tuckett et al., 2008), experience suggests, in effect, that many psychoanalysts seem to develop a kind of allergy when attending to clinical material, especially when presented by someone apparently using a different framework. The allergic response seems to be promoted by feelings of "not like me" or even "not as good as me." Such focus in discussions is sometimes used to produce controversy and spectacle (as, for example, in the argument between André Green and Ted Jacobs at the International Psychoanalytic Association's 1993 congress discussed by Paul Denis [2008]). Usually, it ends in stalemate and entrenched bad feeling.

As mentioned, each group has a moderator to help the group implement the two-step method, as follows. First, the presenter is invited to provide a brief history before presenting the sessions. Ideally this is spontaneous (i.e., not written down), but language and communication difficulties meant we had to be flexible. This introductory period is followed by conventional discussion, which also takes place after each session presented, to allow the group to be comfortable with the material as psychoanalysts and to gain some understanding of the described situation in their own terms. It may mean asking the presenter to explain or elaborate, and so forth. In any case, after presenting what they judge relevant background (Step −1) and then presenting each session with further discussion (Step 0), the analyst sits back and plays only an occasional clarifying role, listening to the discussion as the moderator moves it to the first of the two steps (Step 1).

During the Step 1 discussion, each intervention the analyst made is studied, one by one, in the context of what happened before and after, and an attempt is made to think about which of the six functional categories (Figure 2.1, next page) that we have found useful fits each intervention best.[4] The group is encouraged to disagree with and challenge each suggestion and to give reasons so that different assumptions and interpretations of the analyst's inferences and comments can be surfaced and opened in the group. For instance, if the analyst makes a comment about the patient being frightened of displeasing the analyst, would that be "designating" the transference in the "here and now" (4) or not? The question is a stimulus for different views—such as of what is meant by "here and now." In any case, once two or three hours have elapsed and most (apparently) different kinds of interventions have been explored, so that a pattern is emerging about the analyst's approach, the moderator will judge Step 1 can end. Because the group appears to have a sufficient idea of the kinds of things the analyst does and what she or he listens to or not, it is now ready to begin to focus more intensively on what the analyst's suppositions are.

The moderator now introduces the second step—although in the most successful groups, Step 1 smoothly transitions into Step 2. Now is the time that the group tries to think together about the analyst's suppositions. They should by now have got an idea of the function of what the analyst has been trying to do when speaking, and, as a corollary, at least some idea of how the presenting analyst has set about interpreting the unconscious meaning of what the patient has said. Aided by the moderator the group will then try to build on these ideas to explore each of the five core theoretical issues in Figure 2.2 (p. 33) and decide into which type the presenting analyst's suppositions fit.

The five original components of Step 2 were (1) listening to unconscious content, (2) how analysis works, (3) how a successful process is furthered, (4) what's wrong, and (5) the analytic situation (see Tuckett et al., 2008). Understanding what we meant by each one—recognizing core differences in how analysts approached each task—required a long iterative journey, in which the writing of this book was itself a significant step. Eventually we settled on four components rather than five, cast as suppositions. We will be introducing them and their exact meanings in Chapters 3 to 6.

It is worth noting that some parts of the Step 2 task will always prove harder than others. Group members know quite easily from the presentation what it is that patient and analyst said to each other (and anything the analyst had added by way of

---

4. These categories were developed via discussion and experience from an original thirteen used in 2003 (see Tuckett et al., 2008, pp. 138ff.). They have not changed since 2004 because they seem to work for the purpose—which is to provoke a wide-ranging discussion of what, with that intervention, the analyst was trying to do.

Comments here are likely to be ambiguous, polysemic, and brief–aiming (with a specific idea of Ucs process) to encourage more association or linking but at the **unconscious** level. *So an opportunity to see what is meant by dynamic unconscious and psychoanalytic process.*

For instance–"Walls?" "A mouth with teeth!" "A bedroom!" "Not feeling hateful?"

Note: No comment can escape the conscious or unconscious but some comments are more directed at one than the other. As one participant put it: "a certain type of wording, i.e., repeating a word that seemed to be central, is basically different from, let's say, clarification, or designation of what is happening in the here and now."

Such comments apparently make the patient conscious of some observations and so enable one to wonder why that matters to A. You will recognize them compared to 2 because they are likely to be more saturated (i.e., to have a clear and unambiguous meaning rather than more ambiguous meaning). Compared to a 4 when they concern the analytical relationship they will be more atemporal or apersonal. The discussion why an intervention might not be the 4 or 3 etc. is more important than the outcome.

Examples: "How do you think of a wall?" "What are you thinking?" "What's going on in your mind?" "Do you think there is a pattern in the way you are here and how you are with your wife?" "You quite often seem to be irritated by your boss." "I think you feel you don't want to talk about that." "It seems to me you get anxious when you think about coming to see me." "There was a purpose but it collapsed." "Tell me more about that feeling." "Any associations?" "The process of cutting yourself is happening now" *(Apersonal? But not atemporal so marginal to 4.)*

---

2. Adding an element to facilitate unconscious process.

3. Questions, clarifications, reformulations, aimed at making matters conscious.

1. Maintaining the basic setting.

4. Designating here and now emotional and phantasy meaning of the situation with an analyst.

5. Constructions directed at providing elaborated meaning.

6. Sudden and apparently glaring reactions not easy to relate to A's normal method.

Basic behavior creating the setting in simple ways. For example: "You have forgotten your coat," "My holiday begins on Friday."

There are circumstances where these comments might be 6 or even 3–that's for debate! (*Such debate may help to see how this A thinks of the analytic situation.*)

This category is designed to explore if A has a concept of mistakes (*CT enactment perhaps or the analytic field as bidirectional*) and whether this is noticed or considered in session. The aim is to bring out underlying ideas and rationales. This category should not be used to supervise the analyst–the analysts must see the comment as a mistake in some way.

Example: "We need to understand this!" (An apparently 1 or 3 type remark but eventually judged by A and group to be 6–because what happened before had clearly disturbed the A and this was an enactment of his irritation.)

Example: "That's quite normal"–said in a moment of anxiety by A when there was an external noise, but then realized by A to prevent associations.

Several ideas come together in the sense A talks about things that have been observed together–not necessarily in one session. [*An opportunity to explore why this helps or perhaps not–A's theory of psychic change.*]

Example: "Maybe you set limits to me like you do to your mother. I am becoming like your nagging and oppressing 'mother analyst'; while I nag you with more and more questions you become…"

These comments **must be specific to the emotional or phantasy meaning situation in the current session**–here and now. Distinguish from comments more generally about the analytic relationship. Usually this will mean that the analyst will specify "you" feel "x" about "me" now or vice versa. But precisely this is for group discussion.

Examples: "You feel I am far too interested in you." "I just made you anxious." "You feel you have not paid me today." "I think you feel I have become grandiose and very pleased with myself." "You hate it that I said something just then and you think you should do the whole thing."

Figure 2.1. Step 1. *Source:* Adapted in October 2022 from Tuckett et al. (2008).

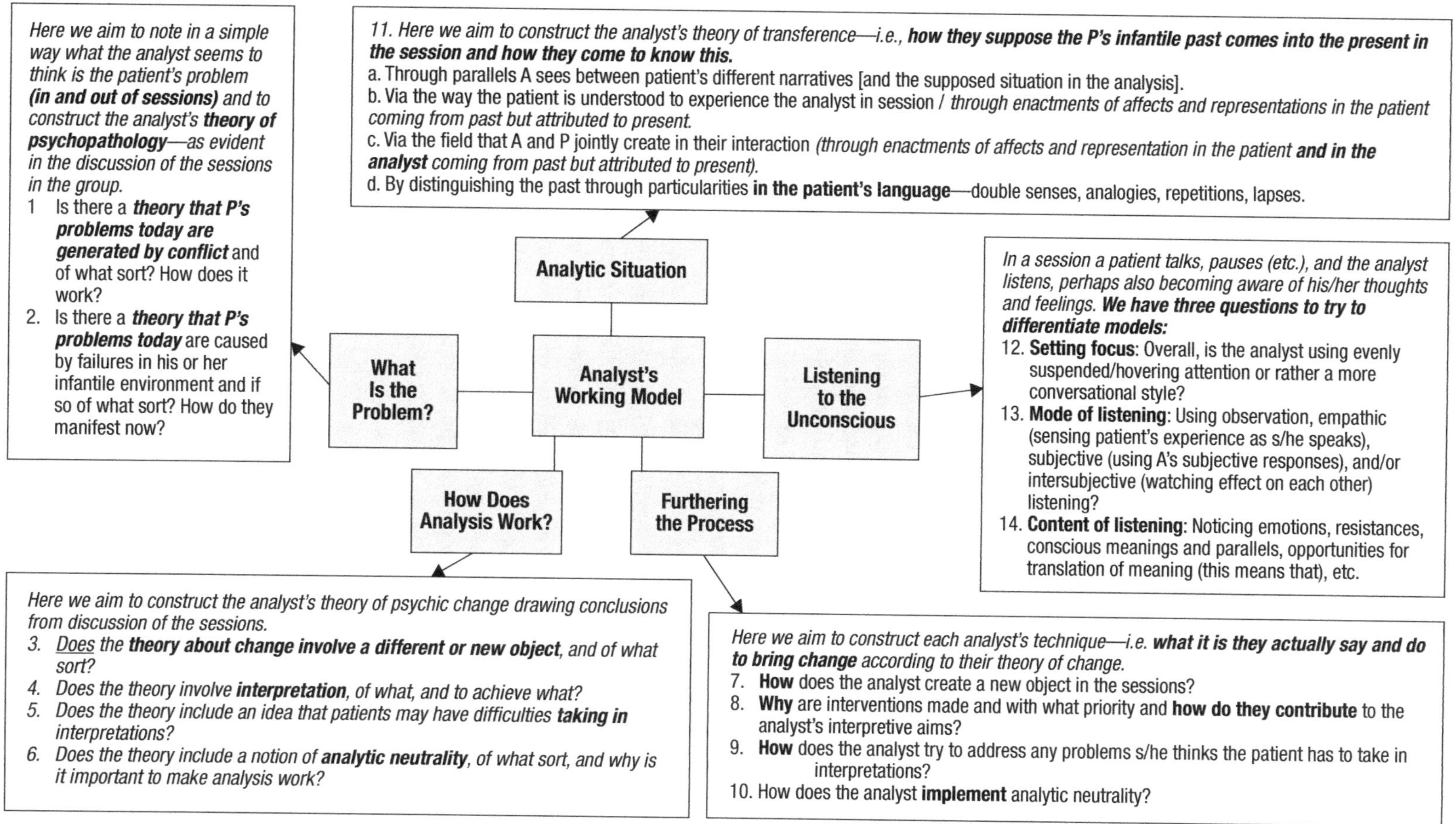

11. Here we aim to construct the analyst's theory of transference—i.e., **how they suppose the P's infantile past comes into the present in the session and how they come to know this.**
a. Through parallels A sees between patient's different narratives [and the supposed situation in the analysis].
b. Via the way the patient is understood to experience the analyst in session / through enactments of affects and representations in the patient coming from past but attributed to present.
c. Via the field that A and P jointly create in their interaction *(through enactments of affects and representation in the patient and in the analyst coming from past but attributed to present).*
d. By distinguishing the past through particularities **in the patient's language**—double senses, analogies, repetitions, lapses.

In a session a patient talks, pauses (etc.), and the analyst listens, perhaps also becoming aware of his/her thoughts and feelings. **We have three questions to try to differentiate models:**
12. **Setting focus:** Overall, is the analyst using evenly suspended/hovering attention or rather a more conversational style?
13. **Mode of listening:** Using observation, empathic (sensing patient's experience as s/he speaks), subjective (using A's subjective responses), and/or intersubjective (watching effect on each other) listening?
14. **Content of listening:** Noticing emotions, resistances, conscious meanings and parallels, opportunities for translation of meaning (this means that), etc.

Here we aim to construct each analyst's technique—i.e. **what it is they actually say and do to bring change** according to their theory of change.
7. **How** does the analyst create a new object in the sessions?
8. **Why** are interventions made and with what priority and **how do they contribute** to the analyst's interpretive aims?
9. **How** does the analyst try to address any problems s/he thinks the patient has to take in interpretations?
10. How does the analyst **implement** analytic neutrality?

Here we aim to note in a simple way what the analyst seems to think is the patient's problem **(in and out of sessions) and to** construct the analyst's **theory of psychopathology**—as evident in the discussion of the sessions in the group.
1 Is there a **theory that P's problems today are generated by conflict** and of what sort? How does it work?
2. Is there a **theory that P's problems today** are caused by failures in his or her infantile environment and if so of what sort? How do they manifest now?

Here we aim to construct the analyst's theory of psychic change drawing conclusions from discussion of the sessions.
3. Does the **theory about change involve a different or new object**, and of what sort?
4. Does the theory involve **interpretation**, of what, and to achieve what?
5. Does the theory include an idea that patients may have difficulties **taking in** interpretations?
6. Does the theory include a notion of **analytic neutrality**, of what sort, and why is it important to make analysis work?

Analytic Situation

Analyst's Working Model

Listening to the Unconscious

Furthering the Process

What Is the Problem?

How Does Analysis Work?

Figure 2.2. Step 2. *Source:* From Tuckett (2012). *Note:* This version of Step 2, developed from versions published in Tuckett et al. (2008) and Tuckett (2012), was first in use in 2017 as a guide to the questions to be asked in workshops and has been used subsequently.

explanation to the group). This provided a reasonably firm foundation from which (1) to start to draw conclusions about how the analyst seemed to be furthering an analytic process, and (2) to draw inferences about how analysis might be supposed to make a difference. Clearly each intervention in one way or another exemplified a way of furthering the analytic process, and because the Step 1 task was a way to think about its function, it provided some kind of grounding.

But it was a more indirect task to picture what presenters had "heard" in the material, what they supposed was the problem from which the patient was suffering, and what were its unconscious causes as well as what they supposed about what was unconsciously going on between patient and analyst in the analytic situation. Although during the presentation and history and its discussion, as well as in the sessions and their discussion, things were said or implied (by presenting analysts or group members) to help the group form an impression about the analyst's different suppositions, there was always room for doubt. The presenters' reactions to group comments and reactions by the group members (who were of course all psychoanalysts themselves) to the presenter, however, often contained valuable clues. Crucially, at each step, the moderator's task was to encourage participants to support their comments and inferences with what they took to be the evidence from the presentation.

After each workshop, the moderator and possibly others in the group would try to summarize what happened in the group as well as to report everything relevant to trying to decide into which type the presentation was judged by the group to fall on each of five core Step 2 issues (Figure 2.2). In doing this, they were asked to ensure that the conclusions in their reports were based on what the analysts had told them or had said or done in the sessions, which was tested when reports were presented.

Because the five issues stayed essentially the same throughout the project and precise definitions emerged later via iteration,[5] the reports summarizing the group's ideas about the analyst's position are a core source of our data. They were often shared back with group participants (including the presenting analyst) for comments and additions before being discussed at regular moderators' meetings one by one (see Tuckett et al., 2008). Eventually we came to realize these discussions were a third, integrative step. And sometimes reports would be discussed and elaborated in fourth, fifth, and further iterations, including in the challenge of preparing summaries of reports for this book.

Methodologically, we suggest that this approach to data collection and analysis is new and significant for psychoanalysis. Moving away from individual inference, it advances from merely idiosyncratic data analysis to make use of the "expert" knowledge of a diverse group of psychoanalytically trained participants to identify the elements needed reliably to infer into which "type" (the shaded inner boxes in Figure 2.2) a particular presentation seems to fit.

To summarize and elaborate, there are three levels of data, as depicted in Figure 2.3: the original account of a session provided by the presenter; the interpretive report from the workshop group, which captures the meanings a diverse group of

---

5. "How analysis works" and "Furthering the process" were eventually combined.

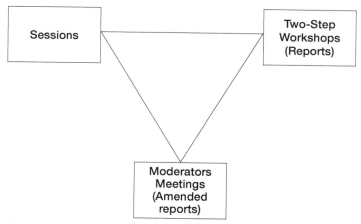

Figure 2.3. Three Sources of Data

professional colleagues gave to the material from the presenter; and a third-level comparative analysis from the moderators. The data, in other words, is not just what the presenters remember of what happened in the sessions they are describing but also the meanings of those descriptions as they have become filtered and developed by successive groups of experienced psychoanalyst peers—first in the workshops and then in the moderators' meetings. We think this triple source of meaning (from the session and from the meaning given to the session in two groups later) is a unique and highly relevant resource for psychoanalytic research, in fact an opinion also shared by two of the other European working parties (Hinze, 2015; Reith et al., 2018), insofar as it extends the work of a presenter from within the framework in which they are usually located into a more general and communicable one.

Of course, like our everyday understanding of ourselves and our patients, progressive clarity of meaning is conceivable, but endpoints to understanding are not. We need to be clear with our readers, therefore, that any conclusions we draw from all this work are an evolved amalgam of a developing understanding of what the presenters recalled their patients saying to them, and vice versa, and then the ideas about it that developed in our workshops.[6] To put it another way, the clinical exemplifications describe the presented psychoanalytic work as successive groups of psychoanalysts understood the psychoanalysis presented.

---

6. Note in this book we do not discuss the status of the analyst's accounts of sessions or the reasons why most psychoanalysts think of the data of psychoanalysis as complex and subjective and so not captured in an authoritative way by "objective" means such as tape recordings or externally validated facts. In the room with the patient, the analyst has "remembered" bits of history and other details and feelings and, of course, thoughts of their own, which may differ from those they may have in another session or later. There are also second thoughts. Different analysts have different views on all this. We see little practical alternative but to suppose that what the analysts and the group discussion produce is the "data" but at the same time that it is open to multiple meanings. Multiple dimensionalities mean we cannot know for sure what happened in the past or even, fully, what is happening in the present. All we can do is make a case for what we think and hope it is useful.

SELECTING DATA TO ILLUSTRATE OUR FINDINGS

The result of all the workshops we ran and then tried to process through our third-level moderator meetings was a literally enormous quantity of fascinating data.

To share it, so that it could paint at least an intersubjective picture for others, we first experimented with creating a series of standardized "thumbnail sketches" of the way our various analysts worked with a patient. We imagined using the thumbnails to make comparisons among ourselves and then to describe them to readers. However, despite laboriously completing more than seventy thumbnails, we were forced to conclude it didn't really work. The thumbnails were stilted and hard to identify with. Two readers didn't necessarily get the same thing from them. Above all, too much depended on the assumptions a reader made when reading a brief account—which typically triggered both multiple conflicting responses and all kinds of emotional reactions. We published five thumbnails (Tuckett, 2012) but then gave up. They just didn't really work for us and so seemed certain not to work for others.

After further experimentation, therefore, we realized that for this book we would have to present our conclusions about how we think psychoanalysts work mainly by telling illustrated stories around each main theme, but constantly referring to what was described by the presenters as going on in the sessions and then trying to spell out the meanings given to it in the workshops and afterward. To try to make sure the arguments in the following chapters make sense and are supportable, we have been making them to each other through the process of sharing drafts, debating, and then, critically, repeating it all in the writing of this book. In this process we have also used *specially made-safe* excerpts from our workshops to tell stories about what we think the analysts did and supposed.[7] The result is no identifiable material in the texts.

We think this process of iteration is sufficiently robust to give confidence in the validity of the main conclusions we will draw. It is for readers to judge. We can assure them that no central point of conclusion relies on one case or inference. What we present does, we think, describe core features of how today's psychoanalysts are working and is also well supported by multiple unpublished examples in our records system.

WHAT DOES THE DATA LOOK LIKE? SIXTEEN BRIEF EXAMPLES

To provide context for what is to come, we start with some very brief descriptions of some limited aspects of the sixteen made-safe cases we will be using to illustrate the

---

7. We allude here to the procedure we have adopted to anonymize and make safe the (previously not published) clinical material in this book. Psychoanalytic case material simply cannot be published directly because what patients say to their analysts must absolutely remain confidential. No case details, therefore, or details of workshop participants can be taken as referring to any patient-analyst pair or any particular workshop. Any resemblance to any actual patient or analyst has been removed in the final editing of the material. The various stories can be taken as based on what we have encountered, attempting to retain the features that matter for the purpose of the book, but they should not be taken as actual encounters. An undesirable but necessary consequence is that any remaining identifying details should not be considered reliable for other research purposes.

arguments in this book. They are summarized to indicate (1) the kinds of patients and problems the analysts were dealing with, and (2) some of the main things going on in presented sessions. The descriptions are introductory and are intended to give readers a flavor of the types of interactions that took place in these analyses. The names given to patients and analysts will be retained throughout the different chapters. Readers who want to follow some of the more frequently discussed examples will be able to use the index to follow them through the book.

Because the data has been made safe by anonymization, the combinations of female-male, male-female, female-female, and male-male pairs depicted are not reliable; nor are any of the identifying details. Indeed, some cases are composites that illustrate the ways of working we encountered via the use of additional material from quite different cases. As a selection of cases, they are based on many cultures of doing psychoanalysis in many different parts of the world.

Readers might wish at this point to identify which of these clinical situations, or something like them, they have been in and how they recall dealing with them. Surfacing such identifications may be useful both to stimulate curiosity about other ways they might have tried and what it is that each of our sixteen analysts was actually supposing that he or she needed to do.

CASES

1. Moira-Marcel (Hard to Win)

Marcel is a very successful man in his forties in analysis for about a year. He has no real friends and cannot find an ongoing romantic partner. In sessions, the pattern was that Marcel associated for quite long periods with Moira listening attentively. She would comment occasionally, seeking to clarify the problems she thought he was revealing there and then in his relationship to her.

For example, in one session Marcel first talked at length about putting his energy into trying to get "this girl" he didn't care about but wanted to sleep with. Then he said it would be better to put his energy "into thinking about things we're talking about here." After that thought, he said he would go back to dating apps and give it a month. He had tried before but it was not to his advantage, he thought. Gradually he shifted to talking how about he was trying to write a profile for the app that was honest and then to the topic of how someone else would perceive him. His boss had said, "How do you have something to talk about every day in therapy?" He added that sometimes he felt a sense of nausea "here" which was not physiological. He thought it was stress and it was exaggerated by coming here: the pressure, getting up early . . . having to come up with something to make the session. His answer to his boss had been "You don't need to come up with something, something comes." At the same time, he said he knew that hadn't changed the fact that he knew he tried to control his analyst's impression. "By the way, at drinks last night I was far more aware of how manipulative I am. I saw it so clearly," he continued. "But the session yesterday had left me unsatisfied. I didn't get what I wanted. There was more in the dream I brought. It was condensed and powerful.

CASES, continued

So, I felt let down and disappointed." At this point Moira mentioned that yesterday, at the end of the session, he had said that what he really wanted was that she would agree with all his interpretations of his dreams and have nothing more to add. He agreed. Further sequences of this kind, as well as further dreams and their discussion, followed in the rest of the two sessions. Moira tried to help him acknowledge and become interested in the deeper competitive and humiliating anxieties he was experiencing being with her in the session and his different ways of defending against them and their consequences.

2. Jana-Nana (Put on the Spot)

Nana is a thirty-seven-year-old woman brought to analysis through a succession of failed pregnancies leading to depression and despair. Working in art administration, she has a son under five from a marriage made in her early twenties, which she has recently left. Her own mother gave birth to her while still at school and then had a series of complex and chaotic relationships. As well as being depressed and exhausted, Nana is frightened of dying as well as of losing her son due to her separation. Jana reports two sessions. The first was the last session from a series of initial meetings, which had lasted five months. There was then to be a holiday and then the beginning of analysis "proper." The second was a session from the analysis a bit later and after a holiday. In each session Jana is put "on the spot" before Nana associates freely and at length. Jana mostly responds with elliptical allusive comments and suggestive questions hinting at underlying meanings she senses.

For example, in the second session presented, after a holiday, Nana arrived so exactly on time that Jana beckoned her straight in. But before lying down, Nana said, in a joking tone, "How are you. You do not even let me wait!" Jana stayed silent. After a while, Nana said, "I had a dream at the beginning of the holidays. You were in it." Jana responded, "Me: I was in the dream?" "Yes! In the dream. I went to buy fruit in the market, pitted fruit, a kind of plum without the kernel. You appeared in the dream . . . [Nana then laughed.] And you surprised me . . . Before I had time to get out my wallet, you paid for all the fruit and tell the merchant that it is for your daughter!" Going on rapidly so that Jana felt she was prevented from speaking, Nana recounted details of her medically assisted reproductive history and her decision to stop interventions, leave her husband, and apply for a divorce. She then described her husband as very pressing and childish in his sexual desire for her and how she felt used by him just as a vessel of procreation. Describing her husband's desire as an unbearable pressure and an effort to annex her belly, to force her to be a surrogate mother for him, she gave details of the IVF treatment, described as persecuting, intrusive, and retaliatory and conducted in a banal and casual way by the medical team. After much medical description, she summarized. "We block the pituitary to avoid the explosion of ovulation after stimulation, otherwise it would go in all directions!" Here, Jana intervened with a brief but suggestive remark: "in every way?"

3. Robert-Paul (Spicy Food)

Paul is a young married man in his twenties working in an allied field, who in the first session presented had just agreed to increase the frequency of his sessions to that customary for an analysis. He had relationship difficulties, a tendency to claustrophobia brought on when living with his girlfriend, and some uncertainty as to whether to pursue a career working with people or numbers. In the sessions Robert understands most comments Paul makes to refer indirectly to difficult feelings his analyst creates in him. Sometimes he talks about them directly, but more often he uses indirect channels that they clearly both understand—for instance, using references to spicy food and indigestion as metaphors for an experience of mental invasion and a need to retreat. "I have learned," Robert told the group, that "if I cross the threshold of tolerance to pain, either the work will stop immediately . . . or he will flatten himself before his 'tyrannical superior.'"

In the first session Paul talked about being in a rage due to difficult choices presented by his mother, including a demand about how he should behave. He then told a dream and then spoke about a four-star hotel. Robert linked these comments to Paul's anxieties about the demands he felt from Robert and the more intense analytic arrangement, which made him anxious. In a later session, Paul presented a dream about bombings and trying to save himself, indigestion following lunch at his mother's and then more indigestion after another meal with ethnic food, and how his girlfriend had questioned why he would take her to such a place. Robert talked to him about his feeling that his analyst has been insensitive or hostile and, in essence, throws too many difficult ideas at him.

4. Gabriella-Alice (Crushed)

Alice is a twenty-eight-year-old woman in her first year of analysis said to have the potential to be a very beautiful woman with precocious intelligence but who is anxious, depressed, and full of disturbing ideas. She is having grave difficulties making her way in life as an independent adult and sexual woman able to separate from her family. She is so enmeshed in it that so far she has been unable to leave home. The sessions are characterized by quite long associations from Alice and then occasional and very brief interrogative comments from Gabriella, usually with implicit reference to her hidden sources of disturbing experience with Gabriella.

For example, in the first session, Alice began with complaints about how she had felt after her previous session and how she had almost resigned her job fearing that she might be "ruining everything." She then described how she had stopped unpleasant thoughts by being rational but had then gone to a surprisingly unpleasant film. Her analyst had said, "Why this choice of movie?" After at first answering literally, Alice developed several trains of thought leading on to describing an incident in which someone fell on her and to a dream and associations. Gabriella responded with just one word. The idea behind it was that it summarized many aspects of her feeling then and there.

5. Louise-Georgina (In a Hole)

Georgina, aged fifty, has been in analysis for six and a half years. She is an unmarried, lonely, and very depressed woman who, her analyst reports, keeps coming for sessions although she tends to scorn all efforts made to understand her. She has ideas about suicide. The analysis feels so difficult that after around three years Louise nearly gave up—feeling it was a deadly experience for her and she wasn't helping Georgina. But a consultation with a respected colleague had renewed her efforts, reminding her that somewhere inside Georgina, she has always detected something lively. In the workshop, she presented several sessions from different periods in the analysis, beginning with one session that had proved a turning point. Characteristically, sessions took

Continued on next page

CASES, continued

the form of quite long associations from Georgina, sometimes followed by silence and further associations, followed by rather brief comments from Louise, often linked to feelings and thoughts she had noticed that Georgina had induced in her and often directed toward Georgina's deep experience of her.

For example, in one session Georgina had begun with a dream in which a wounded dog with a broken paw was in a hole in a covered pool and was being dragged around and around by the current. The dog's eyes were glassy, and it was going to die. There were many details, but the look in the dog's eyes reminded her of the look in her mother's eyes when near death. Louise found many ideas "taking shape" in her mind. They led to pictures of large numbers of ways she supposed her patient might experience her, but nothing definite. Meanwhile, Georgina seemed to be becoming cold, distant, and hopeless. She complained that analysis is just words and no use. Realizing that she had fallen into some hole in which she was no use, Louise used this experience to make a simple interpretation about their being in a hole together.

6. Gilbert-Claudia (Fear of Violence)

Claudia, in her late twenties, has been in analysis with Gilbert for two years. She is stuck in her professional training and feeling inadequate, excluded, and ashamed about it, as well as having breathing difficulties. While her boyfriend is described as her only salvation, she is also threatened by the relationship as too close. She lives at home with siblings and her mother and father. In recent months she has trusted Gilbert enough to reveal she sometimes hallucinates at home but meanwhile has been able to go back to her work.

The characteristic of all three sessions brought to the workshop were that Claudia would associate for quite long periods, to which Gilbert would respond with brief comments, such as "It is difficult to find a safe shelter from all this aggression. What comes to your mind?" or "In which it seems to be necessary to hide better and not let yourself be seen too much" or "Claudia, you must have been very anxious." Sometimes Gilbert made longer statements, such as "What could the girl in the dream do? Nothing other than be silent, stunned, petrified, surrendering to a destiny that seems already written. You know this passivity; it is always there in your dreams. Freezing yourself can become a retreat not to be seen."

7. Lucia-Leah (Betrayal)

When Leah first contacted Lucia, Lucia had a very powerful reaction, provoking a set of ideas that turned out to be factually incorrect. They began an initial therapy, in which Lucia reached the conclusion that Leah sometimes "stupefied" herself, but after a year they started an analysis, which has now lasted seven years. A feature of the sessions presented is the very close attention and significance Lucia attaches to her experience being with the patient, particularly where it is "strange," such as in her initial powerful reaction. She uses reflections on her experience as well as the content of Leah's associations both to comprehend what she supposes is Leah's deeper experience and what she is struggling with in sessions and in her life.

For instance, the first session began with a dream. The associations that followed led Lucia to make a brief comment and then to find her thoughts had wandered so that she become preoccupied with a dream of her own, and so forth. When her concentration returned, she used this experience (and other material) to suggest to Leah that she felt that changes in the practical arrangement they had recently made had provoked Leah to feel betrayed by her analyst and that she and her husband were ganging up against her.

8. Lorenza-Flavia (An Awkward Love)

Flavia is a woman in her late forties who initially asked Lorenza for help because she was having difficulties living with a female colleague with whom she was very much in love but with whom she did not yet have an erotic relationship. Lorenza reported how she somehow often found working with Flavia uncomfortable and found it hard to address issues directly.

For example, in the first session Flavia talked of her mother as a very powerful presence but also of herself too as powerful and of how if she could get things clear between herself and her mother, it would be preferable to an overprotective relationship. Lorenza thought this might refer to their relationship, but she said, "Yet the way you formulate it, it's as if you situate the nucleus of autonomy primarily in factors outside your psyche and not so much in factors within it." It prompted Flavia with some further interchange to talk about a comparison with her cousins, trying to break free of ties of dependency and to feeling claustrophobic and miserable. The topic in Lorenza's mind was that Flavia was profoundly questioning her sexuality and her femininity, but this was never raised directly. A session making this more explicit is discussed in Chapter 7.

9. Britta-Margareta (Reluctance to Commit)

Margareta is a highly educated, stylish single woman in her late thirties working in posts below her abilities and at the time in her third year of analysis. She had come following the breakdown of a serious four-year relationship, but by the time analysis started she had begun a new relationship, which continues but with difficulty. She has been reluctant to commit to analysis, can be quite silent, and has complained about being bored in sessions. Nonetheless, she has moved from an initial once-weekly frequency to analysis three times a week. The sessions Britta described seemed to show a rather resentful relationship between Margareta and herself, with Britta working hard to manage the situation and to understand it.

For example, in the first session Margareta was silent for quite a while. She then talked at length, at first about having no desire to be in the session and then about how she had spent the weekend in the countryside and had a good time there. A dream, much of which she said she didn't remember but which involved who was and wasn't being invited to a performance, followed. Margareta then mentioned that she was anxious about how passive she had felt in the dream and at the weekend in the countryside when her parents had visited. She added how generous her parents were in financing the trip for her and her friend and also how her attitude to them had changed. In the past she wanted to keep them at a distance, but now she could imagine even living in the same city. Observing and listening to this, Britta reported that Margareta seemed to her to have arrived in a state of open and unusual anger, such that Britta had at first almost been overwhelmed by it and had struggled to feel sure about various possible sources of it that had occurred to her. When she spoke, she tried to connect Margareta's feeling of passivity in the dream to the same feeling in the session. As the session developed, Britta then suggested that Margareta's state was caused by a feeling that Britta had seemed bored with her because of her weekend absence. In response, at first Margareta said she did not understand, but then she agreed when Britta suggested

Continued on next page

CASES, continued

that the issue was that "everything here between us is false, a performance. And that you aren't yourself, you are what you think you should be, what I want you to be." In part that was true, Margareta said, and then returned to her feeling as to how much she would rather not be there in the session. They continued to struggle with the difficulty.

10. Andrew-Beckett (A Story of Ruin)

Beckett is a man in his fifties in his third year of analysis, described on referral as a fragile, confused person, using a "psychologizing" language that was difficult to understand. One of the latter children in a very large and impoverished family, he is depressed, feeling life has largely lost meaning and with an impending sense of catastrophe. His life has become particularly difficult because a few years ago he suddenly left his wife for another woman. That relationship didn't last, and then his wife died shortly afterward. The sessions Andrew described are characterized by long associations from Beckett, occasionally followed by comments from Andrew—focused on what he thinks Beckett is talking about now and the possible emotional reasons. For example, "I see that in the second-last session before the holidays you are remembering the situation in which you separated from your wife and children" or "But it seems to me that you are not completely clear about who is leaving and who is staying, and who has these feelings, if they exist, of anger and suffering." In response to such remarks Beckett often expresses doubt.

For example, after the comment above, Beckett responded, "But is it worthwhile thinking about that? Or now that we are going to be separated [for a holiday break], isn't it better to stop worrying about it?" Andrew replied, "At the beginning you were talking about putting everything in someone else's hands after the separation, and about becoming aware after that of the risk of being ruined?" Beckett then gave a long association about someone being furious, going from lawsuit to lawsuit, putting the whole matter in someone else's hands to protect himself, and so on, leading at length to more about the sad story of his dead wife and the upset of their children and how he had been unable to face them and his self-criticism. Andrew responded, "All this, it must still be very complicated for you. But when we look at the situation in perspective, we see that from a time when you had your family, wife and children, work . . . something happened, a rupture, and then severe consequences followed, a sort of devastation." Andrew placed this rupture in the emotional context of the holiday break, which Andrew felt it was very hard for Beckett to take in emotionally and have thoughts about.

11. Patricia-Paula (Tragedy)

Paula is a former alcoholic for whom things have gone wrong throughout her life. She reports being abandoned by both parents as a baby, then brought up in institutions and abused there. She was subsequently raped more than once, although one of those responsible felt guilty so that a financial settlement has left her financially independent. She says she can neither sleep, work, nor love. Patricia (who thought hard before deciding to present the case as to whether such a difficult situation really could be a psychoanalysis) feels Paula is very traumatized. She sits on a chair, and Patricia feels she can barely stand being in the same room with another person. Patricia, therefore, must, "tiptoe" through each session. An idea governing her approach is that if she becomes either too present or too absent to her patient, the situation rapidly becomes catastrophic, resulting in massive anxiety. She reported to the group that consequently missteps happened, evident when Paula stayed away for days, although, as things had progressed, Paula would now phone when too disturbed to come, which happened regularly. The sessions presented were clearly difficult for analyst and patient and full of intense emotional interaction and anxiety, with Patricia trying to explore underlying causal ideas.

For example, in the first session presented, on her way to collect Paula from the waiting room and in Paula's sight, Patricia closed the door to another office. She told the workshop she had done it in case Paula, who when in the room would sit in a different chair to the one usually assigned, went in there. Starting, Paula was immediately perturbed and asked what Patricia was doing and why she was doing it, showing that she was greatly alarmed. She worried for some time, then noted that Patricia had not asked the office's owner for permission to close the door and then began to speculate as to why Patricia looked tired—concluding that while there could be a million reasons, it was likely to be one of five possibilities. Patricia indicated that the "five" reasons seemed interesting, but Paula said she would rather not say more, mentioning that she had made a resolution to herself to let such things pass. Patricia then wondered if perhaps Paula was worried about her and what became of her, perhaps connected to the fact Paula had stopped coming to sessions before the beginning of the recent holiday and then, after Patricia had come back, had also waited before coming back. Paula said she recalled feeling very sad. Eventually Patricia suggested Paula had something to say to her that she was stopping herself from saying. The session continued with much innuendo and effort by Patricia to guess underlying content. Eventually Patricia summed up that she thought Paula was telling her that there was a traumatic relationship within her with her mother that often put her "on the edge"—wanting to be with her analyst, on the one hand, but, on the other hand, wanting to stop anything intense from happening between them. Creating distance, therefore, was essential, which was what was going on.

12. James-Jane (Despair and Resistance)

Jane, aged in her late forties, is in the ninth month of an analysis. Although quite successful, she feels she doesn't belong anywhere after both emigration and divorce. Presenting as shy, nervous, and full of pain, despair, and dissatisfaction, she also has severe doubts as to whether she is deserving of help and suffers numerous physical symptoms. When James presented at the workshop, he reported that he often felt unsure about what was going on and sometimes quite angry. At the same he felt Jane was very divided about wanting psychoanalysis. Characteristic of the two sessions he then presented was that he intervened rather frequently with short sentences, sometimes as a question or a repetition of the patient's last sentence, giving the impression of a dialogue more than in many other presentations. He made thirty-three interventions in the first session, twenty-six in the second. A more typical number would be about ten.

For example, the first session began with some minutes' silence before Jane said, "There is a strong resistance in me to come here, to the idea of talking and dwelling on feelings and emotions." James immediately "replied" with the comment "Even though you are so busy with feelings and emotions when you are on you own." Jane then spoke about her positive and negative feelings about James. As she did so, he continued to intervene quickly and very actively—mostly pointing out apparent contradictions in what she was saying. He thought of the contradictions as expressing broken "links" in Jane's understanding of herself and the world outside her.

Continued on next page

CASES, continued

13. Henry-Hermann (Struggling to Be Here)

Hermann is a man about forty-five years old in the third year of his analysis. Married, he had come to deal with problems of alcoholism and depression. The main characteristic of all three sessions Henry presented was that he described Hermann as associating for long periods of time, during which Henry would listen. What came to Hermann's mind during these associations was quite elaborate and detailed. It also included lengthy descriptions of homoerotic or sexualized dreams and many complex memories. When Hermann stopped, Henry would often remain silent so that there were quite long periods of silence between then. Moreover, when Henry did speak, he was usually, quite briefly, making short remarks (e.g., "but not the dream," "there was space in your dream . . . the basement"). Occasionally Henry made remarks that were more elaborated, such as when Henry said, "It is like you don't trust yourself: Is it a memory or a photo-shop?" "If we conceive this in continuity with your dream, it seems like the papier mâché figure became alive," "which makes for you the swing even more extreme," and so forth.

So, for example, the first session began with quite a long set of remarks from Hermann around the idea "As usual, I try first to do the analysis by myself and then afterwards to bring up my associations." He then told of a dream about finding himself in a basement in which either he was waiting for a man or a man was already there—"we would make love." He could remember no more but could recall himself waking up and thinking, "This is the kind of stuff that you should tell your analyst, it's not just armchair philosophy." He then said he felt a little bit awkward. He moved on to describe spending lots of time during his adolescence obsessed with the idea of whether or not he was homosexual and so on. He then talked about two film directors whose movies, he thought, had nothing to do with homosexuality. "They had to do with sexuality, with erotism." Here, Henry intervened with one of the short remarks mentioned and then an elaboration. He said, "But not the dream. . . . Isn't it that you juxtapose one of these films with your dream and you oppose each other."

14. Lesley-Lucie (The Lingering Smell)

Lucie, in her late twenties, had begun analysis several years before. She was brought up in an isolated household, which she experienced as violent following her brother's birth when she was a little girl. She became a much less lively child after that and has been very depressed since her teenage years. Thought by Lesley to be potentially a "beautiful woman," she is inhibited and scared both in the analysis and elsewhere, with a strong tendency to be submissive (sacrificing her own attitudes and extremely sensitive to the needs of others) and an idea that she has no right to her erotic and other feelings. Obviously bright, she nonetheless failed university. She also suffers from stomach dysfunction that causes pain, frequent need to defecate, and a bad smell that lingers in the consulting room after she has left, which has not been mentioned by Lesley. The characteristic of all three sessions presented was that Lucie would mention various situations and feelings about them in her life and then Lesley would make brief interventions to try to pull out or suggest meanings.

For example, in the first session presented, Lucie began by talking about how she had been anxious, with her heart beating fast, and then more anxious and distressed about her work. Next, she talked about spring and how it made her restless and also that the dust on the streets made it difficult to breathe. At the weekend, she had been on social media with two men—one, who sent a message, suggested a date. She said she was too busy for two weeks and could not make it. But they agreed to meet later. At this point, Lesley (who recalled Lucie had been talking about her disappointment with one of the men before and also a feeling he was intrusive) said, "The other one—was he the one who wanted you by his side?" "Yes, that was the first one," said Lucie. "The other one seems to be nice. On Saturday he asked how am I doing? But I got really anxious at that and let him know that I don't dare to see him even after two weeks. I supposed this would ease my distress. But it is not the only cause for distress." She was then silent. Lesley said, "Meaning?"

15. Cynthia-Cecilia (Self-Esteem under Zero)

Cecilia is a quite successful and attractive professional woman in her late twenties except that she lacks confidence and is quite desperate to the extent that she seems quite close to breakdown. In particular, she feels her boyfriend will desert her and thinks of herself as emotionally handicapped with "self-esteem under zero," doubts that seem to Cynthia not overdramatic but realistic. She has in fact been hospitalized for depression and as a suicide risk. Analyst and patient had initially begun working at a lower frequency, but about three years before the presentation the format had been changed to an analysis. A characteristic of the session presented was that Cecilia seemed to reveal rather little, could be silent for some time, and was openly somewhat hostile and combative. Cynthia's comments were mainly aimed at Cecilia's expectations and what was happening between them.

For example, in the second session presented, Cecilia began by saying that nothing had changed since the day before. She had paid Cynthia's bill but felt like checking it. She had just paid. Cynthia asked, "Do you usually check my bills before?" "Yes. I do. But to be honest [she has math skills] I think any miscalculation you make will be more in my favor than yours. It once happened. But I don't want to check any more. If you do not get your correct money, it is your problem. It should not be a dimension in our relationship." Clear responsibilities for each of us, "interpreted" Cynthia. "And the two of us have different responsibilities. I account for the sessions and it is up to you to balance them." Cecilia now said that she and her boyfriend had quarreled. She then cried. "It leads to nothing," she said. "I feel like this baby topic has just become like any other topic, which people quarrel over. No, that is not the truth. It is essential. It is more than a normal dispute. I don't want to talk about it. Talking about it would strengthen my pain. I endure it as best I can. But for me some things are of crucial importance. It is like if somebody committed a crime, say somebody committed a murder, and then would say, 'Let's go for a walk.' But how can I go for a walk with a murderer? Murder is a rupture." "A deed, something unforgivable," "interpreted" Cynthia. "Right, and it has consequences," said Cecilia. "When I don't get the key for the building, I can't get into the building."

16. Ben-Melanie (Ending)

Ben's treatment of Melanie has been taking place for some time. Melanie was brought up by a single mother who met her father on holiday in another country and became pregnant. They tried being together, but he left after about a year. He had never been back, and they had not been in touch. At the first meeting Melanie was in her early twenties, tearful and completely stuck. She was having to take time away from beginning a legal career and indecisive about a relationship. Ben was struck by a very deep

Continued on next page

CASES, continued

level of confusion, including about her origin. However, during the analysis Melanie had progressed, including getting married to Charles, having children, and developing a part-time career and friendships. Nonetheless, discussing a possible end to the analysis had reawakened anxieties, which were felt strongly around the last holiday break. According to Ben, the central issue in Melanie's life was an unconscious, very ambivalent relationship to a hidden fantasy relationship she imagined between her parents and herself, which, despite analytic work around it, inhibited aspects of her ability to "couple" consistently with her husband or her analyst. Ben's theory was that Melanie felt simultaneously controlled by her internal parental figures, now experienced through the person of the analyst, and abandoned and terrified to move on, and this issue was prolonging the analysis.

In the sessions, Ben often made his first intervention when there was a break in the associations, fairly close to the surface—tending to repeat words Melanie had used to open deeper thoughts with very brief, single-word-type comments—for instance, repeating a number Melanie had mentioned in a dream, which Ben sensed had multiple meanings. A detailed session can be explored in Box 6.1.

GROUP PROCESSES AND THE DATA

From the beginning, as described above, the working group has been a fundamental tool of the CCM methodology for understanding how analysts are working in their sessions. At the same time (with some exception in the discussion of the method in our first book [see Schubert, 2008]), explicit discussion and analysis of features that persistently emerge in the group and the function of the group as a container with its dynamics and peculiarities have mostly not been attempted. Here we make some limited comments.

What is a group in so far as it is a CCM group?

A plurality of people working together, united by a common goal, does not by itself make a group into a "real" group. It is also necessary that the people who participate in it take on a shared responsibility, being attentive to what emerges in the common field of the group understood as a unity. In particular, it means that when there are difficulties, the whole group must try to think about the difficulty and recognize that it can be very useful to treat it as occurring in the field, rather than in an individual participant. By field, here, we mean something quite general: the sense of a space created for the purpose of exchange and common elaboration.

To achieve this end, it is necessary that the members of the group accept some reduction of their active individuality to form a common space. It means a transitory loosening of their sense of personal identity and can be anxiety provoking.

Presenters, group members, and moderators may have slightly different experiences in the group.

One presenter remembers the initial persistent feeling that she would never be able to convey to the group the complexity of the relationship with her patient. She felt she just did not have the capacity to make the group understand the nature of the relationship. For her, the intimate and reserved nature of the analytic relationship, its duration of hours and hours of sessions over the years, and the dyadic quality of the relationship, even if immersed in the triad represented by the psychoanalysis in itself, made communication to the outside in the form of a group of unknown colleagues extremely difficult, with the aggravating circumstance for some of not speaking in their own language. This presenter described feeling a sort of mute despair about the possibility of ever making herself understood and therefore helping the group.

In her experience as a participant, however, the same person experienced something different but complementary to her viewpoint as presenter. She saw herself as asked to "violate" the area of the analytic relationship, to speak about something that did not belong to her and the rest of the group.

The experience of being part of a couple and showing that couple to a third party has previously been discussed in general by Jordan-Moore (1994) and Britton (1994) in their discussion of publishing "clinical facts." The point is that publication and discussion of the clinical facts that occur between the two members of the analytic couple raise potentially significant unconscious conflicts usually associated with the Oedipus situation. Such conflicts create the potential to turn a "work group" faced with a task into a basic-assumption group (Bion, 1961), so that in various ways group participants become overexcited or retreat from the prospect of being in the parental bedroom and making a mess (or fearing this will happen).

The two-step CCM method described above is quite explicitly framed to try to create a work group, and in this respect it differs from many psychoanalytic discussion groups. This is why a key moment for CCM groups, and the one that clearly distinguishes it from other methods of work such as classical intervision, is when, after the first hour of fairly conventional discussion of the case, in which it is possible to request further information from the presenter, the moment arrives when the presenter is asked by the moderators to remain silent, while the group moves to the Step 1 task. In the distant past (as described in Tuckett et al., 2008) and sometimes today, considerable resistance is exhibited to this unusual approach, which forces participants out of their usual stance. Sometimes the group becomes frozen or can't elaborate reasons for their suggestions of a particular Step 1 category. At other times the task can be ignored. Sometimes group members seem unable to develop their ideas without turning to the presenter for further clarification, as if he were the interlocutor. So at least for some, involvement in the group task without the presenter actively participating creates a sense of loss, bewilderment, and confusion. It is as if the group were bereft of reference systems, immersed in a lived experience of profound ignorance, the painful emotional condition of not knowing and not understanding.

In fact, if the group, the moderator, and presenter can stick to the method, the presenter usually eventually finds the situation profound, useful, and emotional, particularly over time. The presenter then feels grateful for the attention and the respect that the group has dedicated to his or her case.

When the presenter, as sometimes happens, is left with a vague sense of discontent that the group does not fully recognize or is doing something odd with their work, this seems to connect to a possible misunderstanding of CCM and the initial selection of the case. As discussed above, it is assumed that cases presented in CCM workshops are presented by competent analysts with a sense of how to do things. However, sometimes the presenter may have misunderstood the opportunity to present a case as a potential opportunity to get help and may be hoping to gain a better understanding of what has been happening in the sessions they have brought. This expectation is understandable, but if it is not recognized and resolved so that the group's purpose is understood, it can become a problem for both presenter and group. Sometimes experienced moderators address the help aspect afterward. In most cases, the presenting analyst takes away much on which to reflect in their own time.

The experience of being in the group as a moderator provides yet another perspective on the group dynamics. One of the tasks of the moderator is to protect the position of the presenter; another is to maintain the working group methodology; a third is to sense the working of the group; and a fourth is to try to help the group conceptualize the presenting analyst's working model in terms of the suppositions we have defined. These are all specialist tasks learned from experience, and in recent groups we have often tried to improve moderation by deploying a couple of moderators and worked on the differentiation between their roles, in the sense not that they must play distinct roles already decided a priori but rather that they need to play them in a complementary sense.

With two moderators, a "couple," so to speak, it is inevitable that groups will unconsciously allocate paternal and maternal, male and female, or combined-parent functions to them. A work in progress for the future may be for the moderator couple to learn to glimpse what has been called the "invisible group" (Corrao, 1981) that underlies the rational structure of a group. In particular, one of the two moderators might be able to disengage from the most inherent concerns of the method and tune in to what is happening beneath the surface (i.e., in what Corrao calls the invisible group). The invisible group will often be enacting a common plot aimed at defending itself against difficult experience. A consequence is that group members may find themselves unknowingly acting to remove, to deny, and to split off dangerous ideas from discussion.

Much more might be said about this, but here the fascinating ways these groups functioned are not our main concern. What is of direct interest is the way observations about group phenomena, at least in some workshops, subsequently provided an additional source of data for some of our conclusions.

JANA-NANA (PUT ON THE SPOT)

Jana's work with Nana was briefly introduced above (case 2). It will be discussed at length again in Chapter 4 where it is explained that it was the very beginning of the analysis. As the words used to label this case suggest, it was one in which the analyst was "put on the spot" by a patient who, through words and actions, appeared to be very intrusive. Nana was impulsive, had had repeated miscarriages, and had lived under the shadow of a relative who had committed suicide. Jana also thought she suffered from a constant and pervasive feeling of not being accepted and welcomed by her mother, who was only just an adult when she was born and soon separated from her father.

During the reconstruction of Jana's family history, the workshop group became extremely confused and muddled about the succession of generations in Nana's family. Also, sometimes, they did not easily manage to distinguish the analyst's interventions (which were brief and perhaps not of a kind familiar to many group members) from those of the patient. For example, one was "Fucking in the pile?" and another "Running to the couch?" Once the clinical presentation was over, the group began to feel that the material was messy. Maybe the translation was inadequate or the material was somehow not processed. They felt that it all seemed approximate, and the group began to feel mistreated by the analyst, as if the bad translation showed a lack of respect.

To the moderator-observer's mind, participants became irritated, and some began to lose interest in the material. This meant that the group members found themselves in the heart of an emotional turbulence. Meanwhile, to some in the group, the analyst's efforts in the material presented all seemed directed toward providing a containing and protective atmosphere for a patient who was actually being rather intrusive. They became somewhat agitated that the analyst did not seem to recognize or to interpret the "negative" aspects of the patient's behavior. The analyst, on the other hand, took things in her stride and argued that these were early sessions in which her responses to her patient needed to be delicate.

In a dream (Box 4.1, p. 94) the patient presented once she lay down after her initial uncertainty as to her proper place, Nana dreams of a baby in a cradle. Her parents are present, but the child is not hers. She suddenly realizes in the dream that they are not her parents; it is the wrong house. She is an intruder. This dream wakes Nana up in a strong state of anguish.

Later in the group, the analyst begins to tremble visibly. Something then began to change in the group dynamics. The moderator, observing the group dynamics, now wondered if, in place of the previous dynamics marked by withdrawal from an analyst felt not to be treating them with respect, the dynamic had shifted to concern and protection. Now it seemed that the group might be "thinking twice," so to speak, and must work out the meaning of the assumptions being made. Their comments begin to suggest a reparative huddle around their shaking colleague.

One fascinating question is which emotional constellation had evolved to allow the group shift? Was it that, behind the question of the bad translation, the group was confronting, without yet knowing it, the powerful splitting in Jana's picture of her relationship to the patient? Somewhat implausibly to many in the group, Jana thought of herself, and tried to act, as the mother whom she supposed Nana had never had. Perhaps the negative aspects of the representation of the mother found their way into the group's picture of the analyst giving them bad material. Only when the analyst showed signs of suffering was the group able to emerge from the irritated climate of rejection and to grasp the analyst's inability to remove herself from the position of the ideal mother. Plausibly or not, the tremors then became, in the minds of some members of the group, a metaphor for the contractions of a premature birth of a baby unable to survive outside the mother's womb—perhaps representing Nana's difficult early survival in her mother's mind, evoked by her successive miscarriages.

It is not the workshop task to judge the presenting psychoanalysts' work or to offer better ways of understanding their patients, but feelings are feelings and must be
taken into account. And the task of getting inside the suppositions of another analyst
treating an apparently disturbed patient and apparently using a "strange" technique is
challenging on top of the normal projection and introjection from the sessions into
the group discussing them. In this particular case intrusion and accusations of intrusion were a central and disturbing feature (see Chapter 4).

SUMMARY

This chapter has set out the methodology we have developed over more than twenty
years to answer the question of what psychoanalysts seem to be doing when they do
psychoanalysis, now more than eighty years since Freud's death. Noting that hitherto
there have been no comparable studies (i.e., no efforts at any scale to compare the
work of ordinary psychoanalysts doing ordinary psychoanalysis differently), we have
described the special CCM workshops we developed where psychoanalysts from very
different approaches could present their work and have it discussed by their peers.

These workshops of usually eight to fifteen people used the so-called two-step
method over some ten to twelve hours. Step 1 helps to reorient colleagues to the
task of thinking about how someone else is working, which may be different from
their own way. Step 2 collects the data, which form the clinical stories we will use to
describe the different ways we found people working—differing according to how
they supposed the analytic situation to be constructed, inferred unconscious content,
thoughts about how repetitive unconscious processes created their patients' difficulties, and attempts to further the process. We will be elaborating the concepts and
using them to describe the way analysts worked over the next five chapters.

Meanwhile, we note that our approach has evolved several methodological innovations. First, we set up workshop groups to create a pool of globally relevant
data. Second, we created the two-step method to build a peer group to interpret the
raw data (the presentation of sessions) into something meaningful to psychoanalytic
peers. We have stressed how we achieve this by interpreting what the psychoanalysts
did through the thoughts and feelings of groups of very diverse peers. Third, we
used a further iterative step of moderators' meetings to discuss the product of each
workshop. This allowed us to compare the type of approach used by an analyst who
presented in a particular workshop against a common conceptual frame comprising
four independent axes (Figure 2.3).

Psychoanalytic material contains many embedded references and implicit assumptions and meanings. Like most data, as we cited Widlöcher (1994) pointing out
above, it does not speak for itself—although it is often presented and discussed at
international meetings as though it does. We have tried here to create a language to
describe comparatively the different ways the different psychoanalysts work. Since
Freud's death we have embraced pluralism. These different ways all appear to work at
least to a degree. Our task is to describe them so everyone can reflect on them, not to
judge them. We will return to this issue in our final chapter.

3

The Analytic Situation

Sigmund Freud's invention, with Josef Breuer, of the analytic "hour" has been compared in significance to Galileo's use of the telescope to explore previously unknown phenomena in the night sky (Schwartz, 1996). Regular sessions in which the patient talks and the analyst listens created an instrument that opened an entirely new way to explore previously unknown psychic phenomena—an inner world. In this chapter, we ask about the different suppositions that the psychoanalysts we studied hold about the phenomena potentially revealed in analytic hours, or, as we will refer to it, the analytic situation.

In more conventional terms, our question is how each analyst understands transference as a mechanism for permitting the active past to be visible in and influence the present.

Transference has been a very confusing concept in psychoanalytic practice. As we will see below, definitions vary quite widely in the literature, and Freud's writing itself contains contradictory positions. When twenty-four cases were discussed by 120 psychoanalysts at our first Prague workshop in 2002, although everyone agreed transference was fundamental, there was almost no meaningful agreement as to either what they meant or how it was to be dealt with, if at all (Tuckett et al., 2008, pp. 15ff.).

In this chapter, starting from the proposition that all psychoanalytic sessions in some way or another contain and potentially reveal what we can call an unconscious script from the past driving a patient's lived experience, we introduce four different ways psychoanalysts suppose it works.

The four ideal types, meaning they are abstractions to clarify differences never encountered in pure form, are described using four metaphors to distinguish them: cinema, dramatic monologue, theater, and immersive theater. The metaphors emerged from the triangular methodology described so far—the three processes of discussing many hundreds of sessions in our workshops, reflecting on these discussions in our moderators' meetings, and then looking in detail at Freud's writings on transference, particularly in the original German.

We begin with a brief elaboration of the suppositions behind each of the four metaphors and then illustrate them in more detail with material from the discussion of the work of seven of the analysts in our workshops. We then describe how we have eventually been able both to ground and to elaborate each of the four types in Freud's writing, starting with his early ideas in the collaboration with Breuer through to the discoveries after "Dora" left treatment and in the case of Ernst (the "Rat Man")[1], his metapsychological papers on transference, and his later comments about countertransference. We close the chapter by arguing that the four types clarify some of the difficulties that have hitherto inhibited exchange and learning on this topic and suggest that they can permit every analyst to reflect better on their chosen approach. In later chapters we will also show how, insofar as particular analysts adopt suppositions of any one of the four types, this has a considerable influence on many other aspects of their work.

FOUR TYPES OF SUPPOSITION: CINEMA, DRAMATIC MONOLOGUE, THEATER, AND IMMERSIVE THEATER

The four types of supposition about the analytic situation we now introduce depend crucially on what it is that analysts suppose about location and timing. In essence, "when" and "in whom" do they think the unconscious script pushing for actualization that is at the heart of every psychoanalysis is having an effect? Each of the metaphors tries to capture a difference along these two dimensions.

The timing difference refers to two discernible approaches. In one approach, analysts mainly seem to find evidence of unconscious scripts pushing for actualization in their patients' descriptions of their lives, relationships, and histories, as *reported to* the sessions. We define this perspective as *indefinite* as to "when" (Freud, 1915b). In the other approach, analysts, although they may also find evidence in those reports, mainly find the evidence of an unconscious script in what they observe and experience being unconsciously actualized and so actually being revealed *in* the sessions *now*.

The "in whom" difference is between those analysts who routinely suppose unconscious scripts pushing for actualization will be revealed *via both their own and the patient's unconscious participation* (symmetric) and those who do not (asymmetric).

In this way, we arrive at the four "ideal types," each described by a metaphor and set out in Table 3.1. The columns distinguish *when* it is that the inaccessible script driving patients is mainly revealed, becomes actualized, and is influential. They divide schematically those analysts who mainly suppose that what the patient is experiencing and describing is happening unconsciously now from those who infer it as happening in a more indefinite space (i.e., as a general sign of a displacement of affect or belief).

---

1. Throughout this book we will use the name Ernst—possibly the patient's real name—in preference to the unfortunate nickname, which has stuck to the case.

The rows in Table 3.1 differentiate "in whom" evidence is found or, in other words, how far analysts' recognition of their unconscious participation is supposed as usually necessary, if the unconscious script the patient brings to psychoanalysis is to be revealed.[2] If the analyst's unconscious participation is required, the supposition is that analytic inference has symmetric foundations. If not, the foundations are asymmetric.

Table 3.1. Four Metaphors for the Analytic Situation

	When: Now	*When:* Indefinite
Participation: asymmetric	A Theater	B Cinema
Participation: symmetric	C Immersive theater	D Dramatic monologue

In this way the rows and columns combine to give four types, A through D, each designated by a metaphor. They are briefly defined as follows:[3]

- *Cinema* (script is temporally indefinite; participation is asymmetric): Essentially characterized by the supposition that the dreams, ideas, and situations the patient is describing in the session reveal to the analyst an ongoing unconscious script (and defenses against recognizing it) driving the patient's experience of their world and the persons they encounter in it. Participation is asymmetric in that while the analyst's feelings and intuitions may sometimes be relevant to give color and understanding to how their patients and those they are describing felt, they are not usually understood to be derivatives of the script itself.
- *Dramatic monologue* (script is temporally indefinite; participation is symmetric): Broadly characterized by the supposition that the choice of words used in the patient's stories, comments, responses, and so forth, along with missing links, moments of hesitation, difficulty, embarrassment, and the like, are revealing of hidden affective meanings hitherto unavailable to the patient and their efforts to suppress them. The analyst's unconscious picks up on these, and via the psychoanalyst's unconscious receptivity, broken links of meaning can be recovered, not necessarily consciously or immediately (e.g., via *après coup*). Participation is symmetrical rather than asymmetrical because analysts in effect "lend" their unconscious to their patients so that the script emerges from their mental activity.

---

2. For those familiar with Bion's transformations terminology, all this could be expressed more cogently in his language. In all four suppositions it is equally assumed that there is in the patient an unconscious script, or unconscious ideas, striving for expression and so for realization (and thus forming the basis of the repetition). The differences between them denoted by the metaphors really refer *exclusively to the nature and location of the transformations* (in Bion's sense) that these unconscious ideas undergo during their search for expression in the analytic situation. But as this language is part of a complex pattern of ideas not widely shared, we chose not to adopt it here.

3. The nature of our subject matter here recalls Green's (1998) comment that "the price to pay for thinking is that the thinker is almost necessarily a liar. Bion applied this conclusion to himself. The thinker who had constructed this sophisticated theory, inevitably falsified the experience" (p. 652). In other words, we are reaching toward something we feel to be the case, but we are necessarily and permanently unconvinced we have found the right words to grasp and so communicate it.

- *Theater* (script is now; participation is asymmetric): Characterized by the sup-position that utterances in the session are hidden expressions of a script partially suppressed but made up from unconscious desires, anxieties, imaginations, and fantasies pushing for expression stimulated by and attached to the person of the analyst in a particular session. Participation is asymmetric because it is the patient's unconscious that is pushing for expression, creating the script, and the analyst is an observer, feeling and experiencing what is going on, perhaps with empathy, but not actually creating it. In other words, the analyst's own uncon-scious script is sufficiently known to be kept out.
- *Immersive theater* (script is now; participation is symmetric): Characterized by the same suppositions as theater but with the idea that the utterances in the session are hidden expressions of two interacting unconscious scripts pushing for expression made up from the unconscious desires, anxieties, imaginations, and fantasies stimulated and attached by the patient to the person of the ana-lyst and by the analyst to the person of the patient. Participation is therefore symmetric because unconscious participation from the psychoanalyst, even if more contained, is to be expected. If scrutinized thoroughly by the analyst, a hidden picture they have of each other and their immediate intentions toward, attitudes to, and feelings for each other, prompted by their being together as people now, can emerge.

Here, we want to stress two points. First, there is no hierarchy of superiority in the four metaphor types. As we will show in Chapter 8, between them the seven well-known analysts we discussed in Chapter 1 used three of the four types of sup-positions. Later in this chapter we show how Freud used all four. Each one raises different questions, and exploring these questions opens up more interesting lines of inquiry than a debate about which of the four types is best, as we will suggest in Chapters 8 and 9.

Second, each metaphor is conceived as a particular type of abstraction, called an "ideal type."[4] Applying the typology to instances of analytic practice—that is, using it to classify any session of psychoanalytic work as a particular type—is challenging, because categorizing "reality" is very different from creating abstract definitions, as we shall see when we discuss examples. In any case, the function of the typology is not to label an instance for its own sake. Rather, its purpose is to capture tendencies within an analyst's approach in specific sessions, which are consequential for the way they work.[5] Assignment to an ideal type, therefore, has no value in and of itself. Nor

---

4. A mental construct derived from observable reality, although not conforming to it in detail because of deliberate simplification and exaggeration to bring out a point. Developed by Max Weber (1921), as an analytic tool for his historical studies, it is not ideal in the sense that it is excellent; nor is it an aver-age; it is, rather, a constructed ideal used to approximate reality by selecting and accentuating certain elements. See also Chapter 6.

5. The four metaphors are not designed to capture aspirations (i.e., how an analyst would like to see themselves or be seen as working). Their purpose is to assess particular sessions. As we see in Chapter 8, this then allows an analyst to ask questions around whether they are working in a particular session or phase as they would wish.

does it imply that psychoanalysts in the same type are similar in all other respects. Typification is a thinking aid with the potential to capture differences in a limited number of identified tendencies, and that is all.

In fact, we think that readers who reach the end of this book will find that the differences in psychoanalytic practice that emerge from our typology of ways of supposing the analytic situation are substantial and valuable. We will now attempt to elaborate the sense and meaning of the distinctions made in Table 3.1 to try to work them through with data from our workshop discussions—data that will rapidly show that at best we are capturing tendencies starting from our implicit assumption that our presenters are all practicing a potentially successful psychoanalytic method and, as part of that, are using sessions to discern, in one way or another, unconscious scripts driving their patients.

We start with cinema.

CINEMA

As mentioned, the cinema metaphor applies to suppositions about the analytic situation in which the inaccessible script is identified by noticing, while the patient is associating in sessions, hidden connections and repetitions in the reports the patient brings to the analyst. From these reports, an analyst making cinema suppositions infers an unconscious script operating in the patient's life or inside the patient. For example, one analyst may infer from reports that the repetitive experience a patient has in relationships to men is a highly ambivalent but unconsciously repeated relationship to a father. Another analyst may infer from reports that the experience another patient has of intimate relationships is a repetitive unconscious relationship to the internal image of a mother who was experienced as emotionally dead and enraging. Yet another analyst may infer from reports that a tendency to masochistic submission and then resentment at being badly treated at work or with a partner has its origins in a sense of guilt that gave pleasure in early situations where direct expressions of pleasure were forbidden.

We chose cinema as the metaphor for such suppositions because the analytic collaboration looks like analyst and patient sitting side by side as in the cinema, watching a film in which characters play out a script. The job is to discern themes and meaning in the film—to be a kind of film critic. So the film portrays recorded events and happenings in a drama and narrates the inaccessible script. It has color, emotional involvement, and immediacy and may even be hard for the analyst to hear and watch or for the patient to narrate. And as with a film, meanings and feelings are certainly evoked in both participants as they watch together. They may also discuss their feelings as an audience sometimes will, and they may even discuss difficulties, such as the difficulty in seeing things in a certain way or how sometimes what is being depicted may make it hard to talk to each other—as when the issues that the analyst thinks are raised in the film (e.g., shame or guilt) become uncomfortable, given that the film is about the patient. Possibly they may mention and discuss ways that sometimes their relationship together seems to parallel or otherwise be like that depicted in the film. However much they discuss their relationship, it remains cinema so long as the issue of how the patient might be "casting" the analyst now (e.g., as hostile, seducing, mean) is not explicit.

Lesley-Lucie (The Lingering Smell)

Lesley's sessions with Lucie, discussed in the previous chapter, appear to fit these cinema suppositions. Lesley, as it emerged in the workshop, supposed her patient to be inhibited in developing her love and sexual life by the terrifying but hidden experiences of ambivalence and shame that sexual or loving feelings evoked. But, to judge by Lesley's pattern of responses to the material and what the workshop group was able to understand about what she was hearing and thinking, Lesley reached this assessment from Lucie's various stories and comments in her sessions. They were treated as unconscious descriptions of her beliefs and difficult experiences outside that she could not surface to consciousness. But, as far as could be understood, they were not treated as hidden beliefs *about Lesley* or as Lucie's unconscious experience of Lesley as a person in sessions. The feelings of hurt, anger, shame, being blocked, anxiety, and so forth that she brought through her stories were not supposed as an unconscious picture of Lesley.

The third session, up to Lesley's sixth comment, is presented in Box 3.1. for illustrative purposes. It begins with Lucie's quite explicit complaint about the impact Lesley's holiday is having on her potential love life (threatening the success of a new relationship) and extends into thoughts about whether a man will invite her out, to her fear as to what kind of messages she might be giving out, and then to whether her friends are ashamed of her and where such ideas might come from.

BOX 3.1. LESLEY AND LUCIE (THE LINGERING SMELL): SESSION 3

Lucie: I had another issue I wanted to talk about, but when at the door, pain and anger rose up in my mind about the upcoming two weeks' pause. Just now, when I'm having a difficult time, you would abandon me now, when I am needy. On the other hand, I'm excited—I don't have much program for the other week, only mourning. I tried to arrange more work, with no success. It is going to be that time, when I would contact the boy I met. If he rejects me, it would feel more safe if I could talk about it here. On the other hand, I have to do it right now, but my fear and anxiousness would appear in my message to him. And I have some studies . . . but now that I think about it, perhaps I am only procrastinating . . .

She lapsed into silence.

Lesley 1: Your feeling at the door. I abandon you just now, when you have difficulties and big questions. Do you feel the anger at the moment?

Lucie: Not now, it vanished. Instead came the other thing, the one I was going to talk about. It was about becoming excluded. I have difficult feelings toward my friends J and

A—as if they were ashamed about me in those situations, when I have something going on with a man. There would be something to be ashamed of. I have anticipated that if I had luck with that man, it would resolve this. Open situation, waiting for solution.

Lesley 2: You think that your friends are ashamed about you having contact with a man . . .

Lucie: I am ready to admit that it is partly my own assumption, but at the same time I'm convinced about their shame.

Lesley 3: Would you like to open this up more?

Lucie: That situation, when I greeted the male colleague, they expressed their shame. I didn't understand why. I remained wondering about the reason.

Lesley 4: You are convinced it was about you, not something that's their own thing?

Lucie: They are ashamed of me, the way I am.

Lesley 5: You have other such experiences in mind . . . ?

Lucie: Tells about another occurrence. Gives reasons to her friends' shame.

Lesley 6: And you expect the relationship with that man would resolve the shame.

To judge by the interpretations, Lucie's associations led Lesley, as she confirmed to the workshop group, to try to clarify matters to Lucie. She seemed to want her to be more aware of the feelings and anxieties that she had but did not recognize when she was with people, as well as to grasp their possible origin in her (as yet not adequately known) feelings of shame and other beliefs. To this effect, Lesley initially pursued whether Lucie perhaps recognized that unconsciously she felt anger at her now about the abandonment the holiday was creating and, implicitly, due to her (generalized) fear of rejection. Later, Lesley extended this line of trying to draw Lucie's attention to her feelings by raising the idea that Lucie felt ashamed about something.

In another session, Lucie talked about social media contacts with men and her anxieties about seeing them. She then mentioned trying to buy tickets for a concert that was sold out. It had made her cry. In this session, when Lucie became silent, Lesley raised the idea she was touching on major anxieties—that Lucie was worried about her age, not yet finding a man, and not yet becoming a mother. Lesley put it subtly—"Time passing, you reaching thirty years, anxiousness about approaching a man—[your social media dialogue],[6] your hopes and fears, the child, with a man"—but not in relation to any unconscious complaint now aimed at her analyst. In another session Lucie's anxieties in relationships and her shame again came up. Again, as described so far, Lesley focused on the hidden feelings Lucie seemed to have in those relationships but with no hint she was referring to any shame Lucie felt toward Lesley

---

6. Platform name withheld.

in the session. Lesley was focused on how to help Lucie acknowledge and take responsibility for her feelings generally—such as to recognize her fears about time passing in the moment above or about "how closeness turns to pain" in another—but it seems she was not addressing them as felt about the analyst "now" in the room. For all these reasons, Lesley's suppositions about the analytic situation seem to fit the cinema type.

Although at the time this workshop was conducted, we had yet to refine the ideas being developed in this chapter, the record of the workshop suggests that members very much felt that Lesley was not focused on Lucie's unconscious picture of her "now." They explicitly raised with Lesley and each other how far Lesley thought Lucie was expressing much deeper unconscious complaints about Lesley in the session—for instance, about her absence or lack of response to Lucie's plight now *in this session*, not just her absence for a holiday. Or they wondered if perhaps Lesley thought Lucie was unconsciously giving expression to feelings of shame, guilt, or anxiety about the unmentioned but very present smell she created (perhaps in other than literally olfactory ways). Or, again, they wondered if perhaps hidden in Lucie's words were unconscious worries about the imagined effects on Lesley caused by Lucie's unconscious casting of Lesley as hatefully absent and the deep rage against her associated with it, and so forth. But none of these ideas resonated with Lesley.

Although Lesley did suppose Lucie was frightened of her feelings and hid them when she was with people outside, Lesley did not think this was particularly manifest in the room. In fact, she was waiting for that to be evident. Toward the end of the workshop, she told the group explicitly that, for her, what she called transference (meaning the unconscious feelings the patient has toward the analyst) had not yet "entered the analysis." Meanwhile, she supposed what Lucie said in the room was describing Lucie's general difficulties with her feelings due to her unrecognized ambivalence, which played out in her experience of outside relationships. Insofar as Lucie hid (or denied) any feelings toward Lesley—for instance, out of fear of becoming dependent or hostile and abandoned—it was in the same unrecognized way as she hid from herself the nature of her feelings about people outside.

The hypothesis reached here, characterizing Lesley's suppositions about the analytic situation as cinema (in which the dynamics and difficulties of the patient's life are being told through a script played out on a screen and watched by both together), is also confirmed by what Lesley told the group about the lingering smell. It was a major problem for her that after every session Lucie left a very bad smell in the room due to her digestive problems. Prior to the workshop, apparently, Lesley had not connected it to any of the shame-related issues she and Lucie were talking about and had never thought to raise it with Lucie in the "now." Rather, she saw it as an unmentionable fact she somehow had to bear. In this connection, and more generally related to the issue of symmetrical-asymmetrical influences on the analytic situation that we will consider further below, the possibility that in some way her ideas and approach to Lucie might have some origin in the analyst's (i.e., her own) unconscious participation, which the workshop group sometimes wondered about, evoked no resonance. They got no impression that Lesley had ever supposed that any of her beliefs or understandings about Lucie might unconsciously be driven by her own unconscious responses to her.

For all these reasons, on balance, Lesley's suppositions illustrate the conception of the analytic situation which we use the cinema metaphor to describe.

Britta-Margareta (Reluctance to Commit)

Britta's analysis of Margareta is a second, if slightly different and more complex, example of an analyst proceeding with cinema-type suppositions about the analytic situation.

BOX 3.2. BRITTA AND MARGARETA (RELUCTANCE TO COMMIT): SESSION 1

Margareta is silent for a while and then talks about lacking any desire to be in the session. She mentions that she spent the weekend at a resort and had a good time. She then tells of a dream she had the day before yesterday. There were lots of things in the dream that she doesn't remember. But what she does remember is an intense feeling. There was to be a theater performance at 9 p.m. To go, she had to get the invitations from one friend but had told another they would be going together. Time passed, and she was doing nothing. She thought she would be late and was increasingly, intensely anxious, but still she was not going. Eventually she decided her friend would have to go with someone else . . . it was all confusing.

She then says that actually the performance is tonight. She is going with another female friend.

Margareta then associates to her anxiety of the inactivity she felt in the dream, her inactivity over the weekend at the resort to which her parents had come, the generosity of her parents, and her changed attitude toward them. She has always avoided them, but now she can imagine living in their "little" city.

[Britta told the group that she thought Margareta had come in very angry, which was very unusual and overwhelming. She felt unsure where it came from. But possibilities crossed her mind: Margareta's negative attitudes toward her and her mother were finally more intensely manifest in their relationship, holidays, the session before about her feelings that analysis would control her if she were more spontaneous, her anger at losing her job. As she was unsure, Britta focused on the immediate material of the dream and the transference.]

Britta 1: And you felt the same inactivity in the dream, regarding getting the tickets, and here too, today.

Margareta: Yes, I'm really bored. I don't want to do anything.

Britta 2: I wonder whether the theater has to do with us here.

Margareta: Yes, analysis is like a theater performance. There is the patient. The analyst plays the roles of the mother, sometimes of the brother and father. And there are different interpretations of the performance, depending on the respective analyst. So where is the reality? Is it forty-five minutes, four hours per week, for as many years as it takes? It's all so boring.

Britta 3: Particularly today.

Continued on next page

BOX 3.2, continued

[Britta tells the group that by emphasizing the time element, she is trying to see what associations regarding her previous hypotheses will come up to explain Margareta's emotional state.

Britta ends up making three further comments, each wondering to Margareta about whether and why things are fake:

"I wonder whether you felt that I was bored and that's why I wasn't here yesterday?"

"That everything here between us is false, a performance. And that you aren't yourself, you are what you think you should be, what I want you to be."

"If you say things according to what you want to hear from me, then you control things . . . and you feel that that is false—but on the other hand you don't want to speak freely and spontaneously."]

Box 3.2 extracts part of the first session Britta presented at the workshop, up to her third comment, after which her further comments are summarized briefly. To decide whether Britta's suppositions about the analytic situation fit the cinema rather than the theater type requires that we establish the location and timing that Britta applies to what Margareta tells her. Does Britta suppose what Margareta is revealing is an unconscious script depicting Britta as a particular sort of person in the session now, or is she rather focused on Margareta's depiction and experience of the people she is talking about in her life? Although making such judgments is always an empirical challenge, what we know about what Britta said to Margareta in the sessions, as well as what she elaborated in response to questions and points made in the workshop at which she presented, gives us some data.

In the session, partially extracted in Box 3.2, we can note that after an initial silence and what seems like a provocative comment about why she is in the session, Margareta produces associations. She reports a dream, makes a point of saying she has no associations, and then says that the theater performance, about which she has dreamed, is on tonight. Then she expresses anxiety about how little was going on in the dream and during her weekend, before talking about what she sees as an improved attitude toward her parents.

We can further note that Britta told the group that in this part of the session she had felt very disturbed by the level of Margareta's open anger and negative attitudes and at first didn't know what to make of them. One thought Britta had was that perhaps the "negative transference" toward her and Margareta's mother was being revealed, but she was unsure what to take up. In the end she opted to make a quite open comment about inactivity in the dream and about the inactivity in buying tickets as well as "here too." Subsequent comments she made included "I wonder if the theater has to do with here" (Britta 2) and "Particularly today" (Britta 3). Later in the session she wondered if at the weekend Margareta had felt Britta was bored by her. Later she wondered if Margarita felt everything was false between them and if she was afraid to be spontaneous.

Clearly, there is a sense in which these interpretations are somewhat aimed at Margareta's experience "here." At the same time, they are not very specific and do not really address her experience "now"—especially not her experience "now" here with Britta cast as a particular sort of person. In other words, they do not seem to suggest that Britta has inferred from Margareta's associations that, for instance, she is living inside a set of unconscious beliefs about Britta when in her session, such as that she is someone Margareta unconsciously fears is inactive, ineffective, bored, uninterested in her, hostile, hurt, perhaps cowed, and so on and so forth.

Britta did have an idea that Margareta had inside her an unconscious script in which she unconsciously represented her in a general way as a bored and disinterested mother toward whom she felt ambivalent, but she did not seem to suppose this otherwise inaccessible script was operating in or influencing the detail of how she was being depicted in the session.

In the workshop Britta reported being shocked and overwhelmed by Margareta's initial anger. But during group discussion of her detailed interventions, she made clear that, unlike some in the group, she did not read any of Margareta's remarks as sarcastic toward her; nor did she suppose that her latent ideas behind the dream contained an unconscious script connected to Margareta's fears or potential disappointment that the analysis was going nowhere, and so forth. Also, when in other material discussed in the workshop Britta noted that a core theme in the material was about hiding, she did not pick this up either as Margareta's idea about Britta or vice versa.

Rather than picking up Margareta's unconscious script about a bored and hostile mother from evidence about how Margareta experienced her now, Britta seemed to have arrived at it by listening to Margareta's reports of her life and childhood. In fact, in the workshop, the group established that Britta's way of proceeding and even her comment about "negative transference" were based on her suppositions about the way an analytic process produces change (see Chapter 6), which also seem to be relevant to her suppositions about the analytic situation. According to the moderator's report, Britta supposed that an analyst treating a patient like Margareta (whose mother was, she thought, in fact bored and disinterested in her) needs to be different to the original and not repeat the trauma (see also Chapter 5).

From the workshop data, it seems Britta formed her picture of Margareta's mother not from what she had discerned about how Margareta represented Britta in associations, and so forth, in sessions but from what Margareta had reported when recounting her past. Apparently Britta had concluded that Margareta's mother really was in fact disinterested and bored by her daughter. We can see a similar process of inference implied in the session in Box 3.2 when Britta floated the idea that Margareta *had* felt Britta *was* bored with her and so *had* gone on holiday (using the past tense). It seems to mean that while Britta was inferring Margareta had felt Britta to be bored with her at the weekend, she was inferring that Margareta felt Britta to be bored with her and inattentive now. In short, because Britta reported to the workshop a great deal going on between her and her patient "now" in the sessions, even to the extent that she reported to the group that she felt very overwhelmed indeed by Margareta's anger, the picture as a whole suggests Britta built her understanding of the unconscious script dominating Margareta's experience on her reports of past experience. This may be one reason why Britta was so thrown by Margareta's live anger. Her suppositions about the analytic situation, which we use the cinema metaphor to describe, are not oriented to discerning Margareta's picture of Britta and her attitude to Margareta now. In that context the eruption into the room "right now" of an angry and discontented patient wanting to complain about her analyst challenged her profoundly. In the session she then seems to have gone to some lengths to absorb or ignore Margareta's potential sarcasm or other hostility and to prevent escalation. Perhaps keeping the conversation as a commentary on past happenings and possible hypotheses about what might have been going on was a way, consistent with cinema suppositions, to provide a new and thoughtful environment.

DRAMATIC MONOLOGUE

We use the metaphor of dramatic monologue to characterize suppositions about the analytic situation in which evidence about the underlying script dominating a patient's experience is mainly inferred *via the effect on the analyst* of the patient's selection of words and the polysemic meanings and affects that appear in his or her mind. Analysts making these suppositions sense the effect of an unconscious script via the associative networks that form the thread of the patient's discourse. Or they may sense a repeated situation conveyed through word selection when they sense the patient veering toward or away from apparently seeking to master an internal situation. Or they may focus on obvious displacements of affect or signs of rupture. Whichever it is, the defining point of this approach is that the unconscious script energizing the sessions is supposed to be conveyed through the patient's word selection and its effect *on the analyst.*

In terms of the distinction we made in Table 3.1 between "now" and "indefinite," the suppositions characterized by dramatic monologue refer to indefinite time—that is, to a frozen state that is always and everywhere. In terms of the analyst's participation, suppositions are symmetric. This is because the process of inference works via unconscious-to-unconscious cognition.[7] Psychoanalysts lend their psychic functioning, so to speak, to their patients without necessarily knowing until later, when effects may become observable, what has been brewing.[8]

Gabriella-Alice (Crushed)

Gabriella, in her analysis of Alice, a twenty-eight-year-old woman in her first year of analysis, is one example of an analyst we characterize as making essentially dra-

7. The complex theoretical territory raised by terms like "unconscious cognition," "unconscious receptivity," or "they fall into or touch upon his Ucs," which are central elements of attempts sometimes made to conceptualize the unconscious communication between patient and analyst, are more deeply analyzed below.

8. In Chapter 4 we will discuss Freud's ideas about inferring unconscious content. We write, "The utterings of the analysand, produced in his attempt to adhere to the fundamental rule and associate freely, are understood as disguised emanations of his dynamic unconscious ('unconscious proper'), mainly generated by and consisting of his repressed infantile wishes. . . . When the analyst listens to these associations in a state of evenly hovering attention they fall into or *touch upon* his Ucs. There, they are subjected to the mechanisms that rule this domain of the psyche: displacement, condensation, and symbolization. A working over in the psyche of the analyst takes place without him knowing." It is something like this that we envisage in the statement here defining the dramatic monologue metaphor for the analytic situation.

matic monologue suppositions about the analytic situation. This is mainly because Gabriella focused on *the effect she felt on herself* of the words and phrases Alice selected in the material (or that were suggested in her own mind) as she listened. Like Britta and Lesley, she certainly heard or had ideas about the unconscious script conveyed through the reports from outside and her past that Alice included in her associations. But what really mattered for Gabriella was not making sense of these events and the various parallels that could be drawn from them but rather the words and affects that struck her. In these words and their affects lay the evidence of an unconscious script pushing for recognition in this psychoanalysis.

Gabriella described three sessions in all. The first session is set out in Boxes 3.3 and 3.4 at length so readers can experience the contrast with Britta's and Lesley's sessions. It has, like the other two, two main elements: There are long periods of Gabriella's silence as Alice associates freely and at length. And then, as she listens and notices responses and meanings evoked in her—sometimes strikingly, sometimes even explosively, Gabriella makes occasional and brief interrogative comments prompted by her subjective impressions.

BOX 3.3. GABRIELLA AND ALICE (CRUSHED): SESSION 1

Alice: Begins by complaining of a major anxiety attack with the urge to vomit and an inability to go to her placement [linked to her studies at an institute] at the children's home following our last session.

Finally, she went to the children's home, and it went well. She felt much better. It still happens to her from time to time. She feels better.

"But I still have my head spinning. I wanted to resign, to be off work until the end of the year. I wanted that someone would take care of me, of myself.

"When I go to work, I feel better. Today I won't go to the institute. I think it's due to the stress of the coming exam. I can't wait for it to be done. I don't have any more courses to do. I appreciate it, and I feel like I'm ruining everything.

"I told myself that what happened on Monday was very violent, more than the other times. It was a bit dramatic, perhaps because it is related to what we said about my thoughts concerning my father that bother me. The feeling of disagreeing all the time with myself with a feeling of madness a little. I appeal to my intelligence to realize the reality.

"In fact, Monday night we went to the cinema [with her partner] to see a dreadful film. It was about pedophilia in the church. There was a lot of testimony, including a man who said that since it happened to him, he had tinnitus attacks that made him fall to the ground, and although his intelligence is clearly superior to that of others, he had not found his place despite lots of therapies. The only thing that helps me is the support of my partner. . . . Maybe I will continue like this all the time. I did not expect a hard movie."

[Aggressiveness toward me?]

Gabriella 1: "Why this choice of movie?"

In what workshop participants came to view as a crucial interpretation (Box 3.4), Gabriella used the word "crushed" interrogatively—it seemed almost to come out of nowhere, particularly to some workshop participants who struggled to make sense of it.

BOX 3.4. GABRIELLA AND ALICE (CRUSHED): SESSION CONTINUED

Alice: We were invited to a preview without knowing the title. Nobody expected that. They are usually funny movies. All these testimonies of adults about their past as children chosen by the priest were very disturbing. There was an exciting side to these stories, and I mixed all those thoughts.

I feel exhausted after a day of work! It's very tiring to be afraid. Tuesday I had two hours in a row with a child. For the first time I realized that he was not the most unmanageable. I could calm him. I felt great that it was so easy to manage. Now I'm going to do it every time, but I'm afraid. . . . There is another difficult child. But nearly everyone finds him difficult. . . . This morning again I wanted to throw up.

[Alice then told a quite long story about a relative who says that since her big sister had a baby, their father has been very jealous and how a grandfather's jealousy is weird and hard to think about.]

She goes on to say that she dreamed of the same relative.

Her father was there. She lived in a sort of cellar where people came to see her. But she was embarrassed by her father. She felt danger. She was then walking down the street, which was full of free food. There were some really good things. But she thought maybe they were poisoned and that she might be attacked. There was then an obese man, huge, at a theater show. He was angry at someone else. In fact, he was ridiculous. He got angry because he wasn't allowed to do what he wanted. He was jumping off the stage and falling on her.

At that moment she thought her partner came in, and she woke up.

Speaking of the dream and the violence, she realized that this obese man who fell on her did not target her especially, but . . . "it makes me think of another dream where someone was getting screwed in the stomach and was drained of his blood.

"It makes me think of a colleague who is also preparing for the institute exam. He is big. He came to see me while I was working in my room. I do not know what he wanted, but he showed me what he was working on. He did not ask me if he bothered me. He was confused. . . . He was asking me questions about things I wasn't yet working on. He seemed to know more than me. He said I did not have the right books; he criticized my worksheets; he showed me his stuff. I was jealous because he seems to be better than me. It makes sense since he works a lot."

Gabriella 2: Crushed?

Alice: Yes, I felt crushed by him. It's a pity. I would like to find someone to work with. I would like to do that with him. My partner upset me. He told me that I did not have the same level. But ultimately what he knows is based on what I tell him.

[Gabriella notes to the group, "That's what I pointed out to her, which she takes over."]

But it is certain that I am impressed by the work he does; he often shows it to me. What notes does the colleague have? . . . [I]t would not bother my colleague to work with me. . . . In fact, as he has a more uncertain position, it is not easy for him. He is a little disconnected. It does not go very well with the children he works with. I feel a little superior to him honestly. Is he so good? I could have the same level if I worked. A thought that I did not have last year. But when I do the exercises, I feel like I do not understand anything. But step by step it is going better.

In fact, as it was worked through in the workshop, what seemed to have come together in Gabriella's mind, highly subjectively and suddenly in a kind of explosion into the session, could with interrogation and reflection be (post hoc) constructed from multiple elements in the previous material—among them are the words "huge man," "falling on me," "getting screwed," "did not ask me if he bothered me," "better than me," and so forth (see Box 3.4). The group gradually came to surmise that the specific word "crushed" had unconsciously condensed in Gabriella's mind as the crucial element in the unconscious script dominating Alice's experience at that moment at multiple conscious and unconscious levels beyond the immediate context. For instance, the word could be seen as a stark representation of Alice's situation of feeling overwhelmed both in her sessions (she had said she had felt like vomiting after the previous session [Box 3.3]) and at many other times. In other words, she was someone who felt unconsciously profoundly crushed in the present by a lot of her internal world—including humiliating, exciting, and confusing sexual thoughts linked in that session to earlier associations to pedophilia and other transgressive behavior. At the same time, "crushed" also referred to her continuous inner and outer experience of feeling crushed by the unconscious intrusiveness of her imagined parental figures, of being someone who was crushed by her own thoughts stimulated in the session and also crushed by her experience at that moment—with a hint that it extended to the idea that her analyst had perhaps been experienced as crushing her with her first comment (Gabriella 1: "Why this choice of movie?"), which had rather surprised Gabriella when she made it and perhaps had been felt as intrusively confrontational by Alice.

The example illustrates what we mean in terms of suppositions about the analytic situation characterized by the dramatic monologue metaphor—particularly the emphasis on the script being inferred through the meaning and affective impact of words in the analyst's mind (symmetrical participation) and the indefinite temporal quality of when the script is playing out.

Henry-Hermann (Struggling to Be Here)

Henry's analysis of Hermann, a forty-five-year-old man in the third year of his analysis, also seems best described as conducted under suppositions about the analytic situation that we characterize with the dramatic monologue metaphor, although it is not a canonical example.

BOX 3.5. HENRY AND HERMANN (STRUGGLING TO BE HERE): SESSION 3, PART 1

Hermann: . . . For a moment, as I lay down, I thought: What am I doing here?

Henry 1: It is against your principles . . .

Hermann: . . . Yes, it is . . . [Silence.] . . .
. . . As I was looking at the photos, to choose some for the exhibition, I thought: What am I doing with all these irrelevant pictures? I had another dream, awkward and disturbing, still burlesque, so I said to myself: The comedy helps me to speak it out more easily. Still I continued to doubt: Is there any meaning in the dream? Now, I have forgotten the details, although I remembered it when I woke up: We were in a room, myself, you, and one or two children . . . something like that. Initially, you criticized me, by saying: "Are you serious?" As we were about to arrive toward a conclusion, you began to say bullshit, about the money, and we lost ourselves. This was the serious part; and then came the burlesque part: We were without blouses, and you began to talk like Mania or like my mother; like a mother figure, framed by the two children; a little bit tenderly and a little bit in a baby manner; you were saying: "Come on now, do not whine; we are a family." . . . [Silence.] I am stuck now because I do not remember the exact phrase you said in the dream. [Perplexed.] Now I feel messed up with analyzing. . . . I began to make efforts toward understanding. I discarded the second part as irrelevant, incomprehensible. . . . As for the first part, I wonder: Is it true that I brought up the money issue so as not to discuss something else? Or do I avoid the money issue itself?

Henry 2: . . . The way I was figured, in the second part, was changed . . .

Hermann: . . . It was like a mask . . . like a carnival, paper mask . . . I am not even sure if it was a mask at all, or who was behind the mask. I was rather led by the voice; it was kind of erotic; kind of motherly; I am not sure . . . [Anguished.] . . . Now I am stuck with the body: which was neither male nor female . . . [Silence.] Now I am stuck again, because, among the photos I was looking at, there was a miserable carnival festival, from last year, in a local village, with masks of politician's faces. . . . Well, probably it was a mask in the dream . . .

Henry 3: . . . A mask . . . but you seem anguished. . . . It is like wondering: Where is the primary material?

One reason is that in all three sessions Henry presented (see Boxes 3.5 and 3.6 for details about Session 3), he was very silent. This meant that like Alice, Hermann was left to associate for long periods of time during which words and images he mentioned would catch Henry's attention and form the basis of his minimalist interventions (Henry 2, 3, 4, and 5). Although Hermann brought many complex memories and described dreams at length with homoerotic and sexualized content, which might have provided other analysts with material that they could use to infer many unconscious scripts, Henry made few attempts to explain them or to discuss any meanings he inferred in the workshop. What he did reveal was that he thought it highly significant and a sign of progress that toward the end of the session Hermann had represented an identification with his mother.

BOX 3.6. HENRY AND HERMANN (STRUGGLING TO BE HERE): SESSION 3, CONTINUED

Hermann: . . . Yes, this is true. Since this morning I tried to recall this material. When you photograph something, that it is not as you saw it . . . Yes, this is annoying; it is like you didn't truly see it; and then the play begins: Was it like this? Or was it like that? [Silence.] . . . It suddenly came to me that I was near the river, this morning [he goes there each morning and takes photos, near the house inherited from an uncle, a painter, that he uses as a photo studio.] . . . It is as if I do not trust either the landscape, or my gaze (my looking); I wonder: Do I truly watch what I have in front of me? Is it like this? I began to look at last year's photos; of the flood . . . [inundation] or the year before last; I was thinking that this keeping of records is not a solution . . . except if you photograph scientifically, with a steady, immobile camera . . . without interfering. The other idea is that the person behind the mask was me; speaking like my mother; or like Mania . . .

Henry 4: . . . Your mother, who does not appear so often . . .

Hermann: . . . In my dreams . . .

Henry 5: . . . In your dreams also . . .

Hermann: . . . Now I am stuck . . . because I met with her also the day before last. [Laughs.] . . . This was not by chance; I intended to meet her . . . not just exchange some words . . . [Silence.]

Hermann: . . . I felt pressure by my own self. We had a weekend with Mania's extended family; and then I thought: Am I a sucker (a baby)? I am all weekend with them, and I didn't go to see my own mother?

There was a special reason for Henry's particularly passive approach, which emerged in the workshop when group members became frustrated. Apparently earlier in the analysis, Henry, to his way of thinking, had been drawn into what he called inappropriate conversations with Hermann—inappropriate because they were, so to speak, too "chatty." He had come to regard those moments as countertransference error (i.e., as a mistake he was now overcoming by maintaining a strict analytic stance of abstinence to allow his patient to get back to associating). The explanation demonstrates that Henry held an asymmetric set of suppositions about the role of the analyst's participation, which are somewhat inconsistent with how we define dramatic monologue, which is why this example is not canonical. It meant Henry did not suppose that his "seduction" by his patient, which is what he implied it was, might potentially have revealed the unconscious script energizing Hermann's experience. Moreover, this asymmetric supposition also meant that although he told the group that he was convinced that Hermann suffered from an infancy with a "petrified" mother, who had to be enlivened,[9] he had not wondered whether his own way of participating—particularly his decision

---

9. Something Henry concluded from a story Hermann told him early in the analysis. Apparently, when his father left his mother to fight in the war, his mother became unable to breast-feed her son, to which Henry gave the meaning that her breast was experienced as "petrified."

to limit his comments to Hermann and to avoid "chat"—although making sense within his framework, could in fact, unconsciously, be turning their contact precisely into the petrified early maternal relationship he hypothesized had been Hermann's experience.

Although, therefore, the example is not necessarily a good illustration of all the features we have in mind for the dramatic monologue type, it serves to show, powerfully, that the analyst's suppositions about the analytic situation, specifically the suppositions he makes about "participation" (Table 3.1, p. 53), have a significant effect on his approach. Hermann allowed himself to respond rapidly and unconsciously to his patient but did not reflect on what might be influencing his participation. This aspect of the presentation is taken up again in Chapter 7.

THEATER

Our third metaphor for the way the analytic situation is supposed is theater. In this approach the unconscious script is supposed to be revealed via the patient's unconscious depiction of the analyst as a person now in the sessions. It is therefore characterized by the supposition that utterances in the session are evoked by being with the analyst now. They are taken as hidden expressions of a script made up from unconscious desires, anxieties, imaginations, and fantasies pushing for expression but stimulated by and attached to the person of the analyst in sessions. Participation is asymmetric because it is the patient's unconscious that is pushing for expression, creating the script, and the analyst is an observer, feeling and experiencing what is going on, perhaps with empathy, but not actually creating it. In other words, the analyst's own unconscious script is treated as sufficiently known to be kept out.

Analysts making theater suppositions differ from those discussed so far. They may well suppose as analysts that they are responding affectively to an unconscious script revealed through the words their patient is selecting (as in the dramatic monologue metaphor) or via the events the patient may be reporting (as in the cinema metaphor). But what they principally suppose is going on is that, lying on the couch, their patients are always representing their unconscious beliefs and consequent feelings about being with the analyst now. Theater suppositions mean that patients necessarily "cast" the whole person of their analysts in particular ways evoked in the session "now."[10] So, had an analyst in Lesley's position (The Lingering Smell) made suppositions of this type, she might perhaps have imagined that Lucie was talking about her deep feelings of disappointment about not feeling understood by an analyst who had become cast in her mind as distant and unresponsive. Or had an analyst in Henry's position held these suppositions, he might have imagined his patient was casting him as "petrified" of him—conceivably as his mother had been.

---

10. Note, it may be of interest that one of the meanings of *die Besetzung* (cathexis) can be "cast," as in a cast of characters or dramatis personae. Actors, so to speak, are cast (cathected) into their roles (see the entry "Cast" in the glossary).

Louise-Georgina (In a Hole)

The analysis Louise conducted with Georgina is an example of this different "theater" set of suppositions. The analyst supposed that lying behind Georgina's associations was an unconscious script evoked by her casting of her analyst "now" in terms of experiences that she had had long ago but had been unable to formulate and understand.

Louise presented several sessions from different periods in an analysis that at one stage seemed to have reached a hopeless impasse. In one session, now more than three years into the analysis, which the analyst viewed as pivotal, Georgina began with a dream in which a wounded dog was in a hole in a covered pool and being dragged around and around by the current. In the dream, she felt hopeless, unable to do anything but knowing the dog would die. Louise reported how, following the dream, Georgina associated, out loud—as did Louise, but to herself. Louise found a large number of ideas "taking shape" in her mind, together with ideas about ways *she supposed her patient might experience her at this moment.* But she could be convinced about nothing definite. Meanwhile, as Georgina continued, she seemed to become cold, distant, and hopeless. She was complaining that analysis was just words and of no use. Gradually Louise realized that she, herself, felt like she had now fallen into a hole. So she wondered if perhaps Georgina had needed to communicate a very early, perhaps preverbal experience of hers, which might have occurred when she was left as a baby with a contagious illness that meant her mother could not visit her. With these thoughts in mind, she chose to speak: "Perhaps I am the pot . . . a pot which might contain good things to eat but instead is a hole, sucking you down to the bottom of the stream, where you might go round and round until you drown."

These and other examples of the thoughts and interpretations that Louise told us about show that the best fit for the type of analytic situation she supposes is theater. As analyst, she listens alertly for repetitive scenes that the patient unconsciously stages nearby or in front of them both via associations. She supposes that what she and the patient are watching unfold together is a repetitive way of being that is unconsciously happening in their midst. The script is waiting to be inferred. Because it will repetitively cast Louise in particular ways, it will become apparent. The script, the play in what we define as a theater supposition of the analytic situation, therefore is unconsciously derived from the patient's internal representations of relationships with important people in her infantile past, now revived in the theater of the analytic situation. In this way the patient can be understood to experience the analyst, based on past experiences that now come into and are projected onto the present. Or, in other words, the patient is all the time talking to the analyst as an internal, not (at least not very often) an external, figure.

In contrast to Lesley (The Lingering Smell), whose suppositions caused her still to be waiting for the patient to become conscious and talk about her feelings of frustration with her analyst, Louise supposed the associations to be driven by an internal script (a template set of responses to emotional situations). That script is inevitably evoked in patient and analyst via the mental representations they form of each other in sessions, whether the analyst becomes conscious of them or not. In the particular session from which we have selected the excerpt, Louise supposed that Georgina both experienced and acted toward her analyst as useless. She also supposed that the imagery and feelings she experienced could be hugely influenced by being with Georgina via her reverie—she felt useless; she felt that she was represented as and had actually become "the pot" in Georgina's mind.

The difference between Louise's theater and Lesley's cinema suppositions is that in the theater model the narratives discerned involve the analyst supposing he or she is unconsciously being "cast" now by the patient in a role or set of attitudes and intentions felt to be similar to that of an important figure from the past.

Analysts we describe as making theater-type suppositions consider that the analytic situation is one where the patient necessarily is preoccupied with the person of the analyst, so that references in the patient's associations, remarks, dreams, and so forth are often taken to represent their unconscious response to particular experiences here and now with the analyst. So, for example, if a patient talks about a fear that other people might react badly to them, such an analyst may wonder if the patient is unconsciously expressing a fear that his or her analyst is reacting badly to them now, perhaps caused by a deeper unconscious belief (script) that there is something to reject. For instance, perhaps more deeply, their particular unconscious resolutions of their Oedipal conflicts may have left them feeling guilty in many situations that evoke rivalry or ambivalence.

Moira-Marcel (Hard to Win)

Moira's analysis of Marcel is a second example of the theater type of supposition. Marcel kept describing meetings with women in his life whom he wanted to seduce and marry. He kept telling Moira he could not understand why the women he would take out and lavish with gifts and luxuries, as well as impress with his achievements, would soon tire of the relationship. Moira heard his utterances as indicating in sessions the repeated experience of an internally frightened child driven repetitively and unsuccessfully to boost himself away from a feeling of inadequacy. Specifically, she heard them as a statement about his unconscious fear of the failure of his efforts to impress her and (in a rivalrous way) boost himself (at her expense) right now in the moment. Marcel was externally hugely successful in his work but not in relationships. She supposed he had a half sense that his lavish seduction was not working either outside in his life or with her, fearing that his analyst had become pushed out of contact with him by his accelerating attempts to dazzle her. Beyond this she thought of him as feeling catastrophically dependent and, due to all his dazzling and pushing away of her and people outside, as fighting off a frightening conscious awareness of being lonely, desperate, and potentially despairing. For Moira, therefore, the analytic situation is a place where the patient's unconscious script for seeing and behaving in the world, present since early childhood, is played out in his reactions to her. First, it is observed as happening with her, and then it is drawn to his attention, along with the terrifying feelings evoked by dependency that are also constantly evoked.

Successful analysts who adopt this theater model differ in how far they use awareness of their own feelings, ideas, and behavior in sessions as influenced through their own unconscious (i.e., inaccessible because uncomfortable) responses to their patients. Moira, for example, was undoubtedly sensitive to and aware of the feelings Marcel evoked in her during sessions, but she did not indicate in the workshop that she saw these at this point as part of the hidden script.

At one point, the workshop group explored with Moira whether there was a way Marcel was unconsciously creating a situation with her in which she was made constantly to feel inferior, against which she, perhaps, unconsciously battled by making interpretations. If so, she could perhaps have been understood by him as demanding that he realize how important she was to him, despite his denials.

The idea of a deeper hidden script energizing how she was being cast to the extent it influenced her "role response" (Sandler, 1976) had emerged because at one point Moira volunteered to the group that she had a feeling that she was letting Marcel down. She related this to a feeling that she should have been better at understanding his dreams. She also mentioned a rationale for not putting up his fees. He was very high earning, but she said she did not want to fit into his picture that she and other women were grasping and rapacious. She had also told the group that in the first of the presented sessions, she had made a succession of comments to Marcel that painted a picture to him of his unconsciously wanting things from her, for which he could not ask directly due to his fear of dependence. To an outsider, there was at least the possibility that this succession of comments could suggest that somehow Marcel was stimulating Moira to engage responsively in "boosting" herself, struggling against the unconscious experience induced by Marcel and his attitude that she was not up to much. At that point, Moira hadn't thought about that, but she became interested in the suggestion.

We introduce these thoughts not because we think them correct but because in a moment we want to introduce a further difference in thinking about the analytic situation. It is a difference between analysts who routinely suppose they may have got unconsciously caught up with their patients (e.g., by at first unconsciously fitting into an invitation to boost themselves before realizing it) and those who do not.

On other occasions, successful analysts in this group, like Louise and Moira, might use their own awareness of their behavior more reflexively. For instance, Louise might have connected her actual feeling of having become paralyzed to an idea that for her patient she had apparently become a pothole that sucks in all life. In such instances, such analysts use their own self-observation (perhaps prompted by awareness of discrepancies) as an important source of unconscious inference and perhaps as an indication of some scenario being played out, perhaps in reverse, based somehow on some unconscious repetition from a fixed past relationship. As another example, an analyst may discern in herself a sense of impatience and a tendency to insist perhaps forcefully on something and then wonder if the patient is nudging her into a "dominating" tendency.

IMMERSIVE THEATER

Immersive theater is an experimental form mainly developed explicitly in the twenty-first century and sometimes adapted by prestigious theater companies like the National Theatre in London. It differentiates itself from traditional theater by removing the stage so that audiences are immersed in the performance itself. One way such immersion can be accomplished is by using a specific location set up in relevant ways and then allowing audiences to converse with the actors and interact with their surroundings.[11]

We use the metaphor of immersive theater to characterize suppositions about the analytic situation in which evidence for the unconscious script driving patients' associations is available now, as with theater, but where participation is symmetric. It is therefore characterized by the supposition that utterances in the session are evoked in the patient, and potentially in the analyst, by their being together now. Utterances by either participant are potentially hidden expressions of a script made up from each of their unconscious desires, anxieties, imaginations, fantasies, and so forth. They push for expression and are stimulated by and attached to the person of the analyst for the patient, and to the person of the patient for the analyst, now. The analyst's feelings and intuitions become relevant information. Participation is symmetric because unconscious participation from the psychoanalyst, even if more contained, is expected but can be corrected through conscious questioning and reflection as to signs as of potentially unconscious responses. As a set of suppositions for describing the analytic situation, therefore, immersive theater provides a metaphor to capture an approach to the analytic situation in which "who is believed to be doing what to whom" in the analytic session is open to be thrown into question at any moment. The presupposition is that the analytic situation is inherently an unconscious as well as conscious interaction between an analyst and a patient so that the analyst can never be entirely secure that he or she has not responded unconsciously to unconscious and so unknown scripts driving the patient. Therefore it cannot be taken for granted that the inaccessible script the analyst has the task of inferring is at one moment no more than the analyst's fantasy, imposed on the patient for some as yet unknown reasons. It means that while in principle the unconscious beliefs and behaviors that form the hypothesized inaccessible script that the analyst is inferring might be those pressing for actualization in the patient, they might also be some relational compromise being evoked by the patient and the analyst together in a folie à deux.

Not until the closing minutes at the very end of the workshop to which she presented, just as the moderator was summing up the work, did Louise (In a Hole), who was a distinguished colleague, perhaps by this stage appreciative toward and trusting of the group, reveal what she had not mentioned before and seemed to be a bit ashamed about. Apparently she had nearly given up on Georgina's analysis in despair after about three years. She had only not done so after consulting a senior colleague. That colleague had been encouraging as to her skill and fortitude and, after hearing the material, suggested that her fear she was wasting her time was not to her mind justified by the facts. The implication seems to have been that her feeling was something evoked in the

---

11. Readers interested in understanding more about immersive theater might look at the website of one of the prominent companies developing this medium, Punchdrunk: https://www.punchdrunk.com.

presenter, which could be thought of as part of a yet-to-be understood transference-countertransference development, which could profit from more consideration.

It was interesting, however, that in the Paris group moderator meeting where Louise's sessions with Georgina were relayed, several colleagues, despite the principle that the task was to understand the analyst rather than impose our own preferences, found it very difficult not to be critical of Louise because of the long silences she described herself and Georgina enduring. These colleagues were quite unused to an analyst allowing such long silences and, momentarily deviating from their effort to understand how Louise worked, could not help but suggest they thought her approach was creating a deadly atmosphere. Looked at now, and with the benefit of hindsight, it is possible to think that this response from colleagues had some insight. Had Louise's normal technique to allow silence more than is the case for many analysts from other different traditions (normative in the network in which she worked) in fact produced an interesting analytic situation between them? Could patient and analyst *together* have unconsciously reproduced via their interaction the traumatic situation internalized from Georgina's childhood, which Louise also arrived at by a different route, recognizing it in the way described above?

We know this was not the kind of supposition Louise held about the analytic situation, and as far as anyone became aware in both the workshops to which Louise and Moira presented, it was clear that neither of them supposed that the dynamics of the situation with Georgina or Marcel, respectively, extended routinely to an idea that they might unconsciously enact the role given to them by their patients. However, the idea that such "mutual enactment" (Tuckett, 1997) is potentially routine is precisely the supposition of a final group of analysts whose approach to the analytic situation we characterize with the metaphor of immersive theater.

The immersive theater metaphor does not imply a set of suppositions in which anything goes and roles are lost permanently, as when an analyst breaks boundaries and ceases to function as a psychoanalyst. Rather, as when immersive theater performances of *Macbeth* or *Oedipus Rex* are attempted, analysts characterized in this way still suppose that they are the psychoanalysts and that their task is to detect the script. So they seek to function with an analytic attitude and frame devoted to understanding the patient's script, not to satisfy or indulge themselves. But the given script, unconsciously written by the patient, is still there, like Shakespeare's, to be unraveled, understood, made sense of, and shared. But the crucial difference with the suppositions of ordinary theater is that the analyst cannot be sure whether, in fact, he or she has stayed in the analytic role at any moment or whether, unconsciously, he or she may inadvertently have strayed out of it and begun an enactment. For instance, sometimes, when an analyst supposes a patient is anxious, in difficulty, in need of an interpretation, fragile, hostile, seductive, and so forth, that is possible. But it could also be how the analyst, in reversal, has actually become. Without noticing it, they might have been feeling left out, lost, uncertain, worried, and so forth, and have responded by being active. With an immersive set of suppositions, it is *always* potentially appropriate for an analyst to wonder if the analyst's way of understanding or behaving and interpreting to the patient may be an unconscious enactment of the patient's script via unconscious improvisation.

Robert-Paul (Spicy Food)

The analysis Robert conducted with Paul, a young married man in his twenties with relationship difficulties and anxieties about other people's emotions, provides the clearest example we have of an analyst making immersive suppositions. Robert conceives of the analytic situation as one in which patient and analyst unconsciously as well as consciously affect each other. Both modulate themselves according to their experience of the other and the fantasies about each other that they have. The sessions Robert presented exemplify these suppositions as he skillfully attempts (sensing the links between his own associations as they emerge in response to his patient's free association) to interpret the meaning of their interchange.

For example, after one session during which he had felt dissatisfied with his work and in too much of a hurry to interpret, he resolved to try to be less impatient the next day. The patient arrived with a dream. There were two airplanes, some explosions, some kind of bombing; then some very long teeth appeared. They pierced through people, without killing them, but he managed to save himself by hiding behind a thick wall. Robert immediately heard this as an accurate description of his view of yesterday's session and the unintended effect on his patient of his way of interpreting too much and too quickly. But to translate this understanding to the patient immediately, he thought, would continue the problem. Instead, he asked what Paul thought. Paul wasn't sure. Perhaps it had something to do with emotions. The others were injured, he added, pierced by bullets, whereas he was unscathed. Feeling his understanding confirmed, Robert said, "Have I somehow been a bomber who aimed at you?"

The session continued as in Box 3.7.[12]

BOX 3.7. ROBERT AND PAUL (SPICY FOOD): SESSION 2

Paul: "Actually, you have not! There was a good atmosphere in yesterday's session."

He then added that after he had gone for lunch, he had been attacked by a terrible stomachache. This led to an association about someone who did "not take care of hygiene when preparing food" and a further story about dinner at an Indian restaurant where the food he was given was very spicy. The person with him had said, "Where have you brought me for dinner? I feel like throwing up."

Robert 1: Now made a more allusive comment to Paul about how he seemed to have been given "a double dose of indigestible food."

Paul: Now elaborated accounts of what his mother gave him.

Robert 2: Refrained from speaking at all. [Robert commented to the group that he thought that his effort [Robert 1] had just produced more material along the same lines. So when still more interpretations about the effect of his excessive interpretation

---

12. To preserve anonymity and space, the text is a mixture of direct speech and summarized speech. Direct speech is within quotation marks.

occurred to him yet again, he began to realize that today, despite his best efforts, he had so far just added to the problem of yesterday. In fact, he now felt trapped and began to wonder how to make any interpretation that would be digestible at all.]

There was silence for several minutes.

Paul: Talked about several TV programs involving "cutting thorns and throwing them away," an "abandoned boy" who had to manage on his own, and a "wifeless father and his son" who somehow succeed in fending for themselves.

Robert 3: "I am thinking that perhaps I was 'sharp-tongued' with you yesterday. I snapped at you. I picked and pointed out only the thorns in your words, and threw away the flower, which I should have appreciated."

Paul: "Why would you say that?"

Robert 4: [Now Robert answered at length, providing details of what he thought had happened today and yesterday.]

Paul: "As a matter of fact, what you said did astonish me."

An interchange followed in which what Robert thought and how Paul had responded were shared. Robert stressed to Paul that he had been pushed through a variety of states of mind because of his analyst's "biting" words, which had persecuted him. Paul had ended up abandoned and motherless, having to do all the emotional work himself.

Robert 5: "But I would like to point out that you were able to come out of bombings and loneliness alive, despite all the difficulties."

Paul: "In the movie, I mentioned that the boy, with his father's help, had carried out his projects and had become capable of dreaming."

Robert 5: "We must hope that less heavy food will be served in future."

Paul: Laughed. After a short silence he told a further story about plowing and compacting ground [which made it clear to Robert that he needed barriers to prevent fights but not such strong ones as to prevent any exchange].

After this session Robert concluded to himself and to the group, "When I interpret too much, this may automatically convey a feeling of a well-plowed field on the surface, but in fact it can make a deeper level of the field impermeable and therefore prevent any still deeper levels from emerging."

The example illustrates an analyst, Robert, who supposes the analytic situation to be one in which he may find he has unconsciously participated—an immersive rather than ordinary theater. He recognizes that he may inadvertently cast Paul as someone in his mind, from his own unconscious responses to him, just as Paul may cast him. Although, in Robert's view, what ultimately matters is the unconscious script pushing for actualization in Paul, it emerges via Robert's unconscious response to Paul, as well as vice versa. Paul's utterances, therefore, are supposed often to be an unconscious response to Robert's unconscious responses to him. As the example shows, Robert tries to read them with that supposition in mind.

What is not made completely clear in this example, however, is how far Robert views his responses as technical errors (he did mention in the workshop his general lack of enthusiasm for interpretations that were too much like clever translations) or as unconsciously driven responses to Paul. What is certain is that Robert felt he had been bombing and had the set of suppositions to note and fine-tune his approach from his reflections. With the benefit of hindsight from discussion with Robert (and also the theoretical distinctions being developed in this chapter many years later), it seems rather likely that Robert's impatience to put his understanding into words (which he concluded had effectively bombed Paul with too much "understanding" and been intrusive) might be best considered an unconscious enactment of the script inside Paul that Robert did in fact think was pushing for actualization.[13] Although it was not how he saw it explicitly at the time, the likelihood is that Robert recognized intuitively that he had been unconsciously nudged (Joseph, 1985) responsively (Sandler, 1976) to create Paul's experience of his mother and father, unintentionally overwhelming Paul's sensitive emotional responses. Certainly, back at the time he presented the material, Robert thought that Paul's premature defensive withdrawals were an adaptive mode of functioning that he had developed, which now caused his relationship difficulties. Enacted and surfaced between them, it could be understood.

THE FOUR METAPHORS AND SUPPOSITIONS ABOUT TRANSFERENCE FOUND IN FREUD'S WORK

We arrived at the four metaphors we have just set out to characterize psychoanalysts' suppositions about how an unconscious script of some kind brings the past into the present in a psychoanalysis, using a triangular method. First, presenters and participants in several hundred workshops, using the two-step discussion method, created the clinical data. Second, over fifty moderator meetings discussed the workshop data and attempted to apply the Step 2 classification options for the analytic situation (Tuckett et al., 2008, p. 165). In those meetings and then in the writing of this book, there was an iterative process of mutual clarification. The classification options and their definitions were constantly debated as we tried to fit types to actual practice. Eventually, the four metaphors emerged and became clarified during the writing of this book as ideal types. In this way, they are, so to speak, concepts grounded in psychoanalysts making sense of the data of what psychoanalysts do.

In the remainder of this chapter, we want to add the third leg of our triangular approach (Figure 3.1) by introducing research carried out within our group (especially by Michael Diercks) into Freud's written work in this area, specifically his work in German.

---

13. The terms "unconscious enactment" and "enacted" are used in this paragraph in highly specific ways. See glossary, p. 256.

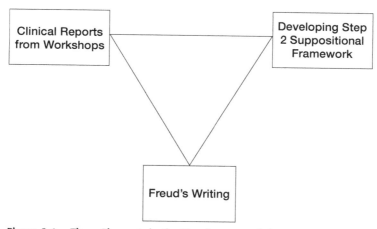

Figure 3.1. Three Elements in the Development of the Four Metaphors

We have found that the four metaphors we developed both help to clarify aspects of Freud's position and are also useful for asking crucial questions about the differences in modern practice raised in Chapter 1.

Recalling Table 3.1, Table 3.2 places some of Freud's ideas about transference within the framework of "when" and "participation" we used in Table 3.1 to differentiate our four metaphor types. Although he emphasized these different ideas on different occasions, none of them seem to have been given up.

One of Freud's (1894) first ideas was that transference was a "false connection" in which affects become disconnected from underlying ideas, rendering them inaccessible to consciousness and leaving them in a kind of frozen state. Via affect-laden words, uttered in the analytic situation, these disconnected ideas can potentially become accessible. This is the principal idea behind the suppositions we use the dramatic monologue metaphor to describe. This is the right-hand column because the frozen state is indefinite or omnipresent. It is revealed via the analyst's symmetric participation, via unconscious-to-unconscious cognition, placing it in Cell D.

A second false connection Freud (1893) had in mind in a passage, which James Strachey notes as the "first appearance of 'transference' [*Übertragung*] in the psychoanalytic sense" (p. 302n), is slightly different. Considering the part played by the relationship to the physician in creating what he called "resistance," Freud (1893) wrote that the sensitiveness and suspiciousness of hysterical patients may occasionally attain

Table 3.2. Different Assumptions Underlying Freud's Transference Theories

	When: Now	*When:* Indefinite
Participation: asymmetric	A Transference to the whole person of the analyst	B Transferences of affect via relationships
Participation: symmetric	C Transference and countertransference	D Unconscious cognition

surprising dimensions "if the patient is frightened at finding that she is transferring on to the figure of the physician the distressing ideas which arise from the content of the analysis" (p. 302).

With this second supposition, transference happens via affective displacements between relationships (the original relationship, the relationship now with the physician, etc.) rather than words. It is the idea behind the suppositions about the analytic situation that we use the cinema metaphor to describe. Once again, the frozen state is indefinite or omnipresent, but it is to be revealed by the analyst making the connections. Participation is asymmetric. This is Cell B. It is the underlying idea well expressed by Moore and Fine (1990) in their glossary of (US) psychoanalytic terms, which has been typical of the neoclassical or ego psychology position to which they are attached, among others. Moore and Fine write that psychoanalysts observe transference as the "displacement of patterns of feelings, thoughts, and behaviour, *originally experienced in relation to significant figures during childhood, onto a person involved in a current interpersonal relationship*" (p. 196; our emphasis).[14]

The third of Freud's suppositions about transference starts to appear in the postscript to Dora (Freud, 1905a). Although Bird (1972) apparently was using Strachey's somewhat inaccurate translation of the most important and telling passage,[15] we view his assessment as highly pertinent:

> In many ways the closest Freud ever came to establishing a formal analytical rationale for transference was his first attempt, in the postscript to the case of hysteria (1905a). . . . These few pages are, in my opinion, among the most important of all Freud's writings. . . . [H]is ideas revealed tremendous insights and promised more to come. (p. 272)

But Bird also perspicaciously stated about Freud that "nothing he wrote afterward about transference was at this level" (p. 273).

In the postscript, transference for Freud is not a false connection from individual "transferences" of affect or relationship (i.e., a set of different false connections such as between Freud with a beard and another man with a beard) but a phenomenon created by the fact that patients cast the whole person of the analyst (now) in terms of their internal unconscious script.

Only once more, in *Beyond the Pleasure Principle*, did Freud (1920a) arrive at a formulation that follows on from that in the postscript: "Patients repeat all of these unwanted situations and painful emotions in the transference and revive them with the greatest ingenuity. They seek to bring about the interruption of the treatment while it is still incomplete; they contrive once more to feel themselves scorned, to oblige the physician to speak severely to them and treat them coldly" (p. 21). This postscript or 1920s view of Freud's is theater, located in Cell A (now, asymmetric).

---

14. The most modern edition now edited by Larry Sandberg and Elizabeth Auchincloss (pp. 266–70) has a much more comprehensive definition—attempting in fact to capture most of the ideas included in this chapter—but with the disadvantage that their contradictory nature is implicit and specificity is somewhat lost.

15. "A whole series of former psychic experiences comes alive not as the past but as the present relationship to the person of the physician" (Freud, 1905a, p. 116; our translation).

Finally, the fourth set of ideas that must be credited to Freud are ones that he does not use in his case studies but clearly anticipated—at least to judge by warnings he made to others (see below) and hints about his own experiences. We have in mind suppositions about the analytic situation as the outcome of a double unconscious casting, by patient of analyst and analyst of patient—in other words, as mutually participatory. Such suppositions are characterized in our scheme by the metaphor of immersive theater. This is Cell C (now, symmetric). As we will show below, although not developed by Freud in any clinical case we know, Cell C suppositions are the logical outcome, once he recognized the inherent contradictions of his idea that free association and evenly hovering attention implied unconscious-to-unconscious cognition. Inevitably, considerations as to the role of countertransference, unconscious reactions to the patient by the analyst in the analytic situation, must follow.

While a full exegesis of the many scholarly works exploring Freud's writing on transference and its sources (e.g., Britton, 1999; Grubrich-Simitis, 1997; Mahony, 2007; Makari, 1992) is beyond our scope, the remainder of this chapter elaborates our reasons for supposing that the four metaphors are a useful way to bring out the struggle Freud experienced while working out his theory of transference and suffering the clinical experience of being its object—something we may all recognize.

In the footsteps of Laplanche and Pontalis (1973), but drawing from the implications of the differences between the suppositions characterizing our four metaphor types, we will try to "recognise the action of the transference in those case histories left to us by Freud by reading between the lines" (p. 456). Our investigation follows three pathways. First, we elaborate on the idea that from the beginning to the end, Freud held internally contradictory ideas. In effect he never made up his mind. Second, we explore one reason we think Freud never entirely made up his mind. Like participants in our workshops, ourselves, and the discipline of psychoanalysis generally, Freud experienced his own discoveries as emotionally very challenging indeed and never fully came to terms with the implications. Finally, we think Freud's inquiry into these matters, as must any other investigation into them, necessarily ran into an irresolvable and problematic contradiction.

DISCREPANT MODELS

What we label as the cinema model conflicts in some essentials with the dramatic monologue just as both conflict with theater. Theater and immersive theater conflict as to whether joint participation (i.e., mutual enactment; Tuckett, 1997) is supposed or not. The conflicts are about when and where the unconscious script is playing out and in whom.

As early as 1893, Freud was already struggling with a conflict between his experience of transference as an obstacle versus his intuition that it was therapeutically crucial. I was "greatly annoyed at this increase in my psychological work" (Freud, 1893, p. 304), he wrote, although a few pages earlier he had also written, "It seems, indeed, as though an influence of this kind on the part of the doctor is a sine qua non to a solution of the problem" (p. 266). Like him, perhaps most of us are more divided in that way. In other words, transference is experienced ambivalently by the analyst as by the patient.

From his first intuitions about it, Freud always conceived transference as a personal relation, at least implicitly felt as playing out in and potentially disrupting the session with the analyst. The view is already there in the remarks quoted above from his chapter on "The Psychotherapy of Hysteria" in 1893. Once patients have decided to put their trust in the doctor, he wrote, "it is almost inevitable that their *personal relation* to him will force itself, for a time at least, unduly into the foreground" (Freud, 1893, p. 266; our emphasis). However, what he means here is somewhat ambiguous. As we saw, in 1893 Freud was writing not about transference to the whole relationship to the analyst but rather about instances of individual transferences (i.e., false connections of ideas or felt relationships observable on a particular day). Nonetheless it's a present experience. The quotation above from 1893 was continued with an explanatory example at length:

> In one of my patients the origin of a particular hysterical symptom lay in a wish, which she had had many years earlier and had at once relegated to the unconscious, that the man she was talking to at the time might boldly take the initiative and give her a kiss. On one occasion, at the end of a session, *a similar wish came up in her about me.* She was horrified at it, spent a sleepless night, and at the next session, though she did not refuse to be treated, was quite useless for work. After I had discovered the obstacle and removed it, the work proceeded further; and lo and behold! the wish that had so much frightened the patient made its appearance as the next of her pathogenic recollections and the one which was demanded by the immediate logical context. What had happened therefore was this. The content of the wish had appeared first of all in the patient's consciousness *without any memories of the surrounding circumstances which would have assigned it to a past time.* The wish which was present was then, owing to the compulsion to associate which was dominant in her consciousness, *linked to my person*, with which the patient was legitimately concerned; and as the result of this mésalliance—which I describe as a "false connection"—the same affect was provoked which had forced the patient long before to repudiate this forbidden wish. Since I have discovered this, I have been able, whenever I have been similarly involved personally, to presume that a transference and a false connection have once more taken place. Strangely enough, the patient is deceived afresh every time this is repeated. (p. 303; our emphasis)

From the point of view of the conflicting suppositions attached to our metaphors, it looks as if Freud's supposition in this passage is that there is potentially a series of false connections as a consequence of the unconscious transfer of a wish from a past relationship to a present one. If so, in cinema terms, an old film, so to speak, has started rolling in the session owing to the compulsion to associate, and Freud is represented in it in a way that causes the patient to draw back. Much depends here on whether, when Freud writes that his patient consciously recalled her wish in relation to himself, he means that she told him about it in the session, suggesting it was provoked now, or he inferred it indirectly from other things she reported. In the latter case it would be "theater," in the former, "cinema."

Moving now to the famous postscript to the Dora case, which was written to understand a failure that hurt Freud very much, we first note the implication of his entire post hoc review: namely, that he now thinks that when with Dora (i.e., while with her in those sessions), he had been blind to her feelings and beliefs *about him*. In the postscript itself, after explaining his failure to interpret transference, Freud is strikingly clear that transference is an "inevitable necessity" for two reasons: "since use is made of it in setting up all the obstacles that make the material inaccessible to treatment, *and* since it is only after the transference has been resolved that a patient arrives at a sense of conviction of the validity of the connections which have been constructed during the analysis" (Freud, 1905a, pp. 116–17; our emphasis).

However, our research suggests the elaboration that Freud offers at this point is significantly obscured by the translation. Strachey's translation of Freud's explanation of transference in the standard edition preserves the sense of it as a false connection. There we find "a whole series of psychological experiences are revived, not as belonging to the past, but as applying to the person of the physician at the present moment" (Freud, 1905a, p. 116).

In contrast we think that the original German should be translated like this: "A whole series of former psychic experiences *comes alive* not as the past but *as the present relationship* to the person of the physician" (Diercks, 2018, pp. 61–62; our emphasis).

To us, the latter conveys a much more vivid sense of Freud's idea, as it comes across in the German. It makes clear that the crucial psychic experience that needs to be understood *is alive as the present relationship to the person of the analyst*. In other words, we are in the theater, not the cinema.

What seems to have happened in Dora's analysis is that Freud supposed he was in the cinema, where things could be reported and talked about, whereas he was in the theater, where they were happening. "I did not succeed in mastering the transference in good time," he wrote. "Owing to the readiness with which Dora put one part of the pathogenic material at my disposal during the treatment, I neglected the precaution of looking out for the first signs of transference, which was being prepared in connection with another part of the same material" (Freud, 1905a, p. 118). Bird (1972), writing about the postscript, argues that "in what seems like a creative leap, Freud made the almost unbelievable discovery that transference was in fact the key to analysis, that by properly taking the patient's transference into account, an entirely new, essential, and immensely effective heuristic and therapeutic force was added to the analytic method" (p. 269). However, as Bird continues, very soon "Freud's conviction seems to have failed him. Nothing he wrote afterward about transference was at this level, and most of his later references were a retreat from it" (p. 273).

One way of understanding all this is to suppose that during Dora's analysis, Freud was somewhat blindsided by his experience of Dora's transference to him (in other words, by his own countertransference and by his lack then of an immersive model), as well as by his operational suppositions. At the time he still maintained what ultimately became an unsustainable separation between remembering (i.e., reporting) and enactment (actualization). Therefore, he thought Dora and other patients at the time would unconsciously *report* disguised forms of their unconscious ideas in their sessions (as in the cinema model) in words rather than *enact* them as deeds (or "as actual relationship"). This hard-to-give-up assumption (at the time), together with what seems likely to have been his countertransference (unconscious, given his then lack of an immersive model), obviously would have slowed up his growing realization that Dora was enacting her fears of him experienced now, in sessions, in the theater.

A further point emphasizes the ambiguity. In the postscript Freud has acknowledged that the experience of transference is important to produce a sense of conviction in the patient. He even goes so far as to say, "Transference, which seems ordained to be the greatest obstacle to psycho-analysis, becomes its most powerful ally, if its presence can be detected each time and explained to the patient" (Freud, 1905a, p. 117). This statement indicates the radical shift to the new view (Bird, 1972, p. 269), according to which understanding and interpreting transference is the decisive and sometimes only means of accessing emotionally loaded remembering and so to finally changing the unconscious script.

What may not be immediately obvious, but whose realization is quite crucial at this point, is that Freud is deeply preoccupied with questions of validation. Is the "truth" of interpretation to be found inside or outside the consulting room? This question is crucial because it lies at the heart of the difference between the theater and cinema suppositions and also because it is at the heart of the related difference between those analysts who think transference dominates a patient's experience of their analyst ubiquitously at all times and those analysts who suppose that transference can be absent (Lesley, The Lingering Smell) or that, sometimes at least, there can be a "real" rather than a "transference" relationship.

An example of Freud's preoccupation with external validation is his question to Ernst about whether he recalled the "passionate temper" of his father, who sometimes couldn't stop his violence, which Freud (1909b) wrote was a "truth" that "to any disinterested mind . . . . would have been almost self-evident" (p. 209) but was not to Ernst!

Freud's hesitation on this point persists. Even as the case history now makes clearer that the issue in Ernst's case is his frightened beliefs that his analyst is cruel and wants to take pleasure in punishing him, Freud is still reporting how he tried to draw on reality to persuade or reassure Ernst that "really" this was not so. "I assured him that I myself had no taste whatever for cruelty, and certainly had no desire to torment him" (Freud, 1909b, p. 166). "I told him I had no intention of tormenting him unnecessarily" (p. 169). Such appeals to reality are reported despite the fact they are quite at odds with Freud's argument to his readers that unmasking Ernst's unconscious experience of Freud as cruel and revengeful in his sessions (conceived clearly now as theater) is crucial to the progress of the treatment.

At perhaps the critical moment, Ernst describes his mother's account of the "elemental rage" he had flown into when his father beat him for biting someone as a child. Freud interprets this scene as incontrovertible evidence of his construction that as a child Ernst must have experienced ambivalent feelings toward his father for interfering with his expressions of infantile sexuality. However, once again, when he tells Ernst, Ernst will have none of it: "With that capacity for being illogical which never fails to bewilder one in such highly intelligent people as obsessional neurotics, he kept urging against the evidential value of the story the fact that he himself could not remember the scene" (Freud, 1909b, pp. 208–9).

Only now does Freud make clear that what follows from this moment is an intensification of Ernst's fantasy that Freud is a cruel analyst who might beat him "now" at any moment. The following passage both makes clear this is how Freud saw things and exemplifies Freud's use of what we characterize as theater suppositions:

And so it was only along the painful road of transference that he was able to reach a conviction that his relation to his father really necessitated the postulation of this unconscious complement. Things soon reached a point at which, in his dreams, his waking phantasies, and his associations, *he began heaping the grossest and filthiest abuse upon me and my family, though in his deliberate actions he never treated me with anything but the greatest respect.* His demeanour as he repeated these insults to me was that of a man in despair. "How can a gentleman like you, sir," he used to ask, "let yourself be abused in this way by a low, good-for-nothing fellow like me? You ought to turn me out: that's all I deserve." While he talked like this, he would get up from the sofa and roam about the room—a habit which he explained at first as being due to delicacy of feeling: he could not bring himself, he said, to utter such horrible things while he was lying there so comfortably. But soon he himself found a more cogent explanation, namely, that *he was avoiding my proximity for fear of my giving him a beating.* If he stayed on the sofa he behaved like some one in desperate terror trying to save himself from castigations of terrific violence; he would bury his head in his hands, cover his face with his arm, jump up suddenly and rush away, his features distorted with pain, and so on. He recalled that his father had had a passionate temper, and sometimes in his violence had not known where to stop. *Thus, little by little, in this school of suffering, the patient won the sense of conviction which he had lacked*—though to any disinterested mind the truth would have been almost self-evident. (Freud, 1909b, p. 209; our emphasis).

Reading this passage and its concluding sentence leaves no doubt about what Freud now considered was required to obtain conviction. But it also emphasizes how that might get lost. First, Freud was focused on explaining why transference, which he had thought of and experienced as resistance, was in fact crucial to cure. Second, he was still mixing this up with the issue of external validation.

Freud's 1912 paper continues his focus on the patient's picture of the analyst but also develops what it seems he certainly had learned from Dora and then Ernst—namely, that what is particularly present now and distressing about the associative process that takes place in sessions under the influence of transference repetition is that a patient is exposed to betraying their ambivalent feelings and thoughts about the analyst to the analyst: thoughts and feelings that here and now the person they entrust to help is precisely the person they feel is so negative toward them.

We find in the end that we cannot understand the employment of transference as resistance so long as we think simply of "transference." We must make up our minds to

distinguish a "positive" transference from a "negative" one, the transference of affectionate feelings from that of hostile ones, and to treat the two sorts of transference to the
doctor separately. . . . Bleuler has coined the excellent term "ambivalence" to describe
this phenomenon.[16] (Freud, 1912a, pp. 104–6)

By now Freud is emphasizing that the distress felt in sessions was not just resistance
to elaborating *any* unwelcome knowledge but specifically discomfort at any awareness
of unwelcome and so repressed thoughts about the analyst and his or her intentions
and the feelings that these thoughts produce. In this view the experience of the session
now produces sets of uncomfortable and incompatible unconscious beliefs (taken by
the patient as facts) evoked by unbearable ambivalent wishes and feelings toward the
psychoanalyst.[17] This is transference supposed as theater, which, so long as ambivalence is inevitable, is inevitable.

Insofar as Freud now took this view, transference experience (i.e., ambivalent responses necessarily evoked in session dynamics) can easily be linked to the eruption
of infantile sexuality and the core of the Oedipal conflict, whether the ambivalent
relationship is posited as toward mother or father.[18] Here, Freud's journey had now
potentially brought him to the position that ambivalent unconscious beliefs must
turn up in sessions and will be experienced toward the analyst, precisely because these
ideas, typically ideas based on their "solutions" to their infantile conflicts, are those
giving patients troubles in their other relationships and in their history.[19] Along these
lines, Freud clearly supposed the analytic situation to be characterized by what we
call theater. Problematic beliefs appear dynamically in sessions so that they can be
experienced and transformed presently. After all, as he famously put it, "no one can
be slain in absentia or *in effigie*" (Freud, 1912a, p. 108; our translation).

---

16. Laplanche and Pontalis (1973) note, "The term of ambivalence was borrowed by Freud from
Bleuler, who introduced it. Bleuler had considered ambivalence under three heads: first, ambivalence
of the will (*Ambitendenz*), as when the subject wants to eat and not to eat at the same time; secondly,
intellectual ambivalence, involving simultaneous adherence to contradictory propositions; and lastly, affective ambivalence, in which a single impulse contains both love and hate for the same person. Bleuler
treats ambivalence as a major symptom of schizophrenia 2, but he acknowledges its existence in normal
subjects. The novelty of the notion of ambivalence as compared to earlier evocations of the complexity
of the emotions and the fluctuations of attitudes consists on the one hand in the maintenance of an opposition of the yes/no type, wherein affirmation and negation are simultaneous and inseparable; and, on
the other hand, in the acknowledgement that this basic opposition is to be found in different sectors of
mental life. Bleuler eventually gives pride of place to ambivalence of feeling, however, and this emphasis
is inherited by the Freudian usage" (pp. 26–27).

17. In our introduction, we noted that André Green's (2000) patient wanted not to lie down and
continue when his mind was plagued by ambivalent thoughts.

18. See Freud's formulation in his last known report of a treatment (Freud, 1920b).

19. Note this formulation of the Oedipus complex in the words of Blass (2001): "The boy's love of
his father stands in a terrible conflict with his wish to be rid of him in order to attain the full love of his
mother. Given the love of the father, there is no way that he can allow himself to attain this. Thus, he
abandons his sexual desire for his mother, and in the face of this conflict-triggered loss he internalises his
beloved father. He gives up on an external beloved object and attains an alternative internal one. In this
process, he is internally enriched. He gains a new internal source of strength which not only makes up
for his loss, but also in a secondary way furthers the restraint of the sexual wishes" (p. 1113).

EMOTIONAL STRAINS

The ambivalent emotional impact on Freud of his discovery of transference will have come through already in what we have just described. He disliked his patients developing strong feelings for him. He seems to have resisted his realization of how suspicious Dora was of him and then tried desperately to avoid being characterized by Ernst as cruel.

In fact, in Ernst's case, the extraordinarily novel insights contained in the pioneering passage above ("And so it was . . . ") convey a striking sense that Freud (empathically) rather regrets the necessity that in various sessions his patient has to relive his former psychic experiences of terror at his father's believed intentions in his relationship to Freud. Freud regretfully acknowledges its inevitability in the case, alongside his decisive shift to recognizing that the repressed childhood scene is repeated in the patient's psychic experiences *in the sessions*. Tolerating such regret, as well as tolerating the patient's perhaps felt-as-outrageous view of oneself, is a sine qua non of conducting an analysis with theater suppositions and, therefore, a constant challenge for any of us making such suppositions, just as it was for Freud. In short, it is as challenging for the analyst to recognize how he is being cast by the patient as it is for the patient to recognize the casting. Many, if not all, psychoanalysts clearly prefer to be represented by their patients as "good" objects, just as patients often hope to meet such ideals.

Finally, although Freud viewed Ernst's case as a success, later analysts have criticized him for not being sufficiently alert to Ernst's experience of him as a cruel father. And indeed, there are certainly moments when Freud does not seem very alert to the role in which he is being cast, such as in the session where Ernst first tells the story of the cruel captain, showing great reluctance. He is even less aware of how, by his constant pressing of Ernst to reveal all that comes to his mind, he might (unconsciously) have been reenacting precisely the captain's part (Diercks, 2018; Mahony, 2007). Here, of course, are the emotional as well as conceptual difficulties of recognizing countertransference, necessarily required if an immersive theater model is supposed as potentially operative.

AN IRRESOLVABLE CONTRADICTION

In the next chapter we will examine Freud's ideas about free association and the fundamental rule and particularly their origin in what he thought was his decisive methodological step—when he found he could detect the (Oedipal) unconscious script in his own dreams.

To anticipate that discussion in the present context, the crucial step Freud had to take was to develop his idea that when an analyst listens to the patient in a state of evenly hovering attention, the patient's associations *fall into or touch upon the analyst's unconscious system of functioning*.[20] There, working over in the psyche of the analyst

---

20. Strictly the system Ucs.

takes place without him knowing—much as in the suppositions characterized by dramatic monologue.

In this way, for Freud, the analyst's activity reverses the original transformation of unconscious to conscious, which the patient necessarily performed in "free association." The difference is that while the patient is supposed to say everything that occurs to him, the analyst, remarkably, perceiving the emanations of his own unconscious stimulated by the patient's associations, "reconstructs" the unconscious of the analysand.

There are two crucial points here for our discussion of the analytic situation. First, by connecting the basic rule of "free association" with the idea of "evenly hovering attention" in 1912, Freud had described for the first time and in a revolutionary way a methodical procedure that was to enable one person (trained to do it) to *recognize* the unconscious of another person, to *re-create* it, and finally to *formulate* it linguistically in the form of an interpretation. He is envisaging a concept of knowledge that goes far beyond the usual empirical-positivist concepts of science. Second, by recommending that the analyst listen to his own unconscious during the session, Freud is confidently assuming that the analyst's unconscious will recognize the patient's.

However, taking this position does inevitably lead Freud to an irresolvable contradiction with significant implications. The reason is that the unconscious in any individual will inevitably press to create an expression satisfying for itself *in consciousness*. Therefore, the "free associations" starting from the analysand but heard through the analyst's unconscious logically *can only serve the latter's unconscious*. If the processing of the patient's associations in the unconscious of the analyst could ultimately lead to the reconstruction of the unconscious of the patient, this would only be logically conceivable if the unconscious of the analyst were no longer pressing for conscious expression, a contradiction in terms. Basically, it would mean that the analyst would no longer have an unconscious worthy of the name.

Freud seems both to have known this objection and not to have known it at the same moment, a phenomenon he later described in his work on splitting of the ego (Freud, 1938b). We argue this because it is precisely in 1912, the year of the paper on transference, when this theoretical dilemma becomes evident, that the demand for the analyst's own analysis, the training analysis, turns up. The explicit idea that it might "purify" the analyst directly and immediately follows the idea, in the work of both Freud (1912c, p. 116) and later authors (see, e.g., Racker, 1982, pp. 26–27), that the analyst's unconscious can reconstruct that of the analysand. We return to the conundrum in the next chapter.

Freud's initial insistence on self-analysis on the part of the analyst was logical at this point of his developing theory. In consequence, the topic of countertransference, a term dating back in his writing to 1909, now inevitably had to enter discussion. It clearly extends the range of possibilities as to how to suppose transference is revealed in sessions.

Bearing in mind Freud's (1905a) increasing certainty that in sessions the analysand unconsciously tries to avoid remembering/becoming aware of conflictual and repressed experiences and the resulting unconscious fantasies by letting them "come alive . . . *as the present relationship to the person of the physician*" (our translation; see also Bleger, 2012),[21] it surely follows that, as long as an unconscious worthy of the name is at work in the analyst, one must assume that he, like the analysand, will tend to avoid the evocation of his own repressed experiences and fantasies and instead tend to let them "come alive *as the present relationship*." It really must follow that what comes alive in the analyst in sessions does so "to the person of the" patient!

The implication is clear. To infer another person's unconscious script from sessions, the most competent analyst must accept to struggle with unconscious reactions at the beginning of treatment (see also Reith et al., 2018) and perhaps throughout. It is also likely that analysts will often not immediately be able to use the material provided by an analysand and may even misuse it. Putting their whole person at the disposal of the method, so to speak, will trigger their own repressed mental experiences and the resistances that inevitably exist within them.

From all this it follows logically, necessarily, and indispensably that an entanglement of the analyst in an unconscious "enactment," to a degree, is likely unavoidable. Whereas in the immersive theater approach to the analytic situation, such enactments, following Paula Heimann (1950), Heinrich Racker (1982), José Bleger (1967), Willy Baranger and Madeleine Baranger (1969), and Wilfred Bion (1962), are taken for granted, in the other approaches they are not. An advantage of the immersive theater viewpoint, therefore, not open to Freud with Ernst or Dora, is that it enables analysts to be on the alert for countertransference abnormalities and resistances, supposing that they then can become vehicles carrying information for unconscious inference.[22]

Although nowhere in Freud's writing or case histories does he show that he supposes an immersive theater model of the analytic situation as such, it could be said that he suspected it. We find his first mention of the term "countertransference" in 1909, in the course of a warning to Carl Jung about his patient's effects on him. He wrote,[23]

> Such experiences, though painful, are necessary and hard to avoid. Without them we cannot really know life and what we are dealing with. I myself have never been taken in quite so badly, but I have come very close to it a number of times and had a narrow escape. I believe that only grim necessities weighing on my work, and the fact that I was ten years older than yourself when I came to psychoanalysis, have saved me from similar experiences. But no lasting harm is done. They help us to develop the thick skin we need and to dominate "countertransference," *which is after all a permanent problem for us*; they teach us to displace our own affects to best advantage. They are a "blessing in disguise." The way these women manage to charm us with every conceivable psychic perfection until they have attained their purpose is one of nature's greatest spectacles. Once that has been done or the contrary has become a certainty, the constellation changes amazingly. (Freud, 1909a, p. 231; our emphasis)

---

21. In German: "eine ganze Reihe früherer psychischer Erlebnisse wird nicht als vergangen, sondern als aktuelle Beziehung zur Person des Arztes wieder lebendig" (Freud, 1905a, 280). Strachey's translation—"a whole series of psychological experiences are revived, not as belonging to the past, but as applying to the person of the physician at the present moment"—falls short of the German original.

22. This idea is taken up further in Chapter 7.

23. Freud's symbols ΨA and ψα in these letters have been replaced with "psychoanalysis" and "psychoanalytic," respectively.

His second reference is in a similar letter, but this time to Sándor Ferenczi, written on October 6, 1910, a year later.

> Of course, I knew very much or most of what you are writing about and now need to give you only a few clarifications pertaining to it. Why didn't I scold you and in so doing open the way to an understanding? Quite right, it was a weakness on my part; I am also not that psychoanalytic superman whom we have constructed, and I also haven't overcome the countertransference. I couldn't do it, just as I can't do it with my three sons, because I like them and I feel sorry for them in the process. (Freud, 1910b, p. 221)

Given that both letters follow Freud's experience with Ernst and may or may not be related to his own direct experiences "analyzing" both colleagues (Bergmann, 2004; Winnicott, 1964), we can read between the lines to suppose experiences of the kind to which he is referring personally were profound. Perhaps, as with the hint of regret we suggested as he reached his conclusions about transference, we can sense the same regret and the same determined struggle to face facts in his views about countertransference. To our reading, it is clear that, in embryo, Freud here must have had in mind suppositions of the immersive type.

A DIAGRAMMATIC REPRESENTATION

Tuckett (2019a) uses Figure 3.2 to represent the logic of transference dynamics. It can be used to show some of the issues discussed so far.

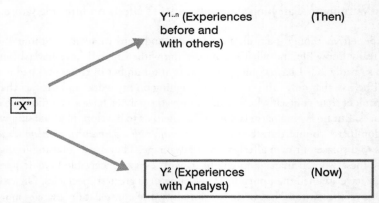

Figure 3.2.   Transference as an Unconscious Causal Template.
Source: Tuckett (2019a). Reprinted with permission.

The essential proposition behind the idea of transference is that the same unconscious internal template for representing and acting on the world (X), built in unconscious iterations from infancy, repetitively influences experience here and now in sessions (Y^2) as well as in past and present experience in the world ($Y^1 \ldots Y^n$). This works slightly differently for the cinema, dramatic monologue, and theater suppositions.

For all three suppositions, affects and beliefs that become "evident" in the analytic situation, via signs of discomfort, are evoked by an unconscious internal template

X—the inaccessible script pushing for actualization. It forms a fixed and inaccessible filter to "explain" experience when it is encountered by the subject, and treated as fact, it drives representations, feeling, and action. It is this filter and its daily operation in producing repetitive troubles that psychoanalytic investigation might seek to modify.

The difference between cinema suppositions, on the one hand, and dramatic monologue and theater suppositions, on the other, is marked by the box surrounding Y^2—representing the "when" in Tables 3.2 and 3.3. Analysts making dramatic monologue and theater suppositions identify X by prioritizing evidence of inaccessible internal templates driving the associations in session (now),[24] whereas those using cinema suppositions tend to identify X from evidence reported to them from elsewhere (then).

It is important to note that this formulation is a *construction of psychoanalysis*. It rests on a theory of transference construction—namely, that the picture of the analyst that the patient builds is derived from his or her internal template X via projective or other processes that influence perception. In fact, the technical task is the opposite. Once the analyst intuits an impression of the unconscious role in which the patient is casting her, unless she thinks the intuition can just be imposed on the patient from her side, it must first be discovered between them.

In other words, analysts of all three types must take two logical steps. First, they must intuit evidence of the patient's perceptions of themselves or others from the data they are given. Second, they must then construct the processes that they believe bring the pictures about. Figure 3.3 depicts this inferential task to demonstrate that, as inferenced, causal relations are reversed. The template X (intuited as causal) is in fact the outcome of an analyst's inferences about what happens in the consulting room and/or what is reported from outside.

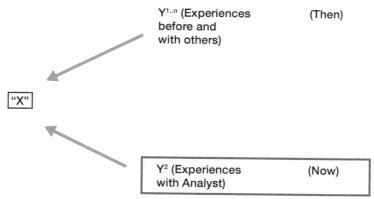

Figure 3.3. Transference as an Unconscious Causal Template: The Direction of Inference

---

24. Strachey wrote, "For the prime essential of a transference-interpretation in my view is that the feeling or impulse interpreted should not merely be concerned with the analyst but that it should be in activity at the moment at which it is interpreted. Thus an interpretation of an impulse felt towards the analyst last week or *even a quarter of an hour ago* will not be a transference-interpretation in my sense unless it is still active in the patient at the moment when the interpretation is given. The situation will be, so to speak, a dead one and will be entirely without the dynamic force which is inherent in the giving of a true transference-interpretation" (Symposium 1937, p. 139; our emphasis).

This logic, as we will discuss further in Chapter 6, means that when "transference interpretations" take the form of constructions, like Freud's "he was avoiding my proximity for fear of my giving him a beating," it may be wise to separate intuition and evidence lest the intuition becomes an imposition. If the patient, as well as the analyst, has first noticed, for instance, his avoidant behavior, then it may be much easier to become convinced of its link to the picture of his analyst that his analyst is suggesting he has. The implication, logically, is that prior to, or contemporaneously with, interpreting the picture of the analyst that the patient appears to have, the analyst may need to establish the evidence with the patient, as Strachey's (1934) contribution makes clear. It means the patient *really* does need (1) to feel the analyst is someone who he thinks will beat him, and (2) to have realized that this is a belief that can be discussed rather than an unbearable fact. Unconscious belief is fact (Britton & Vaihinger, 2009) and can only be questioned once recognized as belief.[25]

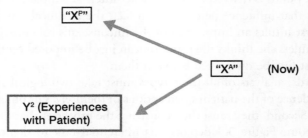

Figure 3.4. Countertransference Influence on an Analyst's Suppositions

The diagrammatic representation in Figure 3.4 attempts to represent the further logical possibility that follows from the immersive theater model of the analytic situation, premised on the existence of an unconscious casting of the person of the patient by the analyst, not only the other way round, as in theater. In Figure 3.4 there are now two inaccessible templates influencing the pictures being formed. First, there is the analyst's own internal template (X^A) "casting" the patient, which potentially filters the analyst's experience of being with the patient (Y^2) and so their intuitions about X^P, the patient's internal template. As already cited, analysts like Heimann, Racker, Bleger, Baranger, and Bion have elaborated such potential for unconscious "mutual enactment" (Tuckett, 1997) between patient and analyst. Similarly, but via the affective resonance produced in them by the patient's words within an otherwise predominantly dramatic monologue approach, analysts like Claude Le Guen (1982) and Pierre Fedida (2002) have described becoming aware, as we would put it, that they are in an immersive theater, realizing, retrospectively, that their interventions (coming unconsciously from X^a) have been unexpectedly highly disturbing to patients. The disturbance has then revealed new versions of X^P.

With immersive suppositions the analytic situation is an unconscious dynamic field. Whatever takes place between analyst and patient is supposed as influenced

---

25. "Initially in our development we treat beliefs as facts and it is only with emancipation from an inner certainty that we can see our beliefs as requiring reality testing" (p. 924).

by it. So, for example, just as it becomes possible to imagine Freud mutually enacting the transference with Dora and Ernst, so it might have been happening to Kurt Eissler and his patient (Chapter 1) or indeed in other cases discussed throughout this book.

In the next chapter, with these foundations for understanding differences in the suppositions that psychoanalysts bring to their conduct in the analytic situation in mind, we will turn to psychoanalytic inference. What suppositions do psychoanalysts make about the unconscious meaning of what they hear and experience in sessions? How from this raw material do unconscious scripts, beliefs, impulses, or fixed patterns of behavior that are influencing their patients, whether in their sessions or outside in their lived lives, emerge into the analyst's mind?

SUMMARY

In this chapter, we have looked at the different suppositions the psychoanalysts we studied hold about the analytic situation or, in other words, how they understand transference, the latent unconscious script being actualized to bring the past into the present analysis.

We introduced four ideal type sets of supposition that we found analysts use to recognize their patients' unconscious scripts. We use four metaphors to distinguish between the types. They are cinema, dramatic monologue, theater, and immersive theater.

The four types differ as to what analysts suppose about timing and participation—in essence "when" and "in whom" they think the unconscious script is having an effect. Each of the metaphors tries to capture a difference along these two dimensions.

Using material from the workshop discussions of seven different analysts' work, we described into which type of supposition their work seemed to fall.

We then looked at Freud's writings on transference over his career, bringing together our developing concepts (the four metaphors) and our study of Freud, particularly in the original German. In doing so we found that support for each of the four characteristic sets of suppositions, all used in contemporary psychoanalysis, is contained in his writings. We argue that for a mixture of theoretical and emotional reasons, Freud's thinking does not reach a conclusion. He struggled to develop his ideas and to apply them, never resolving his stance even if, logically, a direction seems clear.

We will return to this topic in Chapter 8, in which we will also apply the four metaphors to what we know about the suppositions regarding the analytic situation held by the seven analysts we introduced in Chapter 1. We think the value of this typology is not to resolve the issue of how any analyst *should* think about the analytic situation in general but to suggest useful questions any psychoanalyst might ask to explore where, after any given session, they suppose they have been standing on this crucial question. In this way we hope the four metaphors can have practical value. To reflect on how transference is being handled may be a much more useful activity than trying to impose a single view of what it is or how it should be handled.

4

How Do We Recognize What Is Unconscious?

In this chapter, we move from the suppositions we make about the analytic situation to look in more detail at processes of psychoanalytic inference. What suppositions do psychoanalysts make about the procedures that are necessary to identify the unconscious meaning of what they hear and experience in sessions? How from the raw material of a session do unconscious scripts, beliefs, fantasies, impulses, or fixed patterns of behavior that are influencing their patients, whether in their sessions or outside in their lived lives, or both, emerge into the analyst's mind?

We begin by exploring four examples of psychoanalytic inference from the workshops. Together, they illustrate differences in the sources of inference psychoanalysts draw along three axes represented in Figure 4.1 (next page): (1) what content in their patients' associations they treat as expressing hidden beliefs, fantasies, impulses, or fixed patterns of behavior, which the special features of a psychoanalytic session are supposed to make accessible; (2) whether and how their own thoughts and feelings in sessions caught their attention and were reported as relevant information; and (3) whether and how, in the workshops, they indicated they took a third or reflective position toward what was going on so that they became curious about possible relationships between (1) and (2), which could enable them sometimes to transform meaning reflexively (see glossary) and arrive at new inferences.

In Figure 4.1, to an extent, all three boxes reflect the outcome of the analyst's mental processing—or they would not be registered at all. But the two top boxes represent sources of near raw experience. The bottom box represents more developed mental processing—potentially transformative or reflective processes *deepening* understanding.

After exploring the different sources of inference drawn on by four of the analysts in our workshops to detect the unconscious scripts within their patients pushing for expression, we use the remainder of the chapter to place our findings in the context of the research we have undertaken into the evolution of Sigmund Freud's written ideas on this topic.

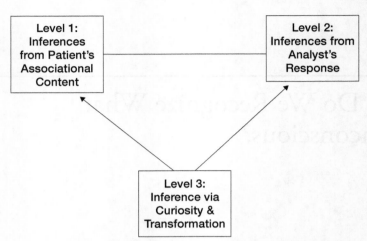

Figure 4.1. Sources of Inference. *Note:* **The idea is that all three sources of inference may arrive in the analyst's mind consciously, partially consciously, or unconsciously.**

As in the previous chapter, we have found it useful to create a dialogue between what we found our presenters doing and what Freud wrote about psychoanalytic technique grounded in his initial discovery of a method to infer the unconscious beliefs or fantasies present in his own dreams. It was this discovery he elaborated as "the" psychoanalytic method when it came to writing his encyclopedia article (Freud, 1923). In his formulation in that article, he firmly positions *freier Einfall* (free association) and *gleichschwebende Aufmerksamkeit* (evenly hovering attention) as the foundation of psychoanalytic investigation (Freud, 1926a). We look at what he seems to have meant by these German terms, arguing that perhaps translation issues have sometimes obscured underlying ideas. We then address the difficulties that emerge, whether for Freud or psychoanalysts today, if those ideas are put into practice in sessions. Picking up points introduced at the end of Chapter 3, we show how unconscious inference based on *freier Einfall* and *gleichschwebende Aufmerksamkeit* must inevitably depend on unconscious-to-unconscious cognition. Therefore, it must raise questions of countertransference, defined, following Chapter 3's discussion, as responses to the person of the patient *in the analyst* of which the analyst *is not aware*, except perhaps via some kind of self-analysis, and then only partially. This brings us to the question of how psychoanalysts assess the validity of their inferences. We end the chapter by relating these ideas and our findings to modern controversies.

JANA ANALYZING NANA (PUT ON THE SPOT)

Jana's analysis of Nana was titled as "Put on the Spot." It illustrates an analyst who, as we see it, tries to seek hidden (i.e., unconscious) meaning in what the patient says and/or does, notices her own reactions, and reflects to a degree on the implications of the thoughts that arrive in her mind and the situation she feels "put in." She then tries to use all that to transform the situation and to offer new meanings to her patient.

The first session presented was the last of an initial exploratory period (using two chairs facing each other) and began unexpectedly. Nana, once she got into the consulting room, chose not to take her usual seat but to lie on the divan Jana uses as a couch—quickly and without a word. Jana sat behind her. Silence settled. After a while Jana (1) asked, "How can we think of what is happening this morning, here, and what we are living together?" Nana replied, apparently without any discomfort, that she did not know why she had chosen to lie down. "It just took me like that! I remember that we said that after the holidays, that is what I would do. But now I am lying here like this, I await your reaction. Are you going to laugh or get angry?" The session is continued in detail in Box 4.1.

BOX 4.1. JANA AND NANA (PUT ON THE SPOT): SESSION 1

Jana 2: "Here we are in a complicated situation. What to do with your move this morning? And what we had agreed? Either I refuse it and I am a frustrating mother like the one who did not welcome your impulses, or I accept and give you a feeling of being all powerful?"

[Nana listens attentively and is very still but then moves to half sit up on the couch.]

Nana: Oh! right? "Can I stay like that?"

Jana 3: What do you think of your position and mine now?

Nana: On your lap I suppose. [She laughs as she gets back to the chair. Silence.] I had a dream tonight.

Jana 4: A dream . . .

Nana: "In the dream I am with my two parents with my maternal grandparents. There's a baby. I see that he has been prepared for, a cradle. I approached [she laughs loudly]: It is not possible! It must be me as a baby and yet not! They call him by a boy's first name."

Jana 5: "A masculine first name?"

Nana: Continuing the dream, suddenly she realizes she is not in the right family; the characters are not her parents; it's not the right house; she is the intruder. She wakes up very anguished, sweaty, and perhaps sick. She goes to drink and finds herself passing her small son's room to check if he is asleep. She goes back with difficulty.

Jana 6: [Remains silent.]

Nana: Now comments on her sense of being underground, adopted, her fear of being illegitimate, and how she always struggles to be heard. "I speak loudly; I agitate; I rush into the heap."

Continued on next page

BOX 4.1, continued

Jana 7: Fucking in the pile? What could it make us think? [Silence.]

Jana 8: Running to the couch?

Nana: [Laughs.] "I think you're talking about my way of arriving here earlier . . . and how being impatient like that might have made me rejected by you."

Jana 9: I do . . .

Nana: But it was OK, wasn't it?

Jana 10: [Smiles inviting her to continue.]

Nana: Because you had not explained to me what I was doing was not just provocation . . .

Jana 11: You would have provoked what?

Nana: Rejection . . . you here but also those who do not hear me. . . . Not just a provocation but an attempt to make me admit and show you how hard it has been for me.

Nana is now moved, cries for quite a long time, and takes handkerchiefs from the coffee table. She says: "It's a hell of a task to start thinking like that."

Jana 12: [After allowing silence] "And the dream?"

Nana now explains that her parents could (by implication) have aborted her and waited for a boy? She gives a boy's name. Him not me. Easy! She then relates this to the miscarriages she had via ectopic pregnancies, saying that at the beginning of her pregnancy she could not stand that her husband wanted choice of first names and how they never agreed.

Jana 13: Your place in the cradle, your place now in the analysis, your fears about where you will be living.

Nana: It would be me who will leave you! I would be able to call! She laughs and then mentions two films and some details. Two children, one to be saved, the other to be sacrificed. She thinks of her young suicidal aunt (who shared a name with one of the film characters) and the folly of her grandfather.

Jana 14: "Abuse of power of the adult over the child." [Pause.] How they were both trapped by the madness of this man . . .

[It's time, and Jana mentions the restart date after her holidays].

Jana explained to the group that she had found herself thinking something like, "Here we are in beautiful sheets!"—a thought she did not put into words to her patient but which she could relate to Nana's experience of both her parents' promiscuity, which Nana had told her about previously. Nana had also been promiscuous. Furthermore, the thought made Jana think of the absence of maternal care in Nana's childhood—something she had surmised from the story so far.

Summarizing what lay behind her responses, Jana told the group she had felt the situation she faced was a "double impasse"—meaning that all moves seemed problematic. She supposed that if she accepted the situation Nana had created by action, then she would passively accept that Nana was the one in control. But if she insisted Nana went back to the chair, it could communicate that Jana did not welcome Nana's initiative, although its origin might be the unconscious impulse of an abandoned child desperately trying to lodge herself in her (her mother's) arms.

The problem she inferred, Jana explained to the group, was Nana's unconscious need to be carried by a mother-analyst who would also be neither too seductive nor too abandoning and who could also provide rules to govern the analysis in a safe and ethical way. She thought of her interpretation (Jana 1) as recognizing this predicament in simple words. She reported that Nana appeared to get the point. From Box 4.1 we see that indeed she takes her assigned seat and after some silence mentions she has had a dream, which Jana encourages her to tell.

Further insight into Jana's suppositions can be then derived from how she responds to Nana's complex and detailed dream. Midway through Nana telling the dream, Jana (5) interrupts her—to emphasize that a boy's first name has been mentioned. When Nana continues telling the dream, Jana is silent. Nana begins some associations. But Jana (7) now says, "Fucking in the pile? What could it make us think?" Now Nana is silent. Jana (8) adds, "Running to the couch?" In response Nana laughs and seems to understand that Jana is referring to her way of arriving here, her impatience, and perhaps her fears of rejection and that her demanding behavior will cause her to be rejected. Anxiously Nana asks if what she did was OK and then tries to justify it. Eventually she seems to become moved and upset at the contact between them. After some silence, Jana (12) then asks about the dream. Nana explains about her belief that she had been at risk of being aborted, her parents' preference for a boy, her arguments with her husband about it, and her own miscarriages. Using the language of "place," Jana (13) comments about Nana's profound unconscious uncertainties, implicitly never modified from infancy. "Your place in the cradle, your place now in the analysis, your fears about where you will be living." Nana then mentions two films. Jana (14) eventually takes up Nana's (unconscious?) fears about abuses of power (implicitly by her analyst) and how her parents seem to have been trapped by the madness of her grandfather.

During the discussion in the workshop group, Jana elaborated on several underlying ideas she was processing in her mind at a reflective level.

Her guiding inference, it seems, rested on the idea that this session was being dominated by Nana's experience of beginning an analysis at this moment and the unconscious beliefs or fantasies this commitment was evoking—in terms of Chapter 3, therefore, Jana supposed they were in the theater. Specifically, Jana said she thought the main unconscious experience being evoked in Nana by being with Jana was one of "confused belonging." She had elaborated this in the workshop in several ways. The session, like Nana's life so far and particularly her experience of being her mother's and father's daughter, faced her with uncertainty. Was it organized by her analyst really for her or not? In Jana's words, "if there is a substitution in the dream," "a baby in the place of another," is that not also a way to disguise "the violence of her cradle deficit"?[1] "Nana was not a baby expected." According to Jana, Nana tries to escape the pain of experiencing such thoughts and linking them to her own inability to accommodate other babies (in her stomach). Later, Jana was to go on to argue how she thinks Nana has the fantasy of having protected her parents from her destructiveness but of not managing to do the same for her babies, when faced with the painful fact of her failed pregnancies.

Thinking about her inferential mode, we can note that Jana does not conduct sessions in the style of an ordinary conversation. In fact, she sometimes allows thoughts almost to burst out of her. But she is also reflective to herself. She wonders what Nana is conveying, she struggles with the meanings of her own responses, and she sometimes keeps silent rather than responding. We can say that in these ways Jana treats Nana's words as free association and that she attends to them as having multiple meanings beneath the surface. Her attention hovers to reflect on those associations and her own responses, all admitted as data. In fact, she noted a temptation in herself to react rather quickly in one or the other way, which she sometimes gave in to but mostly resisted. The evidence is that Nana took in this analytic response of listening and containing as something new in her experience—changing her position, becoming moved and tearful at her analyst's response, ceasing provocation, and indicating at some level that she had "heard."

The session also illustrates some of the ways Jana is willing to let herself get (unconsciously) overtaken by her own responses, alternating between an action and a reflective mode under the pressure of the situation. She creates the conditions to reach and infer unconscious content both by facilitating her patient's associations and by allowing herself to participate unconsciously by saying things she had not yet thought through. In doing so she dips in and out of a reflective capacity, such as to recognize and negotiate the double impasse and to draw on her theoretical preoccupations. Several aspects of the detail make this a bit clearer.

First, as an example of how she could deploy theory to reflect on what was going on at different levels, Jana told the group that she "chose to emphasize the 'regressive' aspect" and to "resist" the temptation to relate to the "provocative, summoning, superego (i.e., judgmental) aspects." She said she thought that what had happened in this beginning session of a beginning analysis was that an initial unconscious situation between them was being established that would be a potential foundation for

---

1. An ambiguous and very indirect way of referring to the subjectively felt murderousness of being told (or believing) a boy, not the patient, a girl, was wanted.

the future of the treatment, given that Nana's inner world was overwhelmingly preoc-cupied with the psychodrama of unconsciously feeling wanted or murderously not wanted and all the suffering, wishes for revenge, and uncertainty that was creating for her in her life. This seems to show that Jana's responses were triggered by her own inner perception that the provocative aspects of the patient's behavior were used as a defense against more dangerous "regressive" tendencies—that is, Nana's wish to be seen and to feel comfortable on the analyst-mother's lap. At the same time, it was also evident that Jana's responses were strongly influenced by ideas she had formed as to the cause of Nana's problems. The group report notes that "the analyst explained that in her mind Nana missed a good symbiosis with her mother" and that Jana thought that this lack had emerged immediately in the analysis.

Second, as an example of a willingness to "let go," her question to interrupt the telling of the dream—"A masculine first name?" (Jana 5)—is an example of her willingness to risk enactment in the service of the process. Whether it will prove use-ful or not, in this instance Jana lets her unconscious speak about a belief that Nana had a problem with her sexual identity she was eager to address. She does this at the potential cost of not waiting (with evenly hovering attention) to see what meanings would emerge *in Nana's mind*. The dilemma introduces an inevitable consequence, if an analyst supposes unconscious-to-unconscious cognition, to which we will return.

Third, the previous point notwithstanding, Jana does facilitate Nana's associations. When Nana finished her report of her dream ("the characters are not her parents . . . she is the intruder and wakes up very anguished") Jana (6) stays silent, as if recover-ing from her instantaneous and perhaps unconscious reaction to the baby's name and now readopting a more reflective or contemplative attitude. However, when Nana vividly says, "I speak loudly; I agitate; I rush into the heap," Jana is prompted to think of Nana's acting out at the beginning of the session and again suddenly seems to jump in. She exaggerates Nana's metaphor "rush into the heap" by making what might seem a provocative comment, "Fucking in the pile?" (Jana 7), quickly followed by an immediate "What could it make us think?" (Jana 7), as if trying to attenuate the situation. When Nana keeps silent Jana fills the gap, somewhat elaborating for Nana what she has in mind: "Running to the couch?" (Jana 8).

The fascinating outcome of all this is that through the various stages of the session, we can begin to see how Jana has combined her mental processing of the patient's words and behaviors, the feelings and thoughts they prompted in her, and a reflec-tive process to elaborate inferences about her patient's unconscious script. She has connected the "acting out" at the beginning with Nana's unconscious predicament, now that she knows she is starting an analysis "properly" after the break, and also to Nana's depiction of the troubles her uninhibited character and overexcitement have created in her life. The whole sequence indicates a way of analytic listening that again and again seems to shift from passive evenly hovering attention toward active and possibly unconscious action and then onward to a more reflective state of attention. By the end of the session, it seems clear that something about Nana's unconscious template for experiencing her life and her analysis (and its possible origins) has been inferred and that it has been achieved specifically by investigating what lies beneath the exchanges. Nana has used all three sources of inference depicted in Figure 4.1 via her conscious and in part unconscious responses.

LESLEY ANALYZING LUCIE (THE LINGERING SMELL)

Lesley's analysis of Lucie was introduced in Chapter 2 and also explored in Chapter 3. Box 3.1 (p. 56) provided detail about the third session presented. Looking at that third session from the viewpoint of the three sources of inference set out in Figure 4.1 (p. 94) suggests interesting differences between Lesley's and Jana's approaches and helps to pinpoint them.

First, Lesley proceeds with a much more normal "conversational style" than Jana. Looking at Box 3.1, with the exception, perhaps, of Lesley's first comment (which is ambiguously phrased by design: "Your feeling at the door. I abandon you just now, when you have difficulties and big questions. Do you feel the anger at the moment?"), it can be characterized as a kind of conversational back-and-forth. In contrast, looking at Box 4.1 and as just discussed, in Jana's session, we can note that Jana (specifically, Jana 4, 5, 6, 7, 13, and 14) repeatedly uses comments (aiming to prompt associations from which she can infer fantasy meaning) that in an ordinary conversation might well be experienced as out-of-place non sequiturs.

Second, whereas we showed above that Jana relies on all three sources of unconscious inference in Figure 4.1, Lesley seems almost entirely to rely on the first level, that is, her interpretive understanding of the meaning of Lucie's remarks, which is that Lucie's utterings reveal half-hidden unconscious shame about herself in her relationships and in her difficulties with beautiful women. She seems to do this based on her clinical intuition and knowledge of the patient but does not seem to have in mind any signs of shame being expressed in the session. It is interesting that although Lesley did report her feelings about the "lingering smell" to the workshop and likely had several thoughts as she listened, she did not count it as "data" from which to draw inferences—although, if raised, it might have led to much more direct awareness of Lucie's shame in the room and possible ideas about Lesley's response to her. In short, Lesley's inferences rely on one source—her intuitions about the hidden meaning of the stories her patient told.

To add some substance to these points, the moderator report mentions that Lesley told the workshop group that she thought Lucie had not yet formed a (transference) image of Lesley herself—apparently the first question (Lesley 1) was an attempt to explore the possibility. Was Lucie angry with her? Lucie replied, "Not now." Lesley then seems to have been preoccupied in Lucie's associations with signs of present but not available feelings about the people in her stories—in part informed by the idea that she couldn't acknowledge she had feelings for her analyst either.

Importantly, it is also unmistakable that Lesley's way of listening, her technique of interpretation, her ideas about the analytic situation, and her ideas about the repetitive problems in Lucie's life all fit together. The suppositions she makes about the "analytic situation" as cinema (discussed in the last chapter) direct her to wondering about repetitive patterns in Lucie's reported relationships. Her assumptions about unconscious repetition (Chapter 5) direct her to her ideas about Lucie having a feelings deficit. Her ideas about how to further an analytic process (Chapter 6) focus on trying to be experienced as different to the primary figures in Lucie's past, as she supposed them to have been.

Of particular interest is that Lesley said she was frightened (elaborated further in Chapter 5) that Lucie might suffer a dangerous regression. She told the group that a state of confusion between them had happened in several past sessions and that she had found this to be a frightening dissolution of boundaries between them. It seems likely that this anxiety constrained her but did not serve as a source of inference. She might have drawn very different inferences if she had had different suppositions about the analytic situation. For instance, as discussed in Chapter 3, she might have thought more about her discomfort about "the lingering smell" and its implications or the influence of her own beliefs on how she heard Lucie. As it is, as she made clear to the group, when they inquired, she actively tried to avoid such regressive entanglement precisely by inviting the patient to a "conversation."

The conclusion is also confirmed by the quite explicit remarks that Lesley made to the group about her approach being, as she put it, "talk oriented." It is also relevant that it emerged in the workshop that, in fact, Lesley arrived at her inferences via some strong intuitive conclusions she had reached about Lucie during their seven-year analysis (to date), based on a particular set of theoretical presuppositions about deficit like those discussed in the next chapter. They had formed strong priors by now. Lesley argued in the workshop that there had never been room for conversation in Lucie's family and that Lucie had seemed always to be faced with two bad alternatives: in one she is entangled in a symbiotic fusion with her mother; in the other, if separate, she is faced with the feeling that something is wrong with her. These suppositions about Lucie's difficulties, inferred from what Lucie had told her about her childhood and life so far in the analysis, also led Lesley to avoid any kind of what she saw as entanglement in sessions in a symbiotic confusion with Lucie.

A final point concerns Lesley's reaction to Lucie's quick defensive responses, her (apparent) denial of feeling (not answering questions about her anger), and what Lesley called Lucie's always lamenting without insight. Lesley made clear to the workshop group some of her frustration with all this. She also indicated that she both carefully controlled her reactions and tried to circumvent what she saw as Lucie's evasions. In this way, Lesley obviously does not suppose that her sense of frustration (about the patient's resistance) could be a potential source of data—for instance, for understanding some unconscious pattern that, perhaps, Lucie is forced to repeat with her analyst. Instead, consistently with her approach, she tries to confront Lucie rather gently with her behavior (first session: "You went to social media?"; second session: "Not preferable but possible"; third session: "Would you like to open up this more . . . ?").

Our third example of an analyst's method for inferring unconscious ideas also has features of the "conversational," but it is also rather different.

GILBERT ANALYZING CLAUDIA (FEAR OF VIOLENCE)

Gilbert's work with Claudia was introduced in Chapter 2. There we noted that all three sessions brought to the workshop were characterized by long periods of associations from Claudia, to which Gilbert would respond with brief comments. The first session Gilbert presented is set out in slightly shortened form in Box 4.2.

BOX 4.2. GILBERT AND CLAUDIA (FEAR OF VIOLENCE): SESSION 1

Claudia begins by saying she feels like shit after seeing other people her age going to work or university, while she is doing nothing. She has had two disturbing and bloody dreams. Out walking with a friend and two dogs. Two guys chased her. She just got away, but they were pushing at the door. Then when she let one dog off her lead to pet her, the dog jumped at her neck. She didn't feel pain but was scared and wondered what was happening? Also, her friend seemed unaware. She couldn't free herself and woke with her heart racing and feeling something clutching her neck . . .

Gilbert 1: "It is difficult to find a safe shelter from all this aggression. What comes to your mind?"

Claudia: "Norma is a spoiled and self-centered dog but she is not aggressive: yesterday I yelled at her and slapped her because she jumped on a table in my father's shop. She is intelligent. She sat away from me with her eyes cast down, an almost human reaction that made me feel so guilty. Then I petted her and she was fine. After I woke, I went back to sleep and had another dream." She elaborates about a celebration at a shopping center. She was with friends, and her parents were sitting at another table. Two men were cooking meat on a barbecue, but there was not enough, and she went to check. The men were eating the meat without giving it to anybody. As usual she was the only one to notice the problem. She was shocked to look at the men and left, walking away with her mother to her father's shop. He was there holding a pincer, and her grandfather, a kitchen knife. What did they intend? "My mother knows everything. Then a chubby, wealthy guy arrives with his girlfriend, who looked like a supermodel wearing a red dress: he follows my father and my grandfather into the attic. It reminds me of our attic, but also of the attic of my mother's family mansion. I hear terrible screams. My parents are beating the man to death. They kill him. I am petrified. For my mother the plan was already formed, but I was unaware of it. My father and my grandfather come back full of blood. They wash it off as if nothing has happened, as if . . ."

Gilbert 2: "Like mafia."

Claudia: "Yes, just like that. Then some other shady guys came in, they were looking for the guy to kill him; at the same time some policemen arrived to investigate the murder. They see each other, mafiosi and policemen, but they don't recognize each other. Now I am reminded of a scene. I don't know if I dreamed it or if I saw it in reality: the image of a girl with blood-stained jeans sitting with her legs under a table, she had killed a person and she believes that other people cannot see the blood splashes. I tell her that the blood is visible and that she should hide better. This is another scene; it is completely disconnected from everything."

Gilbert 3: "In which it seems to be necessary to hide better and not let yourself be seen too much." [There is a long silence.]

Gilbert 4: "Claudia, you must have been very anxious."

Claudia: "I needed some time to recover when I woke up; I struggled to tell myself it was a dream. In the dream I didn't see any bloody scenes, but I could hear the screams and my father and grandfather going on and on. . . . I remember the noises of those tools hitting the body and the broken bones."

Gilbert 5: "It's truly the scene of a mafia killing, and there is a lot of silence, a conspiracy of silence. What comes to your mind?"

Claudia now talked about the victim, the escalation of violence, and her terror at what was happening. She saw the second scene as her typical suffering in silence with no voice and just staring at what is happening with no control over it, while her parents ignore her problem.

Gilbert 6: "It's difficult to save yourself in front of so much violence; how could you react, do something? You can only feel powerless. And this happy couple? It looks like they just happened to be in the wrong place at the wrong time."

Claudia: "He was a stranger, and she was his girlfriend; they were just like a couple visiting us; they were happy and smiling. The wife, like a trophy wife, had no idea of what was going on. I was passive even though I was aware . . ."

Gilbert 7: "That something terrible was going to happen; you understand it and it freezes you up."

Claudia: "In both scenes I understand, but I do nothing; I just shut up. I experience it in silence; I have no voice: when my mother was there, I looked at her, and I understood that I couldn't say or do anything because it was already decided. The people in the shop were not aware of anything either, just me."

Gilbert 8: "Something persecutory is chasing you in both dreams as it often happens to you with your thoughts: the fear of everything leads you to be hypervigilant and to live in the continuous fear that something will happen that you cannot control; you are powerless. Even the policemen are . . ."

Claudia: "Yes. Policeman and mafiosi were ignoring each other."

Gilbert 9: "They are supposed to recognize each other, one to run away, the others to catch them. In the confusion there is a subversion of common sense: you observe, but you don't feel that you are considered, you don't matter; it's as if you didn't exist."

Claudia: "It occurs to me that I feel bad if I am among people who know me. Among strangers who know nothing about me, I have no problems."

Gilbert 10: "What could the girl in the dream do? Nothing other than be silent, stunned, petrified, surrendering to a destiny that seems already written. You know this passivity; it is always there in your dreams. Freezing yourself can become a retreat not to be seen."

Claudia now gave two examples that came to her mind about not being happy on her birthday and her boyfriend's effort to take her out for dinner, which "cost her" a lot because she left her parents at home. It led to scenes with her mother and disaster as well as feeling guilty about everything. [She cried desperately and resignedly, which often happens during sessions.]

Gilbert 11: "You are telling me about your difficulty in going out, in changing; even your friends who try to get you out of the house are bothering you. At the same time, you are talking about the need not to be too much indulged in your staying in there but, on the contrary, to be helped to get out of it."

They say good-bye, and Claudia leaves after wiping away her tears.

Looking at it, first, we note Claudia associates freely for some time and quickly proceeds to tell a dream. At this point Gilbert intervenes immediately with a comment in two halves: (a) "It is difficult to find a safe shelter from all this aggression" and (b) "What comes to your mind?" (Gilbert 1). The first half (a) summarizes an aspect of an unconscious script pushing for expression that Gilbert thinks he detects in the dream. But this intervention is apparently made with some urgency (rather like some of Jana's remarks—for instance, 4, 5, 7, and 8 in Box 4.1) that we characterized as the outcome of allowing herself to be overtaken by her unconscious reactions. Possibly the "suggestion" was driven by an urgent wish to express empathy with his troubled patient. The second part (b), however, looks like a recovery from what was in fact an interruption of Claudia's associating. Now Gilbert steps back and asks her to go on. With this invitation, Claudia talks about her friend's dog before offering a second dream. The same pattern of urgency is then repeated in Gilbert's next response. He interrupts Claudia more starkly, while she is still telling her dream, by making the sudden and short intervention: "Like mafia" (Gilbert 2). And both dreams of course are recounting "bloody" and frightening events.

In the workshop Gilbert elaborated that he felt the violent atmosphere of the dream, and a picture of a mafia killing came to him, which for him was also an allusion to the picture he has been building up of Claudia's experience of suppressed violence in her family, in which she feels people are living on top of each other but are always very secretive.

A second session, which we do not present here, had similar features. Claudia complained about a girlfriend by whom she felt treated condescendingly. Then she told of a dream in which she was camping with her grandparents. Later she tried to perform an antiworm treatment on her mother's old furniture but then realized that her grandfather had chosen a wrong and useless product. Gilbert had ended the session with a comment about this: "What an exhausting effort, Claudia! How many old, dry things you have to clean and disinfect! It appears that there is now a desire to dedicate yourself to this casting, to new experiences, to live and to learn."

BOX 4.3. GILBERT AND CLAUDIA (FEAR OF VIOLENCE): SESSION 3

Claudia arrives five minutes late. She says she had to run to make it. I take my glasses from the table.

Claudia: "I should wear them too, but not because I don't see well; it's because I see too much! More than ten out of ten, and that is not a good thing."

Gilbert 1: "So you think you're seeing too much; you might want to see less."

Claudia: "I would rather not only not see but also hear less: my mother is happy to hear less; she suffers from otosclerosis. I wanted to tell her that talking here with you about Elisa helped me; it made me feel much better; it made me much more relaxed, while it doesn't work with my mother; I just get nervous when I talk to her. I am happy because I can get better, and I feel like I have some power over myself and my personality. I hope it works at my job as well, that I can stick to my guns."

Gilbert 2: "Well, you are definitely putting me on my toes today."

Claudia: "No, no. I must learn to talk about some stuff; it's never happened to me before. The guy at the workplace is very clever. My mother, who has worked in a company all her life, made a rather racist comment: his name is Efrem, and she told me that he offers uncompetitive prices on the market because he is Jewish and he is stingy. I had not thought of that. I have a feeling of repulsion and annoyance toward him; one of my high school friends used to tell me, it 'stinks.' And he speaks in a low-volume voice, and I can't hear; my mother wants me to tell him to raise his voice. I don't like him, his face, his body."

Gilbert 3: " . . .'It stinks' is also a way to say that something doesn't add up."

. . .

Gilbert 11: "The anger you accumulate turns annoying people into threatening and terrifying monsters. With more powerful sight you might see and hear too much. Even in your dreams you always see and feel things that others don't see. There is such strong sensuousness, smells, noises."

A third session began with an interaction not unlike that at the beginning of Jana and Nana's session (Put on the Spot). It is abridged drastically in Box 4.3. Arriving late, Claudia notices that her analyst is picking up his spectacles from the table. She uses her observation quickly to mention an anxiety that she sees and hears too much. Then she talks about her mother and complains about colleagues, one of whom she sees as perverted. Gilbert's main interpretation (Gilbert 11) in this session came much later but draws on this initial part. In it, he made a construction taking up the topics of hypersensitivity, anger, and projection, linked to what can be seen and not seen with many hints to deeper material. Similar constructions emerged in Session 1 (Box 4.2, Gilbert 8–11).

Although trying to work out any analyst's mental processes as they participate in sessions is bound to be challenging, the raw material of what was said and the kinds of things Gilbert told the group about what he does and doesn't say in response to Claudia's associations, how he says them, and what the group teased out in the workshop gave enough evidence to identify Gilbert's suppositions for inferring unconscious beliefs, fantasies, impulses, and wishes.

As noted, there is an element of a conversational style but also some interjections that would be surprising in a typical conversational exchange. Gilbert has strong intuitions about the unconscious script emerging in the sessions and its origins, which is particularly clear in the last interpretation (Gilbert 11, Box 4.3). What are his sources of inference considered from the viewpoint of Figure 4.1?

Looking at Box 4.2 and starting from the lengthy discussion in the group, it seems that, while listening to the dream, Gilbert associated from his subjective response to the atmosphere of the killing in the dream as a typical mafia execution. Importantly, he told the group that he was himself surprised by how sharp and sudden his short remark sounded as he made it.[2] And he had noted that to himself. He also said that afterward he started to think about it. He wondered if he had reacted to aggression in his patient. Significantly, he thought that perhaps he had found an important new spontaneous image for the tight family atmosphere with so many secrets. Clearly, in terms of the three sources of inference recognized in Figure 4.1, all this shows that Gilbert's suppositions allow him to make intuitive sense of Claudia's associations, suggesting meaningful unconscious scripts at new levels, and to begin to make theoretical constructions about how they have come about. He clearly attends to and uses his own responses and regards them as data (e.g., recognizing his sharp tone).

How far does he suppose a need to reflect on and transform this raw material? Although, for instance, the intervention "Like mafia" and his thoughts about it were very thoroughly discussed in the workshop group, it was not clear what inferences Gilbert himself really drew from this or other occurrences of a similar type. He did not volunteer thoughts about any countertransference enactment (i.e., indicate that the arrival of this image in his mind might have been stimulated by some idea of a mafia situation promoted by his own response to the "person of the patient"). When asked about such possibilities in the workshop, Gilbert was unsure. Probably at this point in the analysis he had sensed something new emerging but perhaps could not yet mentally process, transform, and articulate it. Perhaps for this reason the pattern repeats itself when he reacts again rather quickly with the idea that Claudia has been hiding something (Gilbert 3). Claudia is then silent for a long time. Gilbert noticed that and broke it but not by questioning it. Rather, his comment (Gilbert 4) tries to carry on a discussion of the dream almost as if it were an outside event ("you must have been very anxious") rather than address the silence and its transference meaning between them directly. Other examples can be found in the beginning of the third session and are excerpted in Box 4.3. Three interpretations there are rather spontaneous.

The course of Session 3 (Box 4.3) shows that the first intervention was embedded in Gilbert's understanding of Claudia as being very paranoid and suspicious, which was already a theme in his thinking in Session 1. But when he gave the interpretation (Gilbert 1), he told the workshop he was not consciously aware of the background. Interestingly, when shortly afterward Claudia mentions, "It stinks," another very quick response (Gilbert 3) opens up a whole area of unconscious mistrust and cheating. Such examples suggest Gilbert allows himself to slide spontaneously into something like a state of evenly hovering attention, rather like Jana, and not to be inhibited from expressing its results. In this way, it seems to be a central element both of his receptive frame and his source of intuition. It looks potentially transformational.

But returning to his suppositions about the third level (Figure 4.1), what are Gilbert's suppositions about a routine need for reflective awareness? Certainly, he reflects

---

2. See Chapter 7 for a discussion of potential "nodal moments."

about his unexpected reactions and follows them a bit, but in these sessions and the workshop, further conceptualization was not elaborated. His thoughts did not lead, for example, to ideas about what might be going on in terms of disturbed or corrupt internal object relations in Claudia's mind, perhaps then actualized outside or in the analytic relationship—where perhaps they would produce paranoia. One reason for this, we think, is that Gilbert's suppositions about the analytic situation cannot be characterized as "theater" or "immersive theater." Such suppositions would likely have alerted him to the potential beliefs or fantasies that patient and analyst might have been unconsciously imposing on each other in the session.

Gilbert's suppositions might best be characterized as cinema or alternatively as tending toward "dramatic monologue." Consistently with the latter, he allows himself to be overtaken by his responsive unconscious (i.e., by the script being inferred through the meaning and affective impact of Gilbert's words in his mind in symmetrical participation). But if so, he seems to treat the script as having an indefinite temporal quality rather than as playing out now. Certainly, whether cinema or dramatic monologue, his view of the analytic situation seems to have framed the inferences he drew about what Claudia was revealing and at the same time to have closed off some avenues of enquiry about Claudia's unconscious experience of her analyst and vice versa.

Inevitably, given that workshop groups are always composed by analysts of multiple viewpoints who react emotionally, an intense discussion began at one point in the group about the way Gilbert used his spontaneous intuitions and whether or not they were in some sense countertransference enactments not yet understood or used by Gilbert. During that discussion, another example "popped up" when Gilbert suddenly remembered how Claudia had first called him to ask for help. In this telephone call Claudia had commented that Gilbert's office was too far from where she lived. Gilbert had spontaneously answered that it was not a good idea to choose an analyst too near one's own house! The story suggests that the analysis had started as it was to go on. Even in the phone call Gilbert did not function as if this first contact was a normal conversation and allowed his unconscious reactions to come out. At that stage, of course, it was Gilbert's unconscious. But did it already have a connection with Claudia's unconscious processes? Gilbert told the group he was aware at the time of his own spontaneous aggression, but as with the other instances, he had not had further ideas as to what meaning to place on it.

Gilbert's interesting approach, still more than Jana's, and the discussion in the group about it raise fundamental questions about psychoanalytic inference that we will be returning to. If an analyst allows his own unconscious to put his intuitions into play, for example, by finding a word that captures his impression of the dream atmosphere, is the analyst then reliably drawing inferences about the patient's unconscious, or is she imposing her own?

In this project, we can describe the way analysts listened to their patients to infer unconscious content, but when we try to draw conclusions about their approach, the boundaries between countertransference or mutual enactments, on one hand, and

between making inferences and interpreting from a state of some kind of freely float-
ing or evenly hovering attention, on the other, can become quite blurred.

We now move to the fourth example.

LOUISE ANALYZING GEORGINA (IN A HOLE)

Louise's work with Georgina was introduced briefly in Chapter 2 and discussed in
greater depth in Chapter 3, where we discussed our reasons for thinking Louise's suppositions about the analytic situation were best characterized by the theater metaphor.
Here we look at Louise's inferential mental processing by looking at what she saw as
the pivotal session using the three source-level concepts in Figure 4.1. The session,
which began with a dream, is set out in almost complete form, as presented to the
workshop in Boxes 4.4 and 4.5.

BOX 4.4. LOUISE AND GEORGINA (IN A HOLE): SESSION 1

Georgina: In a covered pool, a big wounded dog with a broken paw is being dragged
round and round by the current. Its eyes are glassy, and it is going to die. I feel helpless
and go away; then I come back because I can't let the dog drown like that, but I don't
know what to do.

Louise to herself: "Round and round," as Georgina so often in the analysis.

[Pause.]

Georgina: On a trip abroad a long time ago, I saw a wounded dog dying while pass-
ersby looked on indifferently. I would have liked to ask for help, but I couldn't speak
because I didn't know the language of the country.

[Silence.]

Georgina: [With a distant tone of observation] The look in the dog's eyes in my dream
reminded me of the look in the eyes of my mother. She is very old, ninety years old.
She stays in her bed; she cannot get up; she is near death. I try to go and see her each
day, but I never know what to tell her. I would like her to ask me something; she asks
nothing for herself; she never complains. She was always like that. Sometimes I help her
to eat, but it is by obligation; I feel no feelings for her, no love, no tenderness.

[Silence.]

Georgina: That reminds me of something dramatic that happened near the place where
I used to go on holiday as a little girl. The current had made holes in the mountain
stream, and these formed whirlpools that sucked things down to the bottom; they were
called "pots." A couple was out walking with a dog. The dog fell into one of these holes,
and the man dived in, to save it, but he drowned with the dog.

Louise to herself: A large number of associations took shape within me, the analyst. I saw myself in a number of diverse transference roles and was unclear about the level on which I might interpret. I waited with a feeling of trust and some relief.

[Small silence.]

Georgina: [Suddenly, in a distant, cold tone of voice] Analysis is just words; analysis is no use.

Louise to herself: I immediately felt swamped by a collapsing sensation, as if I were falling into one of the pots in the mountain stream. I thought: Georgina had said, "I couldn't speak." Perhaps had she unconsciously needed to communicate an early, preverbal experience to me and projected it into me? I remembered that Georgina several weeks ago told me a very confused history. She had no direct memory of what happened. Her parents told her that when she was a small baby, she was placed alone in a clinic, because her mother had a contagious illness (?!). That had lasted for several weeks. Nobody went to see her except her grandmother. She always had a special link with this grandmother. According to the family's account, when they were reunited, Georgina had turned her head aside and refused to look at her mother.

[Silence.]

Georgina: I really wonder what use you are to me in the analysis!

Perhaps the most obvious feature of the session is that it is the most unlike a normal conversation so far. For a start, Louise is in no hurry to speak, creating a great deal of space for both her patient *and herself* to observe their thoughts. Georgina takes advantage of the opportunity and associates at depth and to many things and sometimes stops and remains in silence, which Louise does not necessarily attempt to break. Eventually in her last two comments at the end of Box 4.4, Georgina expresses a growing hostility to Louise and wonders what use she really is to her in her analysis. The analyst's inactivity has been allowed to build in this session against a background of three years' work, including, as discussed in Chapter 3, the creation in the analyst of despair, contained only with the help of a consultation with a colleague.

A second feature is that, at the risk of creating anxiety and negative feelings toward herself in Georgina, Louise is giving herself plenty of time to reflect. She allows her feelings, mental states, and thoughts to flow into her mind. She suspends judgment. She finds she has memories. She also brings to bear conscious reflections on their meaning and significance, being curious as to what they are doing in her mind and linking to presuppositions she now has about Georgina's history. Also note that in her last thoughts in Box 4.4, Louise is experiencing something of an anxious collapse within herself—perhaps not unlike what Lesley (The Lingering Smell) was frightened of experiencing with Lucie. Within Louise's (theater) suppositions about the analytic situation, she deals with it differently, comfortable to maintain the tension between them in the room rather than moving toward a less disturbing and more ordinary conversation.

BOX 4.5. LOUISE AND GEORGINA (IN A HOLE): SESSION 1, CONTINUED

Louise 1: [With deep conviction] Perhaps I am the pot.

Georgina: [Exclaims incredulously] Whatever do you mean?

Louise 2: Yes, the pot, which might contain good things to eat but instead is a hole, sucking you down to the bottom of the stream, where you might go round and round until you drown.

Georgina: Remains silent, concentrating hard, quite calm.

Louise 3: And you turn your head aside, as a way of telling me about all the sadness and anger you are feeling and how much I disappoint you.

[Louise told the group: Here, to enable Georgina to reexperience what was happening in her on this early level, I was trying to start from the action—turning her head aside—so that, by recovering the accompanying sensation, she could discover its emotional meaning.]

Georgina: I turn my head aside?

Louise 4: When you tell me that I cannot do anything for you, it is rather like turning your head aside from me, as you did when your mother came to collect you after your separation.

[Silence.]

Georgina: [Manifestly moved] No one has ever sensed before that I really have a hole deep down inside me . . . a sadness [silence] . . . I think that that's why I feel I am looking after my mother out of duty, as if she were still the presence of an absence.

The session continues in Box 4.5 where, finally, Louise makes verbal interpretations. We can now see, using the multiple levels of inference represented in Figure 4.1, how she has been sensing an unconscious script in Georgina's unconscious mind pushing for (some sort of) expression in her conscious mind. The analyst uses her imagination, her reverie, her own bodily feelings, and her theories to construct unconscious meaning from the latent text of the patient's associations. She lets herself be immersed in and taken over by her fantasies and feelings triggered by Georgina's associations and treats them as data, at one point recognizing that she is herself very anxious and despairing. At the same time, she takes a third position, in which she reflects on and weighs what she thinks, deploying her capacity for conceptual and logical thinking.

In her state of mind Louise eventually realized that she had actually, so to speak, fallen into the psychological equivalent of the pothole in the mountain stream and that somehow this had brought about the experience of not being able to speak. Now, wondering if this was what Georgina had been trying to convey about her unconscious experience of despair and depression all these years, she hypothesized from her emotional conviction, allied to her theoretical preconceptions (such as projective identification), about whether Georgina had needed to communicate an early preverbal experience by projection.

Her mind now cleared by these understandings, she then remembered that Georgina had in fact talked about how, when she was a small baby and due to a contagious illness, she had been placed alone in a clinic where her mother was unable to visit her. Only after all these complex internal processes had taken place inside her did she formulate her first intervention: "Perhaps I am the pot . . .yes, the pot which might contain good things to eat, but instead is a hole, sucking you down to the bottom of the stream where you might go round and round until you drown." The intervention captures her idea of the patient's experience now in the session and at the same time draws attention to the horrors of suffering ambivalent feelings of hatred toward a loved object.

Through all this, one can observe how Louise's state of attention and the kind of reverie she allowed in her mind are tightly connected with more formal thoughts about Georgina's early development and preverbal traumatization, as well as her conceptual thinking about the analytic situation. In the previous chapter, we characterized her view of the analytic situation with the metaphor theater. This is because, for her, it was a place where a patient is driven to actualize in relation to the analyst hitherto unsymbolized early preverbal experience that now can find verbal expression.

This vignette also demonstrates how the analyst draws inferences from the totality of the communication field. She does more than listen to words. She also attends to other things, such as bodily signals. Louise said, "And you turn your head aside, as a way of telling me about all the sadness and anger you are feeling and how much I disappoint you." It is interesting to see how this intervention led to a deep emotional reaction in the patient. Georgina ended the session with "No one has ever sensed before that I really have a hole deep inside me . . . a sadness. I think that's why I feel I am looking after my mother out of duty, as if she were still the presence of an absence." In the discussions in the workshop, Louise repeatedly stated that she "listens with her body," explaining that many of these preverbal and early experiences of Georgina could only be "heard" as a bodily experience. This again underlines that "listening to the unconscious" is only a shorthand description of all the verbal and nonverbal signals crossing the space between analysand and analyst.

As we can see, Louise's way of "listening to herself" has considerable depth, with a kind of constant iteration between the three levels identified in Figure 4.1. She considers her own thoughts, fantasies, feelings, bodily sensations, and other experiences to be evoked by Georgina's images, deep unconscious memories, experiences, and fantasies. Like the other three presenters discussed in this chapter, Louise certainly relies on her intuitions. But due to her theater suppositions, these are tested and unfolded in the session as it develops in present time rather than being presented as interpretations of past or present events.

WHAT WE HAVE LEARNED SO FAR

We have explored the suppositions that four psychoanalysts in our workshops seemed to make about the unconscious content in their patients' mental lives by looking at three possible levels. This led us to become aware that all of them draw inferences about the repetitive unconscious scripts pushing for expression in their patients' associations by intuiting hidden meaning in a variety of ways. Clearly these meanings can emerge *in the analyst's mind* consciously, partially consciously, or unconsciously with more or less detailed mental processing. All but one of the analysts (Lesley) also quite consciously included in the evidence a second level: they took into account their own responses, such as feelings, thoughts, memories, tone of voice, and so forth. Three of them also drew to an extent on a third level—that is, they worked on the sense they were making from the "data" from the patient and their responses reflexively to transform their ideas via further mental processing, albeit to somewhat different degrees. This latter level of processing obviously allows for questioning and second thoughts, which may be important because, by the definition of the word "unconscious," one person cannot reliably know what the unconscious beliefs or thoughts of another or themselves really are—a topic we will return to when we explore Freud's psychoanalytic procedure in a moment.

Thinking about Freud's procedure, it is interesting to note that it was hard to know from the workshop reports (although drawing conclusions about it was part of the two-step protocol) how far any of the analysts aside from Louise had provided their patients with the "fundamental rule" or aimed to apply its equivalent—evenly hovering attention (*gleichschwebende Aufmerksamkeit*)—to themselves. Nor was it easy to tell whether they waited consistently for signs of resistance to free association before intervening. Jana and Gilbert seemed to wait more than Lesley (who was trying to an extent to provide an experience of conversation), except when they allowed themselves to be taken over by pressing thoughts of their own. Louise clearly waited the longest, observing thoughts rather than doing or "thinking" for much of the time and allowing discomfort to build up and be experienced by both.

Finally, as we have just noted, ideas about the unconscious of the other in a session *must* involve the analyst's subjective, and therefore potentially countertransference-influenced, responses. Given the role played by the analyst's intuition, in any claim to information about another's unconscious, it could not be otherwise. Hinz (1991) refers to Helene Deutsch's view on this topic. Deutsch (1926) writes, "In a certain sense during a psychoanalysis the psychic processes in the analysand and in the analyst are analogous. In both of them a parallel revival of infantile patterns/aspirations happens" (p. 423; our translation). The same spirit runs throughout Sharpe's (1930) lectures on technique.

FREUD AND UNCONSCIOUS INFERENCE

As we already saw in the last chapter, Freud developed and modified his ideas over the years or left ideas incomplete. Nowhere are there definitive final working examples of either *procedure* or *method*, and his announced plan for a systematic work on psychoanalytic technique, to be titled "General Methodology of Psycho-analysis" (Freud, 1910a, p. 142n), never materialized. But what we do have is the series of papers published between 1912 and 1915 (Freud, 1912a, 1912c, 1913, 1914, 1915a) in which he created and coined what have often been considered the cornerstones of the method: the "fundamental rule" of "free association" and the concepts of "evenly hovering attention," "resistance," and "transference," which we already encountered. These works followed the case of Ernst (the "Rat Man"), which does give detail, as we have discussed. Later cases provide fascinating conceptualizations of clinical situations that Freud went on to encounter (e.g., Freud, 1920b) but do not provide a detailed account of how he actually derived inferences from his patients' utterings—although he lived and wrote for about twenty-five more years.

Perhaps a useful starting point are his encyclopedia articles:

Psycho-Analysis is the name (1) of a procedure for the investigation of mental processes which are almost inaccessible in any other way, (2) of a method (based upon that investigation) for the treatment of neurotic disorders and (3) of a collection of psychological information obtained along those lines, which is gradually being accumulated into a new scientific discipline. (Freud, 1923, p. 235)

The quotation makes clear that "psycho-analysis" is unequivocally a procedure for an investigation into mental processes *that are almost inaccessible in any other way.* Two questions become obvious:

1. What is the procedure Freud has in mind and why?
2. If there are alternatives, what characteristics do they need to contain if they are to solve the problem of how to identify what is potentially inaccessible, whether to patient or analyst or both?

We start with the first question in this chapter and will touch on the second later.

FREUD'S PROCEDURE FOR INFERRING UNCONSCIOUS BELIEFS

Freud makes clear in several places that he developed his psychoanalytical procedure from his experiences with his hysterical patients in the work with Josef Breuer (e.g., Freud, 1924). But his understanding had to wait until he had begun to interrogate himself in the self-analysis of his dreams, into which he then put a great deal of energy shortly after. In Anzieu's (1986) words, "Freud invented psychoanalysis between the ages of forty and forty-five by studying his own dreams" (p. 4; see also Meltzer, 1978, p. 24).

Accurate and important as this remark is, in our view, what Freud was doing at this point was so extraordinary, so original, and so foundational that it needs to be understood precisely. It was not the study of his dreams but the method he adopted for doing so that is of the utmost significance. We think this is crucial, although it seems to have remained in important ways hidden in the modern debates about psychoanalytic technique that we will come to in a moment. Crucially, and recalling the last chapter, Freud not only examined his own dreams but made *his whole person the object of his investigation.* We can see this as he described what he was doing to his principal interlocutor of the time, Wilhelm Fliess.

Consider his letter to Fliess on August 14, 1897, from his holiday in Aussee (Austria): "After having become very cheerful here, I am now enjoying a period of bad humour. The chief patient I am preoccupied with is myself. . . . The analysis is more difficult than any other" (Masson, 1985, p. 261). Then two months later, on October 3, 1897, he writes, "My self-analysis, which I consider indispensable for the clarification of the whole problem, has continued in dreams and has presented me with the most valuable elucidations and clues" (p. 268). Twelve days later, on October 15, 1897: "My self-analysis is in fact the most essential thing I have at present and promises to become of the greatest value to me if it reaches its end" (p. 270). And still later, on October 27, 1897: "And so I live only for the 'inner work.' I am gripped and pulled through ancient times in quick association of thoughts; my moods change like the landscapes seen by a traveller from a train" (p. 274). From this viewpoint, the importance of Freud's self-analysis for the invention of psychoanalysis and specifically for the task of inferring unconscious content can hardly be overestimated.

Crucially, in the way he executed it, the *subject and object of the investigation became one*: Freud "freely associated" to the various elements of his dreams, slips, moods, and symptoms, trying to register his associations while, quite crucially, *adopting an attitude of neither judging nor rejecting any of them*. He allowed them to evoke powerful, emotionally charged ideas and fantasies that had hitherto remained unconscious to him. Although he remained discreet in his written reports, there can be no doubt these ideas were embarrassing and otherwise very discomforting. He knew what he had called "resistance" and was to call "ambivalence" personally.

In *The Interpretation of Dreams* Freud (1900) later described his discovery in this way: "The whole frame of mind of a man who is reflecting," he wrote, "is totally different from that of a man who is *observing* his own psychical processes." While the former is "exercising his critical faculty," the latter "need only take the trouble to suppress his critical faculty. If he succeeds in doing that, innumerable ideas come into his consciousness of which he could otherwise never have got hold. . . . In this way the 'involuntary' ideas are transformed into 'voluntary' ones" (pp. 101–2; our emphasis). The English term "observing," which we have italicized, is crucial here, as is Freud's insistence that it is different from reflecting. Whereas the former expresses a passive stance, the latter is active.

These formulations, particularly his distinction between observing and reflecting, are quite clearly the precursors for the moment when he comes back from his self-analysis to the task of formally describing his procedures for conducting a psychoanalysis in his "Recommendations to Physicians Practising Psycho-analysis" (Freud, 1912c) using the concepts of *freier Einfall*, usually translated as "free association," and *gleichschwebende Aufmerksamkeit*, which we translate as "evenly hovering attention." As can be seen in Box 4.6, he coined the term *gleichschwebende Aufmerksamkeit* to capture the specific way of listening that he had discovered in his self-analysis and now recommended as a kind of "basic rule for the analyst."

As he further makes clear, the term is "the necessary counterpart to the demand made on the patient that he should communicate everything that occurs to him without criticism or selection." In other words, it denotes the antithesis of the "fundamental rule of free association," or *freier Einfall*, that he had set for the patient.

In Box 4.7 we highlight Freud's description of that fundamental rule for the patient and his explanation of how the patient is to be informed to play his or her part in the

BOX 4.6. FREUD'S PROCEDURE FOR THE PSYCHOANALYST: *GLEICHSCHWEBENDE AUFMERKSAMKEIT* (EVENLY HOVERING* ATTENTION)

The technique, however, is a very simple one. As we shall see, it rejects the use of any special expedient (even that of taking notes). It consists simply in not directing one's notice to anything in particular and in maintaining the same "evenly hovering attention" . . . and we avoid a danger which is inseparable from the exercise of deliberate attention. For as soon as anyone deliberately concentrates his attention to a certain degree, he begins to select from the material before him; one point will be fixed in his mind with particular clearness and some other will be correspondingly disregarded, and in making this selection he will be following his expectations or inclinations. This, however, is precisely what must not be done. In making the selection, if he follows his expectations he is in danger of never finding anything but what he already knows; and if he follows his inclinations he will certainly falsify what he may perceive. It must not be forgotten that the things one hears are for the most part things whose meaning *is only recognized later on*. It will be seen that the rule of giving equal notice to everything is the necessary counterpart to the demand made on the patient that he should communicate everything that occurs to him without criticism or selection. If the doctor behaves otherwise, he is throwing away most of the advantage which results from the patient's obeying the "fundamental rule of psychoanalysis." (Freud, 1912c, pp. 111–12)

---

*Our preferred translation, amended from "suspended."

BOX 4.7.
THE FUNDAMENTAL RULE FOR THE PATIENT: *FREIER EINFALL* (FREE ASSOCIATION)

One more thing before you start. What you tell me must differ in one respect from an ordinary conversation. Ordinarily you rightly try to keep a connecting thread running through your remarks and you exclude any intrusive ideas that may occur to you and any side-issues, so as not to wander too far from the point. But in this case you must proceed differently. You will notice that as you relate things various thoughts will occur to you which you would like to put aside on the ground of certain criticisms and objections. You will be tempted to say to yourself that this or that is irrelevant here, or is quite unimportant, or nonsensical, so that there is no need to say it. You must never give in to these criticisms, but must say it in spite of them—indeed, you must say it precisely because you feel an aversion to doing so. Later on you will find out and learn to understand the reason for this injunction, which is really the only one you have to follow. So say whatever goes through your mind. *Act as though, for instance, you were a traveller sitting next to the window of a railway carriage and describing to someone inside the carriage the changing views which you see outside.* Finally, never forget that you have promised to be absolutely honest, and never leave anything out because, for some reason or other, it is unpleasant to tell it. (Freud, 1913, pp. 134–35; our emphasis) procedure. Using the metaphor of a traveler describing the view from a railway car to someone else, Freud once again emphasizes that this is passive observation. Thoughts and feelings flow past.

Importantly, Freud (1924) himself makes it perfectly clear that *freier Einfall* is in no sense free. Rather, he wrote that when providing the rule, he was led by an expectation that "the so-called 'free' association would prove in fact to be unfree, since, when all conscious intellectual purposes had been suppressed, the ideas that emerged would be seen to be determined by the unconscious material. This expectation was justified by experience. When the 'fundamental rule of psycho-analysis' which has just been stated was obeyed, the course of free association produced a plentiful store of ideas which could put one on the track of what the patient had forgotten" (pp. 195–96).

We are highlighting the two German phrases, *freier Einfall* (free association) and *gleichschwebende Aufmerksamkeit* (evenly hovering attention), to English readers for two reasons: (1) because in English they may not have the strikingly new connotations that they should, and (2) because we think there are no good ways to translate these terms in English. In German, they imply that their subjects (patient and analyst) should both take up a passive stance, something that Freud had learned the value of in his self-analysis.

In a footnote in the standard edition, James Strachey tried to make the translation issue clear by commenting on a story Freud tells of a slip made by a speaker in the lower house of a German parliament, who was asked after the incident what thing had occurred to him. Strachey, in a footnote to Freud's Lecture III on parapraxes, writes,

> The phrase "thing that occurred to him" here stands for the German word "Einfall," *for which there is no satisfactory English equivalent.* The word appears constantly in the course of these lectures[3]—two or three times in the present passage, repeatedly in Lecture VI, and at many points elsewhere—so that some comment on it will be useful. It is customarily translated "association"—an objectionable term, since it is ambiguous and question-begging. If a person is thinking of something and we say that he has an "Einfall," all this implies is that something else has occurred to his mind. But if we say that he has an "association," it seems to imply that the something else that has occurred to him is in some way connected with what he was thinking of before. Much of the discussion in these pages turns on whether the second thought is in fact connected (or is necessarily connected) with the original one—whether the "Einfall" is an "association." So that to translate "Einfall" by "association" is bound to prejudge the issue. (Freud, 1916, p. 47n1)

At this point in the development of Freud's procedure, therefore, the technique comprises two complementary rules for the inner attitude of both participants in the psychoanalysis that both justified their respective "mental behavior" within the framework of the analysis and at the same time related their respective attitudes to each other in a corresponding way. Freud (1912c) summed it up in Box 4.6: "The technique, however, is a very simple one. . . . It consists simply in not directing one's

---

3. This footnote was designed to inform the reader that Strachey is referring to Freud's introductory lectures (Freud 1917a).

notice to anything in particular and in maintaining the same 'evenly-hovering atten-tion' . . . in the face of all that one hears" (pp. 111–12).

But, in line with the points being made, this recommendation contains a much deeper and farther-reaching meaning than merely serving to protect the analyst from overloading his memory function with data and details. In this same paper, Freud makes this clear when he finally sums up as the aim of all the rules he put forward "to create for the doctor a counterpart to the 'fundamental rule of psycho-analysis,' which is laid down for the patient." Just as the patient must communicate everything that his self-observation provides him with and withhold all objections to it, so the analyst must use everything communicated for "recognizing the concealed uncon-scious material without substituting a censorship of his own. . . . [H]e must turn his own unconscious like a receptive organ towards the transmitting unconscious of the patient" because "the doctor's unconscious is able, from the derivatives of the uncon-scious which are communicated to him, to reconstruct that unconscious, which has determined the patient's free associations" (Freud, 1912c, pp. 115–16).

This idea, when allowed to have its full meaning, seems to us downright breath-taking as to the ambition in Freud's procedure. But perhaps its full significance has become obscured by debates in recent times, particularly around the analyst's author-ity. It may be useful to look more closely at the argument.

Since *The Interpretation of Dreams* (Freud, 1900), the specific characteristic of unconscious activity was known to Freud as the primary process, governed by dis-placement, condensation, and symbolization. In a later paper Freud (1912b) stated that "the latent thoughts of the dream . . . by entering into connection with the unconscious tendencies during the night . . . have become assimilated to the latter, *degraded* as it were to the condition of unconscious thoughts, and subjected to the laws by which unconscious activity is governed" (pp. 265–66; our emphasis). Given, however, that in the same year he nevertheless wrote that he considered *the system Ucs an organ or an instrument of knowledge, capable of reconstructing the patient's uncon-scious*, it seems useful to elaborate and better understand Freud's view on this process of gaining knowledge.

The utterings of the analysand, produced in his attempt to adhere to the fun-damental rule and associate freely, are understood as disguised emanations of his dynamic unconscious ("unconscious proper"), mainly generated by and consisting of his repressed infantile wishes and what we called the "unconscious script," or template X in Chapter 3. When the analyst listens to these associations in a state of evenly hovering attention they fall into or *touch upon* his Ucs. There, they are subjected to the mechanisms that rule this domain of the psyche: displacement, condensation, and symbolization. A working over in the psyche of the analyst takes place without him knowing. In his mind he unconsciously reverses the original transformation inside the analysand, which was performed on his unconscious material in order to make pos-sible its appearance in "free associations." Eventually, emanations inside the analyst ensue from this process, which can be perceived and acknowledged by his conscious thinking. According to Freud, these emanations enable him to reconstruct the uncon-scious contents that determined the analysand's utterings.

As already stressed, what Freud is doing here is postulating an identical mental procedure for both protagonists in the psychoanalytic encounter, in that both should devote themselves to perceiving the emanations of their respective unconsciouses and drop any inner censorship as far as possible. The initially identical mental state of both protagonists in the psychoanalytical situation is supposed to enable the derivatives of both of their unconsciouses to come onto the scene. It is only in the further handling of this that a decisive difference subsequently emerges. While the analysand is supposed to say everything that occurs to him, the analyst perceives the emanations of his own (!) unconscious stimulated by the patient's associations, "reconstructs" the unconscious of the analysand from this, and finally communicates this reconstruction to the patient in bits and pieces in the form of interpretations (i.e., he shares it with him). As we discussed in Chapter 3, there can be no doubt at this stage that Freud is recommending that the analyst listen to his own unconscious during the session because he is confident that the analyst's unconscious will recognize the patient's. We want to stress here that Freud is envisaging a concept of knowledge that goes far beyond the usual, empirical-positivist concepts in cognitive science.

By arriving at this position Freud set the following condition for the psychoanalyst wanting to practice psychoanalysis—here called "the doctor":

> But if the doctor is to be in a position to use his unconscious in this way as an instrument in the analysis, he must himself fulfil one psychological condition to a high degree. *He may not tolerate any resistances in himself which hold back from his consciousness that which is recognized by his unconscious;*[4] otherwise he would introduce into the analysis a new species of selection and distortion which would be even more detrimental than directly exerting conscious attention. It may be insisted . . . that he should have undergone a psycho-analytic *purification* and have become aware of those complexes of his own which would be apt to interfere with his grasp of what the patient tells him. . . . [E]very unresolved repression in him constitutes . . . a "blind spot" in his analytic perception. (Freud, 1912c, p. 116; our emphasis and translation)

To resolve his dilemma, Freud here demands of the analyst that through his own analysis he should have become aware of his unconscious, repressed infantile drive desires and the defenses directed against them to such an extent that they do not falsify the unconscious processing of the patient's ideas, in that they express themselves in the process rather than in the unconscious of the patient. But, for this to work, we must accept what in 2023 we can certainly see is impossible—namely, that after an analysis there is hardly any significant unconscious, repressed content left in the analyst's unconscious.

Therefore, as necessary as Freud's initial demand for self-analysis on the part of the analyst was at this point of his developing theory, just as inevitably the topic of countertransference, a term dating back in his writing to 1909, now has to enter

---

4. We think Strachey's translation obscures meaning here and so have used our own. Freud says in German, "das von seinem Unbewußten Erkannte," which we think is more appropriately translated by "that which is recognized by his unconscious." It is as if Strachey himself could not fully believe what Freud has said!

discussion. As we discussed in Chapter 3, as Freud (1905a) extended his formulation of transference, he became increasingly certain that in sessions the analysand unconsciously tries to avoid remembering/becoming aware of conflictual and repressed experiences and the resulting unconscious fantasies by letting them "come alive . . . *as the present relationship to the person of the physician*" (our emphasis, our translation; see also Bleger, 2012).[5] It surely follows that, as long as an unconscious worthy of the name is at work in the analyst, one must assume that he, like the analysand, will tend to avoid the evocation of his own repressed experiences and fantasies and instead tend to let them come alive, in this case, as the present relationship to the person of the *analysand*, as set out in the view of the analytic situation we characterize with the immersive theater metaphor!

Added to this difficulty, it is a hitherto little recognized fact that Freud uses the German term *gleichschwebende Aufmerksamkeit*, to which we have given such importance and which we have translated as "evenly hovering attention," only twice—the last time in 1924 (Freud, 1924, p. 196). So, neither in the last nor in the second to last of his "papers on technique" (1911–1915), nor in the "Introductory Lectures on Psycho-analysis" (Freud, 1917a), nor even in "Lecture XXVIII: Analytic Therapy" or the "New Introductory Lectures on Psychoanalysis" (Freud, 1933), is there any mention; nor is there in his "An Outline of Psycho-analysis" (Freud, 1938a). Why?

Throughout his life, Freud (1938a, p. 174) held on to the idea of communicating to the patient the unconscious guessed by the analyst. However, in none of his writings after 1913, except the historical reference of 1923, did he ever again mention the specific kind of listening that he had suggested makes this guessing possible for the analyst: evenly hovering attention. Instead, now often mentioned was assisting the patient to acknowledge her or his resistances and helping the patient to overcome them. Such activity, rather than any specific way of listening, becomes the prominent task of the analyst.

MODERN CONTROVERSY

Reviewing some of the literature relevant to psychoanalytic inference since Freud, we can identify three main themes.

First, there are authors, mostly outside North America, who study in depth the analyst's attentional stance and hold free association and evenly hovering attention, along the lines of Freud's 1912 procedures, to be the normative mode. They stress its central role for patient and analyst in psychoanalytic practice (e.g., Bion, 1970; Bion Talamo, 1997; Bollas, 2006; Faimberg, 2007; Green, 2005; Hinz, 1991; König, 1996, among many others). Wilfred Bion's development of a concept of "reverie"

---

5. In German: "eine ganze Reihe früherer psychischer Erlebnisse wird nicht als vergangen, sondern als aktuelle Beziehung zur Person des Arztes wieder lebendig" (Freud 1905b). Strachey's translation—"a whole series of psychological experiences are revived, not as belonging to the past, but as applying to the person of the physician at the present moment"—falls short of the German original.

stresses a fundamental difference between analytic listening and "normal" listening. And other papers that concentrate on the importance of free association in the context of evenly hovering attention (Hristeva, 2018) follow the same line. Tuckett (1994, 2019a) also falls into this category, following Bion's (1967) notion of second thoughts to differentiate listening and reflecting in the session from a more conceptual way of thinking between the sessions.

Second, there are authors who in various ways try to describe and conceptualize some way of holding on to Freud's procedural precepts but at the same time also want to modify them. They tend to suppose some kind of oscillation between evenly hovering and a more focused attention in the sessions (e.g., Akhtar, 2018; Carlson, 2002; Holmgren, 2013; Killingmo, 2013). Such authors generally describe these different modes of listening as distinct entities that can be clearly differentiated from each other in a session.

Third, there are authors who in one way or another consider Freud's procedural precepts to be out of date for one of two reasons. Some, like Brenner (2000), consider that Freud himself moved on from his earlier ideas of evenly hovering attention, which cannot easily be incorporated into a technique, using his later discoveries of transference, resistance, and "working through." In this case Freud's procedure for the analyst set out in Box 4.6, with its specific reasoning to put evenly hovering attention at the center, should be replaced by a fundamental rule of free association for the patient but a detailed, focused, and rigorous observation by the analyst of defenses against the emergence of unconscious meaning in sessions. Other writers, particularly those explicitly focused on therapeutic outcome measurement or alternatively with more relational positions, consider Freud's original structuring of the psychoanalytic hour to be unsound—for a variety of reasons, all of which challenge what they refer to as analytic "neutrality" because they view Freud's standard setting as either objectionably authoritarian, culturally out of date, potentially exploitative, or otherwise ineffective. In the words of Joseph Schachter, a classically trained North American psychoanalyst, and Horst Kächele, a classically trained German psychoanalyst who has pioneered empirical research,

> The original structuring of psychoanalytic treatment is based upon an unsound foundation. . . . We propose that the nuanced use of techniques of explicit support, consolation, suggestion, persuasion, and advice, all used in healing across many ages and societies, be added to traditional psychoanalytic treatment. *These techniques are inconsistent with the analyst's neutrality, a fundamental characteristic of the analyst's stance in the original model. The demonstration that the analyst's own values, beliefs, expectations, and theories profoundly influence all of the analyst's interventions leads us to reconsider the concept of neutrality.* The possible risks associated with using these recommended explicit techniques mandate that their use requires the same discriminating judgment as is used to determine whether and when an interpretation is presented. (Schachter & Kächele, 2007, p. 432; our emphasis)

Their arguments include the idea that an analyst's neutrality and abstinence served an additional unstated function for Freud and his colleagues: codifying a self-imposed inhibition against troublesome erotic feelings toward women patients (e.g., Anzieu,

1986; Glenn, 1986; Moi, 1990; Stone, 1961). Another argument is that Freud, unlike Sándor Ferenczi, was keen to emphasize neutrality not for clinical reasons but to present his work as science, not therapy (Thompson, 1943), and rejected the idea that the cause of neurosis might be environmental, cultural, and social and so perhaps due to the parents' failure to provide the child with needed love, in the form of a human relationship, which the analyst might now provide, and so forth. We will return to these arguments and their implications in the next two chapters. They align, insofar as they reject what we have stated are Freud's main procedural precepts, with different arguments that free association and evenly hovering (i.e., neutral) attention are impossible, as posited by relational analysts such as Jody Messler Davies (2018). Her "constructivist challenge" is aimed at challenging the authority of the analyst and demanding an entirely new relational approach to the analytic situation. She writes,

> To the extent that we all possess an unconscious, our understanding of the meaning, motivation, and impact of our own behavior is limited. The analyst is not only impacted by his own unconscious process in the formulation of any interpretation, not only a full participant in any analytic enactment, but partially blind to the role he plays in helping the patient to understand both of these processes. To put it more simply, relational psychoanalysis takes quite seriously Freud's basic dictum *that the countertransference is by definition unconscious. There is no training analysis in the world that rids the analyst of his own unconscious.* Analyst and patient alike engage with each other in a multiplicity of ways that exist outside of awareness. If there is any single factor that unites relational analysts, it is the fundamental organizing belief that, like everyone else, we never fully know our own minds and therefore we never fully know what we ourselves are up to in the course of conducting an analysis. (Davies, 2018, pp. 653–54; emphasis in original)

This position is undeniable, just as it is undeniable, as noted above, that all analysts' inferences from their patients' sessions must depend on their personal intuitions and that these must, to use the language we have developed, be influenced by the evocation of their own repressed experiences and fantasies that will unbidden "come alive as the present relationship to the person of the analysand," as set out in the view of the analytic situation we characterize with the immersive theater metaphor.

AN ALTERNATIVE MENTAL FRAME

Above, we posed two questions.

First, we asked what Freud's procedural precepts were and why he thought them necessary. The simple answer we have given is that outside his own efforts to analyze his own dreams using the same approach, he could not think of another way of ascertaining the nature of the unconscious beliefs energizing his patients, given his definitional assumption that they were directly inaccessible. He was also, as shown in Box 4.6, clear that unconscious beliefs cannot simply be imposed by "the doctor" on the patient—"if he follows his expectations he is in danger of never finding anything but what he already knows; and if he follows his inclinations he will certainly falsify what he may perceive." There, he also noted, "It must not be forgotten that the things one hears are for the most part things whose meaning *is only recognized later on*," introducing temporal context and the idea of *après coup*, backward action, or *Nachträglichkeit*, through which patterns of meaning evolve unexpectedly in time and create retroactive meaning (Faimberg, 2007; Laplanche & Pontalis, 1973, pp. 11ff.).

Second, we asked whether there are alternatives to using Freud's procedure to identify what is potentially inaccessible, whether to patient or analyst or both.

One way of looking at the contemporary conflict over Freud's procedural precepts is to suggest that it derives from a misunderstanding—not about the obvious facts of the limitations imposed by countertransference (i.e., that which comes alive unconsciously and unbidden in the analyst *as the present relationship to the person of the analysand*) but about how it is dealt with.

One thing clearly at stake in the way that all the analysts work is that they must select what to comment on, when, and how. We saw significant differences among our four presenters. And here it is interesting to bear in mind that Bion (1967), whose account is arguably the most orthodox "Freudian" development of the relationship between free association and evenly hovering attention (Bion Talamo, 1997), borrowed his crucial term for introducing reflexive thinking, "selected fact," from a mathematician and physicist, Henri Poincaré. When analysts speak of the analyst's listening, of evenly hovering attention, we often think exclusively in terms of psychoanalysis. Bion, however, invites us to connect the realm of psychoanalysis with a scientific outlook, especially that of physics and mathematics.

Mathematics and physics have both long since moved on from being mechanical or even fully deterministic. In fact, in order to be creative (to find new patterns and theories) in these fields, a scientist has first not only to learn to internalize the established procedures for reasoning but also (sometimes) to be able to work and think in something like evenly hovering attention, or reverie. Ron Britton (2010) has pointed out that there is an analogy between Bion's idea that analytic interpretation first based on a selected fact can later become an overvalued idea and the ongoing movement Bion also anticipated between states characterized by the depressive position, accepting loss and failure, and back to the paranoid-schizoid position of confusion. Britton envisages an ongoing process through life which he expressed with a formula:

$$PS \text{ or } [\mathbf{Ps}(n) \rightarrow D(n) \rightarrow \mathbf{Ps}(n + 1)]$$

This means that we must tolerate forming and unforming views of ourselves and the relationships and ideas we hold dear, necessarily suffering the pain of loss and being thrown into confusion and splitting before once again working through to a new synthesis.[6] There are many examples of scientists submerging their thoughts sometimes into a state of reverie—for instance, August Kékulé, who became famous

---

6. Readers of a literary bent may be interested in a fictional account of just such a process in Grossman (1995, pp. 346ff.).

for discovering the circular structure of benzene after a daydream of a snake seizing its own tail, described a state of daydreaming in a speech in 1890:

> If we learn to dream, gentlemen, then we may find the truth:
> And who doesn't think,
> It is given to him,
> He has it without care.—(Goethe, *Faust*)

> —but let us be careful not to publish our dreams before they have been tested by the waking mind.[7]

If we return to Figure 4.1 and the three sources of inference we identified as a triangular set of levels that analysts can use to differing degrees, we can connect aspects of the inferential processing we observed among our four presenters to the suppositions they made about the analytic situation, framed in terms of our four metaphors. Jana's (Put on the Spot) and Louise's (In a Hole) suppositions are best characterized by the theater metaphor, while Gilbert's (Fear of Violence) possibly fits dramatic monologue but more likely, like Lesley's (The Lingering Smell), fits cinema.

Consistent with what we characterize as her cinema stance, we saw that Lesley mainly focused on inferring meaning by making sense of the raw material Lucie gave her in the form of the ideas that came to Lesley prompted by stories from outside. She ruled out any supposition that Lucie had yet become aware of her feelings for Lesley as a person with any specificity, and she also treated her own in-session responses as not particularly relevant. In fact, she courageously tried to suppress them as potentially troublesome. Missing that second level necessarily precluded having available the third reflective level, which Louise worked with and had available from her theater suppositions, through which her ideas about what Georgina was conveying about the unconscious relationship between the analyst's and patient's unconscious beliefs led her first to the panicky experience and then to the conclusion they were "in a hole."

In fact, it is possible to reflect on Lesley's (The Lingering Smell) sessions with Lucie (and here we must mention this is purely an imaginary hypothesis) and conclude that, looked at with different suppositions, two things might have been happening in the sessions that she describes.[8] On one level as she saw it, Lesley focused on the inner conflicts between drive impulses and the defenses against them that she identified in her patient's stories. She tried to make them clear to the patient and to support and strengthen her capacity to manage them. However, if she had taken her own responses into account and considered the relationship between these and Lucie's associational

---

7. Lernen wir träumen, meine Herren, dann finden wir vielleicht die Wahrheit:
Und wer nicht denkt,
Dem wird sie geschenkt,
Er hat sie ohne Sorgen—(Goethe, *Faust*)

   —Aber hüten wir uns, unsere Träume zu veröffentlichen, ehe sie durch den wachen Verstand geprüft sind.

8. Note that Lesley's ability to describe phenomena like the "smell" implies that at some level she grasps their significance, even if they are not yet available for reflection, in part due to the way her suppositions render them irrelevant sources of inference.

content (second and third levels of inference), she might have come to wonder whether her previous perspective had concealed from both participants the possibility that their beliefs about each other and their consequent behavior in relation to each other were repeating a far more unconscious belief pattern of Lucie's that emerged in the interaction between them: that of being exposed to a mother who does not understand, who pursues her own emotional goals, and who is only partially capable of picking up her baby's expressions. She might then also have wondered whether the internalization of such an experience has led to a threatening unconscious expectation or fantasy that needs to be warded off precisely by a fantasized and actually sometimes realized enmeshment with an ideal object, an unseparated union that Lucie tries to re-create in the sessions against the strivings of Lesley to avoid it—the signs of which were noticed by her when she told the group that a state of confusion between them had happened in several past sessions and that she had experienced this as a frightening dissolution of boundaries between them (pp. 101).

Like Louise (In a Hole), both Gilbert (Fear of Violence) and Jana (Put on the Spot) set up their procedures so as to "lend" their unconscious to their patients in the manner of evenly hovering attention. Both then allowed their responses to emerge unexpectedly into their attention in sessions. From (mostly) cinema suppositions, Gilbert noticed ideas appearing in his mind but did not suppose them to have been influenced by his unconscious sense of Claudia's unconscious beliefs about what was going on *in the session*. He was focused on inferring ideas more generally about Claudia's violent inner world, which necessarily then limited the scope for reflection at level three.

Jana, however, with her theater suppositions focusing on Nana's potential unconscious beliefs about her analyst, could more easily engage in some third-level reflection, although it was very much less elaborated than what Louise articulated.

Louise very much used the third level of inference. Indeed, much of what she had been struggling to do—over many years—was to create space for herself to observe herself as well as her patient, so that she could deploy her resources of analytic curiosity and conscious reflection. Figure 4.2, which we can label a Bion-Freud framework, and which extends Figure 4.3, may be a useful way to represent this kind of approach to unconscious inference.

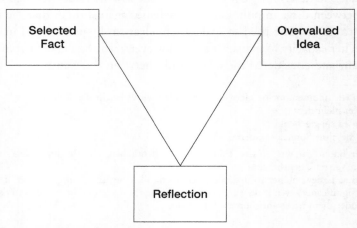

Figure 4.2.   Curiosity

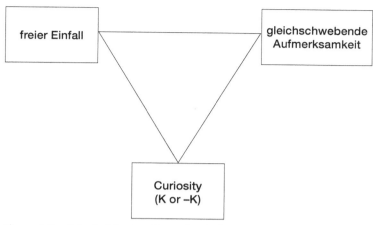

Figure 4.3.   Selected Fact or Overvalued Idea

The core implication here is that suppositions about the analytic situation interact with suppositions about both the sources of inference and the procedures to be created for, so to speak, obtaining the data. The analyst who adopts the procedure of surrendering to his "unconscious mental activity" in evenly hovering attention while the analysand associates freely should expect sometimes to be overwhelmed. As Paul Denis (2008) has put it, "If they are not to limit themselves to indoctrinating their patients with ready-made formulas, psychoanalysts must allow themselves to be taken over by their patient's psychic functioning" (p. 43).

SUMMARY

This chapter started by describing available sources for analysts to draw inferences to identify the unconscious scripts energizing the lives of their psychoanalytic patients. We identified three levels through which meaning could be treated as transmitted and then transformed: (1) the analyst's mental processing of the raw material provided by the patient, (2) the analyst's own responses, and (3) the extent to which they suppose it necessary to add a third level—reflective processing, at least in part conscious, of possible relationships between (1) and (2), enabling new inferences.

Four presentations from the workshops provided an opportunity for comparison. When we considered the ways the four analysts set up the inferential space for themselves, we noted differences in the procedures they invoked (the extent to which they set sessions up as more or less structured like normal conversations or rather used the fundamental rule for their patients and evenly hovering attention for themselves), in the space provided for both parties silently to observe their thoughts and feelings, and in the extent to which the feelings and beliefs put into words were treated as *actually and presently alive and at work*. Our inquiry into the presentations also led us to become aware that all of the presenters in some way drew inferences about the repetitive unconscious scripts pushing for expression in their patients' associations and that this always required intuiting hidden meaning. They varied, however, as to how far they seemed to test their inferences either through their own mental processing or by trying them out in some way with their patients and reflecting on the response.

Clearly meanings can emerge *in the analyst's mind* consciously, partially consciously, or unconsciously, with variable amounts of mental processing taking place between the three levels. Also, it was clear that different psychoanalysts draw inferences in very different ways. Creative empathy with the psyche of another can hardly be legislated. But perhaps its emergence can be facilitated by procedure, as we will discuss in Chapter 7.

In any case, after looking at Freud's procedures for practicing psychoanalysis and the inherent difficulty behind the interacting notions of free association and evenly hovering attention, defined as passive observational states, an important conclusion to highlight, inevitably as in the previous chapter, is that we arrive at the problematic of countertransference and its influence on the status of one person's intuitions about another.

In this way a clear connection began to emerge between the way the analysts drew inferences (and what they chose to draw inferences about) and the way they conceived of the analytic situation, as characterized by our four metaphors. Conversely, it seems likely the way they conceive of the analytic situation will govern their attention to and mental processing of different material.

All this said, we wish to remain clear that the inquiries we have attempted in this chapter and the last are not intended to privilege any one of the four suppositions about the analytic situation, or any one of the various levels of unconscious inference, or one set of procedural setups over another. We are convinced effective work can and was being done using all modalities. At the same time, it does seem likely that whichever suppositions an analyst holds about inference and the analytic situation do have implications. Most psychoanalyses stumble and perhaps need to—Louise, after all, nearly gave up. The real issue for us all, therefore, is recovery and resilience. Here, we think that perhaps understanding and knowledge of the different potential suppositions we have outlined may be useful. For example, phenomena of the kind we hypothesized might have been happening to Lesley and Lucie (The Lingering Smell) might also explain features of Gilbert's situation with Claudia (Fear of Violence) or what happened between Louise and Georgina (In a Hole), with Henry and Hermann (Struggling to Be Here), or with Britta and Margareta (Reluctance to Commit), as with many others. Knowledge of alternative suppositions at such points might help.

Our central point in concluding this chapter derives from the conclusions we reached about Freud's thinking in this chapter and the last, which we think translation and other issues may hitherto have obscured.

The point is that to infer another person's unconscious, the most competent analyst must accept the need to struggle with *unconscious* reactions *to the whole person of his patient*, particularly at the beginning of treatment (see also Reith et al., 2018), just as Freud struggled with himself in his self-analysis. It means all of us must also realize we will often not immediately be able to use the material provided by the analysand and may even misuse it. Putting the whole person of the analyst at the disposal of the method, so to speak, will trigger repressed mental experiences and the resistances that inevitably exist within them. This is to be expected and cannot be avoided. But it can become food for thought—providing the opportunity for belief to be transformed into some degree of knowledge via triangulation.

If we accept that logically, necessarily, and indispensably an entanglement of the analyst in an unconscious "enactment," to a degree, is usually unavoidable in an analysis, then knowledge of the suppositions about the analytic situation built into the theater approach seems likely to be an advantage. The additional benefit of the immersive theater viewpoint is that it potentially enables analysts to be on the alert for their own countertransference-driven beliefs and resistances, so that from the outset they are aware of and look out for the possibility that their own responses and emotional states are potentially essential vehicles carrying information for unconscious inference.

But we should not pretend here that any supposition "solves" the underlying problem. Even if analysts make immersive suppositions in principle and use all three levels of inference, and so forth, they may not get alerted in practice.

Perhaps we can say that those analysts deploying cinema and, to an extent, dramatic monologue metaphor suppositions are most at risk of imposing rather than deriving inferences about what is inaccessible in the other: the former because they are focused on their beliefs about the outside stories rather than what might be happening in front of them, unless the patient makes it very explicit; the latter because, if they rely on unconscious-to-unconscious cognition but do not suppose the possibility of countertransference (or do not regularly subject their countertransference and the validity of their inferences to conscious questioning and curiosity), they may get caught up in mutual enactment (Tuckett, 1997) of an unbidden and inaccessible-to-them *present relationship to the person of the analysand* "coming alive" in the session, preventing them reaching a third position and finding an exit. We will return to these issues in Chapters 8 and 9, revisiting modern controversies and reexamining the work of the seven published analysts we introduced in Chapter 1.

5

From What Unconscious Repetitions Do Patients Suffer?

In this chapter we turn to the suppositions that contemporary analysts make about the troubles their patients have and to what extent they are, or are not, the product of some kind of unconscious repetition of their response to experiences in infancy and childhood. Sigmund Freud, of course, came to think of the "compulsion to repeat" as of crucial importance. He had also originally built psychoanalysis on the proposition that his adult hysterical patients suffered from the ongoing influence of "reminiscences" of which they wished not to be conscious.

Nonetheless, very early on in our workshops it became clear that there were marked differences of opinion among presenters and workshop group members about what the troubles patients seemed to suffer really were and how they came about, as tends to be the case in almost any clinical discussion—a particular implicit feature being who is to blame. It was also evident that these differences were strongly related not only to the suppositions that psychoanalysts made about the analytic situation but also to the inferences they drew from the sessions with their patients and their ideas as to how to further the treatment. But when the workshops tried to understand different views more precisely, it was hard. In what spheres of the patient's life did the presenting analysts think repetitions from the past were evident? Was the issue that patients clung to beliefs generated from unconscious scripts or just behaviors? What sorts of acting out of unconscious scripts were taking place in the analytic situation or in the rest of the patient's life? How exactly, through what mechanisms, were early experiences, often containing severe deprivation, coloring or even creating the present?

As we had to look across practice in different schools and societies, it was not an easy matter either to formulate very precisely what the differences were or to find ways of testing, in the presentation and discussion of clinical sessions, the precise suppositions different analysts were making. As we first mentioned in Chapter 1, like many other professionals, most psychoanalysts do what they do without necessarily being able to formulate it. Moreover, as they gain in experience and skill, they may go well beyond any textbook principles and perhaps often function in their sessions without submitting their ideas and practice to explicit examination. Finally, a great deal of inference is required to go from how psychoanalysts reported themselves listening to and talking to their patients (the content of the sessions they presented for discussion in our workshops) to drawing conclusions about their ideas as to what it was that their patients were repeating to cause their troubles. Additionally, as we will show below, as a consequence of the pluralistic turn in psychoanalysis, it is by no means clear from text books or the literature exactly what different suppositions about how childhood solutions are unconsciously repeated (or their effects) actually exist among analysts of different approaches.

INITIAL EXAMPLES

In Chapter 3 we analyzed seven cases presented in our workshops to try to show differences in analysts' suppositions about the analytic situation, characterized by cinema, dramatic monologue, theater, or immersive theater features. As a way into this chapter's topic, we will look again at some of the presenters discussed in Chapter 3 to explore what we can infer about their suppositions regarding the troubles from which their patients suffered and what unconscious repetition was involved.

Lesley and Lucie (The Lingering Smell)

We used the metaphor of cinema to describe Lesley's approach to the analytic situation. She seems to have taken the view that her patient, Lucie, who had been depressed since her teenage years, was the "victim" of being brought up in an isolated rural house in very difficult family circumstances. She told the workshop a sibling was born when Lucie was a little girl, after which her father apparently became more and more violent toward her mother and Lucie, who then ceased to be "lively." Today, although a potentially "beautiful" and "bright" woman, according to Lesley, Lucie is inhibited and scared. This is true in the analysis as well as outside. She "doesn't bring her feelings" to the analysis, Lesley reported, and is also apparently unaware of them in her social relationships. Lesley also judges her to be submissive and to have the conscious belief that she has no right to her feelings, particularly her erotic ones. Lucie also suffers from abdominal dysfunction, causing pain, frequent need to defecate, and a bad smell. Lesley thinks she is always angry but can't acknowledge it. She also believes Lucie cannot bear to take responsibility for her sexual wishes.

What causes all this? The workshop established that Lesley supposes there is a conflict between Lucie's desires and her internalized prohibitions. In formal terms it could be between id and superego. Lesley also mentioned difficulties Lucie had resolving her infantile Oedipus conflict (i.e., her conflicting wishes relating to her parents), which in some way she viewed as the result of inadequate parental care.

In answer to questions, Lesley elaborated that she saw the problem as early maternal deprivation. In support of this view, she volunteered a theory that bottle-feeding can have direct negative effects on the brain. Additionally, relating to her internal prohibitions, the group understood Lesley to suppose that from early on Lucie didn't dare to live or express, or perhaps know, her wishes for fear of her violent father's condemnation. Therefore, the idea seemed to be that she took refuge in a secretive passive and submissive (sadomasochistic) attitude in which she tried to get permission for her desires without stating them but constantly feared condemnation. This pattern persisted in her relationships and was somehow satisfying but hopelessly frustrating.

As discussed in the previous chapter, Lesley supposed that this constant fear of being violently condemned was not yet consciously or unconsciously present in the analytic situation itself—in other words, Lesley did not think she had evidence that Lucie thought Lesley was condemning. Correspondingly, and because she thought it had never "come in," Lesley had not wondered whether in some way Lucie was unconsciously experiencing and representing her in their sessions as, for instance, the father who beats people up and makes them submit. Her view of the analytic situation, which we concluded was best described by the cinema metaphor, focused her on the problems outside and in the past: what Lucie repeats is reported in sessions. It happens outside and is inferred via descriptions of Lucie's life and experience. In sum, Lucie's problem is that she unconsciously expects to find and experience the deprived situation she has always experienced since childhood and may even unconsciously select people because they fit her expectations.

Louise and Georgina (In a Hole)

To recall, Georgina was a middle-aged, single, depressed academic who found her professional life unsatisfying and felt very jealous of her married friends. Her love affairs had all ended in her being abandoned. She had suicidal thoughts, and her analyst, Louise, described their first three years of working together as "deadly." She felt that the two of them were going round in circles, with her interpretations being rejected as useless. In fact, Louise had been on the point of giving up, until a consultation with a senior colleague, who put her back in touch with her belief that somewhere inside her Georgina was still alive.

As with Lucie (The Lingering Smell), Margareta (Reluctance to Commit), Paul (Spicy Food; see below), and many of the other patients discussed in our workshops, Louise knew that Georgina had experienced trauma—in her case early traumatic separations as a baby when she had spent several weeks apart from her mother, who did not visit her because she (the mother) was suffering from a contagious illness. Once they were reunited, Georgina had reported that she had turned her head aside, refusing to look at her mother. Georgina had also been separated from her parents when her brother was born. He was then seriously ill for several weeks, and she remembered nothing of this time, except the dark entrance to a tunnel close to the house where she stayed, which she associated with a black hole.

As we showed above, Louise supposed Georgina's difficulties to be the outcome of an unconscious belief that her analyst and others around her were useless. They let her down and left her with her anxiety and hatefulness—a "deadly experience" created and re-created in her life and, in a crucial session, in her dreams. It meant she was ambivalent (simultaneously hating and loving) to those she tried to be intimate with. So she established relationships or went to Louise regularly for psychoanalysis in the hope of help but then constantly felt let down and hateful.

We characterized Louise's approach to the analytic situation as best described by the theater metaphor because she supposed that Georgina's experience in sessions of Louise *as a person* represented her experience with others too. Louise and other people evoked in her both love and hate, ambivalence, as her parents once did as well.

Louise recognized that Georgina unconsciously experienced her both as a person who could help and also as a useless and frustrating person who at best was indifferent and at worst hated her. Just as Freud believed Ernst (the "Rat Man") ambivalently sought Freud's love and thought Freud wanted to punish and beat him (via projective processes onto the whole person of the analyst, as discussed in Chapter 3), so Louise supposed that Georgina both thought that Louise could help and hated her as useless. In this instance, what is unconsciously repeated is a template script of ambivalent responses to experience formed in relation to others and their intentions in intimate relationships from childhood.

Britta and Margareta (Reluctance to Commit)

A third example in Chapter 3 was Britta, who worked with Margareta. Margareta was described as a highly educated, stylish, single woman in her late thirties working in posts below her abilities and successively failing to make the lasting relationships to men that she desired.

Margareta was reluctant to commit to analysis, could be quite silent, complained about being bored, and had come to the first session presented feeling very angry, "throwing" Britta into a state of uncertainty about what was going on to the extent that she felt quite overwhelmed and struggled to understand.

Like both Georgina and Lucie, Margareta had trauma in her background. The essential feature Britta was struck by was that she was the child of an unhappy marriage between a very young mother and a much older man. While associating in earlier sessions, Margareta had described how she had a younger brother, who she felt was the mother's favorite. She also claimed her mother had given Britta the firm idea that she got no pleasure from her. Instead, she believed quite consciously that she had had to be a mother (a giver) to her own mother. In sessions, she would express these ideas and her general dissatisfaction with her relationships and her analyst, being uncertain whether she even wanted to come. The central conscious complaint, as Britta identified it, therefore was that she was not given enough by Britta.

Britta understood all this to repeat Margareta's early experiences with her mother. It seems both analyst and patient pictured the mother as someone who did not have enough psychic "milk" to feed her daughter and so could or would not give enough. This picture was linked to an association in earlier sessions in which Margareta described her mother as taking no pleasure in feeding and caring for her. With Britta, Margareta's relationship was said to be quite manifestly full of aggression, complaint, envy, and rivalry all masked by the efforts Britta saw her making to be superficially compliant with Britta's requirements.

Britta certainly thought and felt that her patient was aggressive to her *as a person*, sometimes to the extent of being quite overwhelmed by it. But during the workshop discussion, she did not say anything to cause the moderator to conclude that she conceived the many things said about Margareta's mother to be partially unconscious representations rather than facts—Louise's patient Georgina was also negative about her mother and analyst, but Louise saw another side. Often under clear attack in the sessions (and saying at one point in a very general way that she thought the "maternal transference" was beginning to show), Britta reported her own confusion and uncertainty. However, she did not offer to the workshop any ideas that, in a much deeper sense than suggested by Margareta's accusations, she might *really* be reliving the consequences of Margareta's beliefs about Britta as the inactive and empty mother she, Margareta, needed to give things to. Rather, Britta reported the view that Margareta's mother's relationship to her (Margareta) was deficient—not a mixture of frustrating and satisfying experience (i.e., of ambivalence) but a lack. The mother simply had no psychic milk. From this supposition, along with a view of the analytic situation we characterized as cinema, it was logical that rather than imagine what might lie behind this very negative picture (as well as the interesting but implausible belief that Margareta had been mother to herself), Britta focused her attention on what she saw as the concrete consequences of such an impoverished background. The conflict she reported to the group that she thought Margareta suffered from was not around ambivalent love and hate. It was between her compliant passivity in her relationships (seen as the outcome of an outwardly passive and compliant "false self" created to cope with her situation with her mother) and Margareta's hidden but much more "real" angry and deprived self, which spilled over into everything.

In the workshop, this formulation led to some perplexity and gradually to some quite agitated discussion about why Britta did not consider it useful to talk directly to Margareta about her aggressive feelings toward Britta (which Britta clearly suffered), their possible causes in unconscious beliefs about her, and their unconscious consequences. In fact, the last sessions of the group were described by the moderator as aggressive and confrontational, although the group kept working. Through it all, Britta retained her considered view of the cause of Margareta's troubles. Margareta had been deprived and so had been unable to develop reflective capacity when her emotions were strongly engaged. Britta wanted to try to help her to be more able to think emotionally about the situations she described in her life and to understand how she split off her emotions.

It is possibly quite easy to see why Britta could not see herself as the empty and bored mother although she could talk about maternal transference and suggest that Margareta had concluded that her weekend breaks were a sign of boredom. After all, Britta was doing her utmost to contain a difficult emotional situation with Margareta in which she felt her understanding to be deficient and was nearly overwhelmed. She was working incredibly hard. It seems to have been very hard for her, under fire, to suppose that she might have been the one believed to be inactive, not present, or "out of milk" and actually bored *in those sessions*.[1] So, her view of the analytic situation (described by the cinema metaphor) dovetailed with how she supposed Margareta's troubles to be caused—they were the outcome of a lack of capacity. (We saw in the last chapter how Freud found it very painful to realize that although sadistically punishing Ernst for masturbation couldn't be further from his mind, this is what Ernst feared. The change in his view of the analytic situation took place as Freud gradually realized that reassurance wouldn't do. He had to bring himself to talk to Ernst about Ernst's belief that he really was the cruel captain.)

Paul and Robert (Spicy Food)

Robert's treatment of Paul and the sessions in which he came to see not only that Paul unconsciously felt bombed and stomach poisoned by him and his interpretations but also that perhaps he really had (unintentionally) done so was discussed in Chapter 3. Robert's suppositions about the analytic situation were characterized with the metaphor of immersive theater.

Robert had described Paul (like Lucie, Georgina, and Margareta) as having suffered a difficult early history. He viewed him as someone who came to analysis with a tendency to experience relationships as claustrophobic and intrusive, which would then make him feel forced to withdraw. The trouble affected his work situation, his relationships generally, and his current relationship with his girlfriend. He also appeared (and was) charming but also far too compliant. When Robert was still in his infancy and a sibling was born, he had been sent to live with a maternal grandmother for two years. He reported the experience as "fine," and when he returned home two years later, he would get up early to make breakfast for his "loved" parents and bring it to them in bed. In sessions, consciously Paul had strong positive or even idealized feelings toward Robert, but the latter saw that he hid and was frightened by many paranoid doubts about him and particularly his intrusiveness—reproducing the problems he suffered in other relationships. Robert saw all this as the product of Paul's ordinary strong feelings of love and hate and associated fantasies, which he experienced as overwhelming when in relation to Robert (or intimate acquaintances) and needed help to be able to process. The sessions illustrated Robert's technique for gradually helping Paul to recognize and modulate his feelings and recognize his beliefs rather than engage in autistic withdrawal and the pitfalls they suffered if Robert sometimes caught himself going too fast. Like Louise with Georgina, Robert supposed Paul's troubles to be the outcome of difficulties resolving and experiencing not just any type of feeling but rather the specific feelings of love and hate, which made Paul either withdraw or become compliant for fear of damaging his loved and valued ones, including his analyst.

WHAT BEGINS TO EMERGE FROM THESE FOUR EXAMPLES?

Britta's and Lesley's suppositions about the cause of their patients' troubles seem to contrast markedly with those of Louise and Robert. Louise saw Georgina as strug-

---

1. We could even hypothesize Margareta's mother had felt the same.

gling with difficulties, feeling that she both hated and loved the same people, such as her mother, friends, or analyst, whom she simultaneously believed to be for her and against her. Louise saw this difficulty as *an unresolved internal conflict* originating in childhood but *operationally active in her life and analysis.* She then saw Georgina's compromise activity, secretly hating herself and her analyst in sessions, to be the cause of a severe depression (i.e., as an inability to love herself and others). It is this configuration of hatred and despair resulting in an inability to love that somehow transmitted a deadly atmosphere to the analyst, who was nearly so overwhelmed by it (and perhaps by the effect of having to contain such a negative situation) that she might have been provoked to give up. Robert also thought Paul's difficulties were the product of unconsciously struggling with the difficulty of feeling that he both hated and loved the same people, but in this case the outcome was a kind of emotional autism and withdrawal. Both Georgina and Paul had arrived at their "solutions" to experiencing ambivalence from early situations likely to have caused frustration, rage, and hatred. Both Robert and Louise had periods of being emotionally very involved.

Britta and Lesley were also quite emotionally overwhelmed at times in their sessions and not altogether hopeful about their patients. But their suppositions about the trouble and what was giving rise to it were different from those of Louise and Robert. Simplifying, they configured the trouble as *lack of capacity* for experiencing or knowing feelings rather *generally.* They did not specify that the issue was ambivalence or hatred. They supposed that both Lucie and Margareta lacked the mental capacity to know what they felt, due to some kind of developmental deficit, and it was there they put their emphasis. They supposed, it seems, that their patients hid their feelings even from themselves, particularly the feelings stirred up in the analytic situation. It was apparent from the workshop discussions in both instances that both analysts felt reluctant to mention to their patients the hatred and anger they sensed to be around in the sessions. Neither said anything either to surface these feelings as provoked by the patients' beliefs about their analysts or to try to discuss their patients' unconscious fears about the effect on their analysts of their hatred due to being let down.

The kinds of ideas that Lesley and Britta seemed to hold about what was wrong with their patients and how these difficulties had come about were not unusual among our presenters. But interestingly, more than usually complex emotional interactions emerged in both groups discussing these cases, and this was also the case in other workshops where such suppositions emerged. We think this is relevant to understanding the issues.

It would start when one or another participant raised with other group members whether the analyst involved had discerned the unconscious hatred or destructiveness in their patients that the participant inferred. They or someone else would ask why the analyst had not interpreted "negative transference" or aggression, in the parlance often used. Not infrequently, these discussions would produce discomfort among participants and a certain retreat into taking sides—for and against the analyst and even the patient—leading to a potential breakdown of the frame, which was to look at the analyst's viewpoint! The pressing issue would be whether recognizing and then perhaps talking to a particular patient about their "negative" feelings or thoughts about the analyst directly was a helpful technique or was counterproductive and would make things too "hot," as Britta, Lesley, and others in the groups maintained. The kinds of arguments offered were that patients would be unable to cope with the feelings provoked or perhaps leave analysis.

To be clear, in these circumstances, no one argued that negative feelings should never be interpreted. Rather what was at stake was when and how this should be done. In the presentations discussed above, the presenting analyst's supposition was that it was not yet the right time and that, before such feelings and the beliefs behind them could be successfully reflected on by patients, some further psychic development would be necessary. In effect, the debate was always between those who posited a developmental view of their patients' difficulties and those who thought situations that were active in the room should be addressed. The former approach implied some need for technical measures to produce growth in patient capacity to "think" or to "represent" or to "symbolize" or to "tolerate" or to "metabolize" emotions, particularly emotions such as hatred and aggression, before ordinary analysis of conflicting feelings toward the analyst could be discussed directly. We will return to this dilemma.

Two further examples of presentations not discussed in any depth in earlier chapters may make these various issues clearer.

ANDREW ANALYZING BECKETT (A STORY OF RUIN)

Andrew's patient, Beckett (Chapter 2), was a man in his fifties. One of ten children and sometimes sent away to relatives, he was brought up in situations, as his descriptions suggested, of significant emotional and financial poverty. Another part of his past was that some years before he had suddenly left his wife (V) and children for an affair. It did not last, but his wife quite soon became ill and died. There were recriminations. Later he almost ended his analysis in much the same way. He was now depressed ("devitalized," as Andrew described it evocatively). He was referred after some helpful psychotherapy, although Andrew thought this had a downside in that it taught him a psychologizing language. He was now in his third year of analysis. Boxes 5.1 and 5.2 abridge the first session that Andrew presented. We can see from it both the thoughts that came to Beckett's mind as he associated at length and the way that Andrew responded. From an outside view, the analyst and patient appear in some ways to converse almost in an ordinary way, with Andrew drawing attention to inconsistencies and contradictions in what Beckett has told him, often using a form of indirect speech. He explained this approach as trying to help Beckett to become less fragmented and more in touch with the feelings that go with what he is talking about here and now.

In his interpretations Andrew avoided making guesses about the unconscious meaning of the many details in Beckett's associations. He also did not think it wise to suggest in a direct way anything about what Beckett's unconscious anxieties or ideas were about Andrew in the room at the time. He felt such interpretations would just lead to psychological talk. Instead, he listened and tried to avoid being pulled in, as he put it, to using psychologizing jargon. Rather, he tried to stress to Beckett how, it seemed to him, that Beckett was upset and confused by the emotional consequences for him of Andrew's coming holiday break as well as other departures. It seemed he could not register the feelings meaningfully. Andrew hoped in this way gradually to bring Beckett more closely in touch with his feelings.

BOX 5.1. ANDREW AND BECKETT (A STORY OF RUIN): SESSION 1

B: Dreaming of buildings . . . can't remember very well, also an image of comprehension of my daughter's rage; I wondered how, as a child, she must view the way her mother (V) dealt with the conflict that our separation involved. And I suppose her rage must have been intense; it certainly was in the dream: her rage, and that of her mother (V). She should have tried to ensure it did not become as extreme as her own. Then I saw myself in a relationship with X. . . . I have been feeling less and less self-assured with her, probably because I was still feeling hurt and guilty after separating from V. I let her deal with everything . . . [details]. I would have given up the fight.

I hadn't been able to think about the anger that children might feel, my immaturity, falling in love, being a real bastard. . . . [H]ow could all of that have been going on without me realizing it? And how was I able to hand myself over so completely to X, how could I let her take all the decisions? We were depending on a company who gave us a lot of work. But she said stop, we are going on holiday. I knew it was very risky . . . could mean ending with nothing. She planned everything in advance. The company needed to fulfill orders every day. And X told my children off when badly behaved although never having her own. Why did I put up with it? Not to be hurt? How come I didn't see how the anger of the mother could be passed on to the daughter? In the dream I see this anger in her but not in my son. Some months ago, I took out a photo of V . . . [etc.].

Andrew 1: Yes, there seem to be some things that are not very clear yet as regards what happened at that moment, how you felt about it, and how the others might have felt. In the dream it seems that V and your daughter were very angry. But then you talk about putting everything in someone else's hands and that that is ruining your life.

B: No, it's not quite like that, poor X is not ruining my life, I might be lamenting suffering and death. Huge suffering because of a decision I made, adolescent infatuation, and not being conscious enough. X was not involved with anyone. She just took a fancy to me. I kept blocking her attempts to get closer. But she could also have pulled back. For her too. It was difficult for her too. She was a good person. She found herself with a man who really wanted to be with her; she thought that at last she could start a family when she thought she had missed the boat, because of her authoritarian character. No, the big surprise for me was that she was totally oblivious to other people's feelings. He then speaks at length about his ex-wife V's family and how he should have had nothing more to do with them. Having her child didn't make him have to relate to her family. He complains of the damage at being subjected to all the emotions in that family, the sudden impulses he would have at night to go running, kick the walls and scream. "It must have been an emotional need . . ." His previous therapist had talked to him about the death drive, regression, but he is not so sure. He doesn't feel he should be forced to take responsibility for all these disasters. He has paid a heavy price.

Andrew 2: I see that in the second-last session before the holidays you are remembering the situation in which you separated from your wife and children.

BOX 5.2. ANDREW AND BECKETT (A STORY OF RUIN): SESSION 1, CONTINUED

B: But what sort of separation is this holiday?

Andrew 3: At the moment it seems that you are remembering another separation, and in your effort to recall a moment when there is abandonment and rupture, you are trying to imagine the painful consequences that a separation entails, the consequences that it might have had for V and your children and also for yourself.

B: I see my daughter furious in the dream, and I don't know if her mother has been trying to understand separations, and perhaps thinking about communicating to you but with anger.

Andrew 4: But it seems to me that you are not completely clear about who is leaving and who is staying and who has these feelings, if they exist, of anger and suffering.

B: But is it worthwhile thinking about that? Or now that we are going to be separated, isn't it better to stop worrying about it?

Andrew 5: At the beginning you were talking about putting everything in someone else's hands after the separation and about becoming aware after that of the risk of being ruined.

B: Continues with repetitious material.

Andrew 6: All this, it must still be very complicated for you. But when we look at the situation in perspective, we see that from a time when you had your family, wife and children, work . . . something happened, a rupture, and then severe consequences followed, a sort of devastation.

B: Well, yes. That is what happened in the end, not only bankrupt but with lots of debts. Besides, I was also foolish; instead of diversifying I put all my eggs in one basket, totally trusting the large company to keep supplying me with orders . . . but I was in a bad state . . . I was in a bad state.

Andrew 7: As far as we are concerned, I sense you might fear that when we stop meeting, terrible consequences will follow.

B: [Silence] . . . Perhaps. That there would be a regression, a deterioration. . . . I'm not sure, it follows from what you said (he keeps talking in a rather confused manner about the time when he took over the business and it went downhill). When the holidays come, the loneliness is more acute. When I came back in the summer, the first day after the holidays, I was euphoric; everything was good. And I'm pleased about that. Because in the previous treatment, I was angry when I came back after the holidays. I use the word "separation" because that's what I have always called it; it's curious. I had always called it that, and it's curious that that is what I have always called it.

[Five long minutes of silence]

I'm more absent than present at the moment; I'm thinking that at any moment you are going to tell me that the time is up.

Andrew 8: As if you were already "out" before I have a chance to say that time is up and that "you have to go."

B: Yes, I'm sorry if I have stopped too suddenly, but it was also so as not to put you in the situation of having to stop me when I was still in full flow.

In the workshop, Andrew elaborated on the reasons for his approach. He explained that Beckett's difficulty was that he suffered from a "fundamental lack" in being able properly to symbolize "his inner emotional states." Although Beckett talks and thinks about things in the psychological jargon he has learned, it means little to him. In this way he makes little real contact with people and is both miserable and jumpy—frightened that bad things could happen at any moment, as, indeed, they have.

So how did Beckett get like this and what is the relationship to his childhood experience? Andrew's idea, according to the conclusions reached in the workshop, was that this lack of being in touch with the feelings other people evoke in him originated in a lack of "motherly containment." As noted, Beckett was one of ten siblings, and it seemed to Andrew there *must have been* a lack of understanding, of the metabolizing of emotional experience. He wasn't given appropriate words for his feelings and consequently suffers from a general deficit in being able to experience his emotions. As Andrew explained, Beckett had nearly no space, or at least too little space, in his mother's mind. He got no names for affects and is confused about them. Moreover, he got no language for emotional experiences in relations. Specifically, Andrew told the workshop, "Emotions are not absent, but Beckett's words don't convey them properly. Instead, they only roughly envelop them." Andrew also told us that Beckett may present something of a "false self" (for instance, repeating words and sentences borrowed from the previous therapy that have no "felt" content for him personally) and that Beckett has great difficulties in recognizing and acknowledging other people's feelings and in "mentalizing"—a word Andrew used to elaborate how "the patient can't detect, recognize, and work on emotions." Because Beckett doesn't know how to communicate his feelings or other mental content, he also doesn't know how to recognize them in others. What he does, Andrew feels, is convey what he feels without speaking it, as he does with his enormous sense of guilt and his idea that he is "lethal" to others. He shrinks from the world and those he relates to, like his children and partner, and becomes devitalized—because contact with people and the future is so painful.

During the workshop sessions where Andrew presented Beckett, the atmosphere of the group eventually became very emotionally loaded (as it had with Britta)—so that the moderators' report mentions that "at the end of the Saturday session the group had a longer phase of tension and difficulty—that can be described as an emotional storm." It surrounded the question of whether Andrew was being neutral with Beckett or whether he was passionately involved in the work. The group became quite heated, although the following day they realized that these are not mutually exclusive states. Various accusations of talking too much or being too intrusive were leveled by members at each other, including at the moderators. Apparently, although Andrew remained outside and silent, for several minutes nobody could actually finish a sentence because each person was being interrupted by the following participant. When a reflective space was reestablished the next morning, various ideas were put forward as to what had been happening. No solid conclusion was reached. But it seemed clear that something felt as nonspecifically very dangerous was spilling over into the group and that perhaps the patient's frustration with himself and the failure of his words to make contact with his own feelings or those of anyone else was somehow being expressed. The group, it seemed, had eventually "contained" the situation between them and settled to work. But perhaps it had also learned that Andrew was struggling with feelings that were very hard to contain in the sessions.

Andrew had made clear to the group (at various points) that he supposed that in the analytic situation (unspecified raw) feelings are evoked, which challenge and overwhelm Beckett just as happens in the rest of his life. It was in this context that Andrew also told the group that (like Britta and Lesley) he thinks it largely dysfunctional to talk to Beckett about the ideas and feelings he has about Andrew in the room. Rather, he elects to talk indirectly about Beckett's feelings about holidays or separations or how Beckett feels confused by others. In this way Andrew circumvents exploring in a more direct way the feelings or confusions Beckett might have as a consequence of his ideas about Andrew as a person and whatever it is that might get "too hot."

The group view that emerged was that Andrew, therefore, is trying to provide for Beckett a developmental space—that is, a space of containing that Andrew thinks Beckett lacked as a child. He implied he also supposed that if he talked directly about Beckett's ideas and feelings about himself (for instance, about Beckett's frustration or possible complaints about being confused by his analyst, etc.), he ran a serious risk. He might become for Beckett the "old" intrusive object—that is, the mother and the others who provoked but did not contain. Therefore, like Britta and Lesley, Andrew is trying to build Beckett's capacity to know and bear what he is feeling and feels that he must desist from direct comments until such time as Beckett is more able to think.

In terms of the two metaphors applied to the analytic situation in Chapter 3, Andrew's suppositions are an interesting paradox. Implicitly, he is worried that the sessions will become far too hot. But he did not treat this anxiety of his own as data on which to reflect (as discussed in Chapter 4), in part because his suppositions about the analytic situation would not be characterized by the immersive theater metaphor. Such suppositions, in which the analyst's unconscious reaction to the person of the patient are data, would perhaps have alerted him to the possibility of an unconscious connection between his experience of the clinical situation and how inhibited he feels talking to his patient in the sessions. In effect, by opting not to talk about the situation between his patient and himself more directly, he supposes he can keep what is happening at a distance, as in a cinema, and that this is actually possible.

JAMES TREATING JANE (DESPAIR AND RESISTANCE)

Jane, a woman in her late forties, is in her ninth month of analysis. James described her as able to achieve elements of a successful career but as undermined by an acute sense of not belonging—actualized in impending divorce, actual emigration, and actual separation from her parents. She is shy, nervous, and full of pain and despair, suffering some somatic symptoms. Generally dissatisfied, she says she is uncertain whether she belongs in analysis.

Jane was referred to James by another analyst who shared her mother tongue and who told James that he thought work conducted in that common language would be too emotionally intense ("too hot," as he put it). She was separated, and someone else was funding her treatment.

BOX 5.3. JAMES AND JANE (DESPAIR AND RESISTANCE): SESSION 1

Jane: [Silent two minutes.] There is a strong resistance in me to coming here, to the idea of talking and dwelling on feelings and emotions.

James 1: Even though you are so busy with feelings and emotions when you are on you own.

Jane: I am experiencing in the present moment feelings and emotions, all the time, and I somehow feel that I am bringing here all time stories of history, not of the moment, and this is what I mean by dwelling on them.

James 2: You say dwelling on them . . . kind of devaluating . . .

Jane: Right, digging too much.

James 3: When you talk about feelings you say you talk about the past, you say even history. But then you are talking now, you are telling about these things now, which means now is not history, now is this very moment.

Jane: Yes, but then it is very quickly arriving to . . . anger; life is leading me to not being able to deal with facts; that makes me angry. I see that what I am doing then is analyzing the anger; it is because of this and this and this, and this is the history, and I see it is not bringing me anywhere except for being more angry because when you talk about the past you cannot change it. And the fact is now that I have this ability, I feel the resistance of being pushed, like I try to imagine what these meetings between us are supposed to be, and I feel that, because I can bring whatever I want, is making this weak ego, the one that is driving me crazy and making me sad, the one that is telling me all the time that I am no good, that is running these meetings, that is deciding, OK, now we need to analyze, now we need to tell the story in details, now we need to feel so sorry about myself, but then wakes up somehow a voice that I should not talk too much about sad things and bad things, unhappy things, it is not useful!

James 4: So there is some kind of competition between these two approaches?

Jane: (Abridged:) It is the same as what I always say. . . . [S]omehow I know that the old way (like I am telling you this story or that story, or this is making me angry, or that is making me angry) brings a short relief but then emptiness. . . . I interpret it as sex; it is something you are compelled to do. The minute you get it, you have it. You feel happiness for a moment and then emptiness. And then you want it again. I feel, coming here means that. All the time I occupy myself with how to get help as long as I am still alive. I care about myself, it is good. I am meeting you. I am judging these meetings all the time to check the bottom line—is this helping me? My resistance comes from the worry that it is not only not helping me but in fact strengthening the old patterns, the old weakness, the victim me. . . . [A]bout our meeting today I was thinking it is just like going to the gym, here I am, I feel that the muscles are getting stronger, but the body is sick. . . . I need to do something much more profound. . . . [H]ere in this analysis I feel I am really drowning, and here you are, lying on your raft, looking at me, asking me, tell me what does it feel like now that you are drowning. And I want to say, hey, move away, I need to get out of the water. I should stop it and come back when I have reached a minimum level of strength of a normal human being with problems!

James 5: Well, if we go back to the metaphor of drowning and me lying in a raft watching you drowning and asking you stupid questions of how it feels, what you instead expect from me is to pull you out, isn't it?

As can be seen in Box 5.3, in the first of the sessions presented, Jane begins by referring to her resistance to coming. It comes, she says, from the worry that analysis is not helping but instead is strengthening old patterns. Later, she acknowledges that the analysis is useful but likens it to having sex, which fills up an emptiness but doesn't last. She then adds about the feeling that she experienced when imagining her analyst as watching her drowning from a position on a raft on which there was no space for her. James's interpretation (James 5) is that she expects him to pull her out.

BOX 5.4. JAMES AND JANE (DESPAIR AND RESISTANCE): SESSION 2

Jane: (After a long silence:) I think that I am holding back all the words that want to come out.

James 1: You hold them?

Jane: Yes, I won't say them, then I think about the next, and I won't say those. It's the same all the time—repetitive and complaining like I want to die, I don't belong, and I cannot connect to anybody. I have Q in my head. I am having full conversations with him, and then I am upset about it myself.

James 2: You have the conversation in reality or in your imagination?

Jane: No, no, only in my imagination but all the time. I see that he is all that is left of all the people I could talk to, and then I see, I don't like him, I am just dependent on him because I don't find anything in me, I am dependent on these little leftovers that any human being can give me, and it just happens to be Z. I don't do the things I want to do, I didn't phone this guy in A (the country she came from). I wanted to call him in the last two months, about my money there, what to do, because he knows about money, but I don't do it.

James 3: So in fact what you are saying is that there is now at least, or now again, more than maybe a while ago, a gap between your inner world and the outside reality, a gap which is difficult to bridge . . .

Jane: Totally, totally! It is not happening. I'm trying. I have no one that I really feel connected to, that I feel at home with. I don't have it in me at all. Even people that have it a little bit, for them it is hard, but for me . . . I understand myself but I can't help myself. I don't find anybody interesting enough and I am angry at myself that I don't go where I think I might find someone interesting and try to connect with people. Today I started to be angry again about me and you, that I am so weak. The only connection I somehow have here [in this country] is you. So I stay here because of you. It's not that great. It's not making me happy. I stay here for one person, for one thing. This is why I decided to stay here, and then again I saw the same pattern with Y. I stopped it [the relationship]. At least I stopped it. I saw it coming. I [could see] I would live with him, lying to myself, bringing stories from out of nowhere . . . so at least I could stop it. I am totally not letting my inner strength . . . I was looking at Facebook, a friend of mine from A; she used to be my girlfriend; she has her issues, but the way she lives her life, how she represents herself in front of others, how she stands up for her rights and needs, her mother really took care of her, showed her how to buy a little flat, and then she bought a bigger one, and now she has an amazing apartment. She does what she wants, but she is not aware; she has no compassion; she cuts connections very quickly. We were close friends until I could not stand her attitude anymore. She would judge immediately and not allow you anything. I used to be a little bit like that myself, but then I suppressed it. It is very much connected with the aggressive woman, hurting people, selfish. I could separate and just be assertive and say what I want without judging that now I hurt this person. You serve them all the time and give them what they want. Again it is the border between myself and others, me not knowing when it is okay and when it is not, I don't know or at least not fast enough. So I avoid these connections . . .

James 4: You are avoiding it, because you easily become afraid of . . .

Jane: I don't control . . .

James 5: Yes . . .

Jane: The edges of it.

James 6: Hmm.

Jane: I don't control when it's not nice . . .

James 7: That is what I was trying to say—you are avoiding it because you are afraid that you might have destroyed something without having wanted to destroy it.

More about James's approach to Jane's sessions and how Jane associated can be derived from a further extract in Box 5.4. It is the second of the two sessions presented and begins with a long silence. We have extracted only what happened up to James's seventh comment. After that Jane went on to talk about places to live that feel like home, and James obliquely brought up that Jane might get (or already was) dependent on him. "Someone whom you do not feel connected with?" he said, to which Jane replied, "I am not dependent on you; I am dependent on the story in my head about you, not you yourself." James then suggests that maybe she is trying to bring together dependency on one side and anger and guilt on the other, but she can't because she is frightened to destroy the connection with the person in its entirety. Jane denies this and asks why she is wasting her time "here." She elaborates on how, for her, being needy is equal to being homeless. Then she complains she is a lonely planet, adding that the analyst cannot substitute for real people in her life. Try as she might to be kind, she says, she always feels left out. The session ends with Jane again talking about her lack of her own accommodation.

Explaining his approach to the group, James expressed a concern that things between them could become "too hot." Both sessions began with quite lengthy silences and evidence that Jane felt her thoughts should be kept to herself. In the first session Jane began by mentioning her strong resistance. James's reply (James 1) was immediate and perhaps confrontational: "Even though you are so busy with feelings and emotions when you are on your own." Throughout both sessions, he continued to intervene quickly and very actively—mostly pointing out contradictions. As is relevant to the concerns of this chapter, he told the group that he thought of these comments as "repairing" broken "links" in Jane's understanding of herself and the world outside.

James made it clear to the group that on the one hand he saw Jane as someone who was hungry for contact, feeling herself to be very deprived and abandoned and furious about it, while on the other hand she was terrified of contact, fearing that she would be obliterated by it. What was striking was how active James supposed he needed to be with Jane—there were sixty interpretations in two sessions, which was exceptional. The inference is that James felt it would be risky to leave the patient too much alone, given his idea that she felt neither he nor anyone else *had space for her and could hold her in mind.*

The life raft interchange is exemplary of this aspect. James elaborated to the workshop that he believed that Jane tended to forget what happened between one session and the next, which caused her feeling of isolation, so that part of his task was to help her remember by making links in his interpretations. He further thought that her tendency to forget was due to an inability, which he saw as somehow a developmental deficit (disagreeing with group members that it might be an attack on unbearable links[2]). When he was asked about whether his patient might be suffering from all the unconscious attacks she seemed to be making on him and others, his response was that with "this patient he wouldn't dare to interpret aggression *at this stage of the analysis,*" seeing her as too anxious, with a very fragile ego, to be able to make use of anything like that. He further explained that he was afraid that if he interpreted along such lines Jane might leave the analysis, develop a catastrophic psychosomatic problem, or commit suicide. For him, Jane would be unable to tolerate such interpretations because she had become stuck in her development. Nonetheless, in Session 2 (James 7), he did try, if abstractly, to hint about the cause of the disappearance of connections in her mind. She didn't agree, which he took as further resistance to knowing.

Once again, however, as with Andrew and Beckett, a feature of James's workshop was a very striking disturbance in the workshop group discussing the presentation. A first animated discussion started almost immediately during the analyst's presentation of the patient's history and initial course of treatment. Why had the referring colleague felt that the emotional contact with Jane would be too intense for him? Why were analyst and patient using a third language, which was neither's primary one? A heated discussion also involved the group being unable to restrain itself from expressing strong opinions about the effect of Jane's impending divorce on her analysis. Why wasn't she paying her own fees? Was she able to pay? Then another heated discussion took place between two members of the group. One member stressed the

---

2. Perhaps in the manner of Green's patient, Gabriel, discussed in Chapter 1.

destructiveness of the patient, who, in his opinion, had received many good things in her life but had destroyed everything. That member would not accept her in treatment but also said that if she was in treatment, it would be important that she paid at least something toward the cost from her own means. Another group member responded vehemently to this, "defending" Jane and asking for evidence that she had really got such a lot of good things in her life. The rest of the group stood by, rather paralyzed. Then they recovered. Was this fierce debate a reenactment of the patient's problems? Was there something in the patient that compelled her to go against everything positive? Was the patient enacting her mother's never-ending complaints? Clearly, once again something from the analysis had spilled over into the group in powerful ways.

Reflecting on the report, the moderator group came to wonder if the group too felt powerfully, but perhaps unconsciously, the disturbance of contact and connection that James supposed to be Jane's underlying problem (and perhaps his fear of things becoming too hot). Interestingly, as with Andrew, the most appropriate of our four metaphors to apply to James's supposition of the analytic situation may not be immediately obvious. On the one hand, Andrew makes a lot of here-and-now comments. This might suggest he supposes that the sessions are in a theater with his patient relating to him as a person created by the template X she projects onto him. However, as in Andrew's case, further reflection suggests that this is not the appropriate metaphor to apply. James doesn't suppose his patient is reacting to her unconscious ideas about James as a person (e.g., a person standing by). He also keeps his comments general and even depersonalized ("*Someone* whom you do not feel connected with?"). In this way, although he is manifestly uncomfortable in the sessions, it seems that this is in part because he is trying to preserve it as a safe cinema rather than a dangerous theater. Certainly James does not seem to have treated his own ideas and personal reactions as data from which to draw inferences about unconscious content (as in Chapter 4) and did not reveal to the group any thoughts about his thoughts—such as why things were "too hot" and so forth. As far as we can tell, James did not suppose that his many comments, which often had the effect of shutting down Jane's associations, or his anxiety about being drawn in, or the slightly "edgy" and anxious disagreements between him and Jane could be understood as any kind of unconsciously driven exchange—for instance, one created by both of their unconscious reactions to the person of the other. For these reasons, neither the theater nor the immersive theater metaphor seems appropriate to characterize the analytic situation. It is more like a cinema with some potentially very unruly film critics.

TWO TENDENCIES

To summarize, the descriptions we have arrived at by analyzing the suppositions about patients' troubles and how they came about, which we were able to deduce in six of our workshops, appear to reveal an interesting and significant line of cleavage that differentiates analysts' suppositions about how unconscious repetitions from the past function to cause their patients' troubles.

Some analysts, like Lesley, Britta, Andrew, and James, practice with the apparent supposition that their patients' repetitive troubles in the present derive from early environmental failures, which have left them with a deficiency in their capacity to tolerate and use feelings *generally*. Given the absence of unconscious beliefs and fantasies in these analysts' accounts, this deficiency also seems to inhibit the development of beliefs—for example, thoughts about their analysts as persons with attitudes, beliefs, and desires.

Other analysts, in this chapter so far represented only by Louise and Robert, suppose that their patient's troubles in the present derive not from a deficiency in the capacity to tolerate feelings in general but rather from long-standing difficulties in tolerating and becoming aware of *specific feelings* evoked by others—namely, love and hate—or, in other words, the painful experience of ambivalence. Given the presence of unconscious beliefs and fantasies in these analysts' accounts, such feelings are the product of thoughts containing ideas and impulses that necessarily create emotional conflicts.

We propose it is useful to treat these two sets of suppositions as two tendencies—ideal types in the sense we are using the four metaphors, bearing in mind that ideal types capture a tendency, and there are always variations within a type.

The first group of analysts, adopting a *deficit tendency*, seemed to suppose that a general deficiency in managing feelings due to difficult situations in infancy and childhood is carried into their patients' lives and into the analytic situation, which makes them emotionally fragile. Their analysts are then often cautious in their responses to them, while themselves feeling under considerable strain. For this type of analyst, these early situations have meant that their patients are conceived as damaged, and they use concepts like lacking "ego" capacity. The patients are seen as having somehow been failed by life to date so that they are saturated with too much feeling. Sometimes, it is stated that these patients' development has somehow become arrested at a pre-Oedipal stage and their "thinking" lacks symbolic fluency and is often concrete. They have particular problems with aggression and separation anxiety and in a general sense are unsatisfied and aggrieved. Although analysts whose suppositions are characterized as belonging to this deficit type generally accept the importance of Oedipal or ambivalent conflicts, they tend to consider that their patients are not yet able to experience them because they can very quickly be overcome with anxiety and pushed into destructive behaviors. This supposition causes the analysts to be wary of precipitating negative reactions.

To elaborate a little further, the theory behind one or another deficit type formulation tends to be that an inability to tolerate feelings is the product of rather early pathology. A "not-good-enough" (neglectful, depressed, abusive, self-centered) caregiver was experienced who didn't or couldn't pay the patient the right kind of attention for "normal" mental development to take place. This not only left the patient with an unconscious expectation of a disappointing response from future objects but also made it hard for them to manage their reaction to such responses from them. They did not receive the kind of attention that would have helped them to build up more flexible or robust capacities. They are brittle.

As we have seen in this chapter, suppositions of this deficit type have significant implications for how a particular analyst thinks psychoanalysis works. Those adopting deficit models tend to suppose that before the emotional conflicts associated with rivalry and frustration, usually associated with Oedipal conflict, can be faced in treatment, the analytic setting first needs to provide an opportunity for early failure to be made good. With this supposition, what then becomes important for these analysts is to try to ensure that what happens in analysis *does not repeat* the early failure. We will discuss this further in the next chapter, but it means analysts of this type often suppose they need to try to provide the care that once was lacking and to help their patients to develop the capacity to reflect on or contain their thoughts and feelings developed in their interactions with others, without acting out their feelings. Many analysts who presented in our groups are quite explicit that this or something similar is what they are trying to do (e.g., to make or repair links, to help their patients to be more in touch, to build a different picture of relating).

Within this deficit type set of suppositions, the analyst's understanding of the patient's early situation tends *not* to be treated as a representation or belief (i.e., a way of making sense of experience) but as a reality. There was no milk. Correspondingly, with this set of ideas, the patient's possible beliefs and fantasies about why their early situation was the way it was (and why their situation with the analyst now is what it is) tend to be downplayed, sometimes with the rationale that to treat patients' ideas as beliefs, rather than verified facts, may be felt to be close to "gaslighting" their experience and therefore likely to precipitate strong reactions. A consequence is that such analysts may go to great lengths to avoid being perceived as the not-good-enough or hostile or cruel caregiver. They often find themselves at least implicitly highlighting to their patients (or the workshop groups) the ways in which they are *not like* the disappointing or infuriating or hateful parents that they or their patients picture as the past. As we noted in Chapter 3, Freud did try this with Ernst.

The second group of analysts, characterized as holding suppositions of the *ambivalent conflict* ideal type, also recognize severe difficulties in their patients' early lives and relationships. But they tend to see the repetitive origin of their patients' problems as derived from the "fact" that daily experience, from very early on in infancy to the present day, regularly and necessarily confronts their patients with instances of both frustration and satisfaction, which they have to make sense of *and necessarily develop beliefs about*. Patients build internal templates of beliefs by means of which they make sense of these mixed experiences, which they then apply to experiences in relation to persons, such as parents, intimate friends, employers, and partners. The template is also necessarily applied to experiencing and making sense of their analysts in their analytic sessions.

Noting that these differences reflect two ideal types that describe two tendencies or emphases in the suppositions of those who presented in our workshops, we now turn to the literature to try to understand how these two different and opposed approaches have come to coexist.

FREUD AND AMBIVALENCE

Ron Britton (1998) remarked that unconscious beliefs are facts. As facts, certain beliefs, which are ordinarily inaccessible to consciousness because they threaten anxiety, such as an idea that one is hated or despised or not loveable, influence behavior. They can then "create" vicious circles of dynamic confirmation bias. The purpose of the psychoanalytic procedure created by Freud (and discussed in the last chapter) could be described as bringing unconscious beliefs treated as fact into view—bringing what has hitherto been inaccessible towards awareness. When this happens, beliefs dominating experience, which have hitherto been treated as unchallengeable facts, can potentially be re-examined as hypotheses, taken as facts, that have been influencing one's perspective and behavior or prejudicing one's judgement of experience. Once facts are recognized as constructed by beliefs, their empirical basis can then be explored, particularly and most easily in the analytic situation in which they are configuring the patient's casting of the analyst and then their understanding of the analyst's response. Greater complexity of feeling and belief can then be explored.

Freud's 1914 paper "Remembering, Repeating, and Working-through" describes how the development of psychoanalytic technique revealed the problem of unconscious repetition. In the early days of psychoanalysis, the aim of treatment was described as to help the patient to remember the situation in which their symptoms had first been formed and to reproduce the mental processes involved in that situation to allow them to be discharged (abreacted through a cathartic process). At first Freud tried to achieve the discharge and abreaction through hypnosis, but then, after considering his own dreams, he turned to interpretation of the patient's free associations. The next step was taken when, as Freud (1914) put it, "the analyst gives up the attempt to bring a particular moment or problem into focus. He contents himself with studying whatever is present for the time being on the surface of the patient's mind, and he employs the art of interpretation mainly for the purpose of recognizing the resistances which appear there, and making them conscious to the patient" (p. 147). He claimed that as a result of this development of his technique, patients *were much less likely to remember what they had forgotten or repressed*. What tended to happen instead was that the patient reproduced their hitherto unconscious beliefs that were the repetitive cause of their troubles "not as a memory but as an action; he repeats it, without, of course, knowing that he is repeating it" (p. 150). From this point on, two years after the definitive paper on transference discussed in Chapter 3, repetition comes to characterize Freud's suppositions about psychoanalytic treatment from beginning to end: "Above all, the patient will begin his treatment with a repetition of this kind. . . . As long as the patient is in the treatment, he cannot escape from this compulsion to repeat;[3] and in the end we understand that this is his way of remembering" (p. 150).

In *The Interpretation of Dreams*, Freud (1900) made what remained for all his life his core proposal: "The unconscious is the true psychical reality; in its innermost

---

3. Freud's first use of this term.

nature it is as much unknown to us as the reality of the external world, and it is as incompletely presented by the data of consciousness as is the external world by the communications of our sense organs" (p. 613). Freud also believed, as we will discuss in Chapter 6, that there was an inseparable bond (*Junktim*) between the investigation of unconscious mental processes and cure. "The most complete and profoundest possible analysis of whoever may be our patient," he wrote, will "enrich him from his own internal sources, by putting at the disposal of his ego those energies which, owing to repression, are inaccessibly confined in his unconscious, as well as those which his ego is obliged to squander in the fruitless task of maintaining these repressions" (Freud, 1926b, p. 256). Set in the language of his day, this is the point just made about beliefs and facts. By becoming aware of unconscious beliefs, if the forces keeping them unconscious can be reduced, the patient's thinking and reflecting capacity can be brought to bear, and what were thought to be facts can be recognized as strongly held prior hypotheses and tested.

Once Freud realized very early through a combination of his own *self-analysis* and his clinical experience that not all the traumatic experiences his patients described had actually taken place, he was confronted with the question of what were beliefs and what were facts. As is well known, this prompted him to reevaluate his early trauma ("seduction") theory and led him to conclude not only that psychic reality required due recognition alongside actual reality but that "in the world of the neuroses it is psychical reality which is the decisive factor" (Freud, 1917a, p. 368).

Increasingly crucial among the unconscious beliefs that Freud thought mattered, also deriving from his self-analysis, were ambivalent unconscious beliefs derived from Oedipal conflicts that repetitively shape the ways in which we all interact with others, including when we are with our analysts who are felt to be rivals, judges, empty breasts, seducers, and so forth. The patient's problem, for Freud, is not, by now, what happened to them once upon a time but how their unconscious beliefs about what happened and why continue to shape their current experiences whenever situations, such as those that create frustrations, evoke their past experiences and beliefs.[4]

The reasons why the Oedipal situation remains central to understanding the difficulties that patients experience are not always fully understood. But among them, this situation is a first encounter with four key challenges that no one (unless living alone on a desert island and perhaps not even then) can sidestep in later life: (1) feelings about our differences from those of the opposite sex and sameness with those of the same sex; (2) ambivalent feelings (love and hate) toward the parents and guilt or shame about this; (3) hatred of being small compared with the grown-ups and envious and jealous feelings about this and then guilt or shame as well; and (4) hatred of being excluded from the parents' relationship. Each person's attempts to navigate these challenges produces unconscious internal templates or scripts that drive subsequent representations and actions. If Oedipal issues structure the mind, then ambivalence is at the heart of the matter. Throughout life new situations are unconsciously

---

4. Laplanche and Pontalis (1973, pp. 455–62) are particularly illuminating on this point.

experienced and so given meaning in old ways and are therefore subject to old solutions and beliefs. Such repetitions will therefore inevitably also turn up in the analytic situation, for both patient and analyst, which Freud recognized as presenting both a challenge and an opportunity for transformation.

EGO DEVELOPMENT AND THE WIDENING SCOPE

In a 1976 Congress paper, presented as part of a debate with André Green about the widening scope of difficulties patients were presenting that analysts were then seeing and writing about, Anna Freud (1976) pointed to the difficulties this might create. To do so, she distinguished two types of infantile disorders in which disturbances in later life are rooted and in light of which such disturbances can be understood.

On the one hand, following her father's view just reprised, there are the infantile neuroses, in which, according to Anna Freud, the child's "ego" has done harm to itself by adopting *pathological solutions to Oedipal conflict*. It can be supported to undo this damage and put more adaptive solutions in place.

On the other hand, there is developmental pathology. Here she writes, "Instead of being born with the average expectable physical and mental equipment, reared in an average environment and developing its internal structure at the usual rate, a child can be subjected to deviations in any or all of these respects and consequently develop deviant, atypical or borderline features. There is no question here of the child's ego having done harm to itself; on the contrary, *harm has been inflicted on it by circumstances entirely beyond its control*" (Freud, 1976, p. 259).

She thought that in this second type of case, while the individual's situation could be explored and understood from a psychoanalytic perspective, *the damage could not be undone by psychoanalysis as she understood it* (i.e., through free association and interpretation of resistance and conflict). At best, psychoanalysis could help such individuals to cope better with the aftereffects of what they had suffered. She did not suggest, either then or at any later time, that in such situations the analyst could effect a cure by actively seeking to create a situation that did not repeat the early problematic environment and offering themselves as a new object. In fact, she was explicitly critical of those (such as Green, as she understood him) who believed at that time that "cure" in such cases could be achieved by reestablishing the early mother-infant interaction in the analytic situation: to "use the latter in an attempt to correct the failures of the earlier one." In other words, she specifically opposed the idea that "the analyst/mother" can lend "to the mental apparatus of the patient/infant her own powers of superior functioning, thereby mending structural defects and promoting growth" (Freud, 1976, p. 260).

Anna Freud's view did not carry the day. Particularly in the United States the quite contrary ideas of Heinz Kohut, which became widespread and quite popular shortly afterward, opened the way to efforts to do precisely what she thought could not work.

THE TWO ANALYSES OF MR. Z

Kohut's 1979 paper "The Two Analyses of Mr. Z" sets out the argument.

Mr. Z (not as disclosed in the paper but as later subsequently known [Bromberg & Aron, 2019; Brothers, 2015; Strozier, 1999, 2004]) was almost certainly Kohut himself. In the paper he describes his first (training) analysis, representing himself as Mr. Z, a graduate student who lived with his widowed mother. The second analysis described in the paper seems to be a self-analysis presented as a fictional second analysis (probably also drawing on later analyses conducted by Kohut), constructed to illustrate his views of how he subsequently came to think his own analysis should have been done. For clarity, the following summary of Kohut's paper is presented as if it were a synopsis of a straightforward case report, but it is important to be aware of these complications.

Mr. Z was an only child. Moreover, in early childhood his father fell in love with a nurse who took care of the father while he was seriously ill, and he left the family to be with her for a year and a half, returning when the patient was five years old. Mr. Z presented with mild somatic symptoms and complaints of social isolation and inability to form relationships with women. He had had one close friend with whom he would go to the theater, and so forth, often accompanied by Mr. Z's mother. However, before the analysis began, the friend had formed a new relationship that excluded both Mr. Z and his mother. Mr. Z's sexual fantasies involved performing menial tasks for a domineering woman. Initially his difficulties were understood as consequences of his demand that he should have exclusive control of a doting mother, and the analyst interpreted along these lines, taking the view that these demands were "resistances against the confrontation of deeper and more intense fears connected with masculine assertiveness and competition with men" (Kohut, 1979, p. 8).

Apparently, as his analysis was coming to an end, analyst and patient had agreed that Mr. Z's grandiosity and narcissistic demands had been satisfactorily taken up and worked through, as demonstrated by the emergence of more assertiveness in his career, toward women, and toward the analyst and also by his moving out of the home he shared with his mother to live independently.

However, Kohut reports that toward the end of the analysis, Mr. Z reported a dream in which his father, loaded with gifts, was trying to come into the house, and Mr. Z was intensely frightened and tried to shut him out. This was interpreted, he reports, in terms of Mr. Z's ambivalence toward the father and his wish to retreat to the pre-Oedipal attachment to his mother. His analyst was apparently pleased that Oedipal conflict had manifested itself so clearly.

Five years later, Mr. Z is described as returning for more analysis. Since the analysis ended, Kohut writes, Mr. Z had had some relationships but was still living alone and felt that the relationships he had had in the meantime were emotionally shallow and sexually unsatisfactory. He was also not enjoying his work. Moreover, in the interim, his mother, who was now also living alone, had developed paranoid delusions, and Mr. Z was feeling a pull to resume masturbation, accompanied by his masochistic fantasies. In this second phase of analysis, Mr. Z is described as making very similar demands for perfect empathy and attunement as he had in the first analysis. But these are no longer seen as a defensive avoidance of conflict. Instead, Kohut explains, the analyst had come to regard these demands as "an analytically valuable replica of a childhood condition that was being revived in the analysis" (Kohut, 1979, p. 12). Unconscious repetition of Mr. Z's "enmeshment with the pathological personality of the mother" (p. 12) was now seen as taking place within the consulting room. A picture of the mother as demanding total submission as the price of her love now emerged, accompanied by great anxiety on Mr. Z's part.[5] Kohut writes that he thought that Mr. Z was struggling to disentangle himself from this (really) problematic mother. But he also writes that he thought that as the analysis progressed, Mr. Z, for the most part, did *not* experience his new analyst as like the mother. In other words, he was experiencing his analyst not as the old but as a new object. Technically, it was important, he writes, that Mr. Z should *not* feel the analyst to be like his mother, if the analysis was to progress: "It is my impression that the comparative underemphasis of transference distortions in such cases is not a defensive manoeuvre but that it is in the service of progress. In order to be able to proceed with the task of perceiving the serious pathology of the selfobject of childhood, the patient has to be *certain* that the current selfobject, the analyst, is not again exposing him to the pathological milieu of early life" (p. 13; our emphasis).

From this new perspective, Kohut felt that the theoretical convictions the analyst had expressed and pressed on Mr. Z regarding his infantile drives and conflicts in the first phase of his analysis had been experienced by Mr. Z as "a replica of the mother's hidden psychosis."[6] This had repeated the distorted outlook on the world to which he had adjusted in childhood, "which he had accepted as reality." It was important for the progress of the second phase of analysis that the analyst began to be experienced as a different kind of object in relation to which Mr. Z could establish an independent self-structure, more like the father whom Mr. Z now came to perceive as "an independent man who lived a life independent from the life of the mother." In the final phase of the analysis, the dream about the father bearing gifts was reinterpreted as representing the fulfillment of Mr. Z's wish for a strong father who could provide him with the psychological resources he lacked but who was also feared because these resources would undermine the self-structure he had managed to establish in the meantime, which was "rooted in his attachment to the mother."

Clearly, particularly with knowledge in hindsight that this paper expresses Kohut's view of how his own analyst *should have* proceeded, there are different ways of understanding Mr. Z. Perhaps most obvious is that undoubtedly a problem he and his analyst appear to have had was his rivalry and his deep disappointment with the limi-

---

5. "In contrast to the first analysis, the second one focused on the depression and hopelessness that the mother's attitude evoked in him. She was not interested in him. Only his faeces and her inspection of them, only his bowel functions and her control over them fascinated her—with an intensity, a self-righteous certainty, and adamant commitment that allowed no protest and created almost total submission" (pp. 14–15).

6. That is to say, the theoretical convictions that Kohut's training analyst had expressed and pressed on Kohut himself.

tations of what he felt his analyst had been able to give him. Particularly interesting, perhaps, is that the clinical report Kohut provides makes no mention of any idea that the dream that came at the end of the first analysis might have expressed anxiety provoked by ambivalent and/or rivalrous feelings toward the analyst, such that it might make it a relief to shut him out (break off treatment). Certainly, in Kohut's account as he gives it to us, repetition of a script profoundly driven by unconscious ambivalent beliefs was not seen as taking place within the analytic setting.

For our purposes, what is interesting is the interpretation of Mr. Z's dream. It makes reasonably clear that the writer believed that the first analyst was operating under what we term "cinema" suppositions of the analytic situation—the dream was about the father, not Mr. Z's feelings about his analyst now. Such suppositions seem to have made it impossible to recognize and surface the very difficult situation between them—even more so if his analyst was believed as a person also to be his demanding mother. In particular, although this might be a way to understand Kohut's subsequent trajectory, the dream could not be represented as a picture of Mr. Z's fearful rejection of his analyst's gifts, perhaps now acted out by publishing a description of the superior technique used in the second analysis.

We now turn to another widely discussed case, which elaborates even more specifically ideas about how the analyst can "make up for" the past.

THE CASE OF P

The case of P, also known as the "Cadillac case," reported by James Fosshage (1990b) in *Psychoanalytic Inquiry*, is an example of a case understood at a time when some psychoanalysts in North America influenced by Kohut were transitioning toward the different types of "relational" psychoanalysis evident today quite widely. Fosshage's patient, P, is understood by her analyst to be bringing unconscious expectations that she would have the kind of relationship with him that she had had with previous significant others (relationships in which she had felt emotionally abandoned by a narcissistic object) but also to be unconsciously seeking a new kind of object relationship that would enable the impact of her early trauma to be redressed. This formulation could describe any patient. The issue is how it is that the analyst becomes "new," or, in other words, how repetitive experience of "new" people in a patient's life as versions of the old ones can be interrupted.

Fosshage's crucial assumption is that the patient does not *necessarily* need to experience the analyst as the old object they are expecting to find and that whether they do or not *depends on the analyst's behavior*. In the case example provided, the analyst illustrates his view that P needed to be supported to develop a more positive and cohesive sense of herself (thus addressing a perceived deficit by redressing early deprivation) that would safeguard her against both risky behavior and incapacitating depression. Fosshage's case was published alongside a series of commentaries. As we will see, many commentators have subsequently interpreted what took place in terms of how an analyst approaches the inevitability that an analysis will evoke ambivalent feelings and so ambivalent unconscious beliefs about the analyst, as indeed will be the experience in the patient's life. This is the heart of the cleavage between the two types of analyst we met in our workshops identified above. Let us look at Fosshage's description and what has been said about it.

P, aged twenty-eight, came to analysis after a previous therapy that had helped to reduce her use of drugs and alcohol and her promiscuity but had ended with her in a depressed state, linked in part with her unsatisfied demands that her analyst *show her that he cared* about her. P (was said to have) had a tyrannical father and a mother by whom she had felt emotionally abandoned (the example given was that when she was three years old, she had been hospitalized and not visited by her mother for three days). She had also experienced her mother as extremely needy and self-absorbed. Once in her new analysis, she idealized her analyst and fantasized about marrying him. Fosshage (1990b) reports that he found himself responding to her pressure to show her that he cared for her "more directly than is customary for me" (p. 463).

Fosshage (1990b) felt that the analytic process he provided gave P "a reassuring and steadying experience" (p. 463), which, importantly, was a "fundamentally new relational experience" (Fossaghe, 1990a, p. 602) for her. It enabled her to develop "a more positive and cohesive sense of self" (Fossaghe, 1990b, p. 464). This had been possible, he stressed, due to the "supportive-stabilizing" (as opposed to "expressive-interpretive") elements of the analytic process, which he felt met P's previously unmet developmental need to feel that she was cared for and worthy of care (Fosshage, 1990a, p. 603). Fosshage's (1990b) argument was that if he had not been sufficiently responsive to her, providing her with "recognition, affirmation, and caring" (p. 463), she would have a (transference) experience of him as wooden and "corpselike." And she had, indeed, described her previous analyst as having been like a "walking corpse." To repeat that, he considered, would be a replication of her early traumatogenic experiences.

In the paper, Fosshage reports in some detail a session in which, after some discussion of how she (quite consciously) tends to feel critical of people who care for her—including her analyst—P describes how her good feelings about her relationship with her analyst were lost when she saw a Cadillac parked in his driveway. She tells him that she hates Cadillacs because they are owned by rich, conventional, materialistic people and demands to know whether it is his car:

> Is it your car? Tell me? You're not going to tell me [with a heightened pitch quickly escalating to exasperation]? A—It wasn't my car. [I felt that not to answer directly at this moment, which is the more standard procedure, would be experienced by the patient as a noncaring, unauthentic "technical game" and would serve only to create an unnecessary impasse that would disrupt rather than facilitate the analytic process.] (Fosshage, 1990b, p. 470)

Later, Fosshage elaborates that he decided to answer P's question in order to avoid her having an experience of *not being treated as a person*, which in his view would have been an iatrogenic repetition of her earlier traumatic experiences with her mother.

In their commentary on Fosshage's report, Priscilla Roth and Hanna Segal (1990) raise the question of the meaning of P's communications to the effect that sometimes she despises her analyst, which was what preceded the insistent questioning about who the Cadillac belonged to. They suggest alternative ways to understand the material. For instance, could the analyst have considered that underneath her discontent, P was envious of her analyst's ability to be the kind of person who could afford a Cadillac, perhaps with deeper resonances in jealousy provoked by the "other car," which could be an unconscious representation of beliefs about the analyst's relation to a wife. Again, if perhaps her analyst was being experienced as her mother, was it an expression of almost inaccessible beliefs about the consciously despised and detested father, and so forth? In their commentary, they also wonder what P's unconscious fantasies might have done (in her mind) to the analyst by forcing him out of his neutral observing analytic stance into being a participant who sides with her. They suggest that the dream that P brings in the following session (of a dead or dying figure associated with her analyst who is "writhing in pain") may indicate anxiety derived from otherwise inaccessible beliefs that he has not been able to withstand her critical attacks on him.

Segal and Roth comment from a London Kleinian perspective. Homer Curtis (1990) commented on the case from a classical North American perspective. He also noted a lack of consideration of P's (not directly accessible) fantasies, needs, and defenses. For example, he suggested that her narrative of deprivation and frustration of needs by the self-absorbed parents might have been the outcome of a projection of her own neediness and rage onto them, disclaiming her own.

Fosshage's response to the commentaries on the case clarifies that one thing at stake for him was the different perspectives that analysts have on the origin and causative role of aggressive and destructive feelings. Such perspectives to an extent, he thinks, underpin the differences in their readings of the material. He thinks Roth and Segal's perspective assumes there is a primary intrapsychically generated destructiveness in all children and that perhaps P's parents were unable to digest it. But from Fosshage's (1990a) perspective, P's rage at her parents is not primary but secondary: "In my view, the parents' difficulties precipitated a rage that was a *reaction*, a *protection* from anticipated future injury, and a *reassertion* of her self (from a passive victim to an active agent)" (pp. 608–9).

The implication of Fosshage's view is that different parents (and a different kind of analytic experience) can lead to a different and better outcome. If the analyst can reflect on the ways in which he might be enraging P or at risk of enraging her, he can avoid provoking her. At first glance this might suggest that Fosshage's suppositions about the analytic situation should be described with the immersive theater metaphor. After all, his idea is that what goes on between analyst and patient is "variably shaped by *both* patient and analyst within a two-person field model" (Fosshage, 1990a, p. 604), as opposed, he argues, to thinking of it as influenced by a projection of the patient's unconscious fantasies.

However, if we look at Fosshage's thinking further, it turns out that the immersive theater metaphor does not fit well. The immersive theater metaphor (described in

Chapter 3) aims to characterize suppositions about the analytic situation in which the analyst is careful to inquire of himself whether the inaccessible script he thinks makes sense of the patient's experience might actually fit the analyst's hitherto unconscious fantasy better than the patient's hypothesized unconscious beliefs. It is an interpsychic theory in which a picture of the other is potentially created in fantasy by the unconscious beliefs of each of the two in the room.

In contrast, Fosshage's suppositions rely on what he terms a two-person interpersonal field. This concept relies on the idea of mutual influence and perception and enables him to think about how his patient might consciously perceive him and to adjust his behavior sensitively. But the field concept is not a concept involving representation (i.e., psychically or belief-determined reality). Therefore, although it allows him to monitor his potential effects, it does not provide him with the awareness that he, himself, through his unconscious beliefs may *inadvertently and unconsciously* be participating in the scenes being staged in the sessions. He is not alerted to a potential unconscious fantasy of his own—for example, an omnipotent rescue fantasy.

Oddly, and perhaps at first surprisingly, from the point of view we developed when we were distinguishing the four metaphors, Fosshage's suppositions about the analytic situation are probably best described by cinema. This is because he does not seem to accept that the analytic situation creates a meeting of unconscious beliefs about the person of the other (for instance, templates [X] from the past). For Fosshage, the script underlying the session (the patient managing a hard life after being injured by a tyrannical father and an emotionally abandoning mother) is not a set of beliefs actively evoked in the session via contact with the whole person of the analyst but is out there, captured on a screen. It happened. So, what goes on, so to speak, in the session, might best be described as film criticism, with the analyst adopting a novel but fixed view of the plot, which, if things go well, might indeed be a productive revelation for a patient.

In summary, Fosshage's two person-field model is valued by him not because he and his patient are relating to each other in terms of each's "whole person" (i.e., their conscious and unconscious wishes and beliefs about each other) but because he feels it gives him a sporting chance of finding ways of *avoiding* the risk of replicating the early traumatic experience he has seen unfolding on the screen as fact. His aim is to provide an experience of a new object.

GABRIEL

André Green's (2000) patient Gabriel was discussed in Chapter 1 but will be further elaborated here. We suggest that Green's approach, like that of Louise above, characterizes the other, conflict-focused, ideal type of approach to supposing what is wrong with patients and how it comes about.

Like Fosshage's P and Kohut's Mr. Z, Gabriel undoubtedly appears to have suffered experiences of early deprivation. But Green understands his current troubles as the outcome of his "projection" of ambivalent feelings and impulses onto the description of his key objects linked to beliefs inaccessible to him (but operational throughout his life until the present) until identified by his analyst.

Gabriel had had a lengthy previous treatment with an analyst who in the end had "thrown in the towel," complaining that he was being prevented from doing his work because Gabriel was so silent. This had triggered a life-endangering somatic process, and Gabriel then began analysis with Green for his chronic anxiety. It took a long time to piece together some of the events of Gabriel's early childhood, but Green eventually understood that he had been separated from his parents between the ages of one and three, and his mother had never visited him during this time; he did not recognize her when she finally came to collect him. In early infancy his mother had had an abscess of the breast and had carried on trying to feed him for some time without realizing that he was not thriving; his father had finally had to separate them to get him medical assistance. When he was twelve his parents divorced when his father found out that his mother had been unfaithful; following this, Gabriel lived with his mother, who was depressed and emotionally unavailable until she disappeared abruptly from his life when he was sixteen. Gabriel was afraid both of becoming ill and of going mad—which he connected with feeling linked to his mother by an unbreakable bond that left no room for any other relationship.

In sessions, Green found Gabriel's associations confusing and hard to follow and noticed that when he did manage to pick up interesting themes, they would be accompanied by Gabriel expressing the expectation that Green was bored and on the brink of throwing him out. Green eventually thought that Gabriel was afraid of allowing himself to associate freely. If he did, he hypothesized, Gabriel feared his associations would lead to a cascade of echoes of the various traumas he had suffered. He would be overwhelmed and would go mad, not because of the pain of his memories of deprivation and abandonment but because he would be reconnected with the dangerous rage and destructiveness that these experiences had stimulated. Green describes Gabriel as a borderline patient and suggests that Gabriel was showing destructiveness toward his own psychic functioning. Although this destructiveness was aimed at preventing his awareness of destructive rage or sexual feelings about his abandoning mother, his attacks on his psychic productions also mirrored the hostility toward the mother that he was trying to hide. Green suggests that there had been a murder of the representation of the mother, which then led Gabriel to deny the existence of his own psychic reality ("that isn't in me, it can't be me, it isn't me"). This explains why, according to Green, "such patients can only conceive of their inner world as being shaped by the actions and reactions of others towards them." One example of Gabriel's foreclosure of his own psychic reality was his lack of awareness that a possible reason that his mother had left him when he was sixteen was because she had felt he had made life impossible for her, pushing her away because of his beliefs and accompanying anxieties about her lack of boundary setting.

SUMMARY

All the analysts who presented in our workshops described patients whose early experience had presented them in one way or another with rather severely unbearable impulses and feelings. In this particular chapter, it also seems that the same sorts of problems were evident in Lucie, Georgina, Margareta, Jane, Beckett, and Paul from our workshops and in Mr. Z, P, and Gabriel in the literature.

We can't know for certain, but one consequence is that the differences in the way their analysts characterized their problems and supposed any underlying unconscious repetition to work are best treated as two alternative ways (or perhaps emphases) of thinking psychoanalytically, precisely as discussed by Anna Freud earlier in the chapter. They are, as she put it, rather fundamentally in disagreement. Lesley, Britta, Andrew, James, Kohut, and Fosshage are examples of one type, and Louise, Robert, and Green illustrate the other.

The presentations from the former group, as discussed in our workshops, suggest that these analysts predominantly suppose that their patients' troubles are the outcome of a deficit resulting from suboptimal early experience with caregivers, which has created severe difficulties with the feelings *generally* that they experience when in intimate relationships. In sessions, this type of analyst behaves in a way that suggests they feel that it is premature or even dangerously counterproductive to make patients aware of hitherto unconscious conflicts between loving and hating feelings, and even the existence of hating feelings, if they experience them at all, including toward the analyst.

The presentations from the latter group suggest that these analysts, even if they also consider that their patients suffered deprivation, predominantly suppose that their patients' troubles are the outcome of difficulties permitting themselves to be aware of the conflicting feelings of love and hate they experience, when they are evoked in situations with people they want to love and be loved by, specifically the analyst. This type of analyst supposes that creating some kind of awareness of this ambivalence and its associated beliefs and consequences is the principal work of psychoanalysis.

Although we have found it hard to specify for all presentations, a central aspect of the difference between the two types of supposition appears to rest on what the different analysts suppose about the relationship of thinking (i.e., conscious and unconscious beliefs) and feeling. Analysts in the second group tend to focus on specific unconscious beliefs, particularly around the analyst and his or her intentions and attitudes, and their accompanying feelings. Analysts in the first group, by contrast, very often focus either on conscious beliefs and/or just sensitivities around feelings. Underneath the difference are more or less well-articulated ideas about under what conditions thinking is so overwhelmed by feeling that all that is possible is action—including severe withdrawal.

On the whole, those arguing that their patients have difficulty with feeling in general are particularly hesitant to talk with them directly about hatred and its derivatives or its precipitates—envy, jealousy, rivalry, and so forth. They seem often to suppose that their early experience has left these patients with what are variously described as thinking or reflecting or symbolization or linking deficits, which all have the broad effect of making their experience overwhelming and too real. Some of those with such views (like James and Andrew) then embark on what they call with different names "containing" feelings, or making otherwise missing "links" for their patients, or in other ways helping them to become able to develop a "reflective function." The common feature in all these approaches is that a capacity is missing and must be developed.

Correlated with the difference between the two types of analysts we have noted in their suppositions about what was repeated, we also noticed that they tended to differ in their approach to the analytic situation. Analysts of the first type were usually classified as adopting suppositions to which we applied the cinema metaphor, whereas analysts of the second type tended to adopt suppositions to which we had applied either the theater or immersive theater metaphor.

Reviewing the literature from Freud, through Anna Freud to Kohut and then Fosshage and Green, we traced a development in analytic theory toward an emphasis by some theorists on treating patients as suffering from deficits rather than internal conflicts marked by ambivalence. Some analysts began to doubt whether the repetitions from the past that create the troubles suffered by their patients could be treated by ordinary analysis focused on the analysis and interpretation of ambivalent conflict, at least initially.

We have shown how Anna Freud argued that she did not think the very real deficits that she acknowledged many patients to have could be resolved by a different technique focused on an analyst providing what the early environment had not. But Kohut and Fosshage, in effect, argued to the contrary. (We will discuss all this further in Chapter 6.) The evidence, given the significant number of analysts like Lesley, Britta, Andrew, and James, whom we classify as having suppositions of our first type, is that Kohut's and Fosshage's arguments—often rather loosely also attributed to Wilfred Bion or Donald Winnicott—have gained much traction. This first type, comprising significant numbers of our presenters, to judge by the way their work was understood in the workshop, in one way or another, thought their patients were suffering from deficits that needed to be made good by their trying to be different "objects" from those their patients seemed to reveal they had known in their childhood.

In the next chapter, we will discuss the suppositions of these different types of analysts about how psychoanalysis should be done.

6

How Do We Further the Process?

In the previous three chapters, we have explored the analytic situation, processes of unconscious inference, and the different suppositions of psychoanalysts in our workshops and in the contemporary literature about what drives the repetitive problems that bring patients to psychoanalysis. In this chapter we discuss how psychoanalysts suppose their work in sessions makes a difference: What do they suppose about the way psychoanalysis brings about change in their patients, and what specific activities do they need to undertake to be effective?

Looking at presentations from our workshops, we notice three distinct sets of suppositions about how psychoanalysts make a difference. These are focused on (1) creating a process in which more or less explicit interpretation of a patient's unconscious beliefs is the objective, (2) creating what we might call a discussion around the patient's thinking difficulties and awareness of hidden feelings, or (3) building a relationship with the analyst designed to improve the capacity for relating more generally. While these three approaches are not necessarily mutually exclusive and we are far from sure what proportion of psychoanalysts favor each approach, there does seem to be evidence that, in practice, one or another of these sets of suppositions tends to be favored in the work of any one analyst.

We start by introducing three workshop presentations we have not yet discussed in any detail. We then characterize those approaches and summarize the different methods that we find among some of the psychoanalysts discussed in earlier chapters and report the results of a new experimental type of qualitative data analysis that makes use of what we learned on this topic not so much from the presenters but from the way their work was discussed in the workshops. We look at what Sigmund Freud had to say about how analysis should make a difference and also consider what we find more generally in the literature since his death. Finally, we sum up.

BEN TREATING MELANIE (ENDING)

Ben's treatment of Melanie (introduced as Case 16 in Chapter 2) is, he thinks, coming toward an ending. He talked about two sessions in detail. The manifest issues were Melanie's reactions to his holiday break and then a difficulty making up her mind about her daughter's forthcoming school ski trip. The issue was that the trip had been proposed by a cousin with whom Melanie is friendly but whose sexually precocious daughter neither she nor her husband, Charles, likes or thinks is good for their daughter, Teresa. In the session before the one summarized in Box 6.1, to which Melanie had been late due to traffic jams, Melanie's concern was how to tell her cousin that she and her husband had decided Teresa would not participate. Her associations had eventually dried up completely, leading Ben to interpret in subtle ways that Melanie's thinking had become jammed up because she was finding it hard to own and set out to Ben her own thoughts in the session, fearing them to be different from Ben's while at the same time fearing Ben to be authoritarian and potentially disappointed in her.

BOX 6.1. BEN AND MELANIE (ENDING): SESSION 3

[Brief silence.]

Melanie: Talks about being tired, exhausted, and the hard work in her job that day. Then about how she had bumped into her cousin yesterday in a coffee bar in town. It had been embarrassing as she knew, even though it was a brief conversation and others were there, that she had to bring up the ski trip. In the end, they both had to hurry off, so she was relieved to have avoided the issue but said she would ring later in the afternoon to talk about the trip. It got more and more difficult. She could recognize she did all kinds of other tasks before finally managing to pick up the phone. She didn't know how to tell her cousin . . . it was difficult. . . . In the conversation they eventually had she still went round and round, and also she had the sense that her cousin too was avoiding the issue. In the end they talked about any other subject, still avoiding the issue. She lapses into silence.

Ben 1: Was it difficult to convey what you and Charles had decided—as if in a couple made of two parents you were saying no.

Melanie: I don't think so. . . . [W]hat was difficult was to tell him that we didn't want Teresa to go on the trip with his daughter, because we find her a bad influence and oversexualized. . . . [I]t is hard to say that . . . all the more so because I get along well with him. . . . I could not really tell him these things. . . . But I did finally manage to say we weren't ready to decide . . . that we would think about it . . . that there might be other obligations . . . other children. . . . My cousin asked why we were changing our mind. . . . I said that it was "difficult." . . . [W]e dropped it. . . . Later I talked about it with a friend from work as it kept worrying me. She wondered if in mentioning it was "difficult" I was implying it wasn't up to me but that Charles had overruled it. [Silence.]

Melanie: Well, I don't know why but now I'm thinking about Easter holidays . . . about the idea to go to Egypt. . . . When I told my friend at work about the plan, she asked whether I was afraid of the instability there . . . [Silence.]

Ben 2: Is it the "difficult" aspect that brought this to your mind and has now silenced you . . . ?

Melanie: Perhaps. It is complicated. Sometimes I feel anxious, kind of up and down . . . and it's already happened when I worry about flying. . . . I have overcome it . . . but I can still feel apprehensive.

Ben 3: Your friend seemed to think you were hiding behind your husband with this "difficulty"?

Melanie: I suppose so. . . . [T]here are different ways of seeing things. . . . [M]y work friend is worried about us going to Egypt, then another friend of mine originally from there is not worried at all. . . . [H]e says that there is always instability. . . . [T]hings come and go. . . . Charles is calmer about things . . . but the truth is that there is a risk . . .

Ben 4: But you are still decided to go . . .

Melanie: Yes, it's weird . . .

Melanie then talks at length about various past and present anxieties and the difficulties of being a parent protecting children and inventing terrible scenarios.

Ben 5: A parent who doesn't protect children . . .

Melanie now elaborates on times she felt endangered and the dangers facing her daughter as she moves toward being a teenager and what might have happened to her that she can't remember. Ben makes a comment about whether she is struggling to sort out being confused about feeling protected and being able to give protection (Ben 6).

Melanie: Yes, perhaps. And I realize I made the Egypt decision in the holiday break . . . [Pause.] . . . This is where it gets "difficult" . . . being alone, having to decide. . . . [A]nd before we talked about ending the analysis . . . and how it could be done and be worked through. . . . I had the impression I was progressing and facing up to things and my parents . . . but also that somehow you had decided to abandon me.

Ben 6: I left you all on your own with thoughts that destabilized you and caused blocks in your head and with no protection. But on top of that you have the suspicion that really I am a person who wants to control you and keep you here or let you go just for my convenience . . .

Looking at the interchanges in Box 6.1, we can see how in this session the issues returned. Melanie had remarked how, after yesterday's session, she had by chance met her cousin. They had avoided the topic and prevaricated—"evading" the issue, as she put it. Ben wonders if the difficulty was caused by the necessity to confront a couple (Ben 1), which makes Melanie anxious. Melanie replies she doesn't think so and specified that the difficulty was caused by having to say no to her cousin and to explain their doubts about the daughter. Eventually she had said it was "difficult." Later she talked again about it with a work friend who suggested that the "difficult aspect" could suggest it was her husband alone who was against the trip, not both of them. Going on, she wondered why she was talking about Easter holidays at this point. The same friend had commented that she was planning this far-off Easter visit to an unstable country. She paused, and this was when Ben made his second comment (Ben 2): "Is it the 'difficult' aspect that brought this to your mind . . . ?"

Both interventions (Ben 1 and 2) take an indirect form, hinting at multilevel meanings and conflicts that Ben told the workshop he believes Melanie suffers from, although they are hidden from her. Ben has in mind unresolved ambivalent conflicts of an Oedipal type, deriving from beliefs formed in trying to understand her childhood situation but still active and played out in her sessions.

In fact, at the beginning of the week, as at the beginning of each session, the analyst's strategy seems to have been to start with the surface, tending to repeat words the patient has used to open deeper thoughts. He does this in the third session with the euphemism "difficult" as he had done in similar ways in the first session to bring up the impact of the holiday break and Melanie's extension of it by taking her own holiday. In this way, Ben works at the level of the meanings conveyed by words and confirms an interest in his patient's internal rather than external experience. As he elaborated in the workshop, it allowed group members to see that Ben was not only interested in the creation of meaning but also in affirming Melanie's predicament, her emotional state of mind (subjected to instabilities and jams). He also conveys an analytic attitude of curiosity. In this respect it was noticeable how there was a degree of neutrality in Ben's observational or attentional stance. His way of taking up the extra days Melanie took off for her holidays, focusing only on their effect, seemed to demonstrate curiosity rather than judgment, aimed at helping Melanie to be aware there was something conflictual to think more about.

The second part of the final interpretation, perhaps the crucial comment, which the development of the third session eventually facilitated, was judged to be highly significant in the moderator's report. Ben ended his interpretation saying, "But on top of that you have the suspicion that really I am a person who wants to control you and keep you here or let you go just for my convenience . . ." (Ben 7). The comment makes perfectly clear what was present throughout. Ben supposes the analytic situation to be characterized by what we have called theater. This means he supposes that Melanie's associations, although having manifest content in the form of stories, experiences, and so forth, are compelled internally to reveal an unconscious script pressing for actualization and evoked by her experience of her analyst as a person constructed by her internal template X. Ben's formulation in this final interpretation is that Melanie is in an unconscious repetitive struggle with an idealized yet hated (selfishly controlling) analyst (and working analytic couple). She feels trapped and desperately wants to leave (and needs to leave) but cannot extract herself from it and her excitement in it. It is this that Ben has been leading up to using several short allusive interpretations (e.g., Ben 2, 3, 4, 5) to stimulate associations, based on an assumption that, given freedom to report what is in her mind, Melanie can creatively contribute. This evolution seemed to the workshop group to be a noticeable aspect of this working dyad.

CYNTHIA TREATING CECILIA (SELF-ESTEEM UNDER ZERO)

Cynthia treating Cecilia was briefly summarized in Case 15 in Chapter 2 but has not been discussed since.

BOX 6.2. CYNTHIA AND CECILIA (SELF-ESTEEM UNDER ZERO): SESSION 1

Cynthia reported that Cecilia had "scurried past her" into the consulting room, only lightly shaking her hand. [Silence.]

Cecilia: Today I don't feel like lying down. It is really awkward. I don't want to sit either. I don't want to look at you.

Cynthia 1: [After some minutes being puzzled and wondering what's going on, I said:] Today, you do not expect me to be of any help for you.

Cecilia: Yes, I don't. I came because we had an appointment.

Cynthia 2: [Thinking that like her mother, I reject her. I know her as acting like this. It doesn't persist, so I just said:] Aha.

Cecilia: It has to do with the condition I am in. I made some important steps in my education needed for my job. It won't take long until I will have completed everything formally required. . . . I always took seriously what my chief told me and offered to me . . .

[She continues describing how she thinks to be able to come to an end of this educational process . . . (Suppresses crying when talking.)]

Cynthia 3: [In terms of what she was telling I still didn't know what was wrong. I tried to think of our last sessions but can't find anything which might have been disturbing. Is it something in the realm of termination? On the emotional level and on the level of interaction, I understand at this point that she feels rejected and humiliated.] That sounds like you were at a very critical point, like balancing. Things one does when it comes to a certain point of change. But I hear that the balance is not bad on the one hand . . . so up to now I can't understand what makes you feel so desperate.

Continued on next page

BOX 6.2, continued

Cecilia: Why I don't want to use the couch? Since some time, I am continuously and endlessly angry about my partner. Sometimes my anger and rage ebbs away [tires out]. I don't want to talk about it, and I don't want to look at you.

Cynthia 4: It must be something severe [I have no idea what is going on]. But obviously you don't expect me to understand a strong kind of emotion like anger or rage.

Cecilia: We spent the weekend at our best friend's house. They asked unsuspectingly about our planning to have a baby. . . . I am so furious because he does not want to think about it. I don't want to talk about it. I am not interested in what you say about it. I want to have a baby in my age. If he does not want, OK, then it is over! There are things which need to come true, have to be realized within a certain schedule of time. [Talks furiously.]

Cynthia 5: The baby topic comes up now that you finish your education in the company? [I am really surprised.]

[The group report notes that in the remainder of the session Cecilia brings more material and gradually that her "no" responses to the analyst disappear. This would seem to be the result of the furthering interventions of the analyst.]

An interesting feature of the first session she presented (Box 6.2) is that Cynthia reported that Cecilia had "scurried past her" into the consulting room, only lightly shaking her hand. (Shaking hands before and after sessions was customary in that country, as in several others.) "Today I don't feel like lying down," she then said. "It is really awkward. I don't want to sit either. I don't want to look at you."

This situation is reminiscent of the one faced by Jana (Put on the Spot). In this case, after a silence of some minutes, while she puzzled about what might be going on, Cynthia responded, "Today, you do not expect me to be of any help for you" (Cynthia 1).

It was a difficult situation for Cynthia—how to understand the unconscious communication and what to do? Cynthia conveyed to the workshop that as they sat for those minutes in silence before Cecilia spoke, she had felt particularly taken aback at what she felt was Cecilia's apparent rejection of her. She seems to have experienced it as if a bomb had been thrown into the room and caused some paralysis of her mind. As well as Jana with Nana (Put on the Spot), Britta experienced a similar situation with Margareta (Reluctance to Commit), just as did Otto Kernberg, Wilfred Bion, André Green, Donnel Stern, and Philip Bromberg with their patients (as described in Chapter 1). Such situations are emotional and not uncommon for psychoanalysts. They present significant challenges. One of the issues at stake is whether the analyst takes it personally or supposes that, however strongly felt, it is the outcome of an unconscious script dominating the patient's experience, which is creating a particular picture of the analyst as a person, based on an internal template X, as discussed in Chapter 3.

The way Cynthia understood Cecilia's rejection and how the session proceeded is laid out in Box 6.2. It was a struggle. The presenter, determined to be helpful and straightforward, told the workshop group she had been shocked and paralyzed in the first exchange and reported that she remained unsure what was happening for some time. Like Britta but unlike Jana or Louise (In a Hole) or, indeed, Ben, Cynthia seems to be using cinema suppositions about the analytic situation. This means, it seems, that she is not expecting the experience in sessions to be so "up close" and personal, formed by whatever template X for apprehending her personal experience Cecilia might have—treating Cynthia and not just her boyfriend, for instance, as the person who doesn't give her what she wants.

Cynthia made clear to the workshop that the struggle for her was to think what on earth "could have happened" for Cecilia to get in this negative state. It meant searching for external rather than internal events, while containing herself and her feelings. So she is very careful not to respond too quickly and to create "space" for herself and her patient to come back to some sort of alliance. Eventually, in her third interpretation (Cynthia 3), she admits openly (self-discloses) that she doesn't understand what is going on. But a little later she makes it clear empathetically (Cynthia 4) that what is troubling Cecilia must be something severe. Cecilia responds to this by filling Cynthia in as to what has been happening outside at the weekend and sharing with Cynthia her frustration that her partner is reluctant to have a baby with her. Cynthia is surprised but now thinks she understands why Cecilia is so upset. Gradually Cecilia cooperates, and they seem to rebuild their working alliance.

Cynthia does not in this session suppose what is at stake is an unconscious picture of herself as a person created by an internal template so that clearly she uses a very different approach to Ben's. Rather than rely on interpretations of her patient's silence and discomfort (and indeed outright hostility) by attributing it to some breakthrough signs of some inferred unconscious fantasy content, transference ideas, or internal conflict that are too worrying to speak about—such as Ben suggested to Melanie—Cynthia adopts an attitude of being tolerant, concerned, straightforward, and empathic with her patient. She is clearly aware of Cecilia's ambivalent feelings or even perhaps guilt about treating her analyst as she does, but she does not seem to consider these (or Cecilia's potentially growing disappointment about the success so far of their joint project) to be of primary importance. Nor did she respond to workshop group suggestions about Cecilia's rivalry with her analyst as the cause of her difficulties—Cecilia, after all, is rather high performing and able, and rivalry might feature in her relationships.

In fact, Cynthia told the group that in her view Cecilia's problem with relating was one of deficit. She thought she had been damaged by an unresponsive mother, an intrusive father, an unresolved family history, and an unresolved Oedipal complex dominated by hate for both parents and some kind of attempt to be better than them with her siblings. She thought all this played out in Cecilia's external relationships and her ideas about herself as a failure, which had in the past produced suicidal symptoms. And she saw Cecilia as stuck in this position mainly because, Cynthia inferred, her mother was autistic, and the parental relationship and then divorce had all deprived Cecilia of the chance to work it out and move on.

This meant that Cynthia supposed the therapeutic opportunity now was the chance for Cecilia to have a new relationship provided by analysis and an analyst who was not autistic and was committed to her and empathic. It was this experience Cynthia wanted to provide via being understanding, even when under fire. So, bearing in mind the previous chapter, Cynthia's focus seemed to be on trying to provide a type of new experience.

PATRICIA TREATING PAULA (TRAGEDY)

A third example of an analyst's practice of trying to make a difference is provided by Patricia treating Paula, whom we so far have met only very briefly (Case 11 in Chapter 2). Paula was a late middle-aged and seriously disturbed woman abandoned by her parents and with such an incredible and tragic history of institutionalization, brutalization, unsafe situations, and then rape that many details were not believed by some participants in the workshop. They are withheld here for reasons of confidentiality. Her analysis had been going on for some years.

As with Cynthia and Cecilia, Paula's disturbance and the effect on Patricia was evident from the start of the session when it was clear that Paula was very paranoid, wondering why her analyst had closed a door (see Box 6.3).

BOX 6.3. PATRICIA AND PAULA (TRAGEDY): SESSION 1

Paula is already present in the waiting room, and on her way to collect her, in Paula's sight, Patricia passes and closes the door to another office. [The analyst was afraid that Paula could enter the other doors.]

Paula: What were you doing? I . . . I . . . [stuttering]. What where you doing? Why did you want to do that? [Clearly confused and alarmed.]

[They sit in their chairs. Patricia mentions to the workshop that Paula's is on the other side of her consulting room from her, which she thinks her patient selects because she thinks it must be Patricia's usual chair, because it's located behind and slightly to one side of the analytic couch.]

Paula: Hello [repeating it several times], I was looking forward to seeing you. I wonder why you wanted to close that door. You did not even ask the person's permission. You look tired today . . . very tired today but of course that could be for a million reasons.

Patricia 1: [Patricia reported to the group that she raised her eyebrows to that and thought that she was not aware of looking any different than usual.]

Paula: Yeah, it could be due to a million different reasons, well, maybe not a million but certainly to about five different reasons.

Patricia 2: I'd be interested in hearing those five reasons for my looking different to you today, which perhaps you are worried about.

Paula: I'd rather not say, not go into that. It does not matter. I have made a New Year's resolution to let it go [mumbling].

Patricia 3: Maybe you are worried about me? You left before the sessions were over in December and came back after they began this month. Maybe you worried about what became of me.

Paula: I thought about you. Yes, that is true. And before leaving home I suddenly felt very sad after having left your office.

Patricia 4: True, you left a message on my office phone from the airport.

Paula: [Startled] That was a long time ago, I just barely remember that. . . . I was in A for New Year's Eve. There were four women. Four people. Two couples. Then there was me with my partner.

Patricia 5: Three couples then.

Paula: I prefer to say six people.

Paula: I mean . . . [Gets stuck.]

Patricia 6: There is something you want to say to me but you stop yourself. You seal your lips; you even make a gesture . . . [Patricia demonstrates a gesture Paula has used in past sessions.]

Patricia 7: I should perhaps know what you are referring to.

Paula: Oh, come on! We've talked about this before. You know what I mean. Okay. We won't go into that. Let's not go into that. I've promised myself I'll just let go of it.
Paula: Did you hear that Carrie Fisher died and the next day her mother died, and the same week that George Michael died?

[Patricia reports that Paula begins to grin again, and it's understood by the two of them that the grin has to do with the fact that she very often feels she's got to report all current events to her to keep her at a distance.]

Paula: You should read *Postcards from the Edge* about their mother-daughter relation-ship . . . going on a bit about this mother and daughter.

Patricia 8: I think you are telling me today that there's a traumatic relationship within you with your mother—a traumatic mother-daughter relationship that you often feel puts you on the edge—and when you are with me, you want to be with me on the one hand, but on the other hand feel you've got to stop anything intense from happen-ing between us. I think you want me to know that things can indeed be very intense between us for you, and frighteningly so. At times like that you feel you'd be shattered by the trauma, if you didn't create the distance.

Paula: I do have that mixed feeling of wanting to be with you and at the same time not wanting to be here, but my relationship with my mother was not traumatic. It just wasn't! There was no relationship, I hate to tell you.

Continued on next page

BOX 6.3, continued

Patricia 9: Yes, you're absolutely right. The no-relationship was traumatic, and you bring it here to me to see in our own relationship but then, like so often happens today, have to stop yourself from talking.

Paula: I'm okay about my mother now. That's no longer a problem for me, and it *certainly* has no bearing on my relationship with you. I had a dream that I want to tell you. I told P [a close woman friend] that I would tell you. In the dream you're there, and you want to show me some pictures. You want to show me pictures of your husband and two daughters and a son, but I feel very strongly that I don't want to look at the pictures or to know anything about your family. You confide in me. You tell me that your son is gay and that you and your husband are not okay with that. Something else happens later, but I can't remember what. This dream has something to do with me having promised myself that I'll no longer ask you personal questions. In fact, even though I do ask you a lot of personal questions, I'd rather not know anything about you.

Patricia 10: You imagine me to have spent the holidays with people close to me—with loved ones you assume that I have—and not with you. You think of me as being against a gay son of mine, or maybe against you for being gay, for coming here today just as you are, for feeling so much panic with me often. Us being apart was like a mother-daughter nonrelationship too.

Paula: [Has been watching her phone and looking at it constantly to see the time. It's a new acquisition, and although she doesn't exactly know how it works ("I'd take a picture of you if I knew how the camera works"), she uses it now to keep track of the time. She needs to end the session before I do. She jumps up one minute before the hour. I stand up too]. I've got one minute left [moving toward the door, looking at me constantly. She opens the door]. Good-bye.

[The next session is done by telephone, and then the analyst provides an extra session after recognizing that Paula has become fragmented and despairing.]

This is a very difficult analysis. The analyst is struggling very hard to build a relationship of trust. But the patient, in Patricia's own words to the workshop, seems to be convinced she has either to avoid or to deny getting any closer to anyone due to the certainty with which she believes quite consciously that it can only lead to being let down or mistreated. Patricia assumes that any feeling of contact, of closeness to, affection for, or trust in somebody else would be experienced by Paula, based on her history, as a threatening and unbearable catastrophe. Moreover, she believes that Paula's past manifests itself not so much in her internal beliefs and fantasies about the present as in the action she takes almost automatically to protect herself (for example, in her gesture of sealing her lips).

Although it was the group, not Patricia, who put it this way, Patricia described to them how she had been forced to modify the psychoanalytic setting quite drastically to accommodate what she felt were Paula's needs. Feeling under considerable pressure due to these needs, Patricia had found herself accepting demands from Paula that they speak on the phone between sessions, have telephone sessions, accept Paula may withhold payment, and so forth. Patricia feels that the analysis is constantly under threat and that, if she does not give in and accept the situation, her patient will absent herself and perhaps commit suicide.

Modifications to the standard setting, including Patricia's decision not to use the couch for Paula because she is "too disturbed" (and even Paula's unchallenged action in selecting her chair based on her belief that she sits in the analyst's chair) were suffered by Patricia, who felt that she had no alternative. Behind it all, Patricia made clear to the group, she conceives of herself as a mother and of Paula as a very deprived and abused baby, who now needs the tolerant, "good," and empathic mothering she never had. This is what the analysis can provide to make a difference.

Although at first sight Patricia's preoccupation with the relationship in the room might suggest that her suppositions about the analytic situation are best described by the theater metaphor, closer inspection, as with Cynthia, suggests this is not the case. Certainly Patricia is preoccupied with the intense relationship that she and her patient have with each other and also the influence on it of Paula's history, almost to the exclusion of all else. But looking in detail, Patricia's practice and the reasons she gives for it suggest that the cinema rather than the theater metaphor best characterizes her approach. The main reason is that (rather understandably) she thinks of Paula's beliefs about relationships, including with her, as fixed in the past rather than specifically activated in the present. The descriptions Paula gives her are not taken by Patricia as descriptions of her current beliefs about her analyst. Therefore, rather than accepting the unpleasant fact that Paula's relationship with Patricia is being captured and trapped into an impasse by Paula's beliefs about Patricia, Patricia (recalling Heinz Kohut or James Fosshage in the last chapter) supposes she can instead create ways to be experienced as different, giving Patricia an experience of a new type of relationship. Part of the evidence for this conclusion is that in the workshop group, Patricia gave no hint that she thinks Paula is troubled by beliefs about Patricia's intentions and attitudes—even of her frustration at Paula's suspiciousness and lack of trust. In Patricia's mind there seems to have been no concept of a drama being played out in the sessions with Patricia or others cast in roles because of Paula's beliefs. If Patricia had in fact used the suppositions about the analytic situation we describe with the metaphor of theater, or, still more, immersive theater, she might have been led to wonder if she was being nudged into unconsciously enacting the very role she was trying to avoid—that of the hated past caregivers who had first denied they were abusive and then insisted that they loved Paula and had her best interests at heart. Like Cynthia, Patricia thinks of the sessions in terms we use the cinema metaphor to describe and is focused on stories from outside.

In the workshop, when group members wondered (in various ways) whether templates from earlier times were being stimulated to influence Paula's perception of Patricia in session, or if Paula might be anxious about her (understandable) bullying and threatening behavior toward her analyst,[1] which had seemed to them obvious, Patricia did not follow. She was convinced that what she had to do was somehow to

---

1. Patricia knows her affective relationship to Paula is very difficult to bear. She does not appear to suppose that the analytic situation is an immersive theater—so she does not, for instance, wonder if she is being induced to behave exactly like those who brought Paula up in a highly moralizing but full-of-denial environment, and so forth.

"pull off" being felt as a truly empathic new object. As the moderator noted, Patricia's view of the analytic situation as cinema prevented what group members were talking about from making sense to her.

Although Patricia's suppositions about how to make a difference for Paula were mainly focused on building an empathic relationship, she did also use interpretations: these were devices to help Paula construe and get distance from what her childhood experiences were (e.g., Patricia 8: "a traumatic relationship within you with your mother" and Patricia 9: "The no-relationship was traumatic"). Such interpretations, the group concluded, were aimed at helping Paula to develop a new life narrative, a new story to better understand herself. They were used along with the idea that her analyst, who genuinely cares for her and can withstand her provocations, can be a "new object" and so transform her expectations. From this point of view, we conclude that Patricia supposed that she could make a difference mainly by using her stance and her interpretations to build new ways of relating to Paula's mind—in the sense of giving her better ways to manage her approach-avoidance conflicts in the relationship with Patricia and to help her to engage with Patricia and the potential being offered for a new experience.

TOWARD SOME CONCLUSIONS

Patricia's work with Paula (a severe example of deprivation) is an extreme example of one of our major findings—namely, that a significant number of psychoanalysts, while they do interpret to patients, do not by doing so aim to draw attention to unconscious beliefs, whether in the form of beliefs about the person of the analyst or otherwise. Patricia was attempting to build a new relationship for Paula. Cynthia's approach with Cecilia (Self-Esteem under Zero) and Lesley's approach with Lucie (The Lingering Smell) also seem mainly to have been aimed at making such a difference. Lesley, it will be recalled, thought participation in intimate "conversation" would help Lucie because she had been brought up in such a deadly environment with very little ordinary conversation at all.

Somewhat differently, James (Despair and Resistance), Henry (Struggling to Be Here), and Andrew (A Story of Ruin) tried to make a difference also without touching on their patents' unconscious beliefs. Their approach aimed at increasing what was variously called "thinking," "symbolic," or feeling capacity. In part, this seems to have been because they thought their patients' psychic development, their capacity to think and feel, had been impaired by deficient experience. They seemed to hope to achieve a direct improvement in their patients' capacity to think previously unthinkable thoughts or to feel previously unfelt feelings by being with them and pointing out feelings of which they were not aware. So, for example, Andrew elaborated that he avoided making guesses about the unconscious meaning of what Beckett told him and did not think it wise to suggest in a direct way anything about what Beckett's unconscious anxieties or ideas were about Andrew in the room at the time. He felt such interpretations would lead to psychological talk that was quite distant from Beckett's real experience. Instead he tried to stress to Beckett in context how, at particular moments such as on holidays or weekends, he felt upset and confused and in this way to bring him more closely in touch with his feelings. Similarly, James thought that Jane could not tolerate direct mention of her feelings, particularly her negative feelings toward him or others, and was very easily overwhelmed by emotional contact, which would also cause her to forget what had happened between them. His approach was to make connections for her that had gone missing in her thinking and that he thought she could manage so as to try to reduce the sense of isolation that she otherwise endured.

These six analysts' approaches contrasted with that of others, like Ben (Ending) just discussed above, who directly or indirectly attempted to unearth and convey to their patients what they thought were crucial unconscious beliefs influencing the patients' experience of their analysts and their lives. For instance, Ben suggested that Melanie felt "master-minded" by her analyst and so others. Moira (Hard to Win) suggested to Marcel that he was humiliated by his competitive failures to win over her. Jana (Put on the Spot) was working on revealing Nana's unconscious template for experiencing her life and her analysis, which revolved around her unconscious rage at being "not expected." Louise (In a Hole) worked with Georgina on how unconsciously she felt utterly abandoned and placed in a hateful and horrible position that no one understood, in her analysis or anywhere else. And Robert (Spicy Food) was working with Paul to help him realize and manage how he constantly felt he was having to deal with what he felt, deeply, were his analyst's (and others') intrusive efforts to take him over.

Sometimes analysts who suggested to their patients that they were governed by unconscious beliefs did so explicitly in relation to the beliefs their patients had about the persons of their analysts, derived from an internal template X as discussed in Chapter 3. Moira, Jana, Ben, Robert, and Louise were in this group. At other times, another group of analysts like Britta, Gilbert, and Gabriella were less explicit about what they interpreted. Possibly at that point in their work, they felt they did not know more. In any case, they aimed more generally at unconscious beliefs they thought were influential, such as when Britta suggested to Margareta that her mother had no milk for her, without directly locating her belief in relation to her unconscious picture of her analyst.

We now turn to a second method we used to test how contemporary psychoanalysts suppose they make a difference.

IDEAL TYPE ANALYSIS

In our workshops, participants were given the task of working out how the presenting analysts seemed to suppose they made a difference. The task had two parts. First, they tried to work out how they thought the presenting analysts supposed they should work to help their patients with the problems they supposed them to have (how analysis works). Second, they tried to explore exactly how the presenters supposed they needed to put their ideas into practice to do it (furthering the process). Discussion would usually begin after the Step 1 phase (looking at what seemed to be the function of each of the presenting analyst's comments or perhaps decision to remain silent) was over. The idea was that this would focus group members' minds on what the presenter seemed to suppose based on imagining what was behind what they had done in context. Moderators would keep notes about the main points made in the discussion and then write them up in a report under two headings: "Furthering the Process" and "How Analysis Works."

As remarked before, psychoanalysts "do" it. Explaining how they do it and conveying this to others is hard, even if they have ideas about how they do it. In any case, what was of interest was what they did and *what its purpose seemed to be* rather than what they thought they should be doing. Therefore, the workshop group task was not to have a general discussion about a presenter's theories but to draw inferences from their practice, taking account of any explanations offered but mainly drawing inferences from what the group was able to understand about the function of the analyst's comments—which was discussed at length as part of the Step 1 procedure (Chapter 2, p. 31).

To help them think about different aspects of the way psychoanalysts might suppose they made a difference, workshop groups had the questions set out in Figure 2.2 to consider—questions that had evolved over the years as a result of the thoughts emerging in earlier workshops. The moderator's task was to take the group through these questions systematically and to ask them for evidence from the sessions. After the discussion the moderator prepared a summary (with examples) and usually shared it with the group, including the presenter, before presenting it at later moderators' meetings. This exercise resulted in many written reports!

Because, in practice, to try to understand how one analyst works often required others to put suggestions to them (inevitably based on their ideas), one of us (Georg Bruns) realized that the reports, insofar as they contained a lot of ideas about how a psychoanalyst *could* work, necessarily provided an additional potential source of data. This is because reports would likely contain both conclusions reached by the group as to how the particular analyst was working and also lots of other ideas, potentially capturing how psychoanalysts think in an entirely new, if experimental, way.

Ten moderator reports were sampled for an experimental qualitative analysis that explored this new possibility,[2] selected from workshops attended by the person doing the analysis (Georg Bruns). He focused on the sections of the moderator's report dealing with "furthering the process" and "how analysis worked," which was also referred to as "transformation." First, all the interventions the presenter made, which had been discussed in Step 1, were extracted and compiled, one by one, for each case. Second, what seemed to be similar kinds of interventions, based on the group reports, were placed together, ignoring which case they belonged to. An inductive procedure was then used to develop a superordinate category that seemed to encompass similar interventions, according to group reports, so they could now be grouped together. In a

---

2. Six of the cases are those described in Chapter 2: Cases 1, 2, 9, 10, 12, and 13. The four others are not presented in detail elsewhere, for reasons of discretion.

third step, these superordinate categories were used, linked to the case in which they had occurred, to try to find combinations of characteristics in the way analysts were thought to use interventions. The resulting combinations were treated as types—ideal types. Note these types have been formed largely empirically (i.e., the combinations are data rather than theory driven) using the ideal type methodology sociologists have developed to do qualitative analysis (see Weber, 1904; Gerhardt, 1986; Kluge, 2000). The types, therefore, are those we think we "found" in the data rather than imposed on it.

Obviously, this way of proceeding in psychoanalysis is original to this project in two ways: first, because we attempted systematic analysis; second, because we used the ideas in an "expert" discussion group—comprising the workshop participants—as the data source. The analysis of "what some analysts inferred a presenter was doing" provides an additional angle to that from which we have based our analysis of what psychoanalysts do to this point. Whereas up to now we have focused on making sense of what psychoanalysts do by comparing what they did and how we understood it with the dimensions of the common theoretical framework we developed, here we focus on what it was that the members of the workshop groups considered "made a difference." In other words, we treat the thinking of an experienced group of psychoanalysts, asked to consider what they thought was therapeutic in the analyst's work they were discussing, as valid data in and of itself. In a sense their conclusions provide evidence of what psychoanalysts think that captures everyday expert ideas prevailing among today's practicing analysts about how to further the process and the way analysis works.

The findings that emerge, although very preliminary, confirm the conclusions mentioned earlier in this chapter and in the previous one. Again we find three main approaches. There are (1) those supposing they should try to create a process in which more or less explicit interpretation of a patient's unconscious beliefs is the objective; (2) those trying to create what we might call a discussion around the patient's thinking difficulties and awareness of hidden feelings; and (3) those aiming to build a relationship with the analyst designed to improve their patients' capacity for relating more generally.

From the ten cases, fifty-seven interventions were identified and discussed in Step 1, each of which could be conceived as a type of "psychoanalytic action." Because some types were so similar that they could be grouped together, this worked out to forty-one types of intervention, from which five superordinate more general types were then constructed—by far the largest number falling into one type, verbal intervention, was used by all ten analysts at least once. (Other identified types involved nonverbal actions aimed at securing the framework, creating a supportive atmosphere, etc.).

The verbal interventions are divided into three main subtypes: (1) comments that were trying to address what we termed either a psychic feature of the patient (personality, psychic state, psychic functioning, or way of being in the analytic relationship), the patient's functioning, or the analytic relationship; (2) comments addressing some aspect of self-perception or self-awareness, and (3) comments addressing the analysand's experiences in the analytic situation as a model for other life situations outside. All ten analysts said something in the first category, seven analysts said something in the second, and two said something in the third.

To illustrate the observations that workshop groups made, which were placed in the different categories, the conclusions reached about Moira's (Hard to Win) and Britta's (Reluctance to Commit) approaches to making a difference are summarized in Box 6.4.

BOX 6.4. FURTHERING CLASSIFICATION

Moira (Hard to Win): Moira was classified as showing empathy with Marcel's suffering (analytical action), making comments to show Marcel what he was doing, thinking, or feeling (verbal intervention aiming at self-awareness), engaging in dialogue to make Marcel aware of the meaning in his mind of the situation between him and his analyst (verbal interventions centering on a psychological feature, mentalizing), and trying to create an atmosphere enabling Marcel to reflect about the analytic situation she was describing (a combination of a verbal intervention to reflect and a psychoanalytic action).

Britta (Reluctance to Commit): The moderator reported, "The analyst is giving containment and talking about taking in the feelings and thoughts of the patient. She takes in the anxiety of the patient and names it and takes in the aggression of the patient without being provoked to a direct response. She responds later in the session or in the next or in the session after next."

Quite a few of the workshop group reports mentioned nonverbal psychoanalytic action—defined as intentional nonverbal activity, such as expressing empathy or understanding—as an important part of the furthering technique. Presenters whom the group identified as expressing a helpful or supportive attitude toward the analysand were discussed in these terms. Although such action could be connected to a verbal intervention, quite often it was not. For example, it could be a nonverbalized action. Aspects of Britta's work (Reluctance to Commit) are also summarized in Box 6.5. In her case, the group inferred from studying her sessions that the analyst was "providing time" to allow the patient's feelings to be experienced and recorded by her before trying to incorporate them more directly into a verbal analytic process. Specifically, workshop participants supposed that perhaps Britta spoke about Margareta's feelings only after a delay, after she had psychically processed them.

One subgroup of the analyst's interventions classed as "psychoanalytic actions" was "interaction by means of unconscious-preconscious fantasies." This is the category that could potentially capture ways the analysts were thought by workshop participants to make a difference by focusing on what, traditionally, has been considered the central object of psychoanalysis: making unconscious beliefs or fantasies conscious. In fact, the groups emphasized this sort of activity as important only rarely—in the interventions of two out of the ten analysts. Much more commonly they would identify a broader recurring combination of three characteristics as making the difference: use of verbal interventions to address psychic characteristics of the analysand; expression of a supportive attitude; and use of verbal interventions to address the analysand's self-observation. These three combinations were identified together as important in five out of the ten cases. Two out of the three were identified as important in a further two.

So far, we have summarized the findings of the experimental analysis applied to the furthering part of the moderators' reports. A similar analysis was also applied to the parts of the moderators' reports that were supposed to identify actions classified by the workshop groups as transformative. Moira's, Britta's, and Andrew's transformative efforts, in the view of the workshop groups, although not necessarily those of the analysts, are abstracted in Box 6.5.

In fact, altogether sixty-one transformative actions of one kind or another were mentioned in the ten moderator reports. Those most frequently mentioned as transformative were (1) use of the analytical relationship (8/10); (2) the analysts' attitude and mind-set toward their patients (7/10); (3) interpretation (7/10); (4) trying to become or being a new object; and (5) enabling new experience (7/10). The main conclusion, therefore, is that while workshop members thought that interpretation of some sort was likely to be making a difference in seven of the ten presentations studied, forty-five of the total sixty-one actions they considered transformational were not interpretive in the sense of aimed at revealing unconscious beliefs. Rather, they were aimed at what could be called building relational space.

BOX 6.5. EXAMPLES OF TRANSFORMATIVE ACTION CLASSIFICATIONS

Moira (Hard to Win): "Use of the analytic relationship," including the following: "Moira clearly believed that Marcel's difficulties . . . could be transformed . . . by a combination of experiencing his relationship to his analyst through its various vicissitudes and by giving thorough verbal commentaries to try to achieve meaningful conscious understanding." Two transformative factors are named in this sentence, *use of the analytic relationship* and verbal interventions, listed as *interpretations*. Identifying them together suggests that workshop group members' ideas about how transformations are achieved are based on the interaction of several transformative factors.

Britta (Reluctance to Commit): "The establishment of a helpful relationship," which is also a way of using the *analytic relationship*: An example of this is provided by the following description in the moderator's report: "The analyst is applying several modes to bring about psychic change. A basic mode is her holding function; she seems to deliver a calm and secure atmosphere."

Andrew (A Story of Ruin): "Attitude and mind-set toward the patient": Andrew is identified as supposing that psychic change will mainly come about by accurate understanding of Beckett's actual state of mind and by providing adequate symbolic meaning expressed in words. (For the analyst, an attitude of attention to the analysand's state and accuracy of understanding seems important, combined with a symbolic interpretation—that is, a combination of mental action and verbalizing intervention is identified.)

Andrew (A Story of Ruin): "The experience of the analyst as a new object": Beckett suffers from a chronic infection. He believes that his mother, who died of it, infected him as a child. Andrew appears to see his infection as experienced as a "silent intruder" and to see creating a new object experience as the transformative factor in the analysis. The moderator's report says, "The analyst is a new object (and sees himself as such!) in so far as he maintains a non-judgmental and not intrusive stance, he is 'cautious' not to put himself forward in a way that could be experienced as invasive and disturbing."

We mentioned that in the moderator reports, three transformative factors were mentioned particularly frequently: (1) use of the analytical relationship, (2) attitude and mind-set toward patients, and (3) being a new object/enabling new experience. These are emotional and affective exchange processes that the patient is probably only partially aware of, but which groups seem to suppose nevertheless influence his inner world. Study of the moderator reports suggests that interpretation, which of course also has an emotional content, seems to have been seen by the groups as directed to a much greater extent to a rational and cognitive understanding, to awareness, and to the demand to put things in words.

There are clearly limitations to the meaning and generalizability of the exploratory content analysis we have just been describing. It includes a small number of cases with no claims to being representative. The classification methodology is at a pilot stage. However, it provides a potentially new angle—a way to capture "in vivo" the everyday ways psychoanalysts seem to think about what they are doing and how they communicate with each other about it. It seems to us to extend our current understanding of how psychoanalysts suppose they make a difference in somewhat unexpected ways. When compared with more classical theories of the way psychoanalysts make a difference via interpretation of unconscious beliefs and transference conflict, these findings are rather surprising.

To understand better, we turn now both to Freud, as in other chapters, and to the literature on technique and psychic change that emerged after his death.

THE PRODUCTION OF CONVICTION: FREUD'S INTERPRETIVE PROCEDURE

In earlier chapters, to clarify our ideas, we have found it useful to go back to Freud's writing, particularly in the original German text. This was not in order to establish a definitive or authoritative view but because we found that trying to understand Freud's reported clinical struggles and his changing views of clinical practice in response to the challenges he encountered helped to shed light on the technical problems we all face. This is particularly true when we come to consider how psychoanalysis brings about change. Here we focus on Freud's ideas about how to help patients realize the content of the unconscious beliefs or inner templates (X) enlivening their life experience.

Freud did not publish details of his technique in his own clinical work after 1912,[3] which means that the descriptions he left us (Dora, Ernst [the "Rat Man"], the studies in hysteria, etc.) either predate or perhaps half coincide with, but certainly do not significantly postdate, his momentous but only partly internalized discoveries about transference beliefs—namely, that they involved, during the sessions, a projection by the patient onto *Freud's whole person as the object of his investigation.*

---

3. In contrast with his earlier case histories, his 1920 history of a case of homosexuality in a woman does not provide details of his technical approach or his thinking about how to handle the transference (Freud, 1920b).

As discussed in Chapters 3 and 4, there is no doubt that Freud struggled with accepting the implications of this thinking. This is clear in that he did not interpret the transference in this new sense at all to Dora and did so only partially and reluctantly with Ernst. It is therefore possible that he might have made no transference interpretations to some patients or that he might have offered them other kinds of help, as with Ernst, who we know Freud fed on at least one occasion. He might also have done other things, for example, as he did with Ernst, reported in Chapter 3, when Freud tried to reassure him that he was not the cruel or otherwise unpleasant person that Ernst might have feared. Like all of us who have come after him, Freud undoubtedly struggled to tolerate the transference "imagos" (Strachey, 1934) with which his patients characterized him, as well as their pain at having to recognize the facts when they did so. This is why, rather than arguing that psychoanalysts should or should not slavishly follow Freud's thinking, we think what is crucial is to understand it and, with the help of the common framework we have developed, to use it to ask ourselves questions.

At this point we want to clarify the issue of what psychoanalysts might mean by "interpretation" and how they might suppose it makes a difference.

Whether in German or English, the word "interpretation" (in German *Deutung*) has dual meanings in practice.

On the one hand, whether reading these words or listening to a patient, we are all actively making sense of what we hear or read, whether we recognize we are doing that or not. In other words, we are always drawing inferences that influence our way of being and responding to what we hear. This means that in sessions we "interpret" the meaning of words and phrases patients use, based on a combination, in context, of prior beliefs, knowledge, and associations together with the feelings and associations that the words evoke in us, which will be both conscious and unconscious. Making sense, giving meaning, is always an act of interpretation.

On the other hand, we may also attempt to verbalize the products of this sense making in order to inform a patient about an aspect of his or her unconscious that we have inferred, whether directly or allusively. This is the second meaning of interpretation.

If we look at the literature since Freud's death (and there are nearly two thousand papers discussing interpretation in PEP-Web), there is a great deal more discussion about the second meaning of the word "interpretation" than the first—much of it related to correct interpretations.[4] This is surprising in two ways. First, how the patient is understood particularly unconsciously by the analyst via unconscious cognition, as discussed in Chapter 4, very likely influences an analyst's response. Bion's (1963) theory of container-contained makes use of that idea. Freud's (1926b) notion of *Junktim*—the idea that in psychoanalysis the therapeutic work operates in conjunction with the investigative work—is a second example. Freud seems to have thought that the investigation (interpreting the data) is necessarily entailed in the technical procedure (making provisional interpretations to patients to see what follows). An important implication, different to the idea of interpretation as a correct or otherwise

---

4. There are 1,872 articles in PEP-Web that include the phrase "correct interpretation," and most of them are about what to say to patients and how to judge it correct.

Chapter 6

outcome of listening, is that interpretation is not something that is separate from or outside the method but an essential part of it.

In *The Interpretation of Dreams*, Freud is centrally concerned with establishing a scientific method for researching a previously inexplicable psychical phenomenon. As Giovanni Vassalli has convincingly demonstrated, he draws on an ancient, Aristotelian tradition of knowledge, the Greek *techne*. "Freud actually rehabilitated 'guessing' (zu erraten)—although it has since become a largely overlooked concept in Freud's work—and so sought to place conjectural reason as the definitive form of knowledge for the investigation and treatment of the mind" (Vassalli, 2001, p. 3). This is because Freud's (1893) purpose is "to throw light from different directions on a *highly complicated topic which has never yet been represented*" (p. 291; our emphasis).

As used by Freud, *techne* is very definitely not what we generally understand today by (scientific or science-based) technique.[5] Rather, according to ancient Greek tradition, it is a practice based on the special use of reason held to be appropriate for artistic production called *poiesis* (Vassalli, 2001). In Aristotle, *poiesis* is the name for a skillful activity that accomplishes its purpose *in the production of a particular work*. In other words, when something is produced, the resulting work is not something that exists through necessity, that is already given; it is a thing that can be understood *only as it emerges*, something that is in a process of becoming (*esomenon*). There is no absolute and certain knowledge of it but rather a hunch-based knowledge, for which a conjectural use of reason is appropriate.

In *The Interpretation of Dreams*, which Freud in the Aristotelian tradition specifically titles a technical work (*Die Traumdeutung*), he claims that the mind is only knowable by means that transcend formal scientific calculability. The mind, time and again, he argues, proves to be incalculable, not substantiable, inscrutable. We stress that this is certainly not the same as claiming the need for blind (omniscient) use of intuitive opinion or "anything goes." The point is rather that Freud's investigative procedure, the way he seems to suppose psychoanalysis makes a difference, involves three essential elements (the "fundamental rule" of free association; certain knowledge at the analyst's disposal [e.g., the background ideas of psychoanalysis, such as resistance, repetition, and transference]; and the evenly hovering attention of the analyst), resulting in interpretations that are best understood as provisional conjectures.

Although Freud's practice (such as when he manifestly tried to bully certain patients into accepting his view) may sometimes have belied it, it seems to us important to note that within Freud's theory (although not always within his practice, as shown,

---

5. Vassalli (2001) makes a very interesting comparison between the definition of psychoanalysis in the statutes of the International Psychoanalytic Association (IPA) and Freud's definition in 1926. The IPA states, "The term 'psychoanalysis' refers to a theory of personality structure and function and to a specific psycho-therapeutic technique. This body of knowledge is based on and derived from the fundamental psychological discoveries made by Sigmund Freud" (IPA Membership Handbook and Roster 2001, pp. 27–28, Article 3, §N). This formulation, Vassalli argues, "clearly implies that the scientific field developed from the psychological discoveries. . . . The other striking point is that here the psychotherapeutic method 'finally' is seen as one of the applications of the theory that preceded it. The theory is thus made into a better guarantee of analytic science than the technique could be. But in this the principle of psychoanalysis as technique as Freud understood it is reversed and its origins are obscured" (p. 18).

for example, by his work with Dora) interpretation is not the activity it later became, through which one person authoritatively conveys insight to another, for the other to accept or reject or "work through," as in Eissler's practice, which we discussed in Chapter 1. Rather, it is an integral part of an investigative activity governed by the special use of reason within Freud's particular procedural setup between the two participants, as discussed in Chapter 4. In *poiesis* and so in psychoanalysis, the skill is *guessing* (in German, *erraten*). In a disciplined psychoanalytic investigation, it is guessing in the context of the identification of the sources of a patient's discomfort, which brings experiences together to carry affective conviction. Here is Freud (1926b) emphasizing there is no conviction, no sense of hitting the mark, except via the procedure he recommends: "When you have attained some degree of self-discipline and have certain knowledge at your disposal, your interpretations will be independent of your personal characteristics and will *hit the mark*" (p. 219; our emphasis).

This text emphasizes the demanding and highly specific quality of the analyst's presence, which should enable him to "hit the mark." "Hitting the mark" is what Freud means can be achieved by *erraten* (guessing). "Guessing" is not mere suspicion, which remains indefinite, but a suspicion that expresses itself with a feeling of total certainty and produces a conviction in the other through what is discovered (see Gribinski, 1994). This mental process is fundamentally distinct from a logic that starts out from unambiguous facts, then is developed into a theory, and finally leads to applications (Vassalli, 2001). Framed as *techne*, Freud's notion of guessing unconscious content, in fact, is very similar to that conveyed by Bion's (1962) "selected fact," taken from Henri Poincaré (Bion Talamo, 1997).

On our reading, Freud never deviated from his fundamental proposition that the unconscious was inaccessible except by means of the procedure for inferring unconscious ideas he invented (Chapter 4). "It depends only upon analytic technique whether we shall succeed in bringing what is concealed completely to light" (Freud, 1937, p. 260), he wrote toward the end of his life in *Constructions in Analysis*. In the same work he also rather revealingly compares his technique of psychoanalysis to archaeological method. Archaeology's aims, he writes, are fulfilled in reconstruction, but "for analysis the construction *is only a preliminary labour*" (Freud, 1937, p. 260). He is referring here to his idea that there is no external validation (contrary to the assumptions of the modern empirical scientist), only the analyst's and analysand's conviction will do. As he put it, the analysand has to be convinced by his own experience of the force of the repressed instinctual impulses.[6] Because these impulses are repressed, such realization cannot be immediate. This means that "one must allow the patient time to become more conversant with this resistance with which he has now become acquainted"[7] (Freud, 1914, p. 155). In other words, if the analyst's guess about the content of the inaccessible unconscious is felt to bear little or no relation to the knowledge held and the feelings experienced by the analysand, it has achieved no conviction and is worthless.

6. For instance, of his hatred or love for the analyst and its consequences for how he is represented and so experienced, as in Ernst's case.
7. That is, conversant with his discomfort with his thoughts.

Basing psychoanalytic technique on the technique of his self-analysis and his conviction that words were the essential tool of treatment from its invention (Freud, 1890, p. 283), Freud's idea, therefore, was that conviction, like the conviction he was able to form about his own hitherto inaccessible unconscious conflicts in his self-analysis, comes about under the conditions of his procedure: free association and evenly hovering attention. It is then that words, representing *unconscious ideas* and images, are compelled to appear in the patient's mind and so in their speech. It is then that the "universal characteristic" of unconscious ideas—namely, that "they were all of a distressing nature, calculated to arouse the affects of shame, of self-reproach and of psychical pain, and the feeling of being harmed; they were all of a kind that one would prefer not to have experienced, that one would rather forget" (Freud, 1893, pp. 268–69)—is relevant. The procedure means that during free association, word selection, hesitation, slips of the tongue, and so on betray (*verraten*) the existence of uncomfortable and so directly inaccessible ideas, signifying a need for their content to be guessed (*erraten*) via conjecture, as discussed above.

It follows from all this that if conviction has not been attained—in effect, so long as a patient retains ambivalence to the ideas that are emerging as the patient's beliefs—analyst and patient must repetitively return to curiosity and to the technique to see what emerges anew. Of course, this is a very different model of making a difference to the one Freud had initially used when trying to persuade Ernst or Dora of his ideas; before, that is, he understood and gained the theoretical conviction that what mattered was to interpret the transference to his whole person. It is different also to what Eissler seems to have tried to do with his patient (Chapter 1, pp. 5–7).

Freud's view in this model conveys an idea of strict limits to be placed on the value of interpretation—that is, the limits to knowing when the analyst has both made interpretative sense and conveyed it, *such that it can perhaps carry conviction to patient and analyst*. It is also clear that the "knowledge" of unconscious beliefs that Freud believed could be gained via his procedure and could make a difference is entirely different to the kind of knowledge of bodily states that is possible via the measurement of blood pressure or by examining fMRI scans and X-rays.

A further theoretical point, again belied by instances of practice, is that Freud always retained the position that interpretations must *always* remain provisional.[8] This means that in his view an analyst must beware of believing that he or she "knows" and should be equally cautious about giving the patient an impression of omniscience. What an analyst knows derives only from a procedure of enquiry and learning from experience. Crucially, "the patient is frightened at finding that she is transferring on to the figure of the physician the distressing ideas which arise from the content of the analysis" (Freud, 1893, p. 302). It is transference ideas that come alive "as the present relationship to my person"[9] (Freud, 1905a; our translation). "It is only after the transference has been resolved that a patient arrives at a sense of conviction of the validity of the connections

---

8. "It will all become clear in the course of future developments" (Freud, 1937, p. 265), in the words of Nestroy's manservant, whom Freud quotes in this connection.

9. For Strachey's translation of the same text, see Freud (1905a, p. 116).

which have been constructed during the analysis" (pp. 116–17). Transference resolution here has a clear and vital meaning—it means that the patient "gets" it that the belief she discovers that she has about the analyst is hers, not something her analyst is trying to "stick" on her. It also means that whether or not the analyst would concur with her belief—say, the idea that the analyst despises her or feels cruel toward her—it is for her and only her to decide on the evidence available to her.

THE STATE OF THE LITERATURE

In the first sections of this chapter, we saw what the psychoanalysts that we met in our workshops actually did in their sessions to make a difference and found that it varied across a very much wider range of purposes and interventions than might be supposed to be covered by the word "interpretation." Some used explanations. Some used short allusive statements, leaving the patient to make sense of and develop them. Some tried to help patients have insights into their experience in their relationships either in their current lives or in their childhoods. Some tried to help them to see what was bothering them that they did not know about. Some tried to make their patients feel more comfortable or at ease, and some talked about the way they were with the analyst. Some offered direct and baldly stated interpretations of their patients' unconscious experience of their analysts in particular sessions. Some indicated why they saw their analyst in the way they did. Others addressed their patients' experience of them more indirectly. Some used explicit styles of communications generally. Others were more implicit or allusive generally. Some tried particularly hard to ensure that their patients felt they, the analysts, were well-meaning, open, tolerant, patient, understanding, and caring toward them in ways they thought would be different to those their patients had experienced before. And so on.

Our analysts are drawn from four continents, and today many analysts are trained in psychoanalytical institutes teaching multiple theories, which is reflected in various ways in their clinical work (see Cooper, 2015, 2017; LaFarge, 2017; Zimmer, 2017). Modern institutes tend to accept a plurality of theories and models of psychic change in psychoanalysis and often consider this a welcome development compared to the rigid orthodoxy with which some past practices have been associated, especially in North America. This pluralism is what we have found in the practice of the psychoanalysts who presented in our workshops.

We also find it in the literature. The German psychoanalyst Johannes Cremerius (1979a) gave a pertinent, challenging, and witty lecture reviewing that literature to a seminar in Zurich. In it, he showed just how contradictory written opinions on psychoanalytic technique appeared to be and just how confused he thought any critically discerning candidate had every right to be!

Faced with it all, he thought that one simplifying approach for many candidates was to become a partisan—studiously following one or another approach (such as what they believed to be that of their training analyst or perhaps its opposite) and shutting off everything else. Another outcome might be a "long march" through existing techniques to try to understand them and arrive at a considered independent conclusion. Cremerius's account of how such a candidate would experience the march is not just witty; it captures a dilemma for every candidate or indeed analyst. In another paper, he ends up postulating that actually there are two lines of technique apparently based on two contradictory principles: he dubs one "insight therapy" and the other "therapy of emotional experience" (Cremerius, 1979b, p. 580). Although these two therapies are often presented as alternatives, he believes both are necessary, especially in the case of those whose difficulties go back to a preverbal time (in his view psychoses and borderline disorders), who require additional analytic work able to "repair the early failure in the mother-child relationship."

Drawing on twenty reports by Freud's own patients about his practice, Cremerius (1981) was one of the first to argue that there is a gap between what he advised and what he did and that this was due to Freud's desire to present himself as more scientific than he really was. "Freud's technique was little systematized," he writes, and to him it "appears open, immediate, alive, more artistic than strictly scientific" (p. 349). As examples, he mentions two analysands, who report that, when Freud learns that they write poetry, he asks for these poems (p. 327). He also quotes Maryse Choisy, writing of their first encounter that Freud "gave himself amiably, openly, personally, conveying warmth and protection." At the same time, she says, he was "pleasantly distant" (p. 327). She also notes (what we suspect very likely to be true even if hard to recognize for a patient) that he rarely addressed the transference, treating it as displaced (affect) from the past to the former object (p. 329). Also, apparently, with others he treated anonymity and abstinence generously and talked about himself (e.g., his trip to America). He talked about the family. He also met some analysands in a private setting. Moreover, Freud is recorded as giving the complete edition of his writings to one analysand, Blanton, who does not have the means to buy it. When Blanton also wants to introduce him to his wife, he receives her and later gives him his (friendly) opinion of her (p. 328). For another analysand, Boss, who has to starve in order to pay the fee for the analysis, he reduces the fee to a minimum. Occasionally he even gives him ten shillings (p. 329). With several analysands he goes to his collection of antiques in the next room and explains a problem from the analysis on the basis of a figure (p. 336). In the second analysis in 1919, he treats the Wolf Man free of charge, as he does other analysands (p. 346). He serves breakfast to Ernst (p. 347).

For Cremerius, these are all signs of a division between theory and practice and of Freud's adaptive capacity. In particular, he uses his research to support the idea that building an emotional relationship goes along with interpretive work.

Glen Gabbard and Drew Westen (2003), in a more recent and very thorough review of the extensive literature on therapeutic action that has emerged since Freud's death, reach very similar conclusions to Cremerius. They write that contemporary practice is "marked by a pluralism unknown in any prior era" and that "we no longer practice in an era in which interpretation is viewed as the exclusive therapeutic arrow in the analyst's quiver" (p. 823). Although it is beyond the scope of this chapter to examine the various trends that Gabbard and Westen review in detail, a brief summary of the ideas they summarize, as well as those of two other key contributions

by Hans Loewald (1960, 1979) and Madeleine and Willy Baranger (1969), will help
to make sense of our empirical finding that the analysts in our workshops tended to
focus either on interpretation or on relationship building, broadly supporting Cremerius's distinction.

Loewald's (1960) paper, reprinted in German in *Psyche* as recently as 2017, is
often seen as significantly reformulating the classical topographic and structural
issues related to therapeutic action that emerged in the years after Freud's death. It
is important because he began to stress formally, well beyond the early shifts emphasizing the role of tact and timing that had begun to take place within the North
American–dominated "classical frame" (e.g., Loewenstein, 1958), that relational or
interpersonal aspects of treatment and not just interpretation are an essential part
of the therapeutic effect. Absorbing aspects of Kohut's self-psychological thinking
(which we discussed in Chapter 5), Loewald (1960) argued that a crucial part of
psychoanalytic technique must include demonstrating empathy with the patient.
This means there is a need for an ongoing interrelationship between traditional interpretation and working through of resistances to it with small, even "nonanalytic
actions," if psychoanalysis is to produce psychic change. A second paper (Loewald,
1979) summarizes that position succinctly:[10]

> A therapeutic analysis, as a treatment process extending over a long period of time, is a
> blend consisting, even in the hands of the analytic purist, of *more than verbal interpreta-*
> *tions* of free associations, fantasies, dreams, and other verbal and non-verbal material, in
> terms of transference and resistance. Aside from their content, the timing of interpreta-
> tions, the context in which they are made, the way they are phrased, the tone of voice,
> are important elements of the therapeutic action. Clarifications and confrontations are
> used, historical discrepancies are pointed out, comments and interpretations are made
> that are not or only indirectly related to the analytic transference itself. Tact, basic rap-
> port and its fluctuations, the analyst's breadth of life experience and imagination, the
> manner in which intercurrent events in the patient's life (and before, during and after
> the analytic hour) are handled—all these and other factors are far more than incidental
> ingredients of the therapeutic action. They constitute the actual medium without which
> the most correct interpretations are likely to remain unconvincing and ineffective, so-
> called educational measures, and at times encouragement and reassurance, are used. If
> used judiciously they often make possible and enhance the more strictly psychoanalytic
> interventions in all phases of analysis. Psychoanalysis, *a distinct and unique therapeutic*
> *method*, in actual practice *makes use, if sparingly, of therapeutic measures that are in them-*
> *selves not analytic*, while inspired and guided constantly by the model of psychoanalytic
> method. A clinical analysis and the nature of its therapeutic action are more complex,
> more lifelike than any theory or model. Attempts at conceptualizing the therapeutic ac-
> tion always will stress aspects at the expense of others. (p. 158; our emphasis)

Loewald is making two points. Both are significant, we think, if we are to understand our empirical findings as the direction psychoanalysis is taking. First, he is

---

10. Maurice Bouvet's (1958) concept of distance, taken up by Rudolph Loewenstein as tact, is an
earlier attempt to move in the same direction.

proposing what he thinks of as a portfolio of "not-analytic" measures that a skilled analyst *should* adopt. Second, he is making clear these are not alternatives but adjuncts to what he refers to as psychoanalysis defined as "a distinct and unique therapeutic method." It is important to understand that Loewald thought the unique and distinct features should be retained.

One way to appreciate the implications of this view is by returning to the brief excerpt from Eissler's (1953) clinical work, discussed in Chapter 1. There, it will be recalled, Eissler first "interpreted to himself" (i.e., made sense), via his process of unconscious inference, the hidden existence of his patient's sadistic-aggressive impulse to be unfriendly and cold to his wife and inferred its unconsciously satisfying but problematic consequences for his marriage and life generally, linking it to unconscious means of satisfying impulses from as yet not worked-through infantile sexual conflicts. When, to further the process, he put some of this to his patient, Eissler reported, the patient "showed some understanding of the uncanny sadistic technique with which he manoeuvred his wife" and how this was affecting his marriage. But then, which is the main point of his example for his paper, while the patient could agree that he was behaving in the way he did toward his wife, he nevertheless began to try "to prove to himself and to the analyst that he was not cruel, but justified and that he deserved pity owing to his wife's deficiencies." Eissler could not achieve conviction for them both.

Today, we can only guess as to Eissler's suppositions about what we call the analytic situation or whether this case might have had similar features to the enactments Freud seems to have engaged in with Ernst (discussed in Chapter 3). We also can't validate Eissler's "guess" about his patient's unconscious motivations. But we can note that Eissler's excerpt was included in his paper to support his views on the problem of resistance. For him, resistance, to judge by his account, was the sign not of an internal retreat caused by discomfort during free association as ideas pushed toward becoming conscious in a session but of the patient's refusal to accept his interpretation. In the case he presented, that meant resistance to what Eissler saw as a "correct" interpretive understanding—not a guess about what might be going on. It was in fact in this spirit that technical papers around this time often discussed how resistance to unconscious understanding had to be "worked through" (e.g., Loewenstein, 1958), and it is in this context that additional techniques like tact and timing of interpretations, the need to develop a "working alliance," and so on become adjuncts to psychoanalysis proper (e.g., Bouvet, 1958; Greenson, 1965).

In this way, Loewald's paper exemplifies a consensus emerging particularly within American ego psychology at that time. These analysts sought to distinguish a *distinct and unique therapeutic method* from "nonanalytic" activity. The former was based on free association, evenly hovering attention, neutrality, and occasional interpretation. It was psychoanalysis proper. The latter "nonanalytic" activity was designed to enable analysis.

Loewald's paper, like Eissler's, can be described as maintaining a "one-person" psychology view of psychoanalytic treatment. A second trend capturing key shifts in theory and technique since Freud's death is illustrated by an influential paper by

Madeleine and Willy Baranger. It is among those altering clinical and therapeutic focus to "two-person psychology" (sometimes field psychology) or even (symbolically) "three."[11] The Barangers' paper originally appeared in 1969 in Spanish and then in 1982 in French, before being translated into English for the *International Journal* in 2008. They present the concept of "field," which was taken over from gestalt psychology and from the works of Kurt Lewin and Maurice Merleau-Ponty.

The analytic field concept tries to grasp the full implications of the fact that the analytic situation is comprised of two persons. From a Freudian viewpoint but not necessarily a psychosocial viewpoint, this must mean the interactive conscious and unconscious functioning that emerges. The Barangers' conception is not just about two persons creating the analytic process but also about a variety of spatial, temporal, and functional features of the unconscious bipersonal field that they create. Antonino Ferro (2018) has been a recent exponent of the concepts. But what we want to emphasize here is that what Ferro and the Barangers do is extend insights initiated by Paula Heimann, Heinrich Racker, and many in the Kleinian development. They bring countertransference and the complex process termed "projective identification" (i.e., the projection onto and then actualization of the unconscious beliefs of the subject onto the object) into the center of the therapeutic effort. Joseph Sandler (1976) began much the same journey within an ego psychology rather than a Kleinian view.

In their review of the literature on therapeutic action, Gabbard and Westen (2003) summarize the two lines of development just mentioned and others. They make three main points.

First, they argue the literature suggests that there has been a waning of the "interpretation *versus* relationship" viewpoint (which concerned Loewald) and a move in many places toward wider acknowledgment of what they call the effectiveness of multiple modes of therapeutic action. For evidence, they point to the Menninger Psychotherapy Research Project and particularly Robert Wallerstein's (1986) final report in which researchers found that what they classified as supportive strategies as well as interpretations could result in structural changes in personality. They mention that it led Fred Pine (1998) to suggest that the evidence was that there was no single mode of therapeutic action—one of the points also made by Cremerius (1979b) and later emphasized by Michael Šebek (2014) and Judy Kantrowitz (2014), who both stress additional factors like the characteristics of the fit in the analyst-patient pair.

Second, they argue that there has been a widespread shift in emphasis from focusing on reconstruction of the past and its influence on the present toward interpretation of the here-and-now interaction between analyst and patient, with a parallel shift toward the nonverbal aspects of relational experience and the impact of blocked developmental processes of language and thinking. They make the point that this movement toward the present can be legitimated by Freud's (1914) view that what cannot be remembered will be repeated by action in the here and now. For a long time, "acting out" (rather than verbalizing) was seen negatively. However,

---

11. Other important papers were introducing such a perspective from the interpersonal tradition (e.g., Hoffman, 1992).

particularly once more borderline patients were beginning to be treated, Gabbard and Westen argue that it began to be seen more positively as actualization or enactment of fantasy not yet accessible to consciousness. Important contributors cited for this perspective include Akhtar (2009), Sandler (1976), and Joseph (1985), as well as the many others who write about projective identification (e.g., Rosenfeld, 1987; see also Spillius, 1988). As this view developed, Gabbard and Westen (2003) summarize, "transference-countertransference dimensions of the treatment" became the "primary stage on which the drama of the therapeutic action unfolds" as these enactments are both experienced and their meaning interpreted (p. 824). They argued further that, as this idea developed, it became attached to ideas from developmental thinking about deficit, like helping "the patient to become aware of unconscious patterns expressed in the patient's nonverbal behaviour" (p. 824) or expanding a patient's psychic reality, sometimes called "mentalizing, or developing reflective function" (p. 824; see also Fonagy & Target, 1996). They also specify helping a patient to increase an "ability to perceive himself in the analyst's mind while simultaneously developing a greater sense of the separate subjectivity of the analyst" (p. 824) as an approach that connects the intrapsychic with the interpersonal and which can be linked to the work of Jessica Benjamin (1995, 2018). For her, "intersubjectivity is a developmental achievement in which objects are ultimately replaced by subjects regarded as having a separate internal world from oneself" (Gabbard & Westen, 2003, p. 824).

Gabbard and Westen's (2003) third point picks up the implications of the challenges to the analyst as the authority on the patient's unconscious, including views expressed about the authoritarian implications of the fundamental rule of free association or of being asked to lie down with the analyst behind you (e.g., Aron, 1990a; Schachter, 2018), leading to a proliferation of techniques aimed at what they call "negotiating the therapeutic climate." They cite Mitchell (1997), for whom negotiation and mutual adaptation are central to therapeutic action and the "interactive matrix" (Greenberg, 1995).

Gabbard and Westen (2003) conclude that these three points indicate a need for significant humility as to what psychoanalysts actually know about what works. They also summarize the different ideas they found about what psychoanalysts are trying to do in terms that turn out to be very similar to those used by Cremerius (1979b). He distinguished between "insight" and "emotional" aims, believing a mixture of both was desirable. Gabbard and Westen also identify two strategies: fostering insight and fostering relationships.

To elaborate, the *first strategy* aims to foster insight. Free association, they argue, makes it possible for an analyst to observe defenses in action (as argued by Brenner [2000]; see Chapter 5) and occasionally to learn what is behind them, as well as to see resistances and their resources, making it possible to explore the patient's implicit networks of associations (unconsciousness). To paraphrase Gabbard and Westen, with this strategy analyst and patient work together as cartographers of the mind to create a model of the networks that lead the patient to think, feel, and act in the ways he does under various circumstances. They point to recent developments in neuroscience that implicitly provide a support for this fundamental and, as they see it, classical psychoanalytic technique.

The *second strategy* aims at the relationship between analyst and patient as a vehicle of therapeutic action. They include in this strategy "experiencing a different kind of relationship," learning "to self-soothe through repeated experiences of soothing by the therapist," internalizing "affective attitudes from the therapist" such as by "tempering a hypercritical superego, as when the patient begins to internalize the therapist's interested, exploratory stance," "internalizing conscious strategies for self-reflection" by becoming aware of the analyst's mental functioning, and "identification of prominent transference-countertransference paradigms," allowing relational patterns that reflect implicit procedures and associations people are frequently unaware of to be identified and come to consciousness (Gabbard and Westen, 2003, p. 833).

Finally, it is worth noting that Gabbard and Westen (2003) add to this extensive catalogue of activity a further list of what they call secondary strategies, such as explicit or implicit suggestions for change bolstered by the analyst's authority and example. Another is "efforts to address the patient's conscious problem solving or decision making" (p. 834), practiced particularly with patients believed to have severe personality disorders or problems with their capacity to mentalize (p. 834). Exposure, where the patient is repeatedly confronted with situations provoking fear until he or she is no longer anxious; self-disclosure to encourage a sense of reality and trust; affirmation, following Kohut (1971), to validate the patient's perspective, which is ultimately complemented by the "outside" perspective from the analyst that presents a *different* view (Gabbard, 1997; Goldberg, 1999); and facilitation to make the patient more comfortable in his or her work with the analyst are all examples.

Examination of this literature helps to explain our empirical finding that many psychoanalysts in our workshops suppose a sort of building-a-new-relationship approach to be efficacious—that is, in different ways supposing that the most productive way forward for the patient was to try to create in actuality a better relationship than the patient had had previously. However, what seems to have happened in the literature is not only an increase in the emphasis on relationship building and somehow compensating for developmental deficits but also a significant decline in emphasis placed on the proposition that unconscious beliefs or fantasies can be investigated to produce mutual conviction as to their relevance. Recall that the initial emphasis on the need to attend to the therapeutic relationship was considered an adjunct to the, as it was called, distinct and unique therapeutic method resting on Freud's procedures of free association, evenly hovering attention, and interpretation. Some of the shift away from the "distinct and unique" may be due to the fact that Freud did not leave us with a clear or definitive account of how, by the end of his life, he thought psychoanalysis worked or exactly how a psychoanalysis should be furthered to achieve a "cure." And in fact, as Cremerius (1981) has argued, it is possible to note a marked difference between Freud's written recommendations (e.g., Freud, 1912c) about how an analysis should be conducted and reports from other sources, including from some of his patients, about what he actually did. We return to these issues in Chapter 9.

DESIGNATION AND CONSTRUCTION

We end this chapter by emphasizing Freud's epistemological distinction between *noting the signs of discomfort* caused by (hypothetical) unbearable unconscious ideas and *guessing* or constructing what these ideas are, and we apply it to interpreting transference (i.e., to interpretations as to the patient's current unconscious beliefs about the analyst's intentions and attitudes formed by projection onto his whole person). It seems important because making the distinction provides an interpretive choice (see also Steiner, 1994; Tuckett, 2019a).

We can either "designate" the apparent and current existence of a transference belief by pointing out discomfort, as Ben did to Melanie (Ending) when highlighting her "difficult conversation," and then wait for developments, and/or we can also at the same time offer a guess as to what the belief (inaccessible because unconscious) producing the discomfort might be. We can also go further to suggest how the belief has come about—for instance, via projective identification. The latter activities are constructions of the current transference fantasy giving rise to the signs of discomfort and, if provided as an explanation, a further construction as to cause. (In Melanie's case, the fantasy of a controlling Ben, whom she can't get away from but both hates and loves, is formed by her efforts to manage ambivalence via projection.) As analysts move from noticing signs of discomfort to making guesses about its origin to offering causal explanations, each time they necessarily add concepts and complexity to the more basic shared experience, which is discomfort.

Table 6.1. Types of Interpretation

	Designation	Construction
Implicit	A	C
Explicit	B	D

Table 6.1, based on the distinction just made between interpretations that designate discomfort and those that express the content of guessing or construction, is designed to illustrate the scope for such interpretations to be explicit or implicit. Ben's interpretation to Melanie, "difficult," for example, would belong in Cell C. Nonetheless, Melanie seemed to pick it up and work with it very effectively.

To clarify, by "construction," we refer to any interpretations an analyst makes indicating that specified but hitherto unconscious beliefs are apparent because of mental processes in the patient—such as that a patient has projected his belief that he should be punished onto the analyst, thereby defending against guilt. Interpretations of this kind can be spelled out explicitly or introduced more subtly, as by Ben. The crucial point is that whether explicit or implicit, construction suggests inaccessible connections to the patient *that are made in the analyst's mind*.

By "designation," we refer to statements made only about the patient's direct and usually observable experience of discomfort. It is discomfort in search of a causal explanation to be guessed—namely, a specific unconscious belief (Figure 6.1). Ben's "Is it the *difficult aspect* that brought this up?" or, in the first session with Melanie, his minimalist reference to the length of the holiday picks up discomfort and so offers a route to discovering the underlying belief.

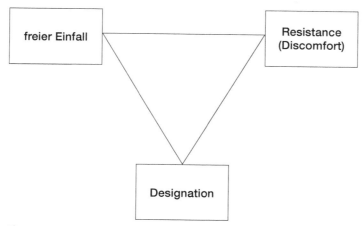

Figure 6.1.   Designating Discomfort

Because construction relies on guessing and linking, particularly when it is explicit, it necessarily makes strong claims. Designation, on the other hand, makes much weaker claims but can prepare the ground for patient and analyst to become interested in constructing the underlying causal beliefs and gaining conviction about them. Recalling Chapter 4, it is based on identifying discomfort in free association (Figure 6.1).

SUMMARY

In this chapter we looked at the suppositions that psychoanalysts have about how to make a difference. We began by comparing three workshop cases not previously discussed in detail and, from there, and also looked at workshop cases discussed in earlier chapters. We noticed that there seem to be three discernibly distinct sets of suppositions focused on either (1) creating a process in which more or less explicit interpretation of a patient's unconscious beliefs is the objective; (2) creating what we might call a discussion around the patient's thinking difficulties and awareness of hidden feelings; or (3) building a relationship with the analyst designed to improve the capacity for relating more generally. We then presented the results of an experimental qualitative analysis designed to test the suppositions among our workshop participants.

Our main finding is that contemporary psychoanalysts adopt a wide plurality of approaches and strategies to make a difference, going well beyond the model of procedure and interpretation that Freud seems to have held to throughout his life. In particular, there has been a quite widespread shift in the use of interpretation to reveal unconscious beliefs and a move toward either relationship-building strategies or ways to help patients articulate their thinking and beliefs. These shifts correlate with the literature we have reviewed, which envisages an expanded role for relationship building and also makes arguments that psychoanalysis has multiple modes of therapeutic action. In Chapters 8 and 9, we will summarize and raise questions about these developments and propose questions for every analyst with which to interrogate their technique and challenge it insofar as they think it valuable to do so. Before that, in the next chapter, we look at one possible route through which change happens in psychoanalytic sessions.

7

Nodal Moments and Their Potential[1]

In the previous four chapters we have set out our common theoretical framework and used it to look at how the psychoanalysts in our workshops practiced and the differences among them. Although we have highlighted ways in which some approaches may be more vulnerable to certain clinical situations than others, we have emphasized that all the psychoanalysts we studied were conducting successful psychoanalyses, all of which were underpinned, to a degree, by the core principles we have explored via our analysis of Sigmund Freud's ideas and procedures. For example, all four approaches to the analytic situation are supported by his thinking about transference—despite their significant differences.

The aspects of analytic work we have described so far are the outcome of innovative methodological decisions we took (1) to assume all the psychoanalysts were doing psychoanalysis, and (2) to build up our understanding of how they were doing it by (a) creating various intensive workshops between peers, (b) structuring the discussion in the workshops using the two-step method to focus attention on the function of the analyst's interventions, and (c) using what emerged to work out the analyst's various suppositions or, in totality, what we may call the analyst's explanatory model—how the analyst supposes psychoanalysis is to be done. The focus, as an adjunct to the more usual focus in discussion groups, which has been to understand the patient and the details of their inner world, seems to us to have thrown essential new light on the choice of framework to adopt for analytic working. In this respect, it has been of great benefit to us personally in our clinical work, teaching, and supervision, and we think it can be to all analysts.

In this chapter, we want to introduce ideas that are the outcome of research that one of us, Olivier Bonard, began when he became curious about what lay behind a

---

1. We are grateful to Sophie Leighton for translating parts of an earlier version of this chapter from the French original.

particular phenomenon—a "type 6" intervention—that he observed when this took place in the first, rather than the second step, in our two-step discussion methodology.

To recall from Chapter 2, after the initial presentation of some sessions and some general discussion, the workshop moderator moves the group to Step 1, in which they examine each "intervention" the analyst made, one by one, and discuss into which of six predefined functional categories it might fit. The purpose is to shift the discussion so that it focuses on the possible functional purposes of the analyst's interventions and to encourage rigor and detail. As described in the first book produced by the Working Party on Comparative Clinical Methods (Tuckett et al., 2008), after some internal controversy, one of the categories into which interventions could be placed during discussion, type 6, included "sudden and apparently glaring reactions not easy to relate to an analyst's normal method." Our three colleagues from Sweden (Tomas Bohm, Arne Jemstedt, and Johan Schubert) had initiated this development because they felt that sometimes such things happened in sessions and were important in ways we otherwise did not capture. They also posed a difficulty that we wanted to avoid—namely, a return to a free-for-all with group members feeling licensed to judge and supervise the analyst. As a safeguard, we agreed what was necessary was to ensure that the analyst herself during the presented session or soon afterward (but not in the workshop) also felt some discomfort about the relevant intervention, feeling that it was somehow "out of synchrony with what he or she liked to do normally."

The analysis we now report suggests that the study of such type 6 interventions turns out to be more valuable than we thought at the time—providing insight into what we will now elaborate are potentially nodal moments in the progress of a psychoanalysis. We describe them as nodal because they mark an instance in time when patient or analyst or both experience shock in their encounter, experiencing in some way, consciously or unconsciously, that they have become temporarily overwhelmed by their response to the "person" of the other.

CATEGORY 6 MOMENTS

Most of the time a Comparative Clinical Methods (CCM) group aims to differentiate the presenting analyst's interventions into five types (1 to 5) according to their objective and their form. In a second step it then builds some hypotheses concerning the analyst's theory of how the patient's difficulties arose and how they manifest themselves in the presented sessions, how the treatment is being conducted, and how the analytic situation frames and allows this.

In our workshops, during Step 1, an additional category, Category 6, can be suggested for a particular intervention, usually hesitantly by a group member but not always. The form of the intervention is often what stimulates a group member's questions: its tone, its possible brusqueness, and its affective quality, but also perhaps a moment of irony or denigration or any other attitude we prefer to avoid in our profession, whether for ethical reasons or due to considerations of technique.

Sometimes the discussion will quickly make clear that the problem has more to do with a difficulty a group member has following what might seem to them the strange approach the presenting analyst is adopting. However, at other times other group members and the presenter will begin to concur. In such discussion, the main issue is the response of the presenting analyst to such suggestions.

A feature of the workshop groups is that the analyst-presenter listens to the discussions of their work for several hours, which for many is an unusual and strange experience that takes time to absorb. Listening to a discussion of your own work from multiple viewpoints can be fascinating but also threatening. Almost all moderators have experienced it as a condition of becoming a moderator. Reactions will always be influenced by the unconscious relationship the analyst has to the person of the patient and its unconscious transmission to the group. In the group, it can become difficult for the analyst to evaluate any unease that he might have felt during or just after the session. One concern, therefore, when we infer a Category 6 intervention and discuss it as a possibility, is the prospect that the presenting analyst might concur with the group's opinion too readily or because they have become aware of ideas or feelings listening to the discussion that had not come to mind during the session, when typically analysts' perceptions are being influenced unconsciously by the transference.

The CCM group moderator has a decisive role when a type 6 is suggested—particularly to use his experience to ensure that the presenter is not wounded by the group's description of his intervention, which sometimes may have arrived into his mind in the session from a disturbing unconscious "return of something repressed" that may be so frightening or disagreeable that it is not yet digestible and ready to be known.

It is also the moderator who tries to ensure that the analyst does not too easily comply with the group opinion in order to keep the peace or to avoid appearing rigidly defended. And of course, such moments in the work are truly delicate because if it was indeed a type 6 intervention, it may have been formulated at a time in the session when the analyst is guessing more than understanding what is happening. As we discussed in Chapters 3, 4, and 6, Freud was convinced about the reality of unconscious-to-unconscious cognition, for all its pitfalls, and considered "guessing," as discussed in the last chapter and as he had also done in his self-analysis (Anzieu, 1986), to be at the heart of his procedure.

Paul Denis (2008) pointed out in the previous book that analysts move in and out of an unconscious relationship to their patients and that this is vital to real psychoanalytic progress. "If he is not to limit himself to indoctrinating his patient with ready-made formulas, the psychoanalyst must allow himself to be taken over by the patient's psychic functioning" (p. 43). He elaborated that because anxiety, guilt, and other emotions are inevitably aroused during the sessions, they are likely to unsettle the "analyst's usual reference-points," to an extent that Denis plausibly considered potentially traumatic.

One implication is that transformation, the recognition of previously hidden beliefs and attitudes, is very likely to involve some form of countertransference enactment (i.e., to be a response from the analyst initially driven by his or her unconscious response to the patient's unconscious). Faimberg (1981) referred to the analyst's listening to the way in which the patient has listened to the interpretation. We might add that the moments of type 6 intervention provide an impetus to listen to the way in which the analyst has listened to the patient—that is, to discover what has unconsciously been generated in him.

At this point, it will be clear to the reader that when a type 6 intervention has occurred, there is a high probability that the analyst has responded in himself to the emergence of an unconscious thought and that this process has been favored by his unusual intervention. But the analyst may also have regretted his intervention and may have considered it to be an error, often an involuntary departure from neutrality.

Below we are going to outline our inquiries into type 6 interventions in three stages: first, by discussing how we become aware of ideas about the clinical moments at which such an intervention has taken place; then, by trying to guess the effect of the intervention on the analyst; and, finally, by formulating some hypotheses.

THE TYPE 6 INTERVENTION: A RELATIONSHIP BETWEEN FORM AND MEANING

Our theoretical starting point is that a type 6 intervention is a sign that the protagonists of the session are each approaching affect-laden unconscious representations that resonate with the unconscious transference and countertransference situation between them. It is likely to have come from both sides, from both the patient and the analyst. The experience of intervening and noticing that something like a rupture has taken place then forces the analyst to attend to what his unconscious movements are telling him about the transference and the representations it generates.

The reader may guess that when type 6 interventions emerge, they are generally in some way a response to some pain felt not only by the analyst but also by the patient. That pain may relate to an emerging conflict, to a feeling that things are too close, or to a regression. In any case one of the outcomes of the type 6 intervention is that it often resolves the painful impression by surfacing it. Experience has shown that when invited to present in a CCM group, analysts often tend to present patients with whom they think they have encountered some difficulties. So it is not surprising that type 6 interventions appear in the clinical reports. We also know that difficulties and the feeling of being able to overcome them are a common feature of the reports from clinical practice that analysts chose to share in their publications (such as those excerpted in Chapter 1). Sharing, if the group is benevolent but willing to speak out, such as when managed by a moderator, makes it easier for difficult issues to be expressed. Both the group and the individual analyst at these times can have recourse to a tolerant superego.

We will now look at three cases that we studied in detail, each of which contained a type 6 intervention according to the Step 1 discussion. Because this research was developed in a later stage of our work, our analysis of these cases will be rather different from that in earlier chapters, relying less on what was discussed in the workshops and more on our own ex post facto analysis. It is, therefore, rather more provisional. What we aim to see is how each analyst reacts to a type 6 intervention, whether he identifies it during the session and presents it as such in his report, whether he describes it and gives it some importance, if he returns to it later, whether he only discovers it during the workshop, and whether he agrees with the hypotheses that are suggested to him. We will also try to understand whether the suppositions that analysts make about the analytic situation as discussed in Chapter 3 differentiate how analysts respond to a type 6—perhaps enabling them to integrate this type of intervention more easily or setting it aside as an accident that would have been better avoided.

LEAH WANTS TO REDUCE THE FREQUENCY OF THE SESSIONS AND LUCIA AGREES

When Leah first contacted Lucia, she gave a very powerful (but factually incorrect) impression of being severely mentally handicapped and part of a sheltered community. In fact, it turned out that she had done brilliant studies in a prestigious university and had a good job but wanted to make sense of her thoughts and experience. After a year of initial therapy, in which Lucia reached the conclusion that Leah sometimes "stupefied" herself, she "embarked," as Lucia put it, on an analysis, which has now lasted seven years. A significant feature to emerge, often addressed, are Leah's worries about being authentic. It has been worked on carefully and effectively; Leah has been able to make some important decisions in life, progress, and emerge from her confusions.

A feature of the sessions presented was the very close attention and significance Lucia attached to her experience of being with the patient, particularly where it is "strange," such as in the initial fantasy she had about Leah after the first phone call. Lucia used reflection on her experience, as well as the content of Leah's associations, both to comprehend what she supposes is Leah's deeper experience and to understand what she is struggling with in sessions and in her life. However, in the past few months, Leah has been asking if she could miss certain Monday sessions—because, she kept saying, her husband could no longer tolerate the restrictions she has been placing on his schedule because she has had to ask him to look after their children during the first session of the week. Having long resisted this change, the analyst finally agreed to cancel the Monday session, for one very specific week only.

Box 7.1 contains extracts from important moments of the Tuesday session after the first cancelled Monday. After Leah has told a dream, Lucia makes a brief interpretation (Lucia 1) to which Leah responds. Lucia then reports that she stopped listening. Her attention returns as Leah is talking about feeling inauthentic and how she had been anxious the day before. Lucia suggests this is related to a possible belief that Leah feels her husband and her analyst have got together to deny her a session (Lucia 2)—a transference interpretation. Lucia has the impression the interpretation is effective in helping Leah identify her annoyance. At the same time Lucia finds herself remembering that when aged ten, Leah had felt caught between her mother and a man she

BOX 7.1. LUCIA AND LEAH (BETRAYAL)

On the Tuesday, Leah reports a dream: she is passionately kissing a colleague who has given her some skis. She tells herself that she is deceiving her husband and making sure that he does not catch her out. After relating the dream, Leah complains about her husband's reprehensible attitudes.

Lucia 1: Points out that in the dream it is Leah who considers herself reprehensible.

Leah: Describes how her manager unfairly criticizes her for taking time off while giving herself time off in a reprehensible way.

[Lucia reports to the group that at this point she knew she had stopped listening. Her attention returned to the patient when Leah was telling her that she had felt inauthentic during an evening with some friends.]

Leah: Said she had been anxious the day before "as if she had not accepted something."

Lucia 2: Said, supposing that this is in relation to the session that she had agreed to cancel, "Was the cancellation of our session yesterday an agreement between you and me or between your husband and me?"

[At the same time Lucia remembers that Leah had said that at the age of ten she had felt caught between her mother and a man she sensed was her mother's lover. She also notices that after her intervention, Leah seems to have a better understanding of her current annoyance.]

Leah: A little later, thinks about a fantasy from the evening before: "I had a strange thought yesterday evening: If you were dead, would your psychoanalytic society give me any assistance?"

Lucia 3: "As if you were thinking: Let her kick the bucket! When you feel betrayed by me."

[Lucia then feels very disconcerted by the brutality of her expression; she had only wanted to show the patient that there was an underlying reason for her aggressive movement.]

Leah: Laughs in an anxious and surprised way and says that was probably what she wanted for her mother.

[In the next session, Leah remembers a skiing holiday when she was ten years old. Her parents were going away with some friends. Leah was given some new skis by one of them. What she might have thought about that, she does not know. She did not feel authentic.]

Lucia 4: "You felt perhaps that you were being deceived."

Leah: Is at first silent, then says, "Yes, I know what I thought: Was it my parents who were giving me these skis or that friend of the family, Jeremy, who I later discovered was my mother's lover? And where is my mother in the scene? Even today, I find her presents annoying; they do not seem intended for me, and I thank her in an inauthentic way."

thought was her mother's secret lover. Leah then mentions a fantasy she had the day before in which she was wondering, if Lucia were to die, whether her psychoanalytic society would help her. Lucia says, "As if you were thinking: let her kick the bucket! When you feel betrayed by me" (Lucia 3). But then she realizes she has said this in an unexpectedly and unintentionally brutal way. Leah too is clearly shocked. Lucia's interpretation is type 6, and this is the nodal moment.

In the workshop, it was clear that Lucia was curious to understand what had made her react so abruptly to her perception of her patient's preconscious aggression, and she created the strong impression that she sensed that she must have specifically chosen this session to present to our workshops.

Interestingly, in this material she shows no inclination to make use of her reaction, although she was certainly conscious of the important impact of the change of setting on her patient's associations and thought that her action in finally complying with Leah's request had intensified the transference and unintentionally increased the opportunity for Leah to justifiably direct the same criticism at her as she had against her mother for introducing a man into her relationship with her daughter.

Our hypothesis about this type 6 interpretation is that it is a sign that the analyst has been captured by a countertransference response to her patient: she has allowed herself unconsciously to provoke and then absorb the anger Leah has been unconsciously directing at her by managing to make her analyst enact the role of a woman who behaves like the mother she unconsciously believes she had—more interested in the man and her relationship with him than in her daughter.

As far as we can tell, Lucia's approach here is intuitive. There is no sign in the session or in the workshop presentation that she was theorizing as we have. But we think she does recognize that her patient's associations in part "cast her" as a person in line with her patient's unconscious beliefs (i.e., she has theater suppositions about the analytic situation), and it seems she has at least some sense of a session as taking a form that is influenced by both protagonists.

FLAVIA IS IN LOVE WITH HER ANALYST, WHO IS FERVENTLY PROTECTING HERSELF AGAINST IT

Flavia was a woman in her late forties described briefly in Chapter 2 (Case 8). An important feature of the workshop was that Lorenza reported to it how she somehow often found working with Flavia uncomfortable—most obviously because Flavia was quite silent and seemed closed off and impenetrable. She also reported feeling awkward about the way Flavia looked at her. During the workshop presentation, both Lorenza and the group were aware of a gap between what Flavia seemed to be talking about and many signs of an unspoken underlying erotic relationship happening between them in her mind, which was difficult to grasp. The topic in Lorenza's mind is that Flavia is profoundly questioning her own sexuality and her femininity, but this is never raised directly.

This means that Lorenza is strongly prompted internally by her patient and her account of her turbulent love life. She keeps in perspective the relationship between

Flavia and her mother, but our hypothesis is that the patient insists on showing her desire to seduce Lorenza, her analyst, who must protect herself against this. Flavia, for example, holds her analyst's hand for a long time when it is given to her at the beginning of the session, information that the CCM group only receives after ten hours of working alongside the presenter, right at the end of the seminar.

Looking at Box 7.2, we see that the type 6 intervention (Lorenza 6) occurs in the second session presented after Flavia has related that she dreamed that one woman she had loved had died in a motorcycle accident. She had then talked about other women she had loved, one of whom had said, after the breakup, that Flavia did not dare to express her desire enough. The analyst told the group that Flavia might be talking about her in an erotized way, but says nothing about it; instead she makes different comments to suggest that Flavia is talking about her feelings toward her former lovers to illustrate her current lover (Lorenza 1–4). It is at this point, after a long pause, that Flavia mentions the wilted flowers in a vase at the entrance to the practice. To her own surprise, the analyst (Lorenza 5) replies, "How do you suppose that happened?" Flavia dodges the question and talks about some other cut flowers that her pupils had found in the school garden. Lorenza intervenes again to her own surprise (Lorenza 6): "Yet it doesn't seem to cross your mind that the flowers in the vase didn't have enough water *because maybe I didn't fill it with water.*" Flavia denies that she might have thought any such thing. She adds that she too might neglect to water flowers, unlike her mother and her grandmother, who are good gardeners.

We abridge the session from this point, but the analyst tells the CCM group that she is still wondering if she might suggest to the patient that she was thinking about her analyst when telling her dream and the thoughts that came to her about the girlfriend who had broken up with her. She gradually approaches an intervention of this kind. Flavia herself tries to soften what she might have thought about the wilted flowers. Then finally Lorenza, speaking in the patient's name as if in psychodrama says, "But my dear Mrs. Lorenza, you tell me that I suppress certain things that I feel. But maybe it's not only me who's responsible for that" (Lorenza 12).

The analyst told the group that she had some difficulty in distancing herself from this session retrospectively and that she was giving this exchange a lot of thought in the following session. She added that Flavia missed the three sessions the following week, pleading first too much work, then illness.

Members of the group thought that the analyst got closer to Lucia's unconscious conflict with her mother through the analyst's countertransference reaction. We do not know, of course, how the analysis evolved after this moment of crisis.

What may be important in this example is that the analyst seems to suppose the analytic situation in terms we characterize as that of a cinema, where she and the analysand are watching the film of Lucia's various love stories unfold. The analyst feels uncomfortable in the sessions presented (this is probably why she chose them for the study), but she does not at this time recognize that this is a consequence of her involvement in the situation. Nor is it a dramatic monologue that she can hear as being specifically addressed to the analyst. And, of course, she does not feel drawn into a theater scene where she participates in the evolution of the situation. But the nodal moment, arguably signaled by the type 6 intervention, has evolved into a kind

BOX 7.2. LORENZA AND FLAVIA (AN AWKWARD LOVE): SESSION 2

[Flavia begins the session saying her subconscious is playing tricks on her because of a dream in which a close female friend (Y) was killed on Flavia's motorcycle, which she'd borrowed without permission. She had been very pleased to awake and realize it was "only a dream." A second dream involved a different female friend, X, and a lot of erotic tension.]

[Lorenza commented to the group that as she listened she felt agitated at the possible transferential dimension: Is she "talking" about how she cannot help suppressing her erotic feelings for me? She doesn't address this directly but tries to open things up.]

Lorenza 1: You feel like you dealt more calmly as regards the intensity of your feelings?

Flavia: Absolutely.

Lorenza 2: Nevertheless, that dream maybe also brings to the surface some elements concerning how X intervened in your life?

Flavia: Talks about how if she had broken up with one female lover, maybe the other would have responded differently and how one relationship can impact another.

Lorenza 3: Talks about whether the dream is an opportunity for the first time for Flavia to talk to Lorenza about all this.

Flavia: Agrees and comes back to the dream, which she thinks makes her confront what you do when you are with a woman you don't want to be with.

Lorenza 4: Comments how last week for the first time "you didn't bring up your usual friend, Z, and then you had the dream."

Flavia: Answers quickly that maybe she should end the relationship with Z as they are not getting what they want from it. Then after a long pause she says, "The flowers in the vase have wilted . . . "

Lorenza 5: How do you suppose that happened?

Flavia: Many days passed by . . . and those flowers seem more delicate than other flowers. . . . And today my students talked to me about some cut flowers they found in the courtyard, and they suggested that I put them in a vase with water. But I thought they would be less likely to wilt if we planted them in a pot. Besides, this is the opinion I myself have about how love can thrive . . .

Lorenza 6: With this comment you introduce the idea that for flowers to thrive, they need soil, water. . . . Yet it doesn't seem to cross your mind that the flowers in the vase didn't have enough water because maybe I didn't fill it with water . . .

Continued on next page

BOX 7.2, continued

Flavia: In fact that never occurred to me . . . that you didn't water them. I just thought that maybe they're delicate. I haven't come to the point where I can ask you questions like that. I didn't think of it because I supposed you watered your flowerpots regularly. Whereas I am liable to forget them. My mother and my grandmother were amazing gardeners—my grandmother even more. Whereas I'm no good at it at all.

Lorenza 7: Is this why you had the idea about the flowerpot in which love could bloom and thrive?

Flavia: Yes, maybe that's why I had the surrealistic idea that buds could bloom in a pot full of soil. [After a long pause she then "hypothesizes" about when love turns to friendship.] If I think about how I've lived my life and how I've experienced my relationships with lovers, I'm certain that in no case whatsoever was the erotic rapport a point of reference for me. This is also intimated in the dream: as if I say, from now on I will get by without love . . .

Lorenza 8: Why?

[While I listen to her, I also ask myself if I could intervene in relation to the transferential dimension of her dream, more concretely in the erotic dimension of the dream.]

[Flavia comes back to the two dreams, and Lorenza tries to engage with them.]

Lorenza 11: Maybe in these dreams something else comes to the surface: as if you yourself provoked something unpleasant, either intentionally or unintentionally, because it was on your motorcycle that X got killed and you're supposed to be the reason why you didn't get intimately involved with Y. In other words, as if you owed something for that guilt. On the other hand, it also seems like you were resisting the guilty feeling: in your dream you're trying to respond to Y's reproaches. As if there were two motions inside you . . .

Flavia: From what it seems these two simultaneous motions characterize in more general terms my life . . .

Lorenza 12: This supplementary reading of the dream maybe we could extend it to our relationship. In other words, we could consider that in this dream you address me while at the same time you are addressing Y and you say something along the lines of "But my dear Mrs. Lorenza, you tell me that I suppress certain things that I feel. But maybe it's not only me who's responsible for that."

[She remains quiet until the end of the session—for about five minutes. I sense that she is in a very pensive mood during her silence.]

of denouement: both patient and analyst have been shocked (at least for now) into re-alizing that it was their relationship that was the origin of the crisis. This may prove to be an opening toward an awareness of the transferential nature of their relationship, which will then lose its "actual" character (Freud, 1896, 1898). If the analyst values these moments of crisis, he or she may welcome the fact that they may be indicated by the emergence of an unusual intervention on his or her part. The analyst can then help to increase the potential for change that the crisis contains.

HENRY, HERMANN'S ANALYST, RESISTS SEDUCTION BY STAYING SILENT

We now discuss a nodal moment in an analyst who seems to present himself some-what differently than the other two discussed so far. Lucia and Lorenza are both rather talkative, although they realize that they are thereby participating in their patients' resistance while wanting to contribute to the development of the process. Hermann's analyst, on the other hand, is a silent analyst who tells us that he adopted this restraint a year ago to move beyond the patient's resistance. His sessions are described and dis-cussed in Chapter 3 and particularly in Boxes 3.5 and 3.6 (pages 66 and 67). A crucial point is that he thought he had talked too much in sessions prior to the presentation, apparently because he had been attracted by the artistic and philosophical themes Hermann raised, which had then involved Henry favoring conscious talk more than he later thought appropriate.

Wishing to avoid being drawn in again, Henry is therefore very quiet during the first two sessions, although Hermann reports several dreams perhaps suggest-ing strong homosexual ties between the two men in them. In the third session, by contrast, the analyst intervenes like lightning at the beginning of the session after the patient has said, while lying down on the couch, that the sessions are useless. Henry is used to this remark, but he seems extremely put out. "You're against analysis on prin-ciple," the analyst very quickly replies. He will confirm to the working group, which suggests a type 6 rating, that he was annoyed by the continual implied reference to the opposition of the patient's father, a military man, to psychoanalysis. The patient then reports a dream: he is in a room with the analyst and one or two children; the analyst is critical of him and ends up talking about money. But then they are both stripped to the waist, and the analyst starts talking in the same way as the dreamer's wife or mother, tenderly and maternally, as if speaking to a baby. On waking, he hears the analyst say, "Come on now, don't whine . . . we're a family."

The patient talks about his unease, and the analyst says, "It seems that the image of Henry changes during the dream." Henry points out that Hermann rarely dreams about his mother, and the patient laughs while saying that he had met her just the day before and that they had a long conversation. He had visited her after having told himself, "I'm an idiot. I spend all weekend with my wife's extended family, without going to see my own mother?"

In the workshop, the group had tried to understand what provoked the analyst's type 6 interpretation at such an early moment in the third session. Henry was, after all, quite accustomed to Hermann making remarks that analysis was useless, as his father had often claimed. What struck the moderators afterward, studying the group report, was that, surprisingly, the comment marked a moment of progress. On reflection, Henry's unusual intervention signaled perhaps a nodal moment—one where Hermann's unconscious (transference) relationship to Henry and Henry's unconscious (countertransference) relation to Hermann became linked and intensified. The hypothesis that seemed possible was that Hermann's affective bond to his analyst had been intensifying (as indicated by the dreams) so that he had needed to hide it from himself at all costs—using as a device to protect himself his many statements that the analysis was pointless and that he could stop it at any time. Of course, this transference belief would very likely affect Henry's countertransference. Possibly, therefore, he reacted quickly and unthinkingly to his patient's defensive distancing, feeling stung by it, by trying to put it aside. We might further suppose this to be a habitual way of responding to Hermann originating in what Henry had so often heard about and so absorbed from descriptions of Hermann's father.

We can further hypothesize that the fact that Hermann eventually recalls that he had managed a visit to his mother the previous day suggests that, perhaps, the frightening intensification of his relationship to his analyst is in fact a feared relationship not to the father but to the mother. In other words, the feared transference link is maternal not paternal. Hermann dreamed of a character who condensed certain traits of his analyst, whom he portrays without a shirt, with characteristics of a mother: her voice, her soft words addressed to a young child. Hermann goes on to say that he wanted to meet his mother and that they had a long conversation the day before the session. Henry noted that his meeting with his mother was a change, both in the external reality and, we can hypothesize, also in the internal dream world. It follows that perhaps the homosexuality depicted in Hermann's recent dreams covered an affection for his analyst, on whom he transferred his hidden love for his mother, and was not about homosexual anxieties at all.

We wrote in Chapter 3 that Henry's suppositions about the analytic situation were best characterized by the dramatic monologue metaphor, although it was not a canonical example. From this study of Henry's type 6 intervention, we can hypothesize that Henry was hampered in making full use of its potential by supposing the analytic situation to be dramatic monologue, because he was reluctant to lend himself unconsciously to receiving Hermann's maternal transference. From this hypothetical perspective, the unusual intervention is provoked by the unconscious urgency of the underlying nodal moment, when the patient's transferential love for his analyst meets the love in return that Henry defends against.

The causes of this defensive attitude are unknown to us, but our general knowledge of the analytic situation allows us to propose hypotheses that may be useful for a better understanding of the difficulties we all have in our practice. Three interrelated explanations may account for Henry's predicament. First, he probably wanted to avoid a reciprocal homoerotic seduction; in this he joins Freud, whose patient Hilda Doolittle (the poet "H. D."; Doolittle, 1956) reported that Freud had told her he disliked being taken for the mother in the transference. Henry could therefore be unaware that his countertransference is a reaction to the patient's love for his mother. Finally, he is led to "petrify" his attitude toward his patient not only to defend himself against homoeroticism but also because he is led by the patient to personify the mother that Hermann thinks he had.

These reflections perhaps help to explain the struggle we had to characterize Henry's suppositions about the analytic situation in Chapter 3. Henry did not fit the theater model because he did not think of his patient as communicating unconscious pictures of his analyst (viewed through his unconscious template) now, in the sessions. It certainly could not be immersive theater. We discounted cinema because he did not seem to use his patient's reports of outside events to construct a picture of his inner template script. We knew it wasn't canonically dramatic monologue but decided that his interest in the patient's words and the space he was giving his patient to develop ideas best fit that approach. However, we can now see that although Henry's suppositions do fit the dramatic monologue in some ways, it was not canonical because it seems he was unprepared for the crucial unconscious participation element now in the session built into that approach. It follows, therefore, that for an analyst like Henry, the emergence of a type 6 intervention has the potential to attract the analyst's attention and to prompt reflection, perhaps creating curiosity and room to reconsider suppositions.

THE NODAL MOMENT: A CRISIS THAT LOOSENS THE CLOSENESS BROUGHT BY THE TRANSFERENCE

The ultimate goal of research through the CCM method is to compare clinical practices and the theories that are attested by them. By comparing the moments of type 6 interventions in three vignettes, we have discovered that they coincide with an affective rupture between analyst and patient.

Despite the great differences between the three analysts chosen to illustrate the idea in this chapter, the course of the analysts' affects appears to be similar in all of them. In the first stage, the analysts are annoyed by the patient and forget that they are very likely driven by the effect on them of the patient's transference, just as they neglect that part of their annoyance is likely rooted in their own unconscious.

In a second phase, alerted by the occurrence of a type 6 intervention, the three analysts react. The patients also react. This surfaces for both parties an unexpected and hitherto unacknowledged unconscious bond between them—formally, transference and countertransference.

Lucia realizes how she was pushed by Leah to act out Leah's transference on her; she was already aware of it a little before, but the strength of the feelings of the two protagonists deepens thanks to the type 6 intervention.

Lorenza was always uncertain about Flavia's homosexual loving transference. But at the end of the session after her type 6 interventions, she makes a theatrical intervention, as in psychodrama. She speaks as if she were Flavia and says, "You, the analyst, are also resisting responding to my impulse for you," hinting strongly at the situation between them.

Henry, perhaps, is the least articulate of the three analysts about his ideas as to the transference and countertransference he believes active. But it turns out that it was after he reacted with annoyance against Hermann that he noticed that the patient spoke about his mother. And it was at this point that the patient told him that he had met her the day before. We have suggested that there may have been a relationship between a defense against closeness between Henry and Hermann and a defense against closeness between Henry and his mother.

Few analysts in our workshops had immersive theater suppositions and neither did Lucia, Lorenza, or Henry. Lucia did make theater suppositions (i.e., she treated associations as about the fantasy situation now) and had a strong intuitive awareness that her patients could influence her response and thinking, which could then, in turn, influence the patient. Before the sessions presented, she was alert to what might have been the consequence of giving up the Monday session.

Lorenza and Henry, on the other hand, did not seem to suppose either that they were participants in revealing the unconscious script or that their patient's associations were about the unconscious situation between them created by the patients' unconscious script now as either theater set of suppositions would require (Chapter 3, Table 3.1). It means that although both analysts have noted the specific features of their type 6 interventions, they have not gone much beyond agreeing it was an unusual intervention for them and then worrying about it. Their theory seems to preclude the idea that they, as well as their patients, necessarily became different under the influence of the transference. They then tend to judge their intervention as an uncomfortable departure from normal technique that they should have avoided (Bourdin, 2007) rather than as an inevitable and unconsciously driven event. Consequently, they do not easily see its revealing and transformational potential.

SUMMARY

Using the CCM group methods to identify and then explore "the sudden and glaring interventions" that were not part of the presenting analysts' normal technique has turned out to be surprisingly rich. When they happen these type 6 interventions seem to constitute a nodal moment between analyst and patient. In fact, there are really two crisis movements that clash: rapprochement and distancing. The transformative potential of the combined crisis lies in its deepening of the relationship between the protagonists and surfacing it to their awareness, at least for a while—raising the importance to each participant of what is going on between them, if the realization can be contained and used rather than retreated from. In formal terms the interlocking of a transference and an unknown countertransference increases therapeutic potential.

The three vignettes chosen to illustrate type 6 interventions involve three very different analysts, both in the attitude they had to events that can be imagined from the clinical reconstruction that they reported to us and in the theory they seemed to suppose as to how an unconscious script becomes legible. We can hypothesize that the more an analyst supposes that the analytic situation is both "now" and "participatory" (Chapter 3) and the more they draw inferences from all three available sources (Chapter 4), the more likely they are to be able to use the crisis moment productively rather than to be frightened by it.

8

Bringing It Together: Some Questions for Every Psychoanalyst

The purpose of this book has been to describe what psychoanalysts do and how they do it. Our starting point was the Comparative Clinical Methods (CCM) Working Party created by the European Psychoanalytic Federation (EPF) in 2004. At the time the EPF Council realized that the differences in the way psychoanalysts worked and the difficulties specifying how they differed could make international meetings and international policy to protect and raise standards of training and clinical work rather problematic (Tuckett, 2004).

Early results from the initial CCM workshops we organized confirmed the problems (Tuckett et al., 2008). Comparing the detailed published clinical work of leading international clinicians, such as the seven discussed in Chapter 1, made it further evident, as did discussions of clinical presentations in leading journals.[1] Since then, the experience of participating in many hundreds of sessions presented in the specialized two-step CCM workshops we refined over the next fifteen years has made it obvious. But what really are the differences between psychoanalysts that we all sense, and could we specify how clinical work differs in ways that are useful?

To solve both issues required a theoretical framework to discern significant differences in the general frameworks or explanatory models that different psychoanalysts bring to the task. An advantage, if we could develop it, would be not just that it would enable us to understand differences but also that it might serve as a tool for every analyst with which to reflect on their practice. This aim is what we will try to achieve in this chapter.

Chapter 2 summarizes in updated form the theoretical framework that we built and published after the first four years of effort (Tuckett et al., 2008). In Chapter 1 we described how we gradually evolved it into a new common theoretical framework to surface and then make sense of the differences in the data we collected in several

---

1. For instance, the *International Journal of Psychoanalysis* Psychoanalyst at Work series (e.g., Rolland, 2006).

hundred two-step-method workshops discussed during fifteen years of iterative meetings—trying to apprehend and understand the differences we could sense from the
workshop materials and fit the clinical data to theory and vice versa. The new framework rests on the presumption that anyone who wishes to define themselves as working as a psychoanalyst must, whether they describe it like that or not, be putting into
practice their version of four sets of suppositions that necessarily govern any psychoanalytic investigation: (1) about the investigation's setting, (2) about how the "otherwise inaccessible" ideas that patients have are to be inferred, (3) about how those
"otherwise inaccessible" ideas and impulses repetitively create a patient's troubles, and
(4) about how the process brings about change. We refer to the thinking governing
these four issues as suppositions about the analytic situation, unconscious inference,
unconscious repetition, and furthering a transformational process, respectively.

In Chapter 1 we also described how we have found that Sigmund Freud's writing,
particularly in German, offered a third pillar to help us progress our efforts. Trying
to conceptualize not only how the presenters in our workshops differed in the suppositions they put into practice, but also how Freud's work evolved, improved our
understanding of our framework and the ways it could be used.

In Chapter 2 we described the methodology we used in our two-step workshops
at which different psychoanalysts presented sessions of their work as well as our
methods of analyzing the workshop proceedings. In Chapters 3 to 6 we elaborated
our general framework and what we found psychoanalysts "doing" in terms of the
suppositions they appeared to have about the analytic situation, unconscious inference, unconscious repetition, and furthering a transformational process. For each set
of suppositions, we were able to develop a distinctive set of "ideal types"—that is,
tendencies in a particular analyst's suppositions in one of the four areas that allowed
us to characterize their working method as in some way similar to or different from
that of others. Proceeding in this way has, we think, enabled us to foreground what
we think are crucial differences in how different presenters "did" psychoanalysis.

We will now summarize our main findings and then argue that our approach
throws more rigorous light than hitherto on two areas: (1) the differences between
psychoanalysts, and (2) questions that every psychoanalyst might use to reflect on
their practice. We think these insights allow us more precisely to consider in what
ways psychoanalysis might currently be at an important juncture in its development
and to frame at least some of the choices to be made about available roads ahead.

THE ANALYTIC SITUATION: WHICH METAPHOR?

Chapter 3 looked at suppositions about the analytic situation, the crucial influence of
which we have then noticed on other aspects of technique.

We began from the proposition that whatever their differences, all psychoanalysts
suppose *in some way* that their meetings with patients reveal ways in which they are
driven by an *unconscious* script. We then identified different ways psychoanalysts

could suppose this unconscious script might be visible in and/or influence what goes on in sessions.

In essence, we tried to discern "when" the presenting analyst in the workshops supposed the unconscious script was having an effect and also on whom: analyst or patient or both? Based on what we found, we developed four metaphors to try to capture the differences between what the analysts supposed, conceived as "ideal types" (i.e., as empirical tendencies), one of which every presenter we studied seemed to us to tend toward quite strongly in the sessions they presented.

The four metaphors for describing an analyst's suppositions about the analytic situation are cinema, dramatic monologue, theater, and immersive theater.

Interestingly, when looking carefully at Freud's writing on topics relevant to the analytic situation, we were able to discern some degree of support for the ways of doing psychoanalysis described by all four metaphors. Importantly, we also presented evidence (particularly from his case reports) that both Freud and his patients suffered personally in the analytic situation. In particular, Freud seems to us to have made it abundantly clear that he and his patients faced significant emotional challenges, particularly insofar as he realized and tried to put into practice his idea that the "whole person" of the analyst is inevitably cast in particular ways by the patient in sessions and then acted toward by the patient accordingly.

Although Freud had understood quite early that the way his patients pictured or felt about people in the past was crucial to the treatment and would be transferred into it, he did not realize its full implications until after Dora had left treatment. It was only then and never consistently that he hypothesized that she had been "casting" him in the roles that she herself had suffered when with others, so that in her mind he (like the others before him to whom she related) was not a helpful figure. Moreover, the harder he tried, the less able she became to regard his comments as neutral and well-meaning.

The retrospective realization that Freud had about the analytic situation with Dora seems to us never to have been fully internalized by him. Certainly, when he was seeing Ernst (the "Rat Man"), Freud was still wavering significantly, as Ernst's associations compelled him repeatedly to hint at his otherwise inaccessible unconscious ideas that he feared cruel punishment for his sexual activity—not just from others but from Freud personally. Indeed, as we have mentioned, to manage the situation Freud at first tried to reassure his patient that he had no such intentions—in the modern parlance discussed in Chapter 5, trying to reassure the patient that he, Freud, was a good object. When eventually he realized that this didn't work and that Ernst's unconscious beliefs or fantasies (his psychic reality) were casting Freud into the punishing role no matter what he did, Freud clearly felt pain—both on his own behalf and that of his patient.

Moreover, Freud never seems to have realized in writing, although his ideas about countertransference prepared the ground for others to do so later, that just as the patient unconsciously casts the person of the analyst into a particular templated role, the analyst must also cast the patient. He himself, in some of the dialogue he describes between himself and Ernst, was clearly (unintentionally) in fact somehow prompted to relate to him by inflicting pain on him, albeit in words (Diercks, 2018).

In fact, if we look carefully at the account of Ernst's case, we can see that Freud supposed the script that was "inaccessible," except by means of psychoanalysis, to be operating successively in the analytic situation via three of our four metaphors—in the patient's speech, dreams, and slips while he was associating, which displayed transferred affects (dramatic monologue); in his descriptions of people in his life that he was sure were punishing him or wanted to do so (cinema); and in his evident fear of Freud (theater). Unsurprisingly, Freud did not see, but the tools he has given now allow us to see, the countertransference enactments in which Freud could not help participating (immersive theater).

THE SEVEN PSYCHOANALYSTS IN CHAPTER 1

We excerpted examples of what seemed to be different ways of working among seven internationally famous psychoanalysts in Chapter 1. Although we have only their reports (written for other purposes) available, we will now try to guess their suppositions about the analytic situation and how might they have influenced matters.

Kurt Eissler's suppositions about the analytic situation seem to be best described more by the cinema metaphor (in which the analytic situation is understood as a place in which the patient reports thoughts, events, dreams, and feelings, which the analyst transforms into unconscious beliefs and fantasies that the patient has resisted "knowing") than by theater, and certainly not by immersive theater.

The evidence is, as far as we can tell, that when his patient was associating, Eissler heard the events narrated about the patient and his wife as revealing an internal template in his patient that involved repetition of infantile ways of managing sexual conflicts transferred into current relationships. Had Eissler's suppositions been those of the theater metaphor, we can suppose he might have heard the same material as describing the application of the same template to the patient's experience of Eissler as a person in the session. He would then have seen his patient as compelled in the session to use his conscious associations, whether about his wife or others and their relationship, to reveal an unconscious script about his experience with Eissler, as cast by his internal template. In other words, we might suppose, which Eissler did not, that it was the whole person of his analyst whose unfair attitudes and behaviors the patient was unconsciously frightened about or gaining pleasure from. Moreover, when the analysis seems to have somewhat descended into a situation where Eissler sought to impose his understanding on his patient, who seemed equally determined to "resist" it, then had "immersive theater" suppositions been applied, he might have wondered whether the patient's internal template was now being matched by Eissler's own unconscious response to him so that they were unconsciously enacting a script between them.

Fred Busch's suppositions about the analytic situation might also be best described more by the cinema metaphor (a place to describe the transfer of affects and unconscious fantasies from the past going on in the patient's life) than by theater. This is because Busch does not suppose that it is useful to treat his patient as inevitably driven to associate about the ways he is casting Busch according to his unconscious script in the session.[2] Rather, he is reporting the transfer of affects and unconscious fantasies from the past going on in the patient's life. However, Busch's scrupulous effort to focus on signs of his patient's discomfort as he associates to events at the weekend and with his wife, never moving too far into any ideas beyond what the patient is conscious of, very successfully leads to his patient making the link directly to his thoughts and feelings about his analyst *at the weekend*. Once, after Busch has pointed out he had become uncomfortable, the patient has courageously brought his unconscious concerns into relationship with Busch at the weekend, it allows Busch to take up how he is (generally) being unconsciously cast by his patient's beliefs (or fantasies) quite openly and then successfully to bring the patient's unconscious (template) experience of previously "not accessible" and unresolved Oedipal and homosexual anxieties and impulses related to his analyst (and influencing his marriage) convincingly into awareness.

The vignette illustrates how when an analyst makes suppositions that we use the cinema metaphor to describe, it can be highly effective in clinical situations provided (1) the patient has been enabled by the process to begin to realize consciously (in this case by being helped to recognize the emergence of discomfort) that he has significant ideas about his analyst's intentions and attitudes toward him, or vice versa, that might be of interest, and (2) that the analyst's countertransference is sufficiently well aligned (i.e., free from unconscious disturbance in the situation with the patient) so that he can recognize the unconscious role into which he is being cast, rather than perhaps denying it and so enacting it without recognition.

Otto Kernberg's suppositions about the analytic situation, on the other hand, are probably best described using not the cinema but the theater metaphor. This is because the vignette suggests he was largely supposing that Karl, his patient, was unconsciously casting Kernberg as a whole person in session in various ways Kernberg described in his account that had derived from his supposition that Karl's inaccessible script played out in multiple indirect associations to his person. This is evident when Kernberg reports, "I proceeded to interpret the patient's image of me as a powerful man, strong, ruthless, and brutal with women" (Box 1.2, OK 2). This comment went beyond anything Karl had said directly and addressed what Kernberg surmised was Karl's image of Kernberg and his unconscious beliefs (fantasies) about Kernberg's attitudes to him in the session. Also of particular interest was the way that Kernberg used his feelings, a sudden sense of power and clarity after months of feeling belittled in the analytic situation, as a source from which to infer this interpretation. It seems Kernberg understood the analytic situation as one in which he both felt and understood that he was cast in a role, as a person, in Karl's mind.

---

2. "My interventions are geared toward representing what Jim is able to associate to. I am not repeating what he's saying, looking for something totally hidden in his thoughts, or attempting to reconstruct the past. It is via the transformation of what is enacted into representational thought that leads to the deeper meanings to this loss of mind" (Busch, 2013, p. 29).

Given the involvement of Kernberg's feelings and his description of his sense of power, can we think of the suppositions he makes about the analytic situation in terms of the immersive theater metaphor? On balance, at least with the information we have, we think rather that his approach is an example of suppositions best described by a particularly rich version of the theater metaphor. This is because nothing in the report suggests to us that Kernberg supposed that at any stage *he had unconsciously been provoked to enact* being powerful, such as by "putting Karl down" (e.g., like Robert, who thought he had "bombed" Paul [Spicy Food] in Chapter 3). Kernberg made his inference by observing and being curious about his feeling of power and earlier his feelings of helplessness and being made impotent—but did not enact reactively (or report that he had at an earlier stage). This difference between using one's feelings and fantasies in the analytic situation and discovering one has enacted them unconsciously (i.e., via countertransference) determines when we think it is best to apply the theater and immersive theater metaphors, as illustrated in the next example.

Wilfred Bion's suppositions about the analytic situation in his analysis of Brian emerge from his initial introduction of the circumstances in which his patient arrived into treatment and then the contrast with what happened. Bion describes how for a time the analysis was apparently going well. His patient associated, he interpreted, and reports from outside reached Bion suggesting that the patient was doing better. But crucially Bion also drew inferences from his feelings in sessions. He reports an uncomfortable feeling that made him suspicious that he *was unconsciously enacting something* (perhaps like the analysts participating in "nodal" situations discussed in Chapter 7). Shortly after he noticed the uncomfortable feeling, it seems Bion's curiosity was aroused, and he began to notice other things. There was a strange and not productive rhythm to the associations. He also increasingly felt as though he was being put in a dilemma: he could break the rhythm, which he sensed would cause irritation, or he could carry on, although he felt that this would be tantamount to giving up and accepting a dead end.

The additional element here, which means that Bion's suppositions are best described by immersive theater, is that his approach to the analytic situation suggests he was both theoretically open to the possibility and then actively alert (through enquiry into himself) to the reality, that *he had become unconsciously immersed* in the role the patient was casting him. In this way, he was able to transform his conscious feeling of unease into an idea about his own unconscious countertransference, understood to be an initially inaccessible or unconscious response, which was leading him to be pulled into an impasse. So then, when a little later the patient suggested the analysis might stop, he was prepared.[3] He recovered the situation by stepping out of the role he had been cast in (and had unconsciously accepted) so that, in reply, he could convey evenhandedly that he could see the patient's point but also wondered what ending treatment really might mean. As we described in Chapter 1, after a prompt

---

3. Spelling it out in this logical way is designed to clarify. The process itself would have been much less so.

to continue association (i.e., after further reestablishing a triangular psychoanalytic situation), Brian's responses allowed Bion, plausibly, to infer a picture of the whole situation and eventually to make sense of it via a construction based on a series of past and present observations that were sufficiently factual for both protagonists that they could be verified.

André Green's account of the analytic situation with his patient Gabriel is a particularly interesting one for our framework. On the one hand, as Green (2000) himself wrote about, he generally sets up the analytic situation to be able "to hear the statements the patient makes and their meaning *outside the framework of the logical connections* associated with secondary *process*" (p. 441; our emphasis). He also believes that (unconscious) meaning will emerge out of dispersion—that is, from being struck by words in the patient's discourse that are defensively dispersed around and loosely connected (via affect) to the (frightening and hidden) ideas that are not themselves accessible. In Gabriel's case some words and images ("the beached whale," "jump out of the bed," "without legs or arms," etc.) emerged into Green's mind, due to his particular quality of attention rather like that of Louise (In a Hole) from our group of analysts, as having dispersed meaning. It allowed Green (again, rather like Louise) gradually to understand his subjective sense of fog as important so that he could transform it into the realization that there on his couch Gabriel was not so much resistant as literally overwhelmed by associations and sensations.

How does this suggest Green supposes the analytic situation? In one way, as for Louise (In a Hole), dramatic monologue is the appropriate metaphor—defined as a situation in which the inaccessible script (pushing for actualization) reveals affective conflicts recognized in the unconscious mind of the analyst, following the idea of the analyst's unconscious receptivity to broken links of meaning (above, pp. 117-19). Certainly, Green supposes Gabriel to be compelled, as he associates, to reference memories and frightening affective conflicts "not accessible" by means other than psychoanalysis. At the same time Green (1999) also wrote, "I hear the analysand's communication from two points of view at once. . . . [O]n the one hand, I try to perceive the internal conflicts that inhabit it and, on the other, I consider it from the point of view of something addressed, implicitly or explicitly, to me" (p. 278). This means that although he uses his unconscious receptivity and how he was struck by words and images to infer the unconscious script, Green's suppositions about the analytic situation are clearly described by the theater metaphor, in which he attends to the unconscious imagos in which his patient is casting him as a person. Recall his interpretation to his then silent patient: "You seem to feel my silence not as if I was listening, not only as if I was not interested, but *as if I took pleasure* to let you down alone and not to give you any help."[4] It was after Gabriel's associations had become even more stuck and he had betrayed still more anxiety about being with his analyst in the room, all of which they both tolerated, that Green became able to construct a picture of Gabriel's situation with his analyst and convey it to him. Gabriel feels

---

4. See Box 1.5 in Chapter 1.

with Green, he suggested, like he had when he was with a frightened mother as a very frightened and helpless little boy.

Gabriel's analysis was long. It is obvious, although not reported directly by him, that Green's stance must have required very palpable internal emotional (counter-transference) work to allow him to stay in a third position between both empathetically observing his and his patient's experience and looking at them together. It was exemplified by the way he kept the setting intact when Gabriel asked for relief and wanted to come off the couch. We do not know whether at any stage Green lost his composure or engaged in enactment. We cannot say, therefore, whether what we think of as his theater view also extended to immersive theater.

Donnel Stern and Philip Bromberg's suppositions about the analytic situation must be inferred from case reports that are rather different from those discussed so far. We included both analysts because they are two significant representatives of an emerging and influential cluster of psychoanalysts in North America, who advocate focus on the relationship between the two protagonists in the analytic couple and rather explicitly reject analysts' claims to be able to unravel their patients' unconscious fantasies.

In their accounts both Stern and Bromberg particularly emphasize the need for the analyst to find relational freedom—that is, to find a way of escaping the pattern of relationships the patient tends to set up with them and others. In a way, this sounds very like what the other five analysts are trying to do. But there is a difference. Eissler supposes it is done by showing patients the unconscious impulses and fantasies that entrap them in repetitive life patterns. Busch is similar but expects these patterns to emerge in relation to him as well. Kernberg, Bion, and Green are also similar, but they suppose the analytic situation to be the place to help their patients to become aware of their unconsciously buried beliefs or fantasies as expressed about their analysts as people. In this way the patients of these three analysts are enabled to understand how they repetitively create their experience and relationships in situ rather than in absentia. In contrast, from a theoretical position mindful of the pitfalls of neutrality claims when constructing someone else's unconscious, Stern and Bromberg try to remove entrapments by actively creating a new experience of relating. An interesting correlation is that many of the crucial developments that both describe in their case reports happen outside as well as inside the consulting room. Stern describes text and telephone efforts to help the patient try to stay in touch. Bromberg becomes hugely challenged by what the patient is doing outside with a rival therapist. Stern (2019) is explicit about how it is an experience of relational spontaneity that makes the difference when he writes, "The revelation of unconscious content is not really the point" (p. 337), and Bromberg (2006) argues similarly when he writes,

> The locus of therapeutic action is not in the material that is told to the analyst, as if it were a buried fantasy uncovered by piecing together the links between a patient's associations. Rather, therapeutic action is organized affectively, through the process of enactment between patient and analyst, where it then has a chance to be symbolized by the verbal meaning attached to the affective perception of what is taking place in the here and now. (p. 172)

Although some more relationally inclined analysts presented in North American CCM workshops, we did not find presenters implementing Stern's or Bromberg's approaches in any of our workshops. This means that what we can surmise about their suppositions are likely to be even more unreliable than those we have suggested for the other five. It looks, however, as though neither Stern nor Bromberg seems to make suppositions to which we could assign the metaphors theater or dramatic monologue—the former refers to the supposition that the sessions express unconscious beliefs or fantasies about the analyst and the latter to the supposition that the patient's association expresses unconscious beliefs or fantasies more generally. So, could they be characterized as typical of those supposing immersive theater? The emphasis on "here and now" "interaction" and mutual relationship at first sight may suggest that this metaphor is appropriate. But the core of the metaphor "immersive theater," like the core of the words "transference" and "countertransference," as we use them, is that they are based on unconscious beliefs about the person of the other, not just interaction. With suppositions we characterize as immersive, an analyst supposes that his or her unconscious beliefs cast the patient so as to influence the sessions in ways that are "inaccessible" to the analyst, unless the analyst gets a hint of what is going on and can then find a way to recognize how his or her beliefs and their enactments are at work—as for example Bion did in his excerpt or Robert (Spicy Food) did in our workshops. Therefore, insofar as beliefs and motivations inaccessible to patients or analysts seem not to be regular constituents of the analytic situation supposed in Bromberg's and Stern's work, although there are sometimes disclosures and admission of assumptions, the immersive metaphor is not a good description of their thinking.

Could Stern's and Bromberg's suppositions, therefore, best be described by the cinema metaphor—the only one of the four remaining?

Analysts we characterize as making cinema suppositions listen to reports of events and responses to them, often with historic and cultural referents, and talk to the patient about them—as Lesley (The Lingering Smell) talked to Lucie about her relationships. Sometimes the views the analysts or their patients have on the subjects (e.g., Eissler's view about his patient's relationship to his wife) become sources of discord, almost as if we could say they are being discussed by two emotionally and personally invested and engaged film critics, debating the movie they are watching. The issue that distinguished cinema from the two theater models is whether or not the analyst explores how the patient may be unconsciously casting the analyst—for example, as hostile, weak, frightened, or dumb—or how the analyst may be unconsciously casting the patient. In this connection recall that Stern, whose patient did not manage to come for long periods, took his patient's word that he wanted to come "really" and left aside the question of whether he might have unconscious anxieties about Stern. And Bromberg, although feeling "on the ropes," did not consider any deeper accusations about himself in Alec's complaint about "slow progress," such as that Alec was reacting to him as a person who "didn't get it." Like Stern, Bromberg's reaction was to be open and tolerant at all costs. He asked and accepted conscious reasons and, like Stern, hung in with significant bravery. Therefore, although it is debatable, and despite the great amount of talk about their relationships within their accounts of the sessions, we think both analysts are best characterized as supposing they are in the cinema, even if not canonically so. This is because we can detect no sign that they are attentive to how they might be unconsciously "cast" by their patients or how they might have been unconsciously casting them. They took what their patients said at face value and treated the analytic situation as an opportunity to comment or prompt elaborations, mostly on general characteristics of their relationships inside and outside the session.

BOX 8.1. TWO QUESTIONS TO TEST HOW AN ANALYST IS USING THE ANALYTIC SITUATION IN A SPECIFIC SESSION

1. *When:* When my patient was talking to me, was I supposing she was conveying the emotional situation *believed to exist between us* (as unconsciously configured in her mind so that it was me *as a person* she had cast as seductive, cruel, fragile, empty, etc.), or was I rather supposing that she was conveying *the situation more generally between herself and others* (as unconsciously configured in her mind as seductive, cruel, fragile, empty, etc.)?
2. *Participation:* If talking about the situation between us or with others, have I wondered whether in some way what I take to be my patient's picture (whether of me or others) is being cast by me? How?

However, rather than trying to resolve how best to characterize these two analysts on the basis of very limited data, we think it is more useful to specify the questions to ask. Box 8.1 suggests two questions to pursue with Stern or Bromberg. More generally, we think the questions might be asked regularly by any analyst about the suppositions they have been making about the analytic situation in any session.

It seems likely that understanding why these questions are formulated in the way they are and asking them rigorously, regularly, and frequently is more important than any answers that may temporarily show up.

UNCONSCIOUS INFERENCE: SOURCES AND PROCEDURES

Shifting to Chapter 4, we moved from the suppositions psychoanalysts make about the analytic situation to look in more detail at processes of psychoanalytic inference. What suppositions do psychoanalysts make about necessary procedures and how to identify the unconscious meaning of what they hear and experience in sessions? How from the raw material of a session do unconscious scripts, beliefs, impulses, or fixed patterns of behavior that are influencing their patients, whether in their sessions or outside in their lived lives, or both, emerge into the analyst's mind?

We begin by exploring four examples of psychoanalytic inference from the workshops. Comparing them, we found they drew on three different sources to draw inferences, as represented in Figure 4.1 (p. 94):

1. Content in their patients' associations that they treated as expressing hidden beliefs, impulses, or fixed patterns of behavior, which the special features of a psychoanalytic session made accessible
2. Content in their own thoughts and feelings in sessions that caught their attention and was treated as relevant information
3. Reflections from a third position toward what was going on, becoming curious about possible relationships between (1) and (2) to enable them sometimes to transform meaning reflexively to arrive at new inferences

Each source reflects the outcome of the analyst's mental processing—or they would not be registered at all. But the first two represent sources of near-raw experience. The last one represents more developed mental processing—potentially transformative or reflective processes *deepening* understanding.

We described how Jana, Lesley, Gilbert, and Louise set about this task. First, we noticed that all four analysts relied on their subjective intuition to infer—that is, to guess—what they thought was significant. Second, we noticed several differences in the suppositions that seemed to underlie how they proceeded. In particular, there seemed to be differences in whether these psychoanalysts seemed to structure their sessions around the complementary setup of the "fundamental rule" of free association for the patient and some kind of evenly hovering attention for the analyst and also how far, from time to time, they seemed sometimes to "turn round" on their own participation—so that they treated what was going on in their minds, as well as their patients', as a matter of additional investigation.

A crude indicator of structure was whether their sessions looked like ordinary conversations or, rather, contained pauses, more extended silences, and so forth. A crude indicator of turning around on him- or herself was whether from time to time the analyst reported observations as to how what was going on between the two protagonists or in the analyst's mind seemed to require second thought, as if the analyst could imaginatively leave his or her seat and triangulate.

Jana (Put on the Spot), for example, certainly did not set up the investigation as an ordinary conversation. She treated her patient's words as free associations, was reflective about herself and her reactions, struggled with trying to work out the meanings of the responses that had fallen into her mind, sometimes kept silent rather than responding, and made comments that in a normal conversation would be non sequiturs. Her account also illustrates a set of complex procedures she used to set about investigating hidden meanings beneath the surface of her patient's conscious words.

Lesley's (The Lingering Smell) approach, on the other hand, seemed very different to Jana's. What she reported looked like a "conversation." The sessions involved a back-and-forth very like a chat between friends in which the meanings of Lucie's utterances and reported impulses are apparently given much the same meaning by Lesley as by Lucie. They talked together, and Lesley took up what Lucie had said rather rapidly and at much the same level. Lesley didn't experience observations or associations falling into her mind or question them. In fact, she described her approach to the session as "talk oriented." This related to an idea she had that she needed to compensate for what she thought had been an absence of talking together in Lucie's childhood. Lesley's account illustrates the idea that what was not accessible, except through psychoanalysis, to Lucie were not Lucie's hidden beliefs but rather her feelings. It was her feelings that were driving her to passivity in her relationships, including her inhibition with her analyst.

Gilbert's (Fear of Violence) approach had some similarities to Jana's. He seems to have set up a situation of free association governed by the fundamental rule (see what falls into your mind) in sessions, and he was mindful of underlying meaning, often responding to Claudia with efforts to draw out themes he thought were hidden behind her free associations—particularly her dreams. A particularly interesting feature of each session was that things did "fall into Gilbert's mind" and then get acted on. On several occasions he reported he had said things in a rather abrupt fashion—surprising himself, as he put it, by comments such as "Like mafia?" or "So you think you're seeing too much, you might want to see less." Such comments had clearly emerged spontaneously from within Gilbert's mind, unbidden so to speak, without forethought and apparently at moments when the situation had become quite emotionally tense.[5] It seems these various sudden interventions captured an aspect of Gilbert's frame of attention and his willingness to allow himself an intuitive and spontaneous modus operandi when listening to Claudia and trying to draw inferences about her hidden beliefs, impulses, and behavior. Gilbert knew such remarks contained information. But at the same time, Gilbert had not, before the workshop, supposed that it would be useful to "turn round" his experience of participation and to use it to make new inferences about Claudia. In part his suppositions about the analytic situation, best described by the cinema metaphor, precluded questions about his own "in session" contribution.

In this respect Louise's (In a Hole) approach was very different from that of Gilbert. She had set up a procedure of free association governed by the fundamental rule for her patient and evenly hovering attention for herself, and she was in no hurry to speak as things came into her mind as well as into Georgina's. She attended to Georgina's words but within an attentional stance designed also to notice and then consider her own imagination, reverie, and bodily feelings prompted by what she heard. These all became part of the "information" from which to infer unconscious meaning from the patient's associations. Aided by her theater-metaphor-type supposition, she also "turned round" her thinking and responses on herself, in the sense of (metaphorically) taking up another chair in the room and observing things going on in her mind.[6] The interpretation Louise arrives at in one session—"Perhaps I am the pot . . . Yes, the pot which might contain good things to eat, but instead is a hole, sucking you down to the bottom of the stream where you might go round and round until you drown"—is an inference about Georgina's unconscious experience of her analyst in the session, with multiple meanings, derived from multiple sources, including Louise's examination of her own associations. It opens a road to a series of unconscious beliefs.

---

5. See Chapter 7 for more about his phenomenon.
6. Our metaphor.

UNCONSCIOUS INFERENCE: THE SEVEN PSYCHOANALYSTS

Turning now to the seven psychoanalysts we introduced in Chapter 1 (and allowing that their accounts provide potentially much less evidence than the details presented in the workshops we organized), we can note that they all also used their clinical intuition and internalized theory to draw inferences about their patients. But the way they structured how they did this varied. The first five analysts appear to have treated what their patients told them as associations to an unconscious script. Eissler specifically cites his use of the fundamental rule. Busch and Green suppose that underlying associations to an unconscious script push to the surface. They are attentive to signs of discomfort (within their patients' discourse suggesting its presence). Kernberg and Bion do clearly suppose that the broad range of what is going on in sessions, including their own responses, is potentially enacting an unconscious script driving the patient's experience. As before, Stern and Bromberg are harder for us to place. They don't seem to use the fundamental rule.[7] They are focused on interacting relationships and recurrent experiences rather than on any underlying beliefs perhaps influencing their interpretation. Consequently, it is hard to know how they use the term "unconscious" in their practice. Meanwhile, their sessions look more like ordinary conversations than do those of the other five.

Turning to the nature of these analysts' attentional states toward their own responses, crudely, the accounts of Kernberg, Green, and Bion all give a strong impression that they observe their own thoughts and feelings. Stern ends up with a sense he has been too active to make a therapeutic relationship with Alan, and Bromberg recognizes that he has been too concerned to do "the right thing" to make one with Alec. Eissler and Busch, based on the evidence we have, seem to focus solely on their patient's words and observable discomfort and their inferred meaning.

Whereas it seems intrinsic to Kernberg and Bion to "turn around" on their own participation and to question it, treating what was going on in their minds, as well as their patient's, as a matter for investigation, this type of reflection seems to come late in the examples of Bromberg and Stern and then only because a crisis has emerged—implying neither "turns around" routinely to the extent that they wonder whether, unknowingly, they are being drawn into a way of responding via their unconscious casting of their patients (as perhaps was the case for Eissler). This stance seems likely to be a consequence of their reluctance to attribute unconscious beliefs to their own or their patient's relational experience.

Box 8.2 lists four key questions for every analyst to ask about how they draw inferences about unconscious meaning in every session. The questions aim to differentiate the types of working that surfaced in our workshops as well as in the work of the seven analysts. Taken together they should be useful as aids to clarifying the unconscious content a particular analyst is trying to infer in sessions and to help them reflect on how reliably they are doing it.

---

7. This has also been noted by Gabbard and Westen (2003): "From a relational perspective, for example, it is not clear why free association would be useful, since it can be a somewhat solipsistic enterprise, and certainly a socially peculiar form of interaction with a person with whom one hopes to develop a meaningful relationship" (p. 832).

BOX 8.2. FOUR QUESTIONS TO TEST SUPPOSITIONS ABOUT HOW AN ANALYST INFERS UNCONSCIOUS CONTENT

1. *Procedure:* Have I created a formal procedure to give my patients an opportunity to observe and recognize the thoughts and experiences that *fall into their minds* in their sessions, or am I setting up something more like an ordinary conversation?
2. *Targets of guessing:* Am I trying to "guess" (1) my patient's inaccessible feelings and impulses, or (2) her unconscious patterns of relational behavior, or (3) the underlying script of unconscious beliefs that create her experience?
3. *Attitude to own thoughts and feelings:* Do my guesses about the meaning of my patient's associations rely to a significant degree, as far as I am aware, on my feelings, responses, and thoughts?
4. *Reflective curiosity:* Have I created a reflective setup in my mind to observe and question how I am arriving at my guesses about my patient's associations and how I am using my own thoughts and feelings?

Question 1 invites every analyst to think about their procedure and specifically how far they are adopting something aligned to the formal procedure expressed via the fundamental rule that Freud devised (through which unconscious content is discerned by taking a passive rather than active stance) or alternatively setting up more of a "normal conversation." The distinctions and their implications were discussed in Chapter 4.

Question 2 invites every analyst to reflect on the source of their intuitive guesses and what they think they are trying to guess. As the days of simple formulas for unconscious inference based on symbols and so forth are long gone, we discussed in Chapter 4 and then again in Chapter 6 how intuition must rest on the analyst's personal investigative framework and, ultimately, some degree of unconscious-to-unconscious cognition with all its perils. As regards the content of guessing, analysts need to take an explicit position on whether they suppose that their patients and themselves are driven by an unconscious script and, if so, how they suppose it can be known. Do they think it is betrayed (*verraten*) via the presence of signs of discomfort during free association, if their procedure follows the fundamental rule, or if not, how? Linking to question 1, if other ways of guessing unconscious content are being used, each analyst might usefully think through how they think their inferential sequence works: What are the raw signs, and how are they transforming them?

The third question to be considered in Box 8.2 is suggested by the implications of the fact that psychoanalysts *must* guess. Not only, as just mentioned, must they necessarily make suppositions about what they are trying to guess, but also they must determine where their guesses come from and, therefore, how they might check their validity: Crucially, how does an analyst suppose that she guards against the kind of countertransference-dominated indoctrination and persuasion of her patient that caused Davies (2018) and others to describe "the analyst" in a traditional approach as an inherently "flawed instrument" (p. 654)?

Our reading of Freud's work is that he always had concerns about validity, which is why we think questions 3 and 4 are useful. In Chapter 4, we argued that, ultimately, because psychoanalytic inference requires "unconscious cognition," Freud had no choice but to come to the radical supposition that the analyst's unconscious is pivotal to infer the unconscious of the patient. The problem was that he then realized, as Davies and others quite reasonably suggest, that analytic inference *can*, therefore, be very wrongly motivated. Certainly, the implications of unconscious cognition bothered Freud. The subsequent institutional proposal that the solution was a thorough training analysis (i.e., in effect the obliteration of a trainee analyst's unconscious) had serious drawbacks. It created unrealistic expectations and hidden omnipotence and, according to Freud's own ideas, was theoretically incoherent. Clearly no training analysis *can* remove countertransference (i.e., unconscious and therefore potentially inaccessible reactions to patients), and the belief that it could would be misguided. The uncomfortable implication is that there must be a continuous possibility that the analyst's ideas about the patient's unconscious beliefs are an imposition by one person who is paid onto another who pays. Worse still, there is always a potential unconscious motivation for the former to dispose of unwanted beliefs and feelings onto the latter, causing more or less serious boundary issues. Any patient can suspect it.

To our way of thinking, the first step here, which is the purpose of question 4, is to recognize the potential problem. The question emphasizes the need to ask and to keep asking the question about where one's guesses are coming from, to keep questioning their validity on an ongoing basis, and to create a structured process to support these efforts. The ideal of analytic neutrality is not one to be assumed but one that should be actively aspired to and constantly checked.

In this way we are led to a core implication of our workshop findings, which is that intuitive assertions about the patient, especially if the analyst is unable to provide some kind of "audit" trail as to how the analyst supposes they got there, are fragile. They must remain the object of inquiry. In Chapter 4, we suggested that one answer to the skepticism Davies and others express (e.g., Greenberg, 2001) is to deploy the concepts of "selected fact" versus "overvalued idea," both of which, like the original concept put forward by Henri Poincaré, depend for their potential validity on their being situated within a very well-defined procedure—for Poincaré the discipline of mathematics; for Bion, Freud's procedure.

Some presenters in our workshops (elaborating on their inferential procedures drawing on the third inferential source mentioned above) presented more auditable ideas than others. For example, although the kind of detailed processes that the workshop group was able to identify supporting the intuitions arriving in the analyst's mind could be elaborated from what Louise (and to an extent Robert, Moira, Gabriella, Lucia, or Ben) presented, details were harder to discover from what Lesley and Gilbert (and also Britta, Andrew, James, Henry, and Cynthia) provided. In these latter instances the analysts had made intuitive interpretations based on guesses as to the meaning of material, but they provided little in their reports and responses that could be the basis for the kind of ex post facto account that emerged in the workshop to which Louise presented—or which we can also recognize, to an extent, in the accounts Busch, Kernberg, Bion, and Green gave us of their inferences, discussed in Chapter 1. It seems likely that insofar as analysts leave their processes implicit, at least in the long run, their inferences are more likely to be at risk of becoming captured by transference-countertransference interaction.

The further role of the third and fourth questions in Box 8.2 is to prompt thoughts about how the ways that psychoanalysts structure sessions (their procedure) may play a part in helping them to make their work more auditable to themselves—by considering their setup, their inferential procedures, and their validity. In the workshop groups the analytic intuitions some psychoanalysts offered in their presentations and responses were much easier to elaborate, understand, and make sense of in the workshops than were others. When, in addition to using something like Freud's procedural structure, they turned around on themselves reflexively using all three sources of data, they could make use of their observations—as, for example, Bion and Kernberg did in the Chapter 1 extracts and Robert did in our workshops. Similarly, Louise clearly supposed the fundamental rule of free association was desirable for Georgina and evenly hovering attention for herself. She then adopted the products of that structure to think and report. Things fell into her mind as she listened.

Of course, adopting the procedures of free association and evenly hovering attention cannot on their own guarantee reliable unconscious inference. But it seems they may create a framework, as Freud had attempted to do in order to understand his own dreams. From this standpoint, the advice to free associate is not so much an injunction not to select or to tell the truth or even to feel free but guidance to adopt a passive attitude to one's thoughts, to let them occur, *to note discomfort*, and, in both analyst's and patient's cases, to create scope for second thoughts—that is, to hesitate before imposing meaning. Recall Ella Sharpe's (1930) suggestions about how a trainee analyst should set up psychoanalytic sessions. She includes an effort to explain to patients what to expect:

> One directs the patient to lie on the couch at once, reiterating again that the position gives greater ease and freedom to the patient, and to the analyst too, explaining that the more freely the analyst can listen, the more easily analysis can proceed. I always then ask what the patient desires analysis to do for him, to formulate his wishes as well as he can. When he has done that, I always say that I cannot fulfil his wishes. *This is essential, because it is true.* I cannot do these things for him. His goal can be reached by a strong determination to co-operate in following what is required of him, and this I tell him forthwith. I then tell him what is required, and I assure him that he will find that *the values he sets upon his words and ideas will not be the values that they will ultimately reveal.* What he judges as silly, unworthy, irrelevant, will not be a judgement that holds valid in such *an investigation* as we are undertaking. We have shifted out of the conventional, logical, moral world into a world of psychological meanings and his task is to say what comes to his mind, and to be assured that as he fulfils this request, so the analyst will keep faith with him. (Sharpe, 1930, pp. 269–70; our emphasis)

Note Sharpe's warning to the patient that his wishes cannot be fulfilled and her use of the word "investigation." For her, psychoanalytic procedure is an undertaking shifted outside "the conventional, logical, moral world" of ordinary human interchange "into a world of psychological meanings" in which the values the patient "sets upon his words and ideas will not be the values that they will ultimately reveal." What a patient does think of or is worried about is not the unconscious belief they seek to keep inaccessible. This is why resistance, the discomfort around associations (see glossary), but not necessarily the thoughts themselves are the clue to unconscious belief, as the extract from Green's analysis of Gabriel in Chapter 1 describes so vividly.

Processes such as Louise described to arrive at her inferences in her presentation (like those of Robert, Moira, Gabriella, Lucia, or Ben) involved observations of different types at different levels that followed from her setup (what Georgina said came to mind; what Louise found falling into her mind, her reflection on it). Her descriptions made the process of inference and its evidential basis quite easy to follow, compared to the difficulty groups experienced when they attempted the same task with what Lesley or Gilbert described. These analysts had intuitive and interesting but nonetheless quite opaque suppositions about their role and that of their patients in the sessions, and we noted above how their sessions seemed to have more of an ordinary conversational quality than the setups described by Freud or Sharpe or in the first five of the excerpts in Chapter 1. A corollary was that it appeared they had little room to observe their patients' words (which were quite often quickly replied to at the same level) and the analysts' own thoughts or feelings about the patients' words—limiting their inferential sources.

Gilbert and Lesley deployed sensitive intuitions (like Britta, Andrew, James, Henry, and Cynthia) but did not offer in their reports or in their responses in workshops any sense of a dialogue between what they had heard said, how they reacted internally, and how they reflected. Consequently, the kind of intelligible ex post facto account that could be constructed with Louise by the group in the workshop to which Louise presented or which we can also recognize, to an extent, in the accounts Busch, Kernberg, Bion, and Green gave us of their inferences, discussed in Chapter 1, was absent. We think a conclusion to draw is that when analysts establish formal roles for themselves and their patients (e.g., the fundamental rule and evenly hovering attention), it creates a richer interaction of levels of reasoning so that intuitions are more legible and explicit rather than implicit for the analysts themselves.

Given these observations, perhaps the main conclusion we are reaching is that current approaches to unconscious inference are marked by an interesting division between those analysts who suppose it is crucial to create a formal setting of free association (for the patient) and evenly hovering attention (for themselves) as distinct but complementary roles and those analysts who adopt a more conversational or even "democratic" approach. The latter often seems to be accompanied by a lot of activity.

For those who adopt the formal setting, the crucial point is that both roles include a vital passive aspect. The task for both patient and analyst is to create room for passive observation rather than active thinking, reflecting, persuading, or explaining. In this way, as in Freud's self-analysis or in Bion's description of his analysis of Brian, "facts" can be accumulated (such as the things that came up in Freud's mind when he wrote down associations to his dreams) and then, in a second step, selectively arranged to give guidance about possible meaning.

Our readers will probably not be surprised that a further clear conclusion is that the way the analysts in our workshops drew inferences and what they drew inferences about were strongly dependent on the way they conceived of the analytic situation. Conversely, the way they supposed the analytic situation also governed what they listened to. For instance, going back to Lesley and Lucie, we might say that two things were happening in the sessions that Lesley described. On a manifest level, it seems that Lesley inferred inner conflicts between drive impulses and the defenses against them and tried to make them clear to the patient to try to support and strengthen her capacity to manage them. But in so doing what may have been concealed from both participants was how their relation might quite unintentionally repeat a far more unconscious pattern of the patient, that of being exposed to a mother who does not understand, who pursues her own emotional goals, and who is only partially capable of picking up her baby's expressions. Very likely the internalization of such an experience has led to a threatening unconscious expectation or fantasy that needs to be warded off precisely by a fantasized and actually sometimes realized enmeshment with an ideal object, an unseparated union that Lucie tries to re-create in the sessions against all the effort of Lesley to avoid it. Lesley's cinema-type supposition that the transference is yet to come into the analysis, based on her expectation that it needs to be verbalized directly, was likely to blind her to such possibilities.

In such cases a model based on the immersive metaphor clearly carries some safeguards when considering countertransference imposition, and models based on the dramatic monologue or cinema metaphors probably reduce sensitivity to possible enactment. Those who use an approach best described by these metaphors may find it harder to answer question 4.

Although we have not been able to explore it in detail, a similar relationship may exist between suppositions made about unconscious inference and those made about unconscious repetition (Chapter 5).

UNCONSCIOUS REPETITION:
LACK OF CAPACITY OR REFUSAL OF AMBIVALENCE

Chapter 5 moved us on to consider the suppositions that contemporary analysts make about the troubles their patients have and in what way they are, or are not, the product of unconscious repetition of their subjective responses to experiences in infancy and childhood.

On this issue, very early on in our workshops, it became clear that there were marked differences of opinion among presenters and among workshop group members. Essentially, after many debates and direct efforts to move away from it, a main line of cleavage kept recurring between two positions about what troubles patients really seemed to suffer and how they came about.

One view was essentially that patients suffered from unavoidable but inaccessible (by other means than psychoanalysis) conflicts. Specifically, what seemed to matter were *feelings of ambivalence*, conflicts in what they felt about mothers, fathers, siblings, partners, or eventually their psychoanalysts. These ambivalent feelings had persisted from their early experience into their present, and patients had so far been unable to resolve them sufficiently in new ways—in part because they were so frightened of one or the other (or both) of their loving or hating feelings that they were often not aware of them. They were dominated by ambivalence but did not know it. Freud's explanation of melancholia as hatred turned inside, so as not to be experienced as directed to loved persons outside (Freud, 1917b), is his classic example, as are his various descriptions of the Oedipus complex once he had completed his own self-analysis. So, in shorthand, this set of assumptions about what is repetitively causing trouble rests on the idea that human subjects have to resolve conflicting feelings about being the same as or different from the opposite sex, feeling love or hate for each parent, feeling generational rivalry and discomforts about different capacities and endowments, and feeling excluded from the parental or other couples. As with the universals of the classical Oedipal conflict, such conflicts are endemic and have to be managed. This position seems broadly to have been taken by Louise (In a Hole), Robert (Spicy Food), and Moira (Hard to Win), discussed in Chapter 3, as well as by others who presented in the workshops like Ben (Ending) or Lucia (Betrayal).

Whatever their differences, Eissler, Busch, Kernberg, Bion, and Green also quite clearly took this first position. Whatever exact language they use, they suppose their patients to be struggling with unconscious ambivalence toward their primary objects rooted in their attempts to resolve their Oedipal conflicts. Eissler, for example, supposed his patient's relationships to be disturbed by his hidden sadism toward his wife, creating guilt and anxiety that he constantly justified and prevented from being worked through by a refusal to give up his satisfaction and his masochistic excitement about being treated unfairly. Busch and Kernberg supposed their patient's marriages and careers, as well as their experiences in the analytic situation, to be disturbed by complex unconscious ideas about their fathers' (and so analysts') sexuality and the desires, anxieties, and defenses they induced. Bion's suppositions led him to discover his patient to be suffering from an (inaccessible) belief that he had a poisonous (contaminating) family inside him linked to a wide range of primitive infantile sexual anxieties believed to be enacted in other relationships. He feared that if he were to have any live relationship with his analyst, because both were sexually "experienced," it would inevitably end in mutual jealousy and hatred. The patient therefore tried to stabilize the analytic relationship into a soporific impasse. So, by a different route, Bion's patient, like the previous three, is supposed by Bion to be suffering the consequences of ambivalent reactions to the Oedipal situation. Finally, Green's suppositions about what is wrong with his patient and the repetitions that maintain his difficulties over his life and a long analysis are similar. His patient had a very difficult and traumatic history (absent father, sleeping in his psychotic mother's bed, etc.). Green discovered in the investigation that Gabriel feared the implications of his own, as it turned out, (inaccessible and) ambivalent sexual thoughts so much that his associations for a long time seemed blocked and choked off (recalling the exact picture other analysts paint to illustrate deficits in representative capacity and feelings). Like Bion's patient, he could not bear to think about or be with the analyst that this set of ideas "created." In summary, although at least four of the five patients appeared to have suffered very difficult experiences earlier in life and appeared to have very depleted capacity that might have looked like deficit, their analysts supposed the problem to be one created by ambivalent expectations about the situations in which they found themselves and their horror of experiencing them.

A second view was to emphasize a much more general problem of a lack of capacity, particularly to experience and label or represent *all feelings rather generally*, especially "negative" feelings. The clear supposition among those holding this view is that patients suffer in this way due to developmental arrest, environmental failure, or trauma, which has made them unable to experience conflicts in sessions (or elsewhere). In this view there is a deficit in mental capacity that must somehow be overcome by providing enough of what was missing. It usually has the implication that what the patient needed was some kind of more nurturing relationship or alliance. In effect this position coincides closely with what we could discover about the suppositions held by Lesley (The Lingering Smell), Britta (Reluctance to Commit), Andrew (A Story of Ruin), and James (Despair and Resistance). It also seems to fit with the view evident in Stern's and Bromberg's vignettes. Both their patients had serious deficits in relating. For these analysts, this difficulty seems to be associated with what they saw as developmental deficits limiting their patients' capacity to possess beliefs. We reviewed some of the theoretical findings for aspects of this view and the supporting clinical material in Chapter 5—discussing Heinz Kohut's two analyses of Mr. Z and James Fosshage's case, P, contrasting them with Green's Gabriel.

Examining the psychoanalytic writing on this topic since Freud's death, particularly in the North American neoclassical tradition, suggests that for some the shift to supposing that patients needed support and nurture began with the idea that some patients were so stuck in their mental functioning that their capacity for speaking their own thoughts, equilibrating their feelings, and managing deprivation was too limited to allow them to develop transference (perhaps meaning sufficient trust in the analyst and the process) to participate in the standard psychoanalytic situation with its various requirements, such as free association in words, tolerance of the analyst's silence, and an interpretive approach.

Based on the literature as well as what we found, it does seem that the tendency to cleavage that we have identified between the two groups of analysts who presented in our groups is an important one. It leads on to the suggestion that two important theoretical issues need to be explored that really divide how psychoanalysts work and why. One is whether analysts suppose patients to suffer from a general lack of access to feelings rather than from a specific lack of access to feelings of love and hate for the same persons (i.e., from ambivalent feelings). The other has to do with whether the feelings causing their difficulties are understood to be caused by inaccessible unconscious beliefs that then provide a template X to give meaning to the situations they are in or, on the contrary, whether repetitions are somehow caused via automatic responses to life situations that operate beyond belief.

The two questions we have formulated for every analyst in Box 8.3 are designed to help tease out to which of these suppositions they are mainly inclined and then to think through the possible implications. The first question addresses whether the problem is supposed to be at the level of a general problem with feelings or a specific problem with ambivalent or mixed feelings. The second question addresses whether or not unbearable or avoided feelings are the product of unconscious beliefs provoked in situations and relationships (i.e., by the template X introduced in Chapter 3). There seems to be the potential in this respect for two positions among those who do not identify repetitive unconscious beliefs as of significance in sessions—one held by analysts like Kohut, Fosshage, Stern, and Bromberg (who consider unconscious beliefs to be unknowable) and another held by analysts who believe them relevant but not yet expressible. In the latter case patients suffer developmental deficits and/or difficulties derived from environmental insufficiencies, such as an absence of maternal containment. Careful prior work may be needed to prepare for an analysis.

BOX 8.3. TWO QUESTIONS TO TEST SUPPOSITIONS ABOUT HOW AN ANALYST SUPPOSES UNCONSCIOUS REPETITION TO BE THE CAUSE OF A PATIENT'S PROBLEMS

1. *Specific or general:* Do I suppose my patient's repetitive troubles in the present derive from a deficit in her capacity to tolerate and access inaccessible impulses and *feelings generally* or a difficulty integrating *specific mixed feelings,* such as love and hate?
2. *Unconscious beliefs or not:* Do I suppose that my patients are *trapped within their **unconscious** beliefs,* so that I know that even if they are hard to detect now, *it must eventually be possible to capture them* so that they become thinkable by us?

We will return to the question of unconscious beliefs and how they become available in the next chapter. Meanwhile, note that those analysts who focus on unconscious beliefs as the cause of their patient's repetitive problems, like the first five analysts in Chapter 1 and others like Louise (In a Hole), Robert (Spicy Food), Moira (Hard to Win), Jana (Put on the Spot), and Ben (Ending) from the workshops, all supposed that the unconscious scripts that create their patient's experience and difficulties are made up of beliefs connected to terrifying feelings they were trying to defend against. Terror in all cases derived from conflicts between loving and hating feelings provoked by unrecognized ambivalence that characterized their relationship with their analyst as well as with others. These analysts supposed relationships are necessarily ambivalent (satisfying and frustrating) and found these beliefs being enacted in sessions and experienced in relation to the satisfactions and frustrations induced by being with the analyst as a person. Busch's, Kernberg's, Bion's, and Green's patients also all harbored unconscious beliefs (about sexual rivalries and fears stirred up in their analyses) that they regarded as facts but could not bear to acknowledge. These caused them to live in constant fear and to take defensive measures. The point is that when unconscious beliefs become elaborated, they can be considered and then become potentially less frightening.

The supposition underlying those who see repetitive problems as a more general problem of feeling is that the process just outlined can only begin when feelings themselves are tolerated. We return to this issue in the last chapter.

MAKING A DIFFERENCE: INVESTIGATING AND INTERPRETING UNCONSCIOUS BELIEFS, BUILDING A RELATIONSHIP, OR ENABLING THINKING?

A common proposition of much psychoanalytic understanding and treatment has been that patients are driven to unconscious solutions to current problems based on responses formed as they grappled with experience in infancy and childhood—whether responses take the form of repetitive beliefs and fantasies or more automated actions.[8] Patients therefore may somehow identify their current situations as if, like Bion's patient, Brian, they are known old situations (in his case of Oedipal rivalry and uncontainable hatred) and apply the old solutions that they feel have worked before (in Brian's case, keeping everything calm and not much happening), or they may, like Mr. Z in Kohut's (1979) presentation, repetitively experience their adult lives as repeating the deprivations they suffered as children.

A second psychoanalytic proposition implied in both Bion's and Kohut's cases is that the process of investigation both identifies a set of experienced "facts" and can be furthered so that these facts become recognized either as regular responses or as the outcome of repetitive beliefs, either of which require curiosity. If responses and/or beliefs are explored, they can then be found not to be context appropriate so that they can be given up. Kohut argued Mr. Z's predicament altered once he was provided with the empathic support he had always lacked, and Bion argued that Brian, once he understood the beliefs he was dominated by, could reassess his situation.

Psychoanalysis, in short, works by exposing unconscious beliefs or repetitive responses, then either allowing beliefs to be explored and renounced or repetitions to be modified by providing new experience and growth.

HOW THE SEVEN PSYCHOANALYSTS IN CHAPTER 1 MADE A DIFFERENCE

As just introduced, in Bion's case working with Brian, the investigation took the form of experiencing and interpreting the operation of Brian's underlying unconscious beliefs, as he experienced them and acted on them in his sessions with Bion as a person. Their consequences gradually emerged in the form of a gently induced soporific impasse whose nature could then be inferred. In Eissler's case, it was through recognition

---

8. The term "response" is used here to preserve the possibility held by some analysts that some unconscious repetitive patterns may be based on some form of automatic rather than belief-generated process, a view that some cognitive psychologists argue (e.g., Chater, 2018) but a strange one for psychoanalysts. We take it up again in the last chapter.

of patterns of belief and impulses in the patient's life, drawing them to his attention, trying to help him to understand his hidden motivations for their persistence, and trying to help him gradually to understand both the gratifications that he had to give up and the potential benefits of a different way of living. Eissler reports the latter proved impossible, which means either that Eissler was correct but couldn't find a technique to help his patient accept it or perhaps that his understanding was wrong.

In Kernberg's and Busch's cases, as in Bion's, the investigations led to understanding of complex Oedipal rivalries and anxieties unconsciously experienced in sessions with their analysts as male persons. Both Jim and Karl eventually understood, and that improved their relationships with their wives. In Green's case, the investigation enabled him gradually to induce Gabriel to become aware of his unconscious terrors based on his childhood traumas and so enabled him first to recover his capacity to think and make connections and second to be able to distance himself from the phobias holding back his sexuality and confidence.

In summary, in all five cases, in one way or another, an investigation took place in which the analysts' gradual interpretation of the patients' words led to an understanding of the patient's otherwise inaccessible beliefs, to their interpretation to the patients, and to new possibilities. In the process the patients' unconscious image of the analysts and their intentions also changed. Within the cases presented at our workshops and discussed in Chapter 6, the one conducted by Ben (Ending) also has roughly the features of understanding and interpretation of inaccessible beliefs played out in relation to their analysts, as do Louise's (In a Hole), Robert's (Spicy Food), Lucia's (Betrayal), and Moira's (Hard to Win), to choose the clearest examples.

However, once more, Stern's and Bromberg's cases in Chapter 1 appear different. Both report that they make no attempt to guess their patient's unconscious beliefs. Rather, they seek to investigate in their sessions with Alan and Alec something that might be described as a repetitive form of nonproductive, nonauthentic relationship, rooted in their earlier experience. Their idea is that their patients need to be able to have a new form of relationship different from those they have had in their lives to date. They need a sense of their agency and authenticity in a different relationship, which their analysts try to create. Structurally, therefore, although the pathways to the position may have been different, there is similarity in these approaches with the arguments Fosshage and Kohut put forward about psychoanalysis as "self" enabling, discussed above and in Chapter 5.

We also used Chapter 6 to introduce in detail the investigations Cynthia (Self-Esteem under Zero), Ben (Ending), and Patricia (Tragedy) conducted with Cecilia, Melanie, and Paula. Whereas Ben's work with Melanie could broadly be described within the frameworks of the investigations conducted by Busch, Kernberg, Bion, and Green, Cynthia's and Patricia's seemed rather different. Patricia's patient Paula was very disturbed and apparently had great difficulty accepting the standard analytic setting—exactly the issue in contention since Freud's death and the so-called widening of scope, which we quoted Anna Freud discussing in Chapter 5, that has taken place since.

Patricia described how she had been forced to modify the way she usually sets up psychoanalysis quite dramatically to accommodate pressure from Paula in the form of demands, phone calls, telephone sessions, withholding payment, and so forth. She felt the analysis to be constantly under threat and that if she did not give in and accept the situation, her patient might commit suicide. Patricia suffered. So, obviously, did Paula. Like Bromberg and Stern, Patricia patiently tolerated the most intense stress through the relationship Paula had with her. But also like them, she did not consider the investigation to be driven by Paula's unconscious beliefs about the situation between them.

Because seeking to investigate and reveal Paula's unconscious relationship with Patricia and how it might have become captured and trapped by Paula's beliefs about Patricia (along the lines Busch, Kernberg, Bion, Green, Louise, or Ben might have attempted) was outside the scope of her suppositions for the analytic situation, and because of her assumptions about deficit, Patricia supposed that to further the analysis she needed to find ways she could be experienced by Paula as different.

In the session described (Boxes 6.3 and 6.4), Patricia finds herself closing a door (in case her patient might use it) and then dealing with an alarmed Paula who wonders why Patricia did that and keeps returning to it—along with ideas that Patricia looks different and what the reasons might be, which she then declines to reveal. Patricia's report and the workshop discussion made clear that insofar as it is possible to tell, in Patricia's mind there seems to have been no concept of a drama being played out live in the session (supposed as theater) between them both. But clearly the sessions could be seen in that way, with Patricia or others "cast" in roles by Paula's unconscious beliefs. Beyond that, in sessions people in Paula's past were described and understood as abusers (as they undoubtedly were), and Paula was understood as an abused baby, as she undoubtedly was. But Patricia, recalling Freud with Ernst, although hinting at related ideas that she was worried that she had perhaps caused her patient's state by letting her down by taking a holiday, could not imagine herself as being cast in such ways—perhaps as a failure who couldn't cope or as a jailer or an abuser locking doors out of fear of her patient or from a wish to trap her and harm her. Heroically, whatever the difficulties thrown at her, Patricia tried to provide a new type of understanding relationship and to provide Paula with a new narrative of herself.

Making the suggestions in the last paragraph, we go slightly beyond the brief we have given ourselves in earlier chapters because, although Patricia's work with Paula is an extreme example, it offers a convenient opportunity to set out and question one of the major findings from the workshops—namely, that a significant number of the psychoanalysts who presented adopted this kind of building a better relationship approach—which is very different from the ways Eissler, Busch, Bion, Kernberg, and Green or Louise, Ben, Moira, Robert, Lucia, and Jana worked, among other examples.

In Chapter 6 we described the ways analysts like Patricia and Cynthia (whose patient Cecilia she thought had been damaged by an unresponsive mother, an intrusive father, and an unresolved family history so that she was still captured by Oedipal rivalries and anxieties) used their investigations to try to provide a better relationship for their patients. We also described how, in North American literature on psychoanalysis, building on earlier ideas by Hans Loewald and others, the "actual" relationship (i.e., the relationship in sessions with the analyst unencumbered by unconscious beliefs about the person of the analyst) gradually became a significant adjunct to psychoanalysis as a "distinct and unique therapeutic method" providing insight. Not long after, however, trying to provide insight was being discussed as one only of several alternative therapeutic modalities.[9]

Finally, we have noted how our experimental analysis of the moderators' reports in our own workshops shows the same movement. When invited to grapple with the mechanics of how presenters thought psychoanalysis worked and how they thought they furthered the process to make it happen, many of the practicing analysts in our groups introduced and debated ideas that seemed to come naturally to them that seemed to forego investigation in favor of action. For example, we reported that workshop group members were most likely to mention the following three factors as what they thought might be making a transformative therapeutic difference in the cases they were discussing (in this order of frequency): (1) analyst's use of the analytical relationship, (2) the analyst's attitudes and mind-set toward patients, and (3) analyst trying to be a new object or to enable new experience (Chapter 6, p. 171).

Findings such as these, as indeed the excerpts from Stern and Bromberg and the account of Patricia's heroic work show, appear to take psychoanalysis a long way from Freud's *Junktim* idea discussed in Chapter 6—namely, that it is psychoanalytic investigation of otherwise inaccessible mental processes (principally beliefs and fantasies) that is therapeutic. Given this context, Box 8.4 sets out three key questions it may be useful for every analyst to ask about what they suppose an analyst needs to do to make a difference.

BOX 8.4. THREE QUESTIONS TO TEST SUPPOSITIONS ABOUT HOW AN ANALYST MAKES A DIFFERENCE

1. *Beliefs or deficits:* Do I suppose that change is brought about by discovering unconscious beliefs that are otherwise inaccessible, or do I rather suppose I need to behave differently to overcome the relational deficits caused by deprivations, neglect, or abuse that my patients experienced in their pasts? If the latter, how do I know I am being different?
2. *Wait for discomfort and address it or not:* When I speak, do I notice if I have waited for evident signs of discomfort in my patient, and if so, do I then try to address them?
3. *Address beliefs about me now or not:* Do I think it essential to help my patients become aware if they are troubled by their unconscious beliefs about me and my intentions in sessions?

The first question directs attention to whether analysts suppose that what matters is to investigate and reveal unconscious beliefs or rather to enable patients to make good deficits in their relational capacity; if the latter, it asks how an analyst can really be different.

---

9. This, of course, would be entirely true if we were discussing a range of psychotherapies rather than specifically psychoanalysis.

The second question focuses on whether and why analysts might wait for signs of discomfort (resistance to thoughts) to become evident, and if they do, what they signify and what should be done.

Finally, the third question asks whether analysts suppose that it is important, to make a difference, that their patients become aware of their unconscious beliefs about the persons of their analysts and so, implicitly, whether analysts believe it is important to test whether they have become, whatever their intentions to be different, immersed in their patients' unconscious beliefs about what their analysts are trying to do with them. Obviously, if patients perceive their analysts via their unconscious beliefs, it is very hard for their analysts to seem different to those they usually experience, however differently they may try to behave.

Of course, as with the previous questions that we have suggested are useful, understanding these ones and asking them rigorously and frequently may be much more important than any permanent answers.

SUMMARY

In this chapter, we have summarized our main findings and tried to show some of the differences between psychoanalysts in a way we think may be both more rigorous and more enlightening than previously.

More specifically we have applied our new common theoretical framework to the clinical work of the seven well-known psychoanalysts we introduced in Chapter 1 and summarized the findings based on the intensive analysis of the sixteen psychoanalysts who presented in the workshops we selected for detailed study and illustration.

We began by applying our metaphor typology to capture the different suppositions about the analytic situation (or transference) that psychoanalysts practice, then summarized our three-source framework for exploring how analysts infer their patients' unconscious repetitions or beliefs. After that we looked at the cleavage that seems to exist between analysts who suppose their patients' problems are fundamentally driven by repetitive beliefs and those who suppose they are driven by deficit mainly in relationships—a set of differences that turned out to be significant in determining whether psychoanalysts supposed they could make a difference by investigating and helping patients to become aware of the unconscious beliefs driving their lives or, alternatively, by building for them a new and different relational experience.

Our summary has led us to eleven questions that we think every analyst might find it useful to ask themselves to clarify and reflect on their approach.

We move now to our final chapter in which we examine contemporary controversies in the light of our common theoretical framework and our empirical findings.

9

Core Issues for Psychoanalysts Emerging from the Work

Now that we have presented our findings about what psychoanalysts do and introduced our eleven-question framework designed to help each analyst to ask themselves how they know they do it, in this final chapter we explore a few controversial issues in contemporary psychoanalysis, viewed in the light of the eleven questions and our findings.

We begin by reflecting on what is "unconscious" in a session. Next, we address the question of deficit and ask how a psychoanalyst can be a "new" relational object. We then move on to ask what a transference interpretation is and what purpose it serves, explore why our findings suggest countertransference has to be at the core of psychoanalysis, and revisit the question of what contemporary psychoanalysts suppose produces psychic change. Finally, we discuss how we might manage ourselves, our differences, and our debates better so as to navigate what we think is arguably a critical moment for psychoanalysis in a productive way, supported by evidence.

WHAT IS "UNCONSCIOUS" IN A SESSION?

The notion of "unconscious" beliefs, that is, beliefs or "fantasies" that subjects find too painful to know and have "repressed" from consciousness but which continue to exert a powerful effect on their lives, was at the heart of Sigmund Freud's "invention" of psychoanalysis. As we discussed in Chapter 4, the idea was sustained and strengthened through his self-analysis and his theory of dreams and then (as discussed in Chapter 3) became central to his theory of transference (in whichever of three forms he expressed it) as well as in his ideas about jokes and mistakes.

The crucial point is that while unconscious beliefs (forming a template through which experience is mediated as fact) are crucial to understanding symptoms or behavior, awareness of them is resisted, because it is emotionally painful—because "knowing" them provokes anxiety, guilt, shame, or any number of subtler uncomfortable emotions.

Freud's procedure for psychoanalytic sessions, discussed at length in Chapter 4 and based on his efforts to understand his own dreams, was explicitly designed to allow the psychoanalyst first to guess that an unconscious belief was nearing consciousness, by noticing the appearance of discomfort, and then to guess its content. As discussed in Chapter 6, guessing that an unconscious belief is influencing a session is likely to be more reliable than guessing its content, because more inference by the analyst (and so more of the analyst's own beliefs, whether conscious or unconscious) is involved in the latter than the former. As discussed in Chapter 4, the analyst can *never* be sure that his own unconscious—that is, his unconscious beliefs evoked by being with his patient as a person (i.e., his countertransference)—has not intruded into the words he speaks. He can, however, reflect on this possibility.

We have argued that psychoanalysts suppose the patient's unconscious *in a session* can manifest itself in four ways, as discussed principally in Chapter 3: through the analyst's response to what the patient's selection of words reveals about his unconscious without his knowledge (dramatic monologue); through the analyst's guesses that identify repetitive patterns in the patient's reported thoughts, dreams, and relationships (cinema); through the patient's manifest discomforts and "resistances" noticed in the sessions by the analyst, suggesting discomfort about how they are casting the analyst and possible reasons for this (theater); and through the analyst's own unexpected thoughts, feelings, and responses (such as "type 6" responses, as discussed particularly in Chapter 7) (immersive theater).

In fact, most of the presenters in our workshops and five out of the seven analysts we discussed in Chapter 1 were trying to identify their patient's unconscious beliefs. However, as we noted in Chapter 6, some of our presenters, like Donnel Stern and Philip Bromberg among the analysts whose work was excerpted in Chapter 1, focused elsewhere. They supposed their patients had been damaged in such a way that they could not formulate their beliefs and feelings about others and so, dissociated from them, tended to express them in actions or behaviors. Such suppositions make it hard to know what is then considered unconscious in Freud's terms. This is particularly so insofar as the sessions they report look like an everyday (but perhaps franker and more intimate) conversation. Both analyst and patient seem to be expressing conscious views, and there is no obvious sense that either's contributions were understood as a manifest indicator of underlying latent beliefs *unknown or unwelcome to the speaker*.

Some of our presenters who tended in this direction may have arrived at differences with Freud and his procedure intentionally. Stern and Bromberg, or Heinz Kohut and James Fosshage (Chapter 5), or others broadly in the US relational tradition, for example, have explicitly articulated a rejection of Freud's procedure and, to an extent, his theories about unconscious beliefs and fantasies. Others may have got to their current practice unintentionally, perhaps via a series of adaptations to difficult clinical situations. The questions introduced in the last chapter (and listed as Table 9.1, p. 237) are designed to help all analysts to reflect on their position on such core issues, using our new common framework.

In fact, none of the presenters in our workshops explicitly adopted a relational technique—like either the ones used by Stern and Bromberg or those used by others.

However, as we described in Chapters 5 and 6, some of them shared the supposition that their patients' capacity to think and feel had been compromised by developmental trauma so that unconscious beliefs seemed absent. We have come to wonder whether a reason for such thinking derives from the suppositions such analysts make about unconscious beliefs and how they manifest themselves in the analytic situation.

Under dramatic monologue or theater suppositions about the analytic situation (of both types) patients' associations are supposed to produce evidence of unconscious beliefs that they *fear to elaborate*. It might be via manifest signs of discomfort, via the creation of atmospheres (such as described by André Green or Wilfred Bion), or by actions such as the behavior Freud described that revealed ambivalence of Ernst (the "Rat Man") toward him. Whatever the manifest signs, the analyst supposes that the patient has an unconscious picture of their analyst as a person here and now. Beliefs are there but repressed and so unknown, but only for now.

Cinema suppositions, on the other hand, require an analyst to detect and guess a patient's unconscious beliefs not as they manifest with the analyst in the room but by making sense of the patient's stories about relationships, memories, and events. This means making links between relationships, memories, and events that the patient has hitherto unconsciously avoided elaborating on and will be actively motivated to obscure because they are frightening or depriving. To make such links manifest and to produce conviction in the patient that an analyst's sense making is "correct," using cinema suppositions, therefore, necessarily requires a great deal of active symbolic processing on the part of the analyst and the patient. To do it successfully requires not just tact and empathy but also that the patient share a significant number of the analyst's assumptions (cultural, epistemological, ideological, and linguistic). This makes analysis in the "cinema" more complex and demanding as a joint endeavor, which is why analysts like Fred Busch (Chapter 1) build up interpretations gradually by noticing and revealing resistances to emerging ideas.

From these viewpoints, it is conceivable that the defects in symbolization or thinking that analysts like Stern, Bromberg, and some analysts in our study suppose their patients suffer from are actually the consequence of their suppositions about what is being manifested in the sessions. We have suggested in Chapter 8 that Stern and Bromberg use cinema suppositions, which was also true of those in Chapter 6 focused on developing their patients' capacities rather than surfacing their unconscious beliefs. Could it be that the problem such analysts have in identifying the existence of unconscious beliefs derives from an interaction between some types of patients and the suppositions they make?[1] Given that surely every patient is aware to an extent of ideas about their analyst in and outside the room (as analysts who have been in a training analysis surely know for themselves), we think that this may be the case.

For instance, Kurt Eissler's patient, discussed in Chapters 1 and 8, had his own ideas and clearly didn't agree with Eissler's interpretations, formed with suppositions about the analytic situation we characterized as cinema. Then Kohut (whose analyst

---

1. Many years ago, Bernstein (1964) proposed that similar divergences in linguistic codes and related institutional arrangements handicapped the education of certain groups of children.

also appears to have made cinema suppositions) also seems clearly to have had his own ideas about his analyst. We cannot know whether Eissler or Kohut's analyst had arrived at correct interpretations of their patients' unconscious beliefs. But we can wonder if perhaps Eissler's suppositions about the analytic situation, together with his theory of resistance and his ideas about working through, meant that he could not adapt his interpretations to the situation in the room. He does not seem to have considered whether, perhaps, his patient unconsciously had cast him in the role of a cruel person (as in theater suppositions) or, perhaps, how he was unconsciously even being stimulated into behaving in a cruel, authoritarian manner (immersive theater). Something similar may have been true of Kohut's analyst. The point is that when faced with impasse, neither Eissler nor Kohut's analyst could "drop the level" of their attention to move away from their focus on constructing links between reported events toward asking themselves about the unconscious beliefs that patient and analyst were using to cast each other in the room.[2] In the end there was no way out for either couple, and eventually the patient's only way out would have been either to submit and idealize the analyst's brilliance or, as Kohut then did with great energy, to dispute the analyst's approach and claims to authority.

Today, it is a fact that among many North American analysts there is significant preoccupation with analysts' potential mistaken use or even misuse of their authority and what they call the "constructivist dilemma." A whole series of papers with this concern have significantly shifted practice away from Freud's procedure (the fundamental rule of free association and evenly hovering and so equidistant attention) and, inevitably as a logical consequence, from the significance of uncomfortable and resisted unconscious beliefs (e.g., Aron, 1990b; Benjamin, 1994; Bromberg, 2009; Greenberg, 1995; Hoffman, 1996; Lothane, 1989; Mitchell, 1998).[3]

Given the fact of countertransference, the "constructivist dilemma," and the challenges of implementing a cinema model of the analytic situation with patients who don't share the analyst's assumptions, the various objections make a certain sense: they are objections to another claiming to see in you things you don't see in yourself and are very much disinclined to see. At the same time, it necessarily creates a logical difficulty. Since patients (and analysts, for that matter) would rather not acknowledge their discomforting beliefs, with some feeling this to be utterly intolerable and emotionally destabilizing, then in the absence of some other more palatable process for knowing them, fulfilling the function of Freud's procedure, Freud's central idea about the role of unconscious beliefs must be abandoned along with much of his other thinking.

As just suggested, theater suppositions about the analytic situation create less of a challenge, particularly if the three sources of inference (Chapter 4 and Q4, Q5, and Q6 in Table 9.1), one of which is explicitly intended to explore countertransference bias, are also used. Clearly neither patient nor analyst can have any certainty as to

---

2. A phrase used by the late Betty Joseph in conversation (DT).

3. Note that as Lear (2017) has pointed out, the fundamental rule is all the more fundamental "because no one can follow the rule" (p. 7). It is precisely when it becomes uncomfortable that it signifies so much, but not because the patient's conscious association is the issue, as Sharpe (1930) pointed out.

Table 9.1. Eleven Questions to Help Decide How a Psychoanalyst Is Working and Why

Q1 (AS1)	*When:* When my patient was talking to me, was I supposing she was conveying the emotional situation *believed to exist between us* (as unconsciously configured in her mind so that it was me *as a person* she had cast as seductive, cruel, fragile, empty, etc.), or was I rather supposing that she was conveying *the situation more generally between herself and others* (as unconsciously configured in her mind as seductive, cruel, fragile, empty, etc.)?
Q2 (AS2)	*Participation:* If talking about the situation between us or with others, have I wondered whether in some way what I take to be my patient's picture (whether of me or others) is being cast by me? If so, how?
Q3 (UI1)	*Procedure:* Have I created a formal procedure to give my patients an opportunity to observe and recognize the thoughts and experience's that *fall into their minds* in their sessions, or am I setting up something more like an ordinary conversation?
Q4 (UI2)	*Targets of guessing:* Am I trying to "guess" (1) my patient's inaccessible feelings and impulses, or (2) her unconscious patterns of relational behavior, or (3) the underlying script of unconscious beliefs that create her experience?
Q5 (UI3)	*Attitude to own thoughts and feelings:* Do my guesses about the meaning of my patient's associations rely to a significant degree, as far as I am aware, on my feelings, responses, and thoughts?
Q6 (UI4)	*Reflective curiosity:* Have I created a reflective setup in my mind to observe and question how I am arriving at my guesses about my patient's associations and how I am using my own thoughts and feelings?
Q7 (UR1)	*Specific or general:* Do I suppose my patient's repetitive troubles in the present derive from a deficit in her capacity to tolerate and access inaccessible impulses and *feelings generally* or a difficulty integrating *specific mixed feelings,* such as love and hate?
Q8 (UR2)	*Unconscious beliefs or not:* Do I suppose that my patients are *trapped within their* **unconscious** *beliefs,* so that I know that, even if they are hard to detect now, *it must be possible eventually to capture them* so that they become thinkable by us?
Q9 (MD1)	*Beliefs or deficits:* Do I suppose that change is brought about by discovering unconscious beliefs that are otherwise inaccessible, or do I rather suppose I need to behave differently to overcome the relational deficits caused by deprivations, neglect, or abuse that my patients experienced in their pasts? If the latter, how do I know I am being different?
Q10 (MD2)	*Wait for discomfort and address it or not:* When I speak, do I notice if I have waited for evident signs of discomfort in my patient, and if so, do I then try to address them?
Q11 (MD3)	*Address beliefs about me now or not:* Do I think it essential to help my patients become aware if they are troubled by their unconscious beliefs about me and my intentions in sessions?

Note: AS = suppositions about the analytic situation; UI = suppositions about unconscious inference; UR = suppositions about unconscious repetition; MD = suppositions about making a difference.

their convictions about each other. Neither can be infallible. But if an analyst like Eissler had imagined that his patient was talking to him not just about his wife but also about his analyst over many repetitions, it might have been possible to designate the transference situation to make it easier for both to see whether, for example, the patient had cast him in the role of beating him up and was secretly enjoying and provoking it. And then, of course, with immersive theater suppositions and a willingness to explore their implications, Eissler could also have asked himself question 2 (Table 9.1) and perhaps noticed type 6 interventions of the kind discussed in Chapter 7.

Our central point is to wonder if those who seem to be rejecting Freud's model of unconscious belief and fantasies do so because of the suppositions they make—both about the psychoanalytic situation and the potential for unconscious inference. Interestingly, this seems to be a particular problem if an analyst uses cinema suppositions with patients who do not share their assumptions.

THE QUESTION OF DEFICIT

As we realized in Chapters 5 and 6, a surprisingly common feature of discussions in our workshops, particularly when presenters or group members were trying to work out their suppositions about how far deficit was responsible for their patients' difficulties,[4] were the twin ideas that (1) there has been a change in the characteristics of patients seeking psychoanalysis, and (2) these newer patients suffer from deficiencies in their thinking about emotional experience or their capacity to experience emotional conflict or transference.[5]

There is a view that such patients perhaps are unsuited to the classical procedures of psychoanalysis, using free association and evenly hovering attention, which, as Kohut described for Mr. Z, can be felt as cold and unhelpful. Such patients may also be viewed as having deficits in their emotional development as the result of trauma so that they produce somatic symptoms, think concretely, have difficulty with symbolization, and so on. Terms like "dissociation" and "vertical splitting" are applied to them in the way that Kohut applied them to Mr. Z. They may then be conceived to have retreated into multiple self-organizations operating independently—exhibiting, for instance, both a compliant and a hostile self, each entirely dissociated from the other.

As well as Kohut, Stern (2019) is once again an articulate spokesperson for such views when he argues that pursuing such patients' unconscious fantasies is unhelpful because what these patients verbalize is not beliefs in the usual sense but states of potential meaningfulness that are actually "vaguely organized, primitive, global, non-ideational, and affectively saturated" (p. 337). As Bromberg (2003) puts it, the locus of therapeutic action is then not in the material that is told to the analyst, as

---

4. That is, a general deficiency in managing feelings due to difficult situations in infancy and childhood (see Chapter 5).

5. Sometimes described as a deficit in representational capacity or deficient capacity for symbolization.

if it were a buried fantasy uncovered by piecing together the links between a patient's associations. Rather, therapeutic action is organized affectively, through the interaction between patient and analyst,[6] where it has a chance to be symbolized by the verbal meaning attached to the affective perception of what is taking place in the here and now.

Cynthia (Self-Esteem under Zero) and Patricia (Tragedy), as well as James (Despair and Resistance), Henry (Struggling to Be Here), and Andrew (A Story of Ruin), did not articulate their approach in the extensive way Stern has. But the suppositions they held, which we described in Chapter 6, suggested they were analysts focused on bringing about change via a mixture of relationship building and "facilitating" their patient's thinking, symbolic capacities, and ability to manage their feelings through their interactions. Like Kohut and Fosshage (Chapter 5), and Stern and Bromberg, as we have been discussing, their idea is that these patients are suffering from deficits caused by deprivations experienced in childhood.

Kohut (Chapter 5) believed "Mr. Z" (in fact, as we have suggested, probably Kohut himself) had been forced to become enmeshed with the pathological personality of his psychotic mother, resulting in a problematic self-structure adaptation created by vertical splitting. In the same chapter, Fosshage's patient P was described as suffering a tyrannical father and a mother by whom she had felt emotionally abandoned. (The example given was that at age three she had been hospitalized and not visited by her mother for three days.) She had also experienced her mother as extremely needy and self-absorbed. Stern's and Bromberg's patients were similarly supposed to have experienced deprivations in their early lives—the results of which were difficulties with affect regulation and symbolization.

Whatever the value of the high-level theories that apparently support approaches that focus on building the patient's relationships or capacities in order to correct deficits, as we see it, the crucial question is the perhaps unintended implications of such theories for Freud's theory of the role of unwelcome unconscious beliefs. Does the analyst suppose the beliefs are there in session, albeit unexpressed and unknown yet trapping the patient, or does the analyst believe they don't exist? An important question for any analyst, therefore, is the one introduced in Box 8.3 in the last chapter, which we label Q8 in Table 9.1—namely, "Do I suppose that my patients are *trapped within their **unconscious** beliefs*, so that I know that, even if they are hard to detect now, *it must eventually be possible to capture them* so that they become thinkable by us?" Experience in workshops and writing such as that of Kohut, Fosshage, Stern, and Bromberg suggest that analysts who start down the

---

6. Bromberg uses the term "enactment," which we have replaced in the above phrasing by "interaction." This is because in our psychoanalytic cultures, the usual psychoanalytic definition of enactment, deriving from Freud's use of the word *Agieren*, has the meaning of the "acting out" or "actualization" of an unconscious wish or phantasy (see glossary, p. 255). For us, but not for Stern, the term implies underlying unconscious ideation. Stern and others also use the words "transference" and "countertransference" very differently—essentially referring (as in the cinema model) to the patient's relationship to the analyst and the analyst's relationship to the patient, but in each case with no explicit implications that unconscious fantasy or beliefs are involved or should be inferred.

deficit road never report later periods of analysis when patients were able to move on to recognize that they suffered from ambivalent beliefs leading them to cast their analysts and so experience them in particular and uncomfortable ways. What is very noticeable, however, is a great deal of commentary about insensitive and defective caregiving. The questions that follow for any psychoanalyst wanting to look at this further are labeled Q9, Q10, and Q11 in Table 9.1.

Meanwhile, if we restrict ourselves to the limited problem of how to do psycho-analysis with adult patients, like the seven patients described by the psychoanalysts in Chapter 1 or those described by analysts who presented in our workshops, our impression is that the development of deficit theories of early psychic functioning, however valuable in general, can be distracting in situations in which the aim is to do psychoanalysis. In any case, the theories do not seem to us to license the idea that an analyst, however sensitively, can deploy intuitions to somehow provide the containing reverie or sense making or self-affirmation that those like Kohut or Fosshage seem to believe was lacking in early experience.

Interestingly, the presenters in our workshops who tried to make a difference by making up what they thought their patients were lacking were all analysts whose suppositions about the analytic situation we characterized as either cinema or, in one instance, dramatic monologue. Andrew was an example. He supposed that Beckett's difficulty was that he suffered from a "fundamental lack" in being able properly to symbolize "his inner emotional states." Andrew then supposed that what he needed to do was to provide Beckett (described as devitalized) with a missing capacity to register symbolic meaning and so to access feelings unavailable to him. Andrew's interpretations (pp. 136) were understood to be efforts to guess absent feelings and the thoughts he inferred that Beckett had but did not know about—he interpreted, for example, "At the moment it seems that you are remembering another separation, and in your effort to recall a moment when there is abandonment and rupture, you are trying to imagine the painful consequences" (p. 138).

In the workshop Andrew also used the word "mentalizing" to describe this effort to translate what Beckett said into what might be more meaningful and to try to bring Beckett into contact with what Andrew was convinced Beckett did not know. He also commented that the situation between them was often on the verge of being "too hot."

Patients like Beckett were manifestly very handicapped and would clearly pres-ent significant problems to anyone—but this was also true of Bion's patient Brian, Green's patient Gabriel, and Louise's patient Georgina. In any case, Andrew's ap-proach in these difficult circumstances was to use quite an active technique remi-niscent of Stern and Bromberg. Like theirs, Andrew's suppositions were judged by us to rest on the cinema metaphor for the analytic situation and the deficit view for unconscious repetition. What is interesting about both suppositions is that what-ever their merits, they direct attention away from any inaccessible beliefs precipiv-tated in the participants in the session that may be leading them to cast each other in particular ways—for example, the workshop members never found out what was really "too hot" in the room and for whom in what way. Under theater suppositions and, still more, immersive theater suppositions, this question would have posed itself. We don't know for sure and mention it only as a possibility, but could Beckett have had inaccessible but frightening beliefs about Andrew's homosexual intentions toward him? Could the many active efforts Andrew made to try to help Beckett know his feelings and thoughts have functioned to create an experience for Beckett of having ideas put into his head, which might, perhaps, have been experienced by Beckett in complex and even sexualized ways? To emphasize, we don't know. The point is that the suppositions made have consequences so that questions such as Q1, Q4, Q7, Q8, Q9, and Q11, if used in situations like that in which Andrew found himself, might help an analyst like Andrew to determine whether he is working in the way he wants to or not.

As a contrast, Green's work with Gabriel (discussed in Chapters 1, 4, and 8) is an example of a psychoanalytic approach to the apparent absence of thoughts and feelings that gradually teased them out. Without doubt the patient had been traumatized. He also appeared to have a deficit in his capacity to associate and to symbolize. But Green's suppositions about the analytic situation, which are characterized as theater based, as well as his adoption of free association and evenly hovering attention procedures with which to conduct the analysis, eventually revealed that the problem was one of unconscious beliefs. It took many years for Green to create the conditions for Gabriel's feelings and thoughts to be "caught" and to become recognizable, because his mental processes rapidly dispersed them to create fog. Similarly, Bion's interpretive work under immersive theater suppositions with Brian, who created a soporific experience for them both and had convinced a previous psychotherapist he needed a lobotomy, eventually captured very relevant but hitherto inaccessible thoughts and feelings in the sessions.

Neither Bion nor Green tried to tell their patients what they were thinking and feeling or to modify their technique in order to conduct the investigation. They both used a broadly Freudian procedure with the fundamental rule and evenly hovering attention, together with guesses about their patients' unconscious beliefs and experiences, specifically interpretations of their patients' anxious but hitherto inaccessible and unthinkable beliefs scripting their interactions with their analysts. Within our sample from the workshops, Louise (In a Hole), who also made suppositions best characterized by theater, also used a Freudian procedure and all three of the sources of inference (discussed in Chapter 4) to the same effect. Like Gabriel and Brian with Green and Bion, respectively, Louise's patient Georgina had been traumatized in childhood and took a long time to reveal her frightening beliefs about her analyst. When they emerged, they were dominating her experience and, like all other unconscious beliefs, were treated by her not as beliefs but as frightening facts until, once recognized as beliefs, they could be tested.

It is beyond our scope to elaborate further, but an additional difficulty with theories that patients do not know their feelings (but their analysts do) is that it seems likely to be both an imprecise and a misleading way to characterize the underlying situation and what we might learn from neuroscience.

From consensus knowledge of current developmental neuroscience, it is reasonable to suppose (1) that the primary motivational systems are affect based, (2) that affect is grounded in either positive (approach, pleasure) or negative (avoid, unpleasure) systems, (3) that in the form of feeling, affect is conscious, and (4) that because affects are activated in the brain stem, the automated defensive patterns developed early on cannot be directly remembered in words (i.e., in the cortex) but evoke feelings that can be made sense of later (e.g., Kernberg, 1979; Solms, 2013). The evolutionary function of feelings of pain, thirst, guilt, anxiety, and so forth is to stimulate attention prior to initiating action programs in the interest of homeostatic survival. If dysfunctional action programs (responses) have been learned early, as in traumatic situations, they are repeated.

From this viewpoint, patients like Gabriel or Beckett or others thought to have suffered early trauma are responding to experience through learned-action programs and are reinitializing responses to unbearable early experience now deployed as rapid responses to emotional dysregulation producing pain or pleasure. Because they are automated responses, stored in brain structures below the cortex, while their effects may be observed repeatedly in the room with an analyst when experiences precipitating them occur, they can become consciously known only by (1) discovering beliefs that may have become retrospectively attached to them in later life, and (2) correctly labeling the underlying situation when it occurs. So, when in adult life early traumatized patients like Gabriel or Beckett find themselves in situations that evoke the old feelings (rightly or wrongly), the old automated responses for managing feelings (which might include mental actions like evacuation) are repeatedly initiated. The implication is that an analyst can closely observe, in ways the patient can recognize, the experiences that occur in sessions—for example, the way Bion and his patient Brian were getting repeatedly into a soporific state or how Green's patient would divert his attention from his thoughts at certain points. Gradually it may then be possible to begin to explore what beliefs may have become attached to these experiences that might explain them. Using a theater or immersive theater set of suppositions about the patient's changing perception of the analyst in the analytic situation seems likely to enable close focus on such repetitions and may allow underlying beliefs that make sense of the repetitions (some of which may occur in the analyst, as Bion's example shows) to emerge. This kind of analytic work creates a process premised on the idea that the underlying beliefs and responses are there but must emerge in the sessions before they can be seen (Q8).

CAN A PSYCHOANALYST BE A NEW RELATIONAL OBJECT?

In Chapters, 5, 6, and 8, we described significant movements in the psychoanalytic field since Freud's death toward the idea that it is the relationship the psychoanalyst and the patient establish together that in a series of ways functions to provide the main therapeutic effect. As we saw in Chapter 6, the development seems to have begun with the idea that the analyst might have to build a psychoanalytic relationship before being able to do psychoanalysis proper, but it gradually evolved into the idea of building the patient's capacity to relate. In this way it has been part of a shift away from what was widely perceived as an authoritarian, cold, and rigid approach to psychoanalysis (particularly as presented in North America but not exclusively), characterized by neutrality, strict procedure, and a claim to know from a position of authority, followed by "working through" of objections to interpretations conceived as resistances. We mentioned above that such an authoritarian stance was experienced as objectionable by some candidate analysts and was seen as at odds with the trend of postmodern philosophy and social thinking. Moreover, as mentioned earlier, developing knowledge in areas like attachment theory, cognitive and affective neuroscience, and knowledge of child development, as well as more general knowledge of the intrinsic nature of human social interaction from birth, is thought to have provided a context for thinking about relationships not available earlier. And finally, as we described in Chapter 6, Hans Loewald and Johan Cremerius, among others, have drawn attention to how Freud, like many after him, did develop broader, more "human" relationships with patients than his formal procedure implies.

Nonetheless, looked at from the point of view of the theoretical framework developed in this book, the supposition that the analyst can progress an analysis mainly by striving to be a new and different relational object—for instance, by being more understanding and supportive, less rigid, or less seductive and distant, as well as more empathetically encouraging, compared to those figuring in the patient's past and present—seems to us highly problematic.

Our reasoning is that on close examination, whatever the good intentions of those who believe they can make up for the relational deficits that patients have (undoubtedly) suffered, this approach is a diversion from the analysis of unconscious beliefs using Freud's procedure. Bearing in mind the doubts we already expressed about psychoanalysis without unconscious beliefs, the tactic of taking what the analyst feels is the patient's side is potentially flawed in two ways. First, a departure from neutrality toward being partisan complicates providing patients with the opportunity for analyst and patient to experience what their analysts (as primary objects) are provisionally feared to be and then to explore it. How does an analyst know that he or she really is good? Second, the claim to know potentially creates a new dilemma. "Knowing" what is good for a patient is a moral stance and must create an inevitable latent authoritarianism.[7]

---

7. The philosophically inclined may notice an echo here of the arguments made in Isaiah Berlin's (1958) critique of liberalism. The core phrase is "if we are not armed with an a priori guarantee of the proposition that a total harmony of true values is somewhere to be found—perhaps in some ideal realm the characteristics of which we can, in our finite state, not so much as conceive—we must fall back on the ordinary resources of empirical observation and ordinary human knowledge. And these certainly give us no warrant for supposing (or even understanding what would be meant by saying) that all good things, or all bad things for that matter, are reconcilable with each other. The world that we encounter in ordinary experience is one in which we are faced with choices between ends equally ultimate" (p. 29). (David Tuckett is grateful to George Soros for drawing this to his attention).

Once again, we suggest that suppositions about the analytic situation can be clarifying. In the theater model, analysts, in psychic reality, are what their patients make them. A "new object" approach within those suppositions, therefore, requires that "really" to experience the analyst as different to past objects (even if the historical situation can be knowable, which is a strong assumption), patients have first to discover how they are casting their analysts and then subject that casting to unprejudiced investigation. Along the way the analyst may well happen to behave like the old object and certainly may get cast in that role.

Being a new object with cinema suppositions is different but in a curious way. In effect, until explicitly brought into the picture by the patient talking about him, the analyst stands outside the action and is a spectator. The film is made. It means, in effect, that so long as that is the case, the question of what sort of object the analyst is does not arise. Such analysts, insofar as they maintain the supposition, remain untroubled and stay outside the script and out of the story. The problem with some patients is that those assumptions don't work, and it seems likely that these are precisely the assumptions that could not be taken for granted with more traumatized patients like Mr. Z, P, and others whose past relationships have been so difficult. With these patients, who perhaps need to cast their analysts in terms of their terrifying (but unarticulated and avoided) beliefs, the pressure is on the analyst to get involved. It is also precisely with such patients that analysts with these suppositions are likely to suffer troubling reactions—likely provoked by the way their unconscious casts the persons of their patients.

In Chapter 3 we showed how Freud's discoveries about the transference, made from 1893 onward, caused him to diverge, if not consistently, from his earlier cinema-type suppositions. Starting with "it is almost inevitable that their *personal relation* to him will force itself, for a time at least, unduly into the foreground" (Freud, 1893, p. 266), he went to "we must make up our minds to distinguish a 'positive' transference from a 'negative' one, the transference of affectionate feelings from that of hostile ones, and to treat the two sorts of transference to the doctor separately" (Freud, 1912a, pp. 104–6) and then arrived at "it cannot be disputed that controlling the phenomena of transference presents the psycho-analyst with the greatest difficulties. But it should not be forgotten that it is precisely they that do us the inestimable service of making the patient's hidden and forgotten erotic impulses immediate and manifest. For when all is said and done, it is impossible to destroy anyone in absentia or *in effigie*" (p. 108).

Insofar as these later ideas are given credibility, as in both theater models, psychoanalysts recognize that they cannot avoid being experienced as both "good" and "bad" objects. If so, it follows that while they cannot choose how they are experienced, they can help their patients to understand, without judgment, the inaccessible (to the patient) beliefs and impulses that cause these experiences.

As we argued in Chapter 3 and then saw in Chapter 7, Freud and all of us after him have struggled with the experience of how our patients see us, as well as the unconscious relationships we are provoked into having with our patients. Patients provoke responses from us of which we are not aware (i.e., in our countertransference). Freud found it (as we find it) hard to tolerate the roles into which his patients cast him, as well as their pain at having to recognize the facts—which is why their beliefs were unconscious.

Insofar as the view just discussed is accepted, the conclusion that becomes evident is that although cinema-type suppositions about the analytic situation can be successful in some situations, they create a vulnerability with precisely the kind of patients that "relational" approaches are designed to help. Psychoanalysts whose beliefs omit the supposition that in sessions their patients are compelled to cast them in whatever unconscious role their objects inhabit may sometimes be blindsided. It is then likely that patients will either escalate their efforts to cast the analyst in this way or give up. Perhaps this tendency was visible in the cases with disturbed patients we discussed where cinema suppositions predominated. In those cases, despite heroic efforts to maintain their composure, analysts like Lesley, Patricia, Gilbert, and Britta (as well as Henry and Lorenza in Chapter 7), just like Eissler,[8] Bromberg, and Stern, came under escalating pressure. However, these analysts' suppositional frameworks seem to us to have made it impossible for them to consider that contrary to their intentions (like Freud with Ernst), they were being drawn into situations in which their patients were struggling with their unconscious casting because (as it usually is) their experience of their analyst was ambivalent. In other words, their problem was the person (as cast) who they felt was in the room with them, not just with their mothers, fathers, and so forth, in the past or outside.

It seems likely that when cinema suppositions predominate (and we should always recall that this may be a temporary feature of an analysis awaiting a type 6 nodal moment), the outcome may become a very explosive experience. Patients may be truly grateful to their analysts for staying in the task and facilitating the intensity, but there is also a risk, so long as ambivalence is kept outside awareness, that a compromise will eventuate with idealization and secret hatred on both sides, in which outsiders will remain villains forever. No new, more balanced view of the past or of the exigencies of life is then possible. This may help to account for the fact that so many abusive or neglectful parents (and the like) are presented in cases where the analyst seems to have bought into the project of trying to be a new and better object.[9]

Unconscious beliefs are facts. Therefore, while a psychoanalyst can become a new object in a patient's mind if the patient's unconscious beliefs, driven by ambivalent feelings, are exposed and gradually recognized to be beliefs rather than facts, and

---

8. Eissler's belief, presumably, was that he was different because he was neutral. It is a consequence, curiously, of the likelihood that psychoanalysts of his type and those of the relational school, as well as strict Lacanians (who deny the influence of their countertransference beliefs), share suppositions about the analytic situation for which we use the term "cinema" or "dramatic monologue."

9. Note that as Bernard Reith (personal correspondence) has pointed out to us, the deficit model may conceal a wish for fusion or enmeshment with an ideal object (as discussed in Chapter 8) but also an infantile (and/or Oedipal and/or narcissistic) wish *to be taken care of* by an ideal, protective, caring parent. If so, the analysand wouldn't be expected to have to do their part in the process as analytic collaborator. A deficit model analyst might be led to take this fantasy concretely and then enter into a chronic enactment.

perhaps also revised in the presence of the psychoanalyst, it does not seem this can be achieved by deliberate efforts to be different from past figures unless the main tenets of Freud's theory of the psychoanalytic situation are discarded. The main reason for this, as we briefly touched on when elaborating an understanding of Patricia's case in the last chapter, is that an analyst's efforts to be different have to be based on the analyst's beliefs (i.e., intuitive guesses) about the patient's internal beliefs about their objects, and these guesses, inevitably, are formed by the analyst's own unconscious response (i.e., countertransference) and the framework she has to recognize and test it.

To become a "really" new relational object in the patient's mind, as far as we can tell, requires an investigation in which what the analyst "knows" is constantly put on one side and revised. It means participating over and over in a psychoanalytic investigation, trying to discover the nature of the beliefs that define the object that the psychoanalyst is unconsciously suspected by the patient to be. Because the suspicions are unconscious and often unbearable (think of Gabriel with Green, or Brian with Bion, or very likely Paula with Patricia), the patient's conscious view (like Ernst's) matters, but it is not reliable. Only the investigation of the inaccessible can hope to approach the hidden and terrified patient.

Therefore, rather than abandoning Freud's traditional framework with its distinct roles for patient and analyst, we proposed in Chapter 4 a better way to address the (constructivist) dilemma. On the one hand, we introduced the value of being fully aware of the suppositions contained within the immersive theater view of the analytic situation. On the other, we introduced the possibility of adopting a triangular framework (Figure 4.3), based on the concepts of the selected fact and the overvalued idea, in which the analyst keeps questioning the sources of inference made within the investigation.

The answers an analyst gives (and keeps reviewing) to the eleven questions in Table 9.1 (p. 237), which brings together the questions we derived in the last chapter about the core suppositions that are necessary for a psychoanalytic investigation to be taking place, may also be helpful. In the specific case of whether an analyst can be a new relational object, an analyst who thinks this may work needs to find a clear answer that they are happy with to Q9, and probably also to Q10 and Q11.

All eleven questions are designed for use for internal supervision on a regular basis or for teaching, supervision, and training. For example, when we review our recent work, does it suggest we have remembered that sessions are opportunities to find out what would otherwise be inaccessible (Q4)? Or, for instance, have we thought about when what is being communicated is happening (Q1)? Relevant to that question, all of us are likely to find from time to time that although we concur with one approach to the analytic situation—for instance, with either of the theater approaches—nonetheless, if we develop the curiosity to inquire, we may find that we have been inadvertently going along for some sessions at a nice distance from the troubles being described and so are actually in the cinema. In other words, and despite our best efforts to talk to the patient "about the patient" (Rycroft, 1956), we may find that we have authoritatively slipped into handing out, in the form of interpretations, our beliefs about their situations with mothers, fathers, partners, or children, at least or until the moment we realize that our inaccessible or countertransference-driven beliefs and anxieties have been in the ascendancy (Q2).

In our view, given the ideas we have reported, to have useful debates about real issues of controversial substance, different implicit suppositions about the analytic situation (Chapter 3), how the unconscious is inferred (Chapter 4), what is unconsciously repeated (Chapter 5), and how an analyst makes a difference (Chapter 6) all have to be carefully understood, defined, and considered when making comparisons. For instance, the claim that Freud's procedure (neutrality, free association, and evenly suspended attention) enables a misuse of analytic authority or that asking patients to lie on the couch is putting them at a disadvantage depends very largely on a particular idea of interpretation (as the analyst constructing meaning by linking elements of what the patient reports) within a cinema framework of the analytic situation. Equally the "constructivist dilemma," in which the fear is that a dominant analyst unaware of his own casting of his patient will impose views on a compliant patient, depends on particular assumptions about sources of inference (no third pillar) and the analytic situation (no practical investigation and exploration of how each participant is unconsciously casting the other).

Given that knowledge of our unconscious is necessarily uncomfortable, rather than abandon Freud's procedure as inherently out of date, we suggest the advantages and disadvantages of different practices are best teased out by using the eleven questions. Important ones relevant to the topics of whether and how an analyst can become a "new" object include those about the analytic situation (Q1, Q2, Q3) but also those about self-audit and the origin of "guesses" (Q5, Q6), as well as those about how I make a difference (Q9, Q10, and Q11.). For example, if we take Kurt Eissler as a representative of the "authoritarian" suppositions challenged by the "constructivist dilemma," we can quite easily suspect that he had not asked (adequately or at all) Q1, Q2, Q5, Q6, and Q11.

In this way, we suggest that many of the controversies around free association, lying on a couch, the analyst's neutral disposition, transference, transference interpretation, and countertransference, as well as the need to be a new object, might usefully be seen as false controversies, albeit about very important issues based on suppositions that have not fully been surfaced and shared. Many of our other most emotionally salient technical debates may have the same origin.

WHAT IS A TRANSFERENCE INTERPRETATION AND WHAT IS ITS PURPOSE?

Back in our first workshops in 2002, we discovered that there were many very strongly held opinions on what a transference interpretation might be and when it should be attempted, with very little common ground on any of the details.

The problem motivated our effort to explore what we have called the different suppositions that are possible about the analytic situation used by the presenters in our workshops and those in published clinical descriptions, such as those of the seven analysts from Chapter 1. As we developed the four metaphors to clarify the suppositions, we then found that they helped us a great deal with the task of "reading between the lines," given that Freud's ideas about transference and its interpretation were inconsistent responses to the personal challenges he faced. It is important to remember that he never published a final definitive view.

The four sets of suppositions about the analytic situation we eventually arrived at allow us to notice that a transference interpretation can be understood and evaluated differently under each one. For instance, under the theater or immersive theater suppositions, the analyst will always eventually be prompted to consider the possibility that the interpretation they are verbalizing must be derived from their intuition about the beliefs and impulses in terms of which their patient is *unconsciously* casting them at a particular moment of a session. When the interpretation is given, it is *claiming* to draw attention to ideas hitherto inaccessible (to the patient) behind this casting of the analyst and his or her intentions. All this makes clear that an implicit claim is being made by the analyst to the patient about the situation between them. Because they are both present, they are both potentially able to note at least some of the evidence and judge it (Q3, Q6, Q10, Q11).

Under cinema and under dramatic monologue suppositions, a transference interpretation is necessarily a rather different sort of claim. In the cinema case, the analyst's intuition about the transference derives from the analyst inferring a transfer of affect from one situation the patient is describing to another through a "false connection" in the patient's portrayal and understanding of the people he is talking about. In fact, it depends on how the analyst has heard the reports and judged the characters and the patient's behavior and does not necessarily include the analyst or the patient's experience of the analyst right now at all. This is so even when the analyst includes himself. For instance, consider a situation where an analyst is going on holiday and believes this is reviving a childhood experience of the patient. He may believe his holiday is subjecting the patient to separation anxiety and discomfort of which the patient is not aware. He may also believe his patient suffered or became enraged and frightened when childhood figures left him and perhaps found experiencing those feelings intolerable. But already we have two beliefs that depend on (1) some evidence or preconceived view about separation for this patient, and (2) further assumptions that the patient somehow equates the situations. There is then an additional question as to what is assumed (i.e., believed) about motivation. Did the patient attribute, for instance, cruelty or indifference to her welfare to her mother so that it stimulated her hatred, which then frightened her, and is that what she now attributes to the analyst, or others, and so forth? In other words, interpretations of this sort typically require a large number of assumptions to be imposed to construct and link events and associations, much of which takes place entirely in the analyst's mind, perhaps with a great deal of intuition and sensitivity but nonetheless requiring many logical connections and explanations, which may or may not be shared by the patient. Our point is that it is a far more complicated and ambitious claim, perhaps far harder for a patient to follow, and far more open to distortion and questioning than interpretations made with theater assumptions based on in-session observations of slips, discomforts, and so on.

In the dramatic monologue case, the analyst's intuition derives from the analyst's unconscious associations as he or she allows him- or herself to be "taken over" by the process through which he or she senses in the wording and flow of associations a transfer of affect from an infantile situation still operative in the patient's mind but stimulated in the session with the analyst. As in the cinema, because the interpretation emerges entirely via the links in the analyst's mind, it is highly dependent on the analyst's intuition and is therefore vulnerable to the influence of his or her countertransference.

Looking closer, in the theater and immersive theater cases, the interpretation makes a claim about inaccessible beliefs about the analyst as a person with intentions here and now. In the cinema case, the claim is about recognized patterns. In the dramatic monologue case, the claim is a suggestion about hidden affect. In all cases, as we have shown, the analyst's transference inferences must be based on construction using the analyst's mental processes—that is, on the analyst bringing things that feel connected together using some kind of guess (*erraten* was Freud's term; *selected fact* might be Bion's). As Freud formulated it, as discussed in Chapter 6, the guess connects things previously unconnected that via betrayal (*verraten*) in free association provide the opportunity for hitherto unrecognized patterns to come together, to make new sense.

Bearing in mind questions about audit (Q6) and evidence (Q5, Q10), when analysts make claims about a patient's beliefs, the issue is whether they are legible to the patient.[10] Transference interpretations embedded in a systematic approach *designating* resistance (Q10)—that is, noticeable discomfort, slips of the tongue, and so on during association—may arguably be legible because they rest on shared observations more obviously than those based on more complex constructions of connections (Tuckett, 2019a), whether explicit or implicit. Complex constructions would seem likely to require more cognitive work and are more distant. In this way, constructions are probably at more risk for being overvalued ideas (Britton & Steiner, 1994) than designations, whether cinema, dramatic monologue, or even theater suppositions are in play. If immersive suppositions, which necessarily warn about countertransference, are being used, particularly alongside the three-source method of making inferences (Chapter 4), things may be safer.

An observation that emerged when reflecting on our workshops was that the most emotionally difficult interactions came up within groups when group members tried to understand why some analysts were reluctant to suppose that transference interpretations should include anxieties caused by "negative transference" (i.e., inaccessible anxieties patients seemed to have because they cast their analysts as cruel, frightened, frightening, hostile, etc.). We mentioned this feature when discussing the workshops at which Jana presented (pp. 48–50). Quite widespread on such occasions was an often implicit idea mentioned by the presenter (or some of the participants) that for the

---

10. We use the term "legible" rather than words like "intelligible" or "understood" to try to convey that whether or not a transference interpretation is "understood" is a complex cognitive and affective process embedded in relationships and procedure.

analyst to raise with the patient the possibility that their casting was causing "negative" feelings about or hostile impulses toward the analyst would make things worse. The belief, in other words, was that to raise the issue was to be *concretely* understood as making a complaint or an accusation, as repeating a trauma, as not relevant, not yet timely, or just too much for patients to take. Implicitly, the further belief was that if such reactions did eventuate, they could not be explored.

To be unable to risk raising negative transference obviously suggests a fragile analytic setup between the participants. It is also incompatible with the interpretation of transference as inherently ambivalent that Freud (1912a) developed. However, once again the difficulty may be explicable due to different assumptions about the analytic situation and about interpretation. Under theater assumptions, and with a focus on designation prior to any construction, the aim is to make legible how the analyst is being cast by the patient based on evidence in the session. In this context interpreting the negative transference means first and foremost drawing to the patient's attention evidence in their sessions for their beliefs about the analyst given away by discomfort, slips, and the like—betraying, for instance, their unconscious casting of the analyst as hostile, cruel, and so on. This is entirely different from suggesting the patient is hostile, cruel, and so forth. Also note that in this formulation, the origin of a patient's beliefs and impulses toward the analyst (such as projection of unwanted attributes) is of secondary importance—to be thought about only once their beliefs about their analyst's attitudes to them and their role in experience are recognized and, if it appears to be a priority, only then to consider where they come from.[11]

A core implication, which brings us to the next question, is that the analyst needs to be able to inhabit the role the patient has cast him or her in sufficiently to take it seriously and empathize with the patient's feeling that they have that sort of analyst rather than to move as quickly as possible to explaining how such a "mistaken" view may come about via projections of unwanted affect, and so forth.

WHY IS COUNTERTRANSFERENCE AT THE CORE OF PSYCHOANALYSIS AND WHAT ARE THE IMPLICATIONS?

Living inside the role a patient has cast one in is a necessary countertransference challenge. In this respect, the titles given to our Comparative Clinical Methods (CCM) annual workshop meetings in Vienna for plenary discussion—"Emotional Storms in the Psychoanalytic Encounter" (2015), "Working under Threat" (2016), "Talking to Patients about Things They Don't Want to Know" (2017)—clearly indicate in hindsight a developing preoccupation with the influence of transference on countertransference and their conjoined effect on the possibility of conducting a psychoanalytic investigation.

At the time, each topic was selected because discussion of the previous year's workshops suggested that countertransference disturbance was a major issue for

---

11. Steiner (1994) has distinguished patient- and analyst-centered interpretations for more disturbed or "split" patients to reduce this risk.

many of us. The theoretical framework of the suppositions that analysts have about the analytic situation, unconscious repetition, unconscious inference, and furthering the process, as well as the comments about how the analytic situation is framed, make clear that management of countertransference is the heart of psychoanalytic work, which despite much discussion is perhaps not fully appreciated. For example, only one of the four metaphors (and the one for which we could find the fewest examples) frames the analytic situation as produced unconsciously by analyst and patient together. And yet, without immersive suppositions, it seems psychoanalysts are always at risk of finding they are imposing more of themselves and their ideas on their patients than they had supposed.

When it comes to suppositions about unconscious inference, we saw in Chapter 4 how Freud realized they must ultimately derive from unconscious cognition and therefore from the analyst's unconscious. To an extent, therefore, they must be influenced by the analyst's repressed responses to the unconscious meanings/messages that express themselves in the patient's utterances.

When it comes to suppositions about furthering the process, the key question is where analysts' guesses about patients' beliefs come from—again this inevitably must be influenced by their own unconscious responses.

Countertransference, therefore, is at the heart of psychoanalytic investigation, inevitably. This then raises the question of what the term means. King (1978) suggests two senses in which the term is used. One sense refers to when an analyst recognizes and tracks that he or she has feelings in response to the patient (as when Britta reported that she felt overwhelmed by Margareta or in the various descriptions Stern and Bromberg gave about their reactions to their patients). A second sense is when analysts realize that they have responded somehow unusually or oddly to a patient (i.e., to the patient's transference relationship to them; see Freud, 1915a) and that this *must have an unconscious meaning for them*, even if unwelcome, as with the various nodal moments described in Chapter 7. In such cases, the cause of the response is inaccessible to the analyst. But, like a patient's inaccessible beliefs or the meaning of Freud's dreams, it can be "guessed" from the original signs through psychoanalytic work linking the analyst's reaction (conceived as a sign of discomfort or resistance) to an explanatory construction. Such a construction might be suggested, for instance, by exploring Q2, Q5, Q6, and Q10 regularly and as discussed in Chapter 7. The second sense underlies immersive theater suppositions about the analytic situation but is left out of the cinema suppositions.

WHERE DOES PSYCHOANALYTIC TRANSFORMATION COME FROM?

Until we got to Chapter 7, we were largely preoccupied with trying to describe what psychoanalysts do, comparatively, and what they know about what they are doing. This focused us on the core suppositions in each psychoanalyst's "explanatory model" underlying their way of doing a psychoanalytic investigation, including Freud's. The eleven questions we have presented are intended as a nonpartisan way to think about the basic technique of that investigation and to internalize it.

What we need to stress here is that although suppositions facilitate and focus the investigation, they cannot produce the interpretive ideas, the guesses, and so forth as to what is going on in the other person and ourselves that ultimately drive the investigation forward.

In Chapter 7 we began to look at where novel or transformational ideas might come from in a psychoanalytic investigation through the concept of nodal moments. They were disturbing phenomena that occurred unexpectedly, according to the analysts who presented their work, but which, we argued, within an investigative framework, were breakthroughs—particularly if the intensification that was taking place could be accepted and worked with.

A point about nodal moments is that they involve in some way a process of unconscious "takeover" of the analyst by contact with the patient of what seems an essential but potentially very disturbing kind. We mentioned that in the first book produced by the Working Party on Comparative Clinical Methods (Tuckett et al., 2008), Paul Denis (2008) wrote about it in a different way. If a psychoanalyst, he suggested, "is not to limit himself to indoctrinating his patient with ready-made formulas, the psychoanalyst must allow himself *to be taken over* by the patient's psychic functioning" (p. 43).

Once again, this kind of idea has different implications according to whether dramatic monologue, theater, or immersive theater metaphors about the analytic situation are supposed by the analyst, rather than the cinema metaphor. The former suppositions alert an analyst to the likelihood that "mistakes" will happen due to the eruption of unconscious beliefs and because anxiety, guilt, panic, and other emotions will be aroused during the sessions. They will be unsettling to the analyst and maybe the patient, but they can become informative if the analyst can puzzle out their meaning and manage the dislocation to the analyst's "own usual reference-points" (Denis, 2008, p. 43).

The scope for such phenomena to be disturbing to the extent of disabling seems likely to be greater for those analysts who rely on cinema assumptions than the others. The cinema framework creates a focus on the patient's difficulties outside or in the past with others not inside the room with the analyst.

Nodal moments are, by definition, unexpected and so spontaneous. To be fully used, they require an analyst to draw on deep internal resources, and it seems likely that the most important are those that allow the analyst to stay curious (or perhaps to realize the need to recover lost curiosity) about what might be going on in sessions. This is why Q5 and Q6, noting one's own thoughts and feelings and reflective curiosity, may be useful to maintain any psychoanalytic investigation.

Haydée Faimberg's (1992) concept of "listening to listening" evolved when she found herself unexpectedly aware of what she later called the telescoping of generations dominating one of her patients' ways of understanding her experience. This is an example of an important idea that makes use of immersive theater–type suppositions about the analytic situation and, specifically, prioritizes the role in the ongoing analysis of the analyst's "own countertransference position"—that is, the disposition toward the patient that the analyst has gradually taken up. As Faimberg puts it in her paper on "listening to listening," in a first stage, the analyst listens to the patient and chooses either to interpret or to remain silent. In a second stage, he tries to listen to how the patient has himself listened to the interpretation or the silence. This second stage is crucial because it "gives retroactive meaning to the first stage and allows the analyst to begin to listen to this barely audible register. Since the patient cannot speak directly about the way he has listened to the interpretations or refer to his unconscious identifications, it is up to the analyst to listen to the way in which these speak" (Faimberg, 1992, p. 545).

Trying to trace with minimal imposition what the patient has "made" of what one just said or did not say with an open mind and finding the courage and inspiration to think what has previously been unthinkable are constant challenges. Changing course may not happen often, and uncertainty that our new ideas may be overvalued ideas is necessary. For the moment, we want only to make the point that making a difference depends on reflexive capacity (Q6) and that the different suppositions structuring a psychoanalytic investigation can impede or further it.

In sum, being aware of the suppositions one is making about the analytic situation and a good-enough experience in one's own personal analysis can prepare an analyst for such moments. We see the role of the eleven questions as providing some structure in which curiosity can take place. But things will always be uncertain—a guess (*erraten* or *selected fact*) can always be an overvalued idea. Importantly, Denis made the point that to avoid becoming disorganized or made too anxious, analysts necessarily undergo a chronic temptation to adopt a fetishistic solution: that is, to cling to the method that has served them. This has been making debate difficult.

HOW CAN WE MANAGE OURSELVES, EACH OTHER, AND OUR DEBATES BETTER?

This work has emerged from the European Psychoanalytic Federation's New Scientific Policy and Ten Year Initiative, launched over twenty years ago in 2002 in Prague (Tuckett, 2002). The idea then was to provide a way for the many psychoanalytic societies (speaking many languages and adapting psychoanalysis to their cultures and medical and intellectual traditions) to learn from each other and to develop policies to further psychoanalytic practice and training on a more solid and less fetishistic footing. At the time it was easy enough to see that mutual understanding between psychoanalysts was rare, that epistemological confusion was widespread, and that the necessary pluralistic breakout from attempts to use authority to solve debates was leading to fragmentation. Evidence about effective practice and training was not accumulating within a framework of uncompelled consensual understanding, and there were clear signs of "anything goes." There was no common observational base and no theoretical scaffolding to allow comparison of clinical methods. This work has tried to make some progress in defining a common theoretical framework for exploring different suppositions about conducting a psychoanalytic investigation. Due to the generous contribution of many presenters, workshop participants, and moderators, as well as many years of effort, we think we have succeeded more than before in sharing a common database experience of doing psychoanalysis while also trying to preserve the anonymity of all involved.

Ambivalence, disagreement, and debate about what psychoanalysts do and should do will continue. To a significant degree, psychoanalysis is at what Fred Busch (2023) has called a crossroads—at least insofar as some of the developments discussed above are threatening to move it away from its essential preoccupation with unconscious beliefs and a specialized procedure for inferring them reliant on the three sources of inference discussed in Chapter 4. It may be that it could be effective to replace investigating unconscious beliefs that are hard to bear with a different approach, but if so, we should be quite explicit about this intention. The eleven questions are one way to test if that is how we want to go.

We hope the CCM two-step method for discussion, together with the common suppositional framework we have presented and put to work in this chapter, are innovations that will provide a way to advance debate and training, providing a better way to manage it and give psychoanalytic candidates the help they deserve. We also hope people will be inspired to go back to reading, debating, and understanding Freud's writing and the development of his ideas about how to investigate mental life. It is not a journey we think is useful if the aim is to appeal to his authority. But for the purpose of understanding his struggle and his rationales, we have found reading his own words and understanding their origin in German to be invaluable.

Glossary

Acting out. *See Enactment.*

Agieren. *See Enactment.*

Ambivalence. The simultaneous existence of contradictory tendencies, attitudes, or feelings in the relationship to a single object (for instance, the picture of the analyst)—especially the coexistence of love and hate.

Cast. A term used in this book specifically to interpret Freud's use of the word *Besetzung* with reference to understanding the specific meaning of transference as the patient casting the analyst (but also vice versa) into a role unconsciously assigned to them by an unconscious script. The German verb *besetzen* and noun *Besetzung* were frequently used by Freud, including in relation to his ideas about transference (Freud, 1912a, 100). These words, commonly used in German as both a noun and a verb, have a multitude of meanings—for example, to occupy a country militarily, occupy or invade a place, seize or squat in a house, cast an actor into a role (the literal translation of the German phrase would actually be "to cast a role with an actor"!), fill a job, and many others. Freud uses it with the very specific meaning derived from neurophysiology—namely, that a psychic object, an idea (*Vorstellung*), or a representation is or gets invested with (emotional) drive-energy. Despite admitting that it was in opposition to Freud's preference for everyday words, Strachey created the rather unhappy neologisms *to cathect* and *cathexis* for English, which, to judge by modern literature, have not stood the test of time. As we see it, "casting an actor into a role" aptly describes the process of transference or countertransference Freud had in mind in 1912, as well as what happens to the object in this process. The expression contains, on the one hand, what Freud describes as a "false connection" (Freud, 1893, p. 303) insofar as an actual object is invested with the drive-energy of a wish formerly directed at a former object, but it goes beyond that insofar as this expression simultaneously designates a pressure that is exerted on the respective other person (to play out the role). This later issue

255

can also be found in Freud. We use the term "cast" because it so aptly and beautifully encompasses these processes. See page 68.

Cinema. Term used in this book to describe a view of the analytic situation characterized by the supposition that the dreams, ideas, and situations the patient is describing reveal to the analyst an ongoing unconscious script driving the patient's experience of their world and the persons they encounter in it. See pages 55–62.

Construction/construct. Terms used in this book specifically to describe an analyst's interpretative (i.e., sense-making) activity when bringing several points together to "construct" a larger meaning. See pages 89–91.

Countertransference. Like "transference," a term that can be used in very different ways. We will restrict its usage so that we mean the analyst's *unconscious response* to the person of the patient. The implication is that while it can be guessed, it can never be known.

Deficit. We use the term, particularly in Chapter 5 but also in Chapter 9, to refer to a broad range of ideas about the difficulties created in the present by various kinds of deficiencies in early experience.

Designation/designate. Terms used in this book specifically to describe an analyst's interpretations to patients when they are limited to pointing out something that both patient and analyst can quite easily notice at the time—for instance, a slip of the tongue, a moment of embarrassment or hesitation, a simple response of dislike, and so forth. See pages 190–91.

Dramatic monologue. Term used in this book to describe the supposition that the patient's unconscious script can *mainly* be revealed/acknowledged/recognized/ reconstructed by means of the analyst's unconscious mental activity while listening in evenly hovering attention to the patient's choice of words, affective tone, moments of hesitation, slips, and so forth. See pages 62–68.

Enactment. A term with different meanings deriving from different traditions. We use it in this book, influenced by Freud's use of the German word *Agieren*, which is best understood in English as "an effort to actualize a wish," that is, as an action that enacts an unconscious fantasy belief. Some analysts in the United States use the term much more generally (e.g., analyst and patient might *enact* a mother-child boundary). For relational analysts the term was used to incorporate both the analyst's fallibility and their potential to become a new object (Cooper, 2004).

Erraten. In simple terms, "guess," but with the meaning that, first, facts and feelings are assembled. See Chapter 6, pages 180–83.

Evenly hovering attention. We use this phrase as the most preferable way to render Freud's *gleichschwebende Aufmerksamkeit* in English. See Box 4.6.

Field theory. Field theory in psychoanalysis derives from two developments: the American psychologist Kurt Lewin and his pupil Harry Stack Sullivan; and the Latin American "River Plate" psychoanalysts (Heinrich Racker, José Bleger, Willy and Madeleine Baranger) influenced by Susan Langer and both Freud and Klein. Modern field theorists include Thomas Ogden and Antonino Ferro and vary as to how far they use the idea.

Freud's procedure. This phrase is used to summarize Freud's argument that a psycho-analytic technique should be based on the fundamental rule and evenly hovering attention. It is discussed in Chapter 4. See pages 113–19.

Fundamental rule. Freud's rule for patients that they should "say whatever goes through your mind. Act as though, for instance, you were a traveller sitting next to the window of a railway carriage and describing to someone inside the carriage the changing views which you see outside." See Box 4.7.

gleichschwebende Aufmerksamkeit. *See evenly hovering attention.*

Guess. *See Erraten.*

Immersive theater. Term used in this book to describe a view of the analytic situation characterized by the supposition that an unconscious script pushing for expression is present in the patient's associations *and* in the analyst's responses. They reveal to the analyst, if scrutinized thoroughly, a hidden picture they have of each other and their immediate intentions toward, attitudes to, and feelings for each other, prompted by their being together as people now. See pages 72–76.

Nachträglichkeit. Translated into English as "deferred action" and into French as *après coup*. The term was frequently used by Freud in connection with his view of psychical temporality and causality: experiences, impressions, and memory traces may be revised at a later date to fit in with fresh experiences or with the attainment of a new stage of development. They may in that event be endowed not only with a new meaning but also with new psychological consequences. To take an example of Bion's, think of a place and your first experience there. Then imagine or recall revisiting the place again with numerous different experiences. Each experience will influence the next, and gradually the place may also feel different retrospectively, colored by experience (Bion Talamo, 1997).

Oedipal situation. We use this term loosely, bearing in mind that Freud (1923) wrote that the Oedipus complex was part of "the principal subject-matter of psycho-analysis and the foundations of its theory" (p. 247) and that his principal understanding of the cause of mental difficulty was that it resulted from the attempt to apply repetitive solutions to repetitively perceived internal conflicts. The Oedipal configuration built up from infancy is central to modern theory not because we all concretely want to sleep with or kill our mothers or fathers (or are stuck in old-fashioned concepts of male and female, etc.). Rather it matters because so much of human life evokes modern versions of the issues we first encountered in infancy—that is, feelings evoked when we recognize our difference from those of the opposite sex and sameness with those of the same sex; rivalrous feelings and ambivalence (hatred and love) toward the parent of the same sex and ambivalence or feelings of lack toward the parent of the opposite sex and guilt or shame about those feelings; hatred and guilt about hatred at the recognition of the existence of time or bigness and smallness, or in other words, of generational difference and capacity; and hatred at the recognition of exclusion from the parents' relationship, or in other words, the primal scene, causing difficulties with the third position.

Reflexive, reflexively, reflexivity. These terms are used (particularly in Chapter 4) in preference to "reflection" or its derivatives. We are creatively adapting the term "reflexivity" from its original use. Anthony Giddens (1991) uses it to address the central sociological issue as to how individuals can be both free and socially constrained by understanding self-identity as a reflexive project. Instead of taking for granted or passively inheriting who we are, we actively shape, reflect on, and monitor our selves, crafting our biographical narratives as we go through life. We treat our identities, then, as a project, something that we actively construct and are ultimately responsible for. George Soros (1987) used the concept to argue that because investors can't base their decisions on (unknowable and uncertain) reality, they base them on their socially shaped perceptions of reality instead. The actions that result from these perceptions have a *reflexive* impact on reality, or fundamentals, which then affects investors' perceptions and thus prices. Our use refers to the reflexive process in the analyst's mind—that is, to the transformation made possible by the third source of data (Figure 4.1). Analysts make sense of patients' words, note their thoughts and responses, and further reflexively transform meaning. This might be via conscious reflection, but because it may involve more than that (i.e., unconscious cognition), not necessarily.

Resistance. Term used in this book to denote a patient's or analyst's feeling or behavioral response to becoming aware of an idea, belief, or fantasy that is unconscious, because once such phenomena become conscious, at least initially, they create discomfort—such as embarrassment, anxiety, shame, guilt, odd excitement, and so on. In this way signs of resistance (changing the subject, forgetting, slips of the tongue, silence, falling asleep, etc.) are signs of something present but avoided so as not to be known to the subject (see Tuckett, 2019b). In this usage resistance makes evident unconscious phenomena starting to surface in the analyst or patient. The term can be used in other ways—such as to express opposition to the analyst and his or her ideas, opposition to attending sessions, and so forth, but this is not the meaning we apply. Historically, there has been much confusion between meanings, and additionally, given that occurrences are defined by analysts, their labeling must potentially be influenced by countertransference. See Schafer, 1973.

Theater. Term used in this book to describe a view of the analytic situation characterized by the supposition that an unconscious script is present and pushing for expression in free associations. These associations reveal to the analyst a hidden picture of the analyst now and of his or her immediate intentions toward, attitudes to, and feelings for the patient. See pages 68–72.

Three sources of inference. A phrase used in this book after its introduction in Chapter 4 to describe three levels of "data" psychoanalysts draw on to infer their patients' unconscious scripts. They can (1) draw on the sense they make of their patient's words and actions, (2) draw on their own feelings and thoughts in response, and (3) draw on a further level by scrutinizing the connections between the first two. See pages 93–94.

Transference. A term Freud introduced as crucial but to which he gave different meanings and which it was clear in our workshops has multiple meanings in psychoanalysis, particularly between psychoanalytic cultures. The purpose of Chapter 3 is to describe what we believe are the four core ways of understanding it—each described by one of the four metaphors we use to consider the analytic situation.

Unconscious. We use the term "unconscious" only in the sense of a dynamic or repressed unconscious consisting of beliefs or fantasies that the subject finds it uncomfortable to be aware of and so resists knowing or elaborating. In this book we also use the terms *belief, fantasy,* and *phantasy* interchangeably.

Unconscious repetition. A phrase used in this book, particularly in Chapter 5, to facilitate discussing different ideas psychoanalysts have about how the present in some way is being influenced by the patient's past—which, clearly, in some way or another, requires a mechanism. To allow exploration we have tried to be agnostic on that aspect.

Unconscious script. A phrase used throughout this book to capture, without making too many assumptions, the idea that unconscious beliefs and fantasies are part of a more overall narrative we all tell ourselves about the situations and people we encounter, which is loosely based on our past sense making and experience. Whether drive theory or an affect regulation theory is adopted as the motivation, we see the script constantly pushing for expression.

Verraten. A German word meaning "to betray." In free association, repressed unconscious meaning is betrayed (against the subject's conscious resistances) through slips of the tongue or other (formal) aspects of language, as well as by the sequencing of "free associations" that cannot help but reveal unconscious beliefs, feelings, and desires, even in terms of their content. See Chapter 6, pages 182–83.

References

Akhtar, S. (2009). *Comprehensive dictionary of psychoanalysis*. Karnac.

Akhtar, S. (2018). *Psychoanalytic listening*. Routledge.

Anzieu, D. (1986). *Freud's self-analysis*. International Psycho-Analytical Library.

Aron, L. (1990a). Free association and changing models of mind. *Journal of the American Academy of Psychoanalysis and Dynamic Psychiatry, 18*(3), 439–59. https://doi.org/10.1521/jaap.1.1990.18.3.439.

Aron, L. (1990b). One person and two person psychologies and the method of psychoanalysis. *Psychoanalytic Psychology, 7*(4), 475–85. https://doi.org/10.1037/0736-9735.7.4.475.

Baranger, M., & Baranger, W. (1969). *Problemas del campo psicoanalítico [Problems of the analytic field]*. Kargieman.

Benjamin, J. (1994). What angel would hear me? The erotics of transference. *Psychoanalytic Inquiry, 14*(4), 535–57. https://doi.org/10.1080/07351699409534005.

Benjamin, J. (1995). *Like subjects, love objects: Essays on recognition and sexual difference*. Yale University Press.

Benjamin, J. (2018). *Beyond doer and done to: Recognition theory, intersubjectivity and the third*. Routledge.

Bergmann, M. (Ed.). (2004). *Understanding dissidences and controversies in psychoanalysis*. Other Press.

Berlin, I. (1958). *Two concepts of liberty*. Clarendon Press.

Bernstein, B. (1964). Elaborated and restricted codes: Their social origins and some consequences. *American Anthropologist, 66*(6, pt. 2), 55–69.

Bion Talamo, P. (1997). Bion: A Freudian innovator. *British Journal of Psychotherapy, 14*(1), 47–59. https://doi.org/10.1111/j.1752-0118.1997.tb00351.x.

Bion, W. R. (1950). The imaginary twin. In *Second thoughts: Selected papers on psychoanalysis (1967)*. In C. Mawson (Ed.), *The complete works of W. R. Bion* (Vol. 6) (pp. 55–72). Karnac, 2014.

Bion, W. R. (1961). Experiences in groups. In C. Mawson (Ed.), *The complete works of W. R. Bion* (Vol. 4) (pp. 95–246). Karnac, 2014.

Bion, W. R. (1962). Learning from experience. In C. Mawson (Ed.), *The complete works of W. R. Bion* (Vol. 4) (pp. 247–365). Karnac, 2014.

Bion, W. R. (1963). Elements of psycho-analysis. In C. Mawson (Ed.), *The complete works of W. R. Bion* (Vol. 5) (pp. 1–86). London: Karnac, 2014.

Bion, W. R. (1967). Second thoughts: Selected papers on psychoanalysis. In C. Mawson (Ed.), *The complete works of W. R. Bion* (Vol. 6) (pp. 45–210). Karnac, 2014.

Bion, W. R. (1970). Attention and interpretation. In C. Mawson (Ed.), *The complete works of W. R. Bion* (Vol. 6) (pp. 211–330). Karnac, 2014.

Bird, B. (1972). Notes on transference: Universal phenomenon and hardest part of analysis. *Journal of the American Psychoanalytic Association, 20*(2), 267–301. https://doi.org/10.1177/000306517202000203.

Blass, R. B. (2001). The teaching of the Oedipus complex: On making Freud meaningful to university students by unveiling his essential ideas on the human condition. *International Journal of Psychoanalysis, 82*(6), 1105–21. https://doi.org/10.1516/0020757011601433.

Blass, R. B. (2023). Why analysts do not debate well and what can be done about it. *International Journal of Psychoanalysis, 104*(1), 161–64. https://doi.org/10.1080/00207578.2023.2162211.

Bleger, J. (1967). Psycho-analysis of the psycho-analytic frame. *International Journal of Psychoanalysis, 48*(4), 511–19.

Bleger, J. (2012). Theory and practice in psychoanalysis: Psychoanalytic praxis. 1969. *International Journal of Psychoanalysis, 93*(4), 993–1003. https://doi.org/10.1111/j.1745-8315.2012.00593.x.

Bollas, C. (2006). Übertragungsdeutung als ein Widerstand gegen die freie Assoziation. *Psyche—Zeitschrift für Psychoanalyse, 60*(9–10), 932–47.

Bourdin, D. (2007). Pour une présence en retrait qui ne soit pas un retrait de présence. Note sur l'altérité de l'analyste. *Revue Française de Psychanalyse, 71*, 719–38.

Bouvet, M. (1958). Technical variation and the concept of distance. *International Journal of Psychoanalysis, 39*(2–4), 211–21.

Brenner, C. (2000). Brief communication: Evenly hovering attention. *Psychoanalytic Quarterly, 69*(3), 545–49. https://doi.org/10.1002/j.2167-4086.2000.tb00574.x.

Britton, R. (1994). Publication anxiety: Conflict between communication and affiliation. *International Journal of Psychoanalysis, 75*: 1213–24.

Britton, R. (1998). *Belief and Imagination*. Routledge.

Britton, R. (1999). Getting in on the act: The hysterical solution. *International Journal of Psychoanalysis, 80*(1), 1–14. https://doi.org/10.1516/0020757991598477.

Britton, R. (2010). Developmental uncertainty versus paranoid regression. *Psychoanalytic Review, 97*(2), 195–206. https://doi.org/10.1521/prev.2010.97.2.195.

Britton, R., & Steiner, J. (1994). Interpretation: Selected fact or overvalued idea? *International Journal of Psychoanalysis, 75*(5–6), 1069–78.

Britton, R., & Vaihinger, A. (2009). Religion und Fanatismus. *Psyche—Zeitschrift für Psychoanalyse, 63*(9–10), 907–24.

Bromberg, C. E., & Aron, L. (2019). Disguised autobiography as clinical case study. *Psychoanalytic Dialogues, 29*(6), 695–710. https://doi.org/10.1080/10481885.2019.1679598.

Bromberg, P. (1986). Discussion of dialogue between Lawrence Epstein and Mildred Schwartz on "Love and Hate in Psychoanalysis." *Contemporary Psychotherapy Review, 3*, 54–68.

Bromberg, P. (2006). *Awakening the dreamer: Clinical journeys*. Analytic Press.

Bromberg, P. M. (2000). Potholes on the royal road: Or is it an abyss? *Contemporary Psychoanalysis, 36*(1), 5–28. https://doi.org/10.1080/00107530.2000.10747043.

Bromberg, P. M. (2003). One need not be a house to be haunted: On enactment, dissociation, and the dread of "not-me"—a case study. *Psychoanalytic Dialogues, 13*(5), 689–709. https:// doi.org/10.1080/10481881309348764.

Bromberg, P. M. (2009). "Speak! that I may see you": Some reflections on dissociation, reality, and psychoanalytic listening. *Psychoanalytic Dialogues, 4*(4), 517–47. https://doi .org/10.1080/10481889409539037.

Brothers, D. (2015). What I learned from Paul Ornstein—and about him. *International Journal of Psychoanalytic Self Psychology, 10*(2), 172–78. https://doi.org/10.1080/15551024 .2015.1005804.

Busch, F. (2013). Changing views of what is curative in 3 psychoanalytic methods and the emerging, surprising common ground. *Scandinavian Psychoanalytic Review, 36*(1), 27–34. https://doi.org/10.1080/01062301.2013.805549.

Busch, F. (Ed.). (2023). *Psychoanalysis at the crossroads: An international perspective.* Routledge.

Carlson, D. A. (2002). Free-swinging attention. *Psychoanalytic Quarterly, 71*(4), 725–50. https://doi.org/10.1002/j.2167-4086.2002.tb00024.x.

Chater, N. (2018). *The mind is flat: The illusion of mental depth and the improvised mind.* Penguin.

Cooper, A. M. (2008). Commentary on Greenson's "The working alliance and the transference neurosis." *Psychoanalytic Quarterly, 77*(1), 103–19. https://doi.org/10.1002/j.2167 -4086.2008.tb00335.x.

Cooper, S. H. (2004). State of the hope: The new bad object in the therapeutic action of psychoanalysis. *Psychoanalytic Dialogues, 14*(5), 527–51.

Cooper, S. H. (2015). Clinical theory at the border(s): Emerging and unintended crossings in the development of clinical theory. *International Journal of Psychoanalysis, 96*(2), 273–92. https://doi.org/10.1111/1745-8315.12249.

Cooper, S. H. (2017). The analyst's "use" of theory or theories: The play of theory. *Journal of the American Psychoanalytic Association, 65*(5), 859–82. https://doi.org/10.1177 /0003065117737069.

Corrao, F. (1981). Struttura poliadica e funzione gamma. In *Orme. Contributi alla psicoanalisi di gruppo* (Vol. 2). Raffaello Cortina Editore, 1998.

Cremerius, J. (1979a). Die Verwirrungen des Zöglings T.: Psychoanalytische Lehrjahre neben der Couch [The confusions of boarding student T.: Years of psychoanalytic apprenticeship beside the couch]. *Psyche—Zeitschrift für Psychoanalyse, 33*(6), 551–64.

Cremerius, J. (1979b): Gibt es zwei psychoanalytische Techniken? [Are there two psychoanalytic techniques?] *Psyche—Zeitschrift für Psychoanalyse, 33* (7), 577–99

Cremerius, J. (1981). Freud bei der Arbeit über die Schulter geschaut.—Seine Technik im Spiegel von Schülern und Patienten [Freud at work—looking over his shoulder.—His technique in the mirror of followers and patients]. In J. Cremerius (Ed.), *Vom Handwerk des Psychoanalytikers. Das Werkzeug der psychoanalytischen Technik [The psychoanalyst's craft: The tools of psychoanalytic technique]* (Vol. 2, pp. 326–63). Frommann-Holzboog, 1984.

Curtis, H. C. (1990). The patient as existential victim: A classical view. *Psychoanalytic Inquiry, 10*(4), 498–508. https://doi.org/10.1080/07351690.1990.10399622.

Davies, J. M. (2018). The "rituals" of the relational perspective: Theoretical shifts and clinical implications. *Psychoanalytic Dialogues, 28*(6), 651–69. https://doi.org/10.1080/10481885 .2018.1538745.

Denis, P. (2008). In praise of empiricism. In D. Tuckett, R. Basile, D. Birksted-Breen, T. Bohm, P. Denis, A. Ferro, H. Hinz, A. Jemstedt, P. Mariotti, & J. Schubert (Eds.), *Psychoanalysis comparable and incomparable: The evolution of a method to describe and compare psychoanalytic approaches* (pp. 38–49). Routledge.

Deutsch, H. (1926). Okkulte Vorgänge während der Psychoanalyse. *Imago, 12*, 418–33.

Diercks, M. (2018). Freud's "transference": Clinical technique in the "Rat Man" case and theoretical conceptualization compared. *International Journal of Psychoanalysis, 99*(1), 58–81. https://doi.org/10.1111/1745-8315.12687.

Doolittle, H. (1956). *Tribute to Freud*. Pantheon.

Eissler, K. R. (1953). The effect of the structure of the ego on psychoanalytic technique. *Journal of the American Psychoanalytic Association, 1*(1), 104–43. https://doi.org/10.1177/000306515300100107.

Faimberg, H. (1981). Une des difficultés de l'analyse: Là reconnaissance de l'altérité: L'écoute des interprétations. *Revue Française de Psychanalyse, 45*(6), 1351–67.

Faimberg, H. (1992). The countertransference position and the countertransference. *International Journal of Psychoanalysis, 73*(3), 541–47.

Faimberg, H. (2007). A plea for a broader concept of *Nachträglichkeit*. *Psychoanalytic Quarterly, 76*(4), 1221–40.

Fedida, P. (2002). Constructing place: The supervision of a psychoanalytic cure. *Bulletin of the European Psychoanalytical Federation, 56*, 17–28.

Ferro, A. (Ed.). (2018). *Contemporary Bionian theory and technique in psychoanalysis*. Routledge.

Fonagy, P., & Target, M. (1996). Playing with reality: I. Theory of mind and the normal development of psychic reality. *International Journal of Psychoanalysis, 77*(2), 217–33.

Fosshage, J. L. (1990a). The analyst's response. *Psychoanalytic Inquiry, 10*(4), 601–22.

Fosshage, J. L. (1990b). Clinical protocol. *Psychoanalytic Inquiry, 10*(4), 461–77.

Freud, A. (1976). Changes in psychoanalytic practice and experience. *International Journal of Psychoanalysis, 57*(3), 257–60.

Freud, S. (1890). Psychical (or mental) treatment. In J. Strachey (Ed.), *The standard edition of the complete psychological works of Sigmund Freud* (Vol. 7, pp. 281–302). Hogarth Press, 1953.

Freud, S. (1893). The psychotherapy of hysteria. In J. Strachey (Ed.), *The standard edition of the complete psychological works of Sigmund Freud* (Vol. 2, pp. 253–305). Hogarth Press, 1955.

Freud, S. (1894). The neuro-psychoses of defence. In J. Strachey (Ed.), *The standard edition of the complete psychological works of Sigmund Freud* (Vol. 3, pp. 41–61). Hogarth Press, 1962.

Freud, S. (1896). Further remarks on the neuro-psychoses of defence. In J. Strachey (Ed.), *The standard edition of the complete psychological works of Sigmund Freud* (Vol. 3, pp. 157–85). Hogarth Press, 1962.

Freud, S. (1898). Sexuality in the aetiology of the neuroses. In J. Strachey (Ed.), *The standard edition of the complete psychological works of Sigmund Freud* (Vol. 3, pp. 259–85). Hogarth Press, 1962.

Freud, S. (1900). The interpretation of dreams. In J. Strachey (Ed.), *The standard edition of the complete psychological works of Sigmund Freud* (Vol. 4–5, pp. ix–627). Hogarth Press, 1953.

Freud, S. (1905a). Fragment of an analysis of a case of hysteria (1905 [1901]). In J. Strachey (Ed.), *The standard edition of the complete psychological works of Sigmund Freud* (Vol. 7, pp. 7–122). Hogarth Press, 1953.

Freud, S. (1905b). Bruchstück einer Hysterie-Analyse: IV. Nachwort. *Gesammelte Werke: Chronologisch Geordnet* 5: 275–86.

Freud, S. (1909a). Letter from Sigmund Freud to C. G. Jung, June 7, 1909. In W. McGuire (Ed.), *The Freud/Jung letters: The correspondence between Sigmund Freud and C. G. Jung* (pp. 230–32). Princeton University Press, 1986.

Freud, S. (1909b). Notes upon a case of obsessional neurosis. In J. Strachey (Ed.), *The standard edition of the complete psychological works of Sigmund Freud* (Vol. 10, pp. 151–318). Hogarth Press, 1955.

Freud, S. (1910a). The future prospects of psycho-analysis. In J. Strachey (Ed.), *The standard edition of the complete psychological works of Sigmund Freud* (Vol. 11, pp. 159–52). Hogarth Press, 1957.

Freud, S. (1910b). Letter from Sigmund Freud to Sándor Ferenczi, October 6, 1910. In E. Brabant, E. Falzeder, P. Giampieri-Deutsch, A. Haynal, I. Meyer-Palmedo, & P. T. Hoffer (Eds.), *The correspondence of Sigmund Freud and Sándor Ferenczi, Volume 1, 1908–1914* (pp. 221–23). The Belknap Press of Harvard University Press, 1992.

Freud, S. (1912a). The dynamics of transference. In J. Strachey (Ed.), *The standard edition of the complete psychological works of Sigmund Freud* (Vol. 12, pp. 97–108). Hogarth Press, 1958.

Freud, S. (1912b). A note on the unconscious in psycho-analysis. In J. Strachey (Ed.), *The standard edition of the complete psychological works of Sigmund Freud* (Vol. 12, pp. 255–66). Hogarth Press, 1958.

Freud, S. (1912c). Recommendations to physicians practising psycho-analysis. In J. Strachey (Ed.), *The standard edition of the complete psychological works of Sigmund Freud* (Vol. 12, pp. 109–20). Hogarth Press, 1958.

Freud, S. (1913). On beginning the treatment. In J. Strachey (Ed.), *The standard edition of the complete psychological works of Sigmund Freud* (Vol. 12, pp. 121–44). Hogarth Press, 1958.

Freud, S. (1914). Remembering, repeating, and working-through (further recommendations on the technique of psycho-analysis II). In J. Strachey (Ed.), *The standard edition of the complete psychological works of Sigmund Freud* (Vol. 12, pp. 145–56). Hogarth Press, 1958.

Freud, S. (1915a). Observations on transference love (further recommendations on the technique of psycho-analysis III). In J. Strachey (Ed.), *The standard edition of the complete psychological works of Sigmund Freud* (Vol. 12, pp. 157–71). Hogarth Press, 1958.

Freud, S. (1915b). The unconscious. In J. Strachey (Ed.), *The standard edition of the complete psychological works of Sigmund Freud* (Vol. 14, pp. 159–216). Hogarth Press, 1957.

Freud, S. (1916). Introductory lectures on psycho-analysis. In J. Strachey (Ed.), *The standard edition of the complete psychological works of Sigmund Freud* (Vol. 15, pp. 1–240). Hogarth Press, 1963.

Freud, S. (1917a). Introductory lectures on psycho-analysis: Part III, General theory of the neuroses. In J. Strachey (Ed.), *The standard edition of the complete psychological works of Sigmund Freud* (Vol. 16, pp. 241–463). Hogarth Press, 1963.

Freud, S. (1917b). Mourning and melancholia. In J. Strachey (Ed.), *The standard edition of the complete psychological works of Sigmund Freud* (Vol. 14, pp. 237–58). Hogarth Press, 1957.

Freud, S. (1920a). Beyond the pleasure principle. In J. Strachey (Ed.), *The standard edition of the complete psychological works of Sigmund Freud* (Vol. 18, pp. 1–64). Hogarth Press, 1955.

Freud, S. (1920b). The psychogenesis of a case of homosexuality in a woman. In J. Strachey (Ed.), *The standard edition of the complete psychological works of Sigmund Freud* (Vol. 18, pp. 145–72). Hogarth Press, 1955.

Freud, S. (1923). Two encyclopaedia articles. In J. Strachey (Ed.), *The standard edition of the complete psychological works of Sigmund Freud* (Vol. 18, pp. 233–60). Hogarth Press, 1955.

Freud, S. (1924). A short account of psycho-analysis. In J. Strachey (Ed.), *The standard edition of the complete psychological works of Sigmund Freud* (Vol. 19, pp. 191–209). Hogarth Press, 1961.

Freud, S. (1926a). Psycho-analysis. In J. Strachey (Ed.), *The standard edition of the complete psychological works of Sigmund Freud* (Vol. 20, pp. 259–70). Hogarth Press, 1959.

Freud, S. (1926b). The question of lay analysis. In J. Strachey (Ed.), *The standard edition of the complete psychological works of Sigmund Freud* (Vol. 20, pp. 177–258). Hogarth Press, 1959.

Freud, S. (1933). New introductory lectures on psychoanalysis. In J. Strachey (Ed.), *The standard edition of the complete psychological works of Sigmund Freud* (Vol. 22, pp. 1–182). Hogarth Press, 1964.

Freud, S. (1937). Constructions in analysis. In J. Strachey (Ed.), *The standard edition of the complete psychological works of Sigmund Freud* (Vol. 23, pp. 255–70). Hogarth Press, 1964.

Freud, S. (1938a). An outline of psycho-analysis. In J. Strachey (Ed.), *The standard edition of the complete psychological works of Sigmund Freud* (Vol. 23, pp. 139–208). Hogarth Press, 1964.

Freud, S. (1938b). Splitting of the ego in the process of defense. In J. Strachey (Ed.), *The standard edition of the complete psychological works of Sigmund Freud* (Vol. 23, pp. 271–78). Hogarth Press, 1964.

Gabbard, G. O. (1997). A reconsideration of objectivity in the analyst. *International Journal of Psychoanalysis, 78*(1), 15–26.

Gabbard, G. O., & Westen, D. (2003). Rethinking therapeutic action. *International Journal of Psychoanalysis, 84*(4), 823–41. https://doi.org/10.1516/002075703768284605.

Gerhardt, U. (1986). *Patientenkarrieren* [Patient careers]. Suhrkamp.

Giddens, A. (1991). *Modernity and self-identity, self and society in the late modern age*. Stanford University Press.

Glenn, J. (1986). Freud, Dora, and the maid: A study of countertransference. *Journal of the American Psychoanalytic Association, 34*(3), 591–606. https://doi.org/10.1177/000306518603400304.

Goldberg, A. (1999). Between empathy and judgment. *Journal of the American Psychoanalytic Association, 47*(2), 350–65. https://doi.org/10.1177/00030651990470021201.

Green, A. (1998). The primordial mind and the work of the negative. *International Journal of Psychoanalysis, 79*(4), 649–65.

Green, A. (1999). On discriminating and not discriminating between affect and representation. *International Journal of Psychoanalysis, 80*(2), 277–316. https://doi.org/10.1516/0020757991598729.

Green, A. (2000). The central phobic position: A new formulation of the free association method. *International Journal of Psychoanalysis, 81*(3), 429–51. https://doi.org/10.1516/0020757001599807.

Green, A. (2005). *Key ideas for a contemporary psychoanalysis: Misrecognition and recognition of the unconscious*. Routledge.

Greenberg, J. (1995). Psychoanalytic technique and the interactive matrix. *Psychoanalytic Quarterly, 64*(1), 1–22.

Greenberg, J. (2001). The analyst's participation: A new look. *Journal of the American Psychoanalytic Association, 49*(2), 359–81. https://doi.org/10.1177/00030651010490020801.

Greenson, R. R. (1965). The working alliance and the transference neurosis. *Psychoanalytic Quarterly, 34*(2), 155–81. https://doi.org/10.1080/21674086.1965.11926343.

Gribinski, M. (1994). The stranger in the house. *International Journal of Psychoanalysis, 75*(5–6), 1011–21.

Grossman, V. (1995). *Life and Fate.* Trans. Robert Chandler. London.

Grubrich-Simitis, I. (1997). *Early Freud and late Freud.* Routledge.

Heimann, P. (1950). On counter-transference. *International Journal of Psychoanalysis, 31,* 81–84.

Hinz, H. (1991). Gleichschwebende Aufmerksamkeit und die Logik der Abduktion. *Jahrbuch der Psychoanalyse, 27,* 146–75.

Hinze, E. (2015). What do we learn in psychoanalytic training? *International Journal of Psychoanalysis, 96*(3), 755–71. https://doi.org/10.1111/1745-8315.12358.

Hoffman, I. Z. (1992). Expressive participation and psychoanalytic discipline. *Contemporary Psychoanalysis, 28*(1), 1–15. https://doi.org/10.1080/00107530.1992.10746734.

Hoffman, I. Z. (1996). The intimate and ironic authority of the psychoanalyst's presence. *Psychoanalytic Quarterly, 65*(1), 102–36.

Holmgren, B. (2013). Two ways of listening to the patient. *Scandinavian Psychoanalytic Review, 28*(2), 110–14. https://doi.org/10.1080/01062301.2005.10592766.

Hristeva, G. (2018). A searchlight on the road to freedom: Why do we still need free association? *Psychoanalytic Inquiry, 38*(6), 435–45. https://doi.org/10.1080/07351690.2018.1480229.

Jordan-Moore, J. F. (1994). Intimacy and science: The publication of clinical facts in psychoanalysis. *International Journal of Psychoanalysis, 75*(5–6), 1251–66.

Joseph, B. (1985). Transference: The total situation. *International Journal of Psychoanalysis, 66*(4), 447–54.

Kantrowitz, J. (2014). Discussion of Paula with "no history." In M. Altmann de Litvan (Ed.), *Time for change* (pp. 237–44). Karnac.

Kernberg, O. F. (1979). Some implications of object relations theory for psychoanalytic technique. *Journal of the American Psychoanalytic Association, 27*(Suppl.), 207–39.

Killingmo, B. (2013). A psychoanalytic listening-perspective in a time of pluralism. *Scandinavian Psychoanalytic Review, 22*(2), 151–71. https://doi.org/10.1080/01062301.1999.10592703.

King, P. (1978). Affective response of the analyst to the patient's communications. *International Journal of Psychoanalysis, 59*(2–3), 329–34.

Kleinman, A. (1980). *Patients and healers in the context of culture.* University of California Press.

Kluge, Susann. (2000). Empirically grounded construction of types and typologies in qualitative social research. *Forum: Qualitative Social Research.* https://www.qualitative-research.net/index.php/fqs/article/view/1124.

Kohut, H. (1971). *The analysis of the self.* International Universities Press.

Kohut, H. (1979). The two analyses of Mr. Z. *International Journal of Psychoanalysis, 60*(1), 3–27.

König, H. (1996). Gleichschwebende Aufmerksamkeit, Modelle und Theorien im Erkenntnisprozess des Psychoanalytikers. *Psyche—Zeitschrift für Psychoanalyse, 50*(4), 337–75.

LaFarge, L. (2017). From "either/or" to "and": The analyst's use of multiple models in clinical work. *Journal of the American Psychoanalytic Association, 65*(5), 829–44. https://doi.org/10.1177/0003065117736513.

Laplanche, J., & Pontalis, J.-B. (1973). *The language of psycho-analysis.* W. W. Norton.

Le Guen, C. (1982). The trauma of interpretation as history repeating itself. *International Journal of Psychoanalysis, 63*(3), 321–30.

Lear, J. (2017). *Wisdom won from illness: Essays in philosophy and psychoanalysis*. Harvard University Press.

Loewald, H. W. (1960). On the therapeutic action of psycho-analysis. *International Journal of Psychoanalysis, 41*, 16–33.

Loewald, H. W. (1979). Reflections on the psychoanalytic process and its therapeutic potential. *Psychoanalytic Study of the Child, 34*(1), 155–67. https://doi.org/10.1080/00797308. 1979.11823004.

Loewenstein, R. M. (1958). Remarks on some variations in psycho-analytic technique. *International Journal of Psychoanalysis, 39*(2–4), 202–10.

Lothane, Z. (1989). Schreber, Freud, Flechsig, and Weber revisited: An inquiry into methods of interpretation. *Psychoanalytic Review, 76*(2), 203–62.

Mahony, P. J. (2007). Reading the notes on the Rat Man case: Freud's own obsessional character and mother complex. *Canadian Journal of Psychoanalysis, 15*(1), 93–117.

Makari, G. J. (1992). A history of Freud's first concept of transference. *International Review of Psychoanalysis, 19*(4), 415–32.

Masson, J. M. (1985). *The complete letters of Sigmund Freud to Wilhelm Fliess, 1887–1904*. Harvard University Press.

Meltzer, D. (1978). *The Kleinian development*. Karnac.

Mitchell, S. A. (1997). *Influence and autonomy in psychoanalysis*. Analytic Press.

Mitchell, S. A. (1998). The analyst's knowledge and authority. *Psychoanalytic Quarterly, 67*(1), 1–31.

Moi, T. (1990). Representations of patriarchy: Sexuality and epistemology in Freud's Dora. In C. Bernheimer & C. Kahane (Eds.), *Dora's case: Freud-hysteria-feminism* (2nd ed., pp. 181–99). Columbia University Press.

Moore, B., & Fine, B. (1990). *Glossary of psychoanalytic terms and concepts* (3rd ed.). Yale University Press.

Pine, F. (1998). *Diversity and direction in psychoanalytic technique*. Yale University Press.

Racker, H. (1982). *Transference and countertransference*. Maresfield Press.

Reith, B., Møller, M., Boots, J., Crick, P., Gibeault, A., Jaffè, R., Lagerlöf, S., & Vermote, R. (2018). *Beginning analysis: On the processes of initiating psychoanalysis*. Routledge.

Rolland, J. C. (2006). A young woman's distress. *International Journal of Psychoanalysis, 87*(6), 1433–42. https://doi.org/10.1516/fj88-henn-atel-2ugn.

Rosenfeld, H. (1987). Projective identification and the psychotic transference in schizophrenia. In *Impasse and interpretation: Therapeutic and anti-therapeutic factors in the psychoanalytic treatment of psychotic, borderline, and neurotic patients* (pp. 220–40). Routledge/Institute of Psychoanalysis.

Roth, P., & Segal, H. (1990). Discussion: A Kleinian view. *Psychoanalytic Inquiry, 10*(4), 541–49. https://doi.org/10.1080/07351690.1990.10399625.

Rycroft, C. (1956). The nature and function of the analyst's communication to the patient. *International Journal of Psychoanalysis, 37*(6), 469–72.

Sandler, J. (1976). Countertransference and role-responsiveness. *International Review of Psychoanalysis, 3*, 43–47.

Schachter, J. (2018). Free association: From Freud to current use—the effects of training analysis on the use of free association. *Psychoanalytic Inquiry, 38*(6), 457–67. https://doi .org/10.1080/07351690.2018.1480231.

Schachter, J., & Kächele, H. (2007). The analyst's role in healing: Psychoanalysis-plus. *Psychoanalytic Psychology, 24*(3), 429–44. https://doi.org/10.1037/0736-9735.24.3.429.

Schafer, R. (1973). The idea of resistance. *International Journal of Psychoanalysis, 54,* 259–85.

Schubert, J. (2008). Experiences of participating: Group processes and group dynamics. In D. Tuckett, R. Basile, D. Birksted-Breen, T. Bohm, P. Denis, A. Ferro, H. Hinz, A. Jemstedt, P. Mariotti, & J. Schubert (Eds.), *Psychoanalysis comparable and incomparable: The evolution of a method to describe and compare psychoanalytic approaches* (pp. 208–33). Routledge.

Schwartz, J. (1996). What is science? What is psychoanalysis? What is to be done? *British Journal of Psychotherapy, 13*(1), 53–63. https://doi.org/10.1111/j.1752-0118.1996.tb00859.x.

Šebek, M. (2014). Transformations in Paula with "no history." In M. Altmann de Litvan (Ed.), *Time for change* (pp. 209–26). Karnac.

Sharpe, E. F. (1930). The technique of psycho-analysis. *International Journal of Psychoanalysis, 11,* 251–77.

Solms, M. (2013). The conscious id. *Neuropsychoanalysis, 15*(1), 5–19. https://doi.org/10.1080/15294145.2013.10773711.

Soros, G. (1987). *The alchemy of finance.* John Wiley & Sons.

Spillius, E. B. (1988). *Melanie Klein today: Developments in theory and practice.* Routledge.

Steiner, J. (1994). Patient-centered and analyst-centered interpretations: Some implications of containment and countertransference. *Psychoanalytic Inquiry, 14*(3), 406–22. https://doi.org/10.1080/07351699409533994.

Stern, D. B. (2010). Unconscious fantasy versus unconscious relatedness: Comparing interpersonal/relational and Freudian approaches to clinical practice. *Contemporary Psychoanalysis, 46*(1), 101–11. https://doi.org/10.1080/00107530.2010.10746041.

Stern, D. B. (2014). A response to LaFarge. *International Journal of Psychoanalysis, 95*(6), 1283–97. https://doi.org/10.1111/1745-8315.12291.

Stern, D. B. (2019). How I work with unconscious process: A case example. *Contemporary Psychoanalysis, 55*(4), 336–48. https://doi.org/10.1080/00107530.2019.1676579.

Stone, L. (1961). *The psychoanalytic situation.* International Universities Press.

Strachey, J. (1934). The nature of the therapeutic action of psycho-analysis. *International Journal of Psychoanalysis, 15,* 127–59.

Strozier, C. B. (1999). Heinz Kohut and "The two analyses of Mr. Z": The use (and abuse?) of case material in psychoanalysis. *Psychoanalytic Review, 86*(4), 569–86.

Strozier, C. B. (2004). *Heinz Kohut: The making of a psychoanalyst* (2nd ed.). Farrar, Straus & Giroux.

Symposium. 1937. "Symposium on the Theory of the Therapeutic Results of Psycho-Analysis." *The International Journal of Psychoanalysis* 18: 125–89.

Thompson, C. M. (1943). "The therapeutic technique of Sándor Ferenczi": A comment. *International Journal of Psychoanalysis, 24,* 182–95.

Tuckett, D. (1994). Developing a grounded hypothesis to understand a clinical process: The role of conceptualisation in validation. *International Journal of Psychoanalysis, 75,* 1159–80.

Tuckett, D. (1997). Mutual enactment in the psychoanalytic situation. In J. Ahumada (Ed.), *The perverse transference and other matters. Essays in honor of R. Horacio Etchegoyen* (pp. 203–16). Jason Aronson.

Tuckett, D. (2002). The new style conference and developing a peer culture in European psychoanalysis. *Bulletin of the European Psychoanalytical Federation, 56,* 32–45.

Tuckett, D. (2004). Presidential address: Building a psychoanalysis based on confidence in what we do. *Bulletin of the European Psychoanalytical Federation, 58,* 5–19.

Tuckett, D. (2012). Some reflections on psychoanalytic technique: In need of core concepts or an archaic ritual? *Psychoanalytic Inquiry, 32*(1), 87–108. https://doi.org/10.1080/07351 690.2011.553169.

Tuckett, D. (2019a). Transference and transference interpretation revisited: Why a parsimonious model of practice may be useful. *International Journal of Psychoanalysis, 100*(5), 852–76. https://doi.org/10.1080/00207578.2019.1664906.

Tuckett, D. (2019b). Ideas prevented from becoming conscious: On Freud's unconscious and the theory of psychoanalytic technique. *International Journal of Psychoanalysis, 100*, 1068–83.

Tuckett, D., Basile, R., Birksted-Breen, D., Bohm, T., Denis, P., Ferro, A., Hinz, H., Jemstedt, A., Mariotti, P., & Schubert, J. (2008). *Psychoanalysis comparable and incomparable: The evolution of a method to describe and compare psychoanalytic approaches*. Routledge.

Tuckett, D., Boulton, M., Olson, C., & Williams, A. (1985). *Meetings between experts: An approach to sharing ideas in medical consultations*. Tavistock.

Tuckett, D., Holmes, D., Pearson, A., & Chaplin, G. (2020). Monetary policy and the management of uncertainty: A narrative approach. Staff Working Paper No. 870. Bank of England. https://www.bankofengland.co.uk//media/boe/files/working-paper/2020/monetary -policy-and-themanagement-of-uncertainty-a-narrative-approach.pdf.

Vassalli, G. (2001). The birth of psychoanalysis from the spirit of technique. *International Journal of Psychoanalysis, 82*(1), 3–25. https://doi.org/10.1516/g7qg-dnhn-vanf-6j07.

Wallerstein, R. S. (1986). *Forty-two lives in treatment: A study of psychoanalysis and psychotherapy*. Guilford Press.

Weber, M. (1904): Die "Objektivität" sozialwissenschaftlicher und sozialpolitischer Erkenntnis. In: *Ders.: Gesammelte Aufsätze zur Wissenschaftstheorie*. 7. Auflage. Tübingen, Mohr 1988, S. 146–214 [Engl.: Weber, M. (2012): The "objectivity" of knowledge in social science and social policy. In: Weber, M. (ed.): *Collected Methodological Essays* (ed HH Bruun and Whimster; trans. HH Bruun). London, Routledge, 100–38].

Widlöcher, D. (1994). A case is not a fact. *International Journal of Psychoanalysis, 75*(5–6), 1233–44.

Winnicott, D. W. (1964). Memories, dreams, reflections: By C. G. Jung. (London: Collins and Routledge, 1963. Pp. 383. 45s.). *International Journal of Psychoanalysis, 45*, 450–55.

Zimmer, R. B. (2017). The analyst's use of multiple models in clinical work: Introduction. *Journal of the American Psychoanalytic Association, 65*(5), 819–27. https://doi.org/10 .1177/0003065117737753.

Index of Cases Discussed

Index

abandonment, 97; analytic situation and, 168–72; in cinema, 56–57; by parents, 168–72, 239

acting out. *See* enactment

Agieren. See enactment

Akhtar, S., 188

alcoholism, 42–43

ambivalence, 240; Bion and, 15; cinema and, 55, 56, 58, 61, 245; defined, 255; Freud, S., and, 148–50; Green and, 84n17; Oedipal situation and, 149–50; in schizophrenia, 84n16; in theater, 70; in transference, 82, 83–84, 84n16, 148; unconscious beliefs and, 148, 149; unconscious repetition and, 55, 135, 146, 147, 148–50, 151, 224–28

analytic hour, 51

analytic neutrality. *See* neutrality

analytic relatedness/relationship, 47, 107–8, 175, 225; authoritarianism and, 243; building, 242–46; inferiority and, 71; questions for, *237*, 246, 247; Stern on, 20; transformative actions in, 177–78; unconscious, 244–45

analytic situation, 51–91; abandonment and, 168–72; anger and, 165; anxiety and, 163, 164; associations and, 162, 164; Bion and, 53n2; as cinema, 53, *53*, 55–62, 70, 107, 244, 245; discrepant models for, 79–84; as dramatic

monologue, 53, *53*, 62–68, 62nn7–8, 66n9, 107; empathy and, 167, 168, 171–72; fantasies and, 167, 233, 238–39; Freud, S., on, 51, 52, 54, *77*, 77–79, 208, 209, 245; furthering process of, 161–91; Green and, 213–14; humiliation and, 165; ideal types of, 51–52, 54–55, 54n4, 76, 173–78; as immersive theater, *53*, 54, 72–76, 241; making a difference in, 228–32; metaphors use and, 39, 49, 51–55, *53*, 208–10; mother and, 167, 169–70; Oedipal situation and, 164; with parents, 168–72; questions for assessment of, *237*, 246, 247; rejection and, 165–67; self-esteem and, 165–67; as theater, *53*, 54, 59–60, 68–71, 171, 240–41; transference in, 51, 247–50; unconscious beliefs/scripts in, 164, 233–38, 244–45; unconscious inference and, 107–8, 125–27; unconscious repetition and, 155–56. *See also* cinema; dramatic monologue; free association; immersive theater; theater; transference; *specific topics*

anger, 41, 42; analytic situation and, 165; Bromberg and, 21, 22; in cinema, 46, 56–57, 59–62, 100; in dramatic monologue, 64; in transference, 100, 101; unconscious repetition and, 56, 57, 130, 137, 142

reflection: of associations, 40; in dramatic
monologue, 65; on dreams, 113–14;
nodal moments and, 197–98; in theater,
71, 98–99, 100; unconscious and, 124;
unconscious inference and, 124, *124*,
216–17; unconscious repetition and, 136
reflexive, reflexively, reflexivity: Bion and,
15; defined, 258
regression, 98–99, 101, 138, 196
Reith, Bernard, 245n9
rejection, 96, 97; analytic situation and,
165–67; in cinema, 56, 57
"Remembering, Repeating, and Working-
through" (Freud, S.), 148
Republicans, 23
resistance, 43, 231, 232; Bion on,
13; defined, 258; Eissler on, 6–7;
unconscious repetition and, 140–45
Roth, Priscilla, 155
rule. *See* basic rule; fundamental rule

sadism: Eissler on, 6–7; Kernberg on, 9
sadistic-aggressive impulses, 6, 186, 250
Sandler, Joseph, 187, 188
Schachter, Joseph, 120
schizophrenia, 84n16
Schubert, Johan, 194
Šebek, Michael, 187
seduction, 67, 70, 149; nodal moments of,
203–5
Segal, Hanna, 155
selected fact: of Bion, 122, 181, 249;
overvalued idea contrasted with, *124*,
125, 221, 246
self-analysis: Freud, S., and, 86, 113–14,
116, 118–19, 149, 182, 195, 233;
unconscious and, 113–14, 182;
unconscious repetition and, 149, 151
self-denying ordinance, 2
self-enquiry, common framework for, 1–25,
3
self-esteem: analytic situation and, 165–67;
depression and, 45
self-observation, in theater, 71
sexual impotence, 9–10
sexuality: associations of, 44; in cinema,
56, 211; in dramatic monologue, 65;

fantasies and, 11; mother and, 41;
unconscious beliefs on, 99; unconscious
repetition and, 130, 151, 152. *See also*
homosexuality
Shakespeare, William, 73
shame, 9, 40; Bromberg and, 22; in cinema,
56, 57–58; in unconscious, 100; with
women, 56–58, 100
Sharpe, Ella, 112, 222–23
silence, 13, 40, 44, 56, 60, 98; breaking,
22, 106; dramatic monologue and, 63;
Green and, 15, 16; in immersive theater,
73, 75; unconscious inference and, 217;
unconscious repetition and, 138, 139,
143
Spillius, E. B., 188
Steiner, J., 250
Stern, Donnel, 5, 214–16, 234, 239n6;
anxiety and, 18–20; associations and, 19;
authenticity of, 19–20; cinema and, 235;
common framework and, 18–20, 18n6;
contributions of, 229; interpretation of,
19
Strachey, James, 77–78, 81, 89n24, 116,
118n4, 119n5
suicide, 48, 167
superego, 98, 130, 196; Eissler on, 7n3;
hypercritical, 189
symbolization, 62n8

techne, 180
technical work (*Die Traumdeutung*), 180
theater (analytic situation metaphor):
ambivalence in, 70; analytic situation
as, *53*, 54, 59–60, 68–71, 171, 240–41;
anxiety in, 68, 109; associations in, 69,
70, 109, 110; cast/casting in, 69; cinema
and, 59–60, 70; defined, 258; depression
in, 111; despair in, 109, 110; dreams
in, 69, 70, 71, 108–9; Eissler and, 210,
238; fantasies in, 54, 68, 97–98, 110,
111; guilt in, 70; hopelessness in, 69;
imaginations in, 54, 68, 71; impasse in,
69; inferiority and, 71; interpretation
in, 69; intervention in, 111; Oedipal
situations in, 70; reflection in, 71,
98–99, 100; self-observation in, 71;

About the Authors

David Tuckett is a distinguished fellow and training and supervising analyst at the British Psychoanalytic Society and emeritus professor of decision-making at University College London (UCL). He is a practicing psychoanalyst as well as a fellow of the Royal Society of Arts and was the founding editor of the New Library of Psychoanalysis series. He has served as editor in chief of the *International Journal of Psychoanalysis*, president of the European Psychoanalytic Federation, board member of the International Psychoanalytic Association (IPA), and chair of the Comparative Clinical Methods (CCM) Working Party. He has contributed books and journal articles in the fields of medical sociology, economics, and cognitive science and developed and published articles in leading journals on conviction narrative theory—a theory of choice under uncertainty, which combines psychoanalytic, neuroscientific, sociological, and economic insights to understand decision making under uncertainty and its wider effects on society, such as in the creation of financial crises. He gave a TED lecture at the University of Warwick and has spoken at significant policy-making events such as the Davos Forum, as well as published on monetary and financial stability policy in the staff working papers series of the Bank of England. He has twice received the Sigourney Award for contributions to psychoanalysis.

Elizabeth Allison, DPhil, is director of the Psychoanalysis Unit at University College London. She is a psychoanalyst and a member of the British Psychoanalytical Society. She is program director of UCL's MSc in theoretical psychoanalytic studies and also supervises students in the Psychoanalysis Unit's doctoral program. She is an editorial board member and editor of the Psychoanalytic Controversies section of the *International Journal of Psychoanalysis*.

Olivier Bonard, MD, a child and adult psychiatrist, is a teaching and supervising member of the Swiss Psychoanalytical Society. He coordinated CCM activities for six years. He teaches postgraduate courses at the Universities of Lausanne and Geneva.

He practices individual psychoanalytic psychodrama with several cotherapists and teaches this technique in Neuchâtel, Barcelona, and Athens. Together with some of his colleagues, he founded the group psychoanalytic psychotherapy training course in Lausanne and Geneva. He is founder of *Tribune Psychanalytique*, an annual Swiss-French psychoanalytic journal.

Abbot Bronstein, PhD, is a psychologist and psychoanalyst. He is editor of the Analyst at Work section and an associate editor for *International Journal of Psychoanalysis*. Co-chair of the Comparative Clinical Methods Working Party in North America, he is a former training and supervising analyst at the San Francisco Center for Psychoanalysis and a board member of the International Psychoanalytic Association. He has been visiting faculty at Emory and Oregon Psychoanalytic Institutes and has taught and presented widely in North America and Europe, including publishing written papers on fetishism, ending analysis, and remote and in-office analysis. Recently he has contributed to collections devoted to IPA working parties and Donald Meltzer's work. He was honored as 2017's distinguished analyst at the meetings of the American Psychoanalytic Association and has led over twenty CCM workshops in North America.

Georg J. Bruns, MD, is a specialist in neurology and psychiatry, a PhD (sociology), a professor emeritus of medical sociology at the University of Bremen, a full member of the German Psychoanalytic Association (DPV), European Psychoanalytic Federation, and International Psychoanalytic Association, and a training analyst; he served as president of the DPV from 2002 to 2004 and as chair of the program committee of International Psychoanalytic Association Congress 2007 in Berlin. He is a member of the CCM moderators' group and associate editor of the *International Journal of Psychoanalysis*. He is author and editor of several books, as well as publications on psychoanalytic, psychiatric, and medical-sociological topics. His scientific fields include psychoanalytic psychotherapy of psychoses, sociology of psychiatry, and application of psychoanalysis in cultural and social fields.

Anna L. Christopoulos, PhD, is a professor emeritus of clinical psychology of the National and Kapodistrian University of Athens, Greece. She is a full member of the Hellenic Psychoanalytic Association, the European Psychoanalytic Federation, and the International Psychoanalytic Association. She is a core member of the European Psychoanalytic Comparative Clinical Methods moderators' group. She is also an associate board member of the *International Journal of Psychoanalysis*. She is author of two books, *Introduction to Adult Psychopathology* and *Research in Psychoanalysis*, both in Greek, as well as numerous articles and book chapters.

Michael Diercks, certified psychologist, is a member of and training and supervising analyst for the Vienna Psychoanalytic Society (VPS) and the IPA. Having been head of the child guidance clinic in Wien-Heiligenstadt from 1989 to 2001, he now works in private practice. He has been a member of the Training Committee of the

VPS since 2005 and was director of training from 2009 to 2013 and from 2018 to 2019. As a member of the European Working Party on Comparative Clinical Methods since 2005 and later of the Comparative Clinical Methods Association, he has facilitated numerous workshops in this framework. Passionate about and committed to training in psychoanalysis, he prepared and chaired visits within the European Visit Programme, created in 2018 to strengthen psychoanalytic training and to ensure and improve its quality. He has published several papers in German on psychoanalytic technique, psychoanalytic listening, and Bion's theory of thinking, as well as a paper in the *International Journal of Psychoanalysis* on Freud's handling of the transference in the case of the Rat Man.

Eike Hinze, psychiatrist and neurologist, works as a psychoanalyst in private practice in Berlin. He is a training analyst and chair of the training committee at the Karl-Abraham-Institute, Berlin, as well as chair of the IPA Committee on Psychoanalytic Perspectives on Aging. Since 2006 he has been active in the development of psychoanalysis in eastern Europe. He has been a core member of the CCM Working Party since 2004 and publishes mainly on psychoanalytic practice and training and psychoanalytic treatment of elderly patients.

Marinella Linardos, PhD, is adjunct professor of medical and health psychology, Faculty of Medicine and Surgery at the Catholic University of Rome, Italy. She is a full member of the Italian Association of Psychoanalysis, chair of the International Psychoanalytic Association Working Parties Committee, member and founder of the Ad Hoc Group of the European Psychoanalytic Federation on Psychoanalysis and Literature, and coordinator for Europe of the Comparative Clinical Methods group. She works as a psychoanalyst in private practice and as a medical psychologist in Gemelli Hospital Oncological Department, Rome.

Marie Rudden, MD, is an assistant clinical professor of psychiatry at Weill Cornell School of Medicine and on the editorial boards of the *International Journal of Psychoanalysis* and the *International Journal for Applied Psychoanalytic Studies*. She is a founding member and training and supervising analyst at the Berkshire Psychoanalytic Institute and an affiliate faculty member of the Austen Riggs Center in Stockbridge, Massachusetts. She coauthored a book, *Psychodynamic Treatment for Depression*, with Fred Busch and Ted Shapiro and has written a variety of scholarly articles in the field of clinical psychoanalysis. Research has been a long-standing interest, and she has conducted and published studies comparing the manifestations of delusional disorder in men and women, observing leadership styles in irrational, regressed groups, and studying reflective functioning in panic disorder. She is co-chair of the North American Comparative Clinical Methods Working Party and has a passionate interest in applying psychoanalytic principles to work in distressed communities; she is also currently cochair of the American Psychoanalytic Association's Task Force on Class and Income Inequality.

Michael Šebek, PhD, CSc, is a training and supervising analyst of the Czech Psychoanalytical Society, and a full member of the IPA. Elected twice as president, he is a former director the society's Psychoanalytic Institute, as well as assistant professor of medical psychology at Charles University, Prague. He has served on the international editorial board of *Psychoanalytic Inquiry*, as secretary for Europe of the IPA, and in various roles for the Han Groen Prakken Psychoanalytic Institute for Eastern Europe. A former Erikson Scholar at the Austen Riggs Center, he has moderated Haydée Faimberg's Forum on Clinical Issues as well as Comparative Clinical Method workshops. Appointed as a visitor on the European Exchange Visit Programme (EVP and EVP2), he has also advised on psychoanalytic training in various societies, including in Moscow. Trained as a psychoanalyst under a communist regime, he has published in English, German, French, Polish, Russian, and Czech on the totalitarian mind, totalitarian objects, the death drive, relations between psychic and external realities, and psychosomatic issues.

Printed in the USA
CPSIA information can be obtained
at www.ICGtesting.com
LVHW081517211124
797133LV00006B/449